TWENTIETH CENTURY

SCHWENKFELDERS

A NARRATIVE HISTORY

TWENTIETH CENTURY

SCHWENKFELDERS

A NARRATIVE HISTORY

by

W. Kyrel Meschter

Pennsburg, Pennsylvania

Schwenkfelder Library

1984

TABLE OF CONTENTS

Introduction

My name appears as author of this history and I hasten to accept responsibility for such inadequacies as the reader may perceive, as well as for opinions and judgments, expressed or implied. With equal haste, however, I must acknowledge the efforts of a host of people who have assisted in the preparation of this book.

These acknowledgements are threefold. First, no pretense is made to original research or scholarship. Rather, an effort has been made to retell in a single volume the story of the Schwenkfelders during the twentieth century, parts of which have been written and published over the years by many authors. Accordingly, the debt to those who have heretofore chronicled events and described individual personalities, is great and pervasive. In the interest of readability, footnotes have generally been omitted.

Second, a large number of individuals have researched various portions of this narrative. Meetings of this group have suggested channels of inquiry and have in general stimulated thinking as to the significance of events and personalities. Their interest and encouragement is gratefully acknowledged. The final chapter could not have been included without the assistance of Dr. Peter Erb.

And finally, I am indebted for suggestions and improvements to those who have patiently read successive drafts of individual chapters as the book gradually assumed its present form.

This history, along with the Colloquium sponsored by Schwenkfelder Library for the week of September 17-23, 1984, grew out of a desire appropriately to celebrate in that year the 250th anniversary of the landing in Philadelphia of the principal band of Schwenkfelder immigrants, and the 100th anniversary of the initiation of the *Corpus Schwenckfeldianorum* project and its outgrowth, the Schwenkfelder Library.

The Schwenkfelders in the late twentieth century are not only a thriving Protestant church in southeastern Pennsylvania; they are a unique religious and social phenomenon. They claim spiritual descent from Caspar Schwenckfeld von Ossig, a nobleman, scholar and theologian who died in 1561. He preached no systematic theology and left no prescription for an organized church. He dwelt upon the moral improvement of individual souls through an experiential knowledge of Christ. Yet his followers maintained an identifiable religious community over a period of almost 200 years in Europe and another 250 years in the new world.

There is a vast bibliography of literature on Schwenckfeld and the Schwenkfelders over this 450-year span. The most readable account of the Schwenkfelders in America is Howard W. Kriebel's *The Schwenkfelders in Pennsylvania,* published in 1904. Developments and events during the twentieth century have been chronicled in the *Schwenkfeldian,* the *Genealogical Record,* the introductions to the several *Corpus* volumes, *Schwenckfeldiana,* and in a multitude of monographs published by the Schwenkfelder Board of Publication, the Mission Board, Schwenkfelder Library, the several churches and related organizations, and in the public press and other sources. The present narrative is designed to set forth in a single readable volume the Schwenkfelder story during the twentieth century, continuing the history from 1900, where Professor Kriebel's history ends, as closely as possible down to the anniversary year of 1984.

This history is addressed to three audiences. Hopefully the general reader, curious as to the Schwenkfelder Church, may here find a contemporary answer to the repeatedly posed question, "Who are the Schwenkfelders?" Secondly it is addressed to non-descendant church members, now comprising a majority of the Schwenkfelder congregations, who should properly have available to them a ready sourcebook informing them as to the traditions and history of the church to which they now belong. And finally, it is addressed to the present generation of Schwenkfelder descendants, more widely dispersed geographically than previous generations, less closely bound by family ties, no longer so persistently indoctrinated by family or church leaders, and generally, I believe, less conscious of, and less influenced by, their Schwenkfelder heritage.

Edmund Burke, appalled at the disruption and anarchy of the French Revolution, described civilized society as an immortal contract which unites generations which have gone before, the living, and generations as yet unborn. Each generation owes an inestimable debt to the past, and correspondingly incurs a sacred obligation to transmit the accumulated wisdom of the ages inherited by it, in its turn, to the generations which follow.

To contemplate our Schwenkfelder heritage in this light, in the religious and social environment of the late twentieth century, must indeed give one pause to think. Ultimately the present history has been inspired by the hope that a review of our heritage in its contemporary setting may inspire present members of the Schwenkfelder community, descendant and adopted alike, to maintain the chain unbroken and to pass along to the next generation those elements that are good and valuable.

Read in this spirit, perhaps the inadequacies of the present history may be charitably pardoned and the burden of its argument thoughtfully contemplated, while the Schwenkfelder story awaits a more serious study by an interested scholar competent in historiography, theology and sociology.

W. Kyrel Meschter

Gwynedd Valley, Pa.

March 1984

Chapter One

The 1934 Bicentennial Celebration

The principal body of Schwenkfelder immigrants landed in Philadelphia on September 22, 1734, affirmed allegiance to their new English sovereign on the following day, and on September 24 gathered in a thanksgiving service celebrated annually to this day as Gedächtnis Tag—Day of Remembrance—the longest running thanksgiving service celebrated by any denomination in America. Two hundred years later in 1934 their descendants marked the anniversary with a summer-long celebration, a Bicentennial Thank Offering to Almighty God, whose guiding hand "hath blessed us on our way, and still is ours today."

The celebration evoked a great outpouring of enthusiasm. Virtually the entire Schwenkfelder congregation participated, for they too, as their forefathers, had much for which to be thankful. They looked back with awe at the steadfast faith of their ancestors, those followers of the "Middle Way" preached and expounded by Caspar Schwenckfeld von Ossig (1489-1561), who had kept alive a community of believers in Europe through 200 years, frequently enduring hardship and persecution. They marvelled at the courage of those forty immigrant families who crossed the sea to establish new homes in an unknown wilderness. They contemplated with wonder the flowering of that immigrant band of some 209 souls into the six organized churches of their day. Combined congregations numbering less than 1500 members were justifiably proud of *The Genealogical Record of the Schwenkfelder Families,* tracing their descent from the immigrants of 1731-1737; of the *Corpus Schwenckfeldianorum,* a critical edition of the works of Schwenckfeld, with thirteen of its eventual nineteen volumes already in print; of Perkiomen School and the China Mission.

Theirs was a grand heritage indeed. It had been recited to them each year in Gedächtnis Tag historical sermons. Now it was to be spread before members and general public alike in breathtaking panorama. It was a great summer to be alive and to count oneself a Schwenkfelder descendant.

The times were propitious. The heady prosperity of the 1920s had given way to the Great Depression. In the midst of social and cultural upheaval people looked to their roots, seeking a sense of identity and stability. During the early years in Pennsylvania the group had naturally been drawn together by their common customs, hertage and language. The rigors of frontier life demanded cooperation, despite the difficulties of travel and communication. They were under the spell of commanding spiritual and intellectual leaders, a remarkable group of individuals for their time.

The strong sense of community among the Schwenkfelders was reinforced by the closeness of family ties. The forty immigrant families bore only twenty-four different family names. There was considerable intermarriage among these families, due in part to their social isolation both before and after the migration, but encouraged also by a fear that worldly influences would weaken the religious faith they so cherished. Balthasar Hoffmann, writing in 1750, questioned the propriety of reading non-Schwenkfelder books, cautioned against employment of non-Schwenkfelders or even admitting them into the home, and warned against outside customs and beliefs. "To what extent can people dabble in the teachings of alien doctrines without incurring damage to the truth? And how soon will marriages to outsiders follow?" A unique example of interrelationship is provided by two seventh-generation descendants who counted forty-eight of the Schwenkfelder passengers on the "St. Andrew" as ancestors, the two being immigrant descendants on both their father's and mother's sides. These two could also visit the burial place of every one of their immigrant ancestors.

To circumstances such as these must probably be attributed the survival of the body as a religious community through the first two centuries in this country. By 1934, however, the isolation of the Schwenkfelder community had long since broken down and the possible consequences of too-close intermarriage had ceased to be a concern. But the Schwenkfelder families had not yet fully experienced the loosening of family ties, the geographical dispersion of members, the intermingling of non-descendants into church membership, and the secularizing influences of the period of World War II and the years following.

In the Schwenkfelder tradition ministers had been selected from within the Schwenkfelder body, and still in 1934 Rev. Lester Kriebel at Palm, Rev. Levi Hoffman serving the middle district, and Rev. Harvey K. Heebner at Philadelphia were of direct immigrant descent. Rev. Robert J. Gottschall at Norristown was not a descendant, but he had married Sue Deysher Schultz, a direct descendant of immigrant Christoph Schultz, and had graduated from Perkiomen School, the University of Pennsylvania and Union Theological Seminary. All these ministers had attended Perkiomen School, where the long-time headmaster, Schwenkfelder pastor Rev. O. S. Kriebel, inculcated in them his own reverence for his spiritual heritage, his strong sense of moral obligation and his enthusiastic visions of the future. Furthermore, such Schwenkfelder scholars as Dr. Selina Gerhard Schultz and Dr. Elmer E. S. Johnson, both of whom had worked in Europe with Dr. Chester D. Hartranft, the original editor of the *Corpus Schwenckfeldianorum*, and were carrying this momentous work toward completion following the latter's death in 1914, were at the height of their powers and influence. Dr. James Meschter Anders, noted physician and in his day perhaps the most illustrious citizen in the Schwenkfelder ranks, presided at several of the bicentennial gatherings. Dr. Samuel K. Brecht, editor of the *Schwenkfeldian* and of the *Genealogical Record*, and Secretary of General Conference, was a member of the Bicentennial Committee. Professor Howard W. Kriebel was winding up a long and productive career as a Schwenkfelder historian. Dr. Oscar S. Kriebel lent his enthusiasm and vision to the early planning but was denied participation in the Bicentennial Celebration by his death in 1932.

In 1934 the Silesian Schwenkfelder homelands still remained in congenial hands, and correspondence and visitation were without obstacle. During the early days of *Corpus* research Dr. Hartranft, Dr. Johnson and Selina Gerhard lived in Wolfenbüttel, Germany, and frequently visited Schwenkfelder landmarks in Silesia. The pilgrimage group who travelled there in 1934 was warmly and enthusiastically received at each stop by town and church officials and by local populations, including many descendants of Schwenkfelder families who had remained behind when the 1731-37 emigrants set out for America. But World War II and its aftermath changed all this. Later visitors to the area encountered only alien Polish speaking peasants eking out a bare subsistence where once prosperous farms had flourished; a sense of congenial homeland could be evoked only with a considerable effort of imagination.

There was ample precedent for a Bicentennial Celebration, for it was at the specially planned 150th Gedächtnis Tag service in 1884 at the Worcester Meeting House that Dr. Chester David Hartranft, professor at, and later president of, Hartford Theological Seminary, challenged the Schwenkfelder descendants, then only some 400 strong, to publish a critical edition of the works of Schwenckfeld.

The *Corpus Schwenckfeldianorum* publishing enterprise so launched had an incalculable formulative and stimulative influence upon the development of Schwenkfelder organizations and institutions over the next seventy-five years. It called forth incredible scholarly effort and dedication. It challenged the patience and resolution of the small body of Schwenkfelders. It sustained interest in the heritage of the past and inspired collection and preservation of the written record of their heritage in the Schwenkfelder Historical Library, now the Schwenkfelder Library. It assured Schwenckfeld and the Schwenkfelders their place in modern reformation historical scholarship. It produced an enduring monument to Caspar Schwenckfeld von Ossig, the reformer of the "Middle Way." And perhaps more than any other factor, it preserved for twentieth century descendants their identity as a Schwenkfelder community.

After two years' study at Oberlin Seminary, Oscar S. Kriebel, the first Schwenkfelder specifically educated and compensated for the ministry as a vocation, took a honeymoon trip to Europe and spent the year 1892 studying at the University of Berlin. His visits to the old Schwenkfelder homelands stirred deep emotions within him; seemingly ever thereafter he cherished the vision of a pilgrimage of Pennsylvania Schwenkfelders back to Silesia. Under new business at the spring General Conference of 1930, held at Palm, Dr. Kriebel formally proposed such a pilgrimage as an appropriate celebration of the Bicentennial year 1934. He suggested that Dr. Johnson's son Rolland, who was planning a visit to Europe that summer, be delegated to make appropriate investigations concerning Schwenkfelder sites and markers, and explore possible arrangements for travel, accommodations, etc. A committee consisting of Dr. Elmer E. S. Johnson, chairman, Mrs. Selina Gerhard Schultz, Wayne C. Meschter, Dr. S. K. Brecht and Rev. Lester K. Kriebel met and drew up a tentative itinerary, duly publicized in an article by Rev. Kriebel in the *Schwenkfeldian* issue of August 1930. Preoccupation with the economic problems of the times seems to have interrupted planning and little further is recorded for the next two years.

At the spring General Conference of 1933 a formal resolution was adopted directing the Moderator to appoint a new (or enlarged) committee "to make arrangements to properly celebrate the two hundredth anniversary of the arrival of the Schwenkfelders in America." By the fall conference the celebration was a principal subject of discussion. A committee consisting of Edwin S. Anders, James M. Anders, Samuel K. Brecht, Robert J. Gottschall, Harvey K. Heebner, Carlotta S. Hoffman, Levi S. Hoffman, Elmer E. S. Johnson, Lester K. Kriebel, Minnie S. Schultz, Oscar S. Schultz, Selina Gerhard Schultz, Christine S. Shearer and Wayne C. Meschter had held an organization meeting at the Valley Forge Hotel in Norristown on September 12, electing Wayne C. Meschter as chairman and Oscar S. Schultz as secretary. Miss Minnie Schultz was subsequently elected treasurer.

An exchange of thoughts at the initial meeting revealed a surprising consensus as to the elements appropriate for inclusion in the celebration. The program for a three-day culmination September 22, 23 and 24 quickly crystallized, largely at the inspiration of Dr. Johnson, who noted that the year also marked the centennial of Hartford Theological Seminary and the 50th anniversary of Dr. Hartranft's interest in the *Corpus*. Rev. Heebner added a word in favor of recognition of missionary activity, and Rev. Hoffman, recalling an earlier dramatic presentation given at Perkiomen School by the Society of Descendants of the Schwenkfeldian Exiles, appears to have suggested a pageant. Selina Schultz suggested the celebration might be initiated with the regular Memorial Day exercises in May, held as usual on the grounds of the old meeting houses. Noting that not all immigrant graves had proper markers she suggested an effort to identify and mark as many such graves as possible.

The desirable extent of public participation and publicity provoked some discussion, Mrs. Schultz initially thinking of the celebration more as a private family affair. She offered no serious objection to a larger affair, however, and in the actual event, prominent non-descendant religious and secular individuals participated. A publicity committee chaired by Rev. Gottschall and including Irma A. Schultz and Herbert Heebner Smith gained wide public interest and recognition.

The initial meeting agreed to recommend to General Conference that 1934 be designated "The Two Hundredth Anniversary Year," that meetings of an historical nature with visits to meeting houses and cemeteries and the decoration of immigrant graves, etc., take place during the spring and summer, and that a three-day celebration over the 200th Gedächtnis Tag (September 24) weekend climax the celebration. Receiving the enthusiastic blessing of Conference on Saturday, October 21, the committee held its second meeting Tuesday evening, October 24, when discussion of organizational details was resumed. It was suggested the Exile Society be apprised of the committee's plans so that it might coordinate its fall meeting. Carlotta Hoffman reported that the Music Committee planned to use at least six German hymns at the several meetings and was considering a Sunday afternoon (September 23) rendition of the Messiah by combined Schwenkfelder choirs. A resolution recommending preparation of a suitable pageant was adopted and Mrs. Shearer was designated chairman of the Pageant Committee. The ministers were charged with preparation of the Memorial Day weekend programs. Oscar S. Schultz was appointed chairman of a committee to identify and properly mark immigrant graves.

At the third committee meeting on December 12, 1933, a report by Mr. Meschter on the contemplated pilgrimage to Germany raised some uncertainty, both because of economically depressed conditions in the United States and because of rising political turmoil in Germany. Dr. Johnson expressed the belief that there would be no difficulty in enjoying free movement provided the usual simple rules for persons travelling as guests in a foreign country were observed. Quite a few people had expressed interest in joining the pilgrimage, but the earlier vision of a group of 100 or more seemed unrealizable for reasons of cost.

By year end 1933 four bicentennial celebration projects were under active development: identifying and marking of immigrant graves; the pilgrimage to Silesia; an historical pageant; and the extended Gedächtnis Tag services September 22, 23 and 24.

Marking Immigrant Graves

It seemed especially fitting, in opening the Bicentennial Celebration, to pay tribute to the memory of the original Schwenkfelder immigrants, whose courage and sacrifice brought them across the sea to these more propitious shores. In the words of Mrs. Schultz, "their strength of character and their purity of faith in God impelled them to carry out their vision of an abundant spiritual life for their children of generations to come. . . . But now, we their children of many generations removed, having come into the precious heritage which they envisioned and saved for us, were impelled by our love and our gratitude to erect suitable monuments, and to carve upon them the names of those fathers and mothers of long ago. That was our first thought in this Bicentennial year. May these memorials and the impressive services conducted at their unveiling help our children to remember to be faithful, and to be worthy of their spiritual heritage, and to give God all thanks. By the past we judge the present and gage the future."

Of 209 Schwenkfelders who left Europe during the years 1731-37, nine died en route. Four more died within a few days of arrival and were buried in Philadelphia's Pilgrim Cemetery—a cemetery reserved for strangers, no longer in existence. Despite the research reported in the *Genealogical Record,* identification of graves proved a complex undertaking. Crude native stones from the soil they tilled marked most of the graves. Howard Kriebel, Lester Kriebel and Grace Urffer at the Historical Library in Pennsburg prepared a preliminary list of some 130 graves, and some sixteen cemeteries were visited, many on a number of occasions. Surviving grave markers were traced on wrapping paper, identified with the immigrant family number assigned in the *Genealogical Record,* and the tracings bound for preservation in the Historical Library.

So that identity of immigrant graves might be preserved for posterity, each grave was to be marked with a small stone and the immigrant number cut into its bevelled surface by sandblasting. Appropriately located in each cemetery, a large monument would list the immigrants buried there, their immigrant number, and where ascertainable, the dates of birth and death. At the top of each monument, beneath an anchor figure flanked by the dates 1731 and 1737, a heading would read: "To the memory of Schwenkfelder Immigrants from Silesia whose remains repose in these sacred grounds." Modern spelling was adopted, leaving devolution of archaic spellings to the *Genealogical Record.* Shape, texture and size of the stones, together with the style, size and spacing of lettering, were carefully worked out. For a low bid of $2,889 (1934 dollars!) Charles J. Schell, a tombstone cutter of East Greenville, executed and erected a consistent, artistically balanced set of markers on schedule for the unveiling ceremonies. Burial places of 141 immigrants were so memorialized on eight monuments and most of the individual graves were identified with the smaller stones. Seven immigrant graves were located but not marked, two in the New Goshenhoppen Church Cemetery near East Greenville, three on a farm near Dr. J. G. Mensch Mill. near Pennsburg, one in the Easton Cemetery at Easton, and one in a private cemetery near Hagerstown, Maryland. Many local church members contributed liberally of their time and energy preparing foundation sites and assisting in erection of the monuments.

Following the tradition of Memorial Day services, unveiling and dedication ceremonies were held Sunday afternoon, May 27, 1934 at the cemeteries adjoining the Kraussdale, Hosensack and Washington meeting houses.

At Kraussdale Rev. Lester Kriebel of the Palm Church presided and read the historical statement, Rev. Heebner offered prayer, Oscar Schultz and Wayne Meschter unveiled the monument, and Mr. Meschter read the biographical sketch prepared by H. W. Kriebel. Eleven immigrants were buried here—four Krausses, two Kriebels, two Yeakels, two Wiegners and one Anders. Among many of note, and typical of the immigrants buried here, was Anna Heydrick Krauss, who was married in 1704 to Melchior Krauss, a farmer in Lower Harpersdorf, Silesia. In 1726 the parents and four children removed to the protection of Count Zinzendorf, in Herrnhut, Saxony. On April 19, 1733 the family, now including five children, set out for America. Melchior died five weeks later in Haarlem, but the widow, 58 years of age, with her two sons and three daughters, proceeded across the sea, arriving in Philadelphia on September 28, 1733, five months after leaving Herrnhut. She lived to the ripe old age of 80, having witnessed the establishment of a homestead, part of which continued in the family down to 1934, and a community bearing her name. Her eldest son, Balthasar, age 27 on arrival, as a lad in his teens had experienced the storm and stress of the Jesuit Mission persecution. He sustained his mother and enjoyed the pleasures and hardships of pioneering in a new country. Balthasar's contemporary, Caspar Kriebel, father of Rev. George Kriebel, shared these experiences. Rev. George Kriebel arrived in Philadelphia with the 1734 migration as an infant of less than two years. All are buried at Kraussdale.

At Hosensack Rev. Kriebel again presided and read the historical statement, Rev. Gottschall offered prayer, Mrs. Elmer Johnson and Mrs. Selina Schultz unveiled the monument, and Rev. Hoffman read Professor Howard Kriebel's biographical sketch. The monument here recognizes three Yeakel immigrants buried in the Hosensack cemetery, and three immigrants (Anna Shubert, daughter of Anna Krauss, John H. Yeakel and Andrew Warmer) buried in the Hans Heinrich Yeakel Cemetery in a field nearby. John H. Yeakel, familiarly known as Hans Heinrich Yeakel, appears to have been a successful breeder of horses, which were much in demand for opening up new farmland, and a land speculator of some renown. He acquired over 1,000 acres, among which were the 500 acres of the Hamilton tract. This he divided into four 125-acre tracts, one for each of his sons. The Yeakel Cemetery lies on the border between two of these tracts; the Hosensack Cemetery is on another of them.

At Washington Rev. Kriebel once again presided and read the historical statement, Rev. Hoffman offered prayer, Elmer K. Schultz and Dr. Johnson unveiled the monument, and Dr. Johnson read the biographical sketch. Thirty immigrants were buried here, including two Meschter groups, two Schultz groups and a Yeakel group. Buried here are three Schultz brothers, George, Melchior and Christopher; the latter had once owned the property on which the cemetery stands. Tradition has it that in 1726, amidst the Jesuit persecutions, their loving parents offered the brothers, then ages 14, 11 and 7, respectively, the choice of flight, leaving goods and property behind, or remaining in Harpersdorf. The family fled to Berthelsdorf, where they lived peaceably for some eight years and where both parents died, the father only two months before departure for the new world. The three orphaned brothers joined the 1734 band of emigrants. Christopher, as a lad of 16, faithfully kept a diary of the voyage from Altona to Philadelphia, later printed as an appendix to the 1771 German printing of his *Erläuterung.* Citizen, preacher, pastor, scholar, author and prolific correspondent, he was shepherd to the Schwenkfelder flock in Pennsylvania and to the remnant of relatives and friends remaining in the old country. He compiled the first Schwenkfelder hymnbook, published in 1762, the catechism, first published in 1763, and the *Erläuterung,* a scholarly defense of the views of Caspar Schwenckfeld, written at once to refute learned criticism abroad and to illuminate young people in this country. He was instrumental in drafting the articles of agreement used as a constitution for the Schwenkfelder School System established in 1764, as well as the 1782 constitution under which was organized the "Society" later to become the Schwenkfelder Church. He died May 9, 1779 and his body was laid to rest in the Washington Cemetery. An original handwritten copy of the sermon preached by Rev. Christopher Hoffmann at the burial service remains extant today in the Schwenkfelder Library.

Similar services were held on Sunday afternoon, June 3, at the Christopher Wagner Cemetery on the John K. Heebner farm at Worcester, where immigrants Anna and Christopher Wagner are buried. All who participated in the ceremony were descendants of immigrants buried here. Rev. Heebner offered prayer, John K. Heebner read the historical statement, Ernest and Lloyd Heebner unveiled the monument and Sadie J. Anders read the biographical sketch.

The services then moved on to the John C. Heebner Cemetery on the Hiram Kriebel farm near Cedars, where four Heebner immigrants lie buried. Curtis Heebner and Henry Ralston Anders unveiled the monument and Doris H. Heebner read the biographical sketch.

At 4:00 o'clock the group moved to the Salford Cemetery, where twenty-nine immigrant graves were recognized. Rev. Gottschall offered prayer, Rev. Heebner read the historical statement, Herbert Heebner Smith and Vincent F. Kriebel unveiled the monument and Oscar S. Schultz read the biographical sketch, as usual the contribution of H. W. Kriebel. Immigrants buried here bore a wide variety of Schwenkfelder names, and included George Weiss and Balthasar Hoffmann, who, along with Christopher Schultz, comprised the great triumvirate of Schwenkfelder leaders during and immediately after the period of migration.

George Weiss, born in Harpersdorf in 1687, married Anna Meschter in 1715. Their only son died when he was about a year old. George Weiss was selected to write a confession of the Schwenkfelder faith in response to questions addressed by the Jesuit Mission upon the mission's arrival in Harpersdorf in 1720. In April 1726 he and his wife fled to Herrnhut, where he was employed as a weaver and teacher, inspiring among others Christopher Schultz. The day after the arrival of the 1734 group in Philadelphia, Anna died and was buried in Pilgrim Cemetery. On December 9, 1735 George was formally appointed the first Schwenkfelder minister and catechist in this country, serving until his early death in 1740.

Balthasar Hoffmann was also born in 1687 in Harpersdorf. A weaver and day laborer, by sheer perseverance he acquired a mastery of Latin, Greek and Hebrew, armed with which he zealously explored the scriptures and the writings of Caspar Schwenckfeld. Balthasar Hoffmann, with his father, joined the 1721 mission in Vienna, where they presented some seventeen petitions on behalf of Schwenkfelders in Harpersdorf at the court of Emperor Charles VI, seeking relief from the Jesuit persecution, which by this time had turned nasty and violent. Finally flatly denied relief, they escaped Vienna with considerable difficulty to find refuge in Berthelsdorf, Saxony, under the protection of Count Zinzendorf. Here was born Balthasar's son, later Rev. Christopher Hoffmann. Balthasar, his wife and three children joined the 1734 emigration. His venerable father, 83 years of age, remained behind, but his mother, Ursula Anders Hoffmann, migrated, seeing the new land for only five days before joining other "strangers" in the already-mentioned Pilgrim Cemetery. Upon the death of George Weiss in 1740, Balthasar succeeded his lifelong friend as a pastor, preaching, catechizing, and officiating at weddings and funerals until physical problems confined him to his study. A biography written by his son enumerates thirty-eight tracts on theology and practical religion, and refers to eighty-three letters, without listing hymns, historical sketches and other writings. He wrote still extant letters to Christopher Schultz, setting forth parallel renditions of Bible texts in Hebrew, Greek and Latin with explanations in German, and the 1761 letter which inspired the *Erläuterung*. This "most consummate scholar" among the immigrant Schwenkfelders died July 11, 1775, aged 89, and was buried beside his wife, Ursula Beier Hoffmann, in the Salford graveyard.

Memorial services in 1934 continued on the following Sunday, June 10, with services held at the Methacton Mennonite Cemetery near Fairview Village, where ten immigrants were buried— Wagners, Heebners, Beyers and one Yeakel. Rev. Gottschall offered prayer, Dr. Samuel K. Brecht read the historical statement, Abram Reiff and A. Lincoln Anson unveiled the monument and Mrs. Christine Schultz Shearer read the biographical sketch.

Services followed at the Towamencin Cemetery, where twenty-nine immigrants lie buried, including Kriebel, Seipt-Reinwald, Anders, Dresher and Wiegner family groups. Rev. Hoffman opened with prayer, substituting for Rev. Edwin Anders, who was unable to be present. Rev. Kriebel read the historical statement, Wilbur Seipt and Warren Kriebel unveiled the monument and Herbert H. Kriebel read the biographical sketch, as usual reflecting the meticulous research of Professor Howard W. Kriebel. The Wiegner family group included Christopher Wiegner, his sister Rosina, and their widowed mother, Susanna Heydrick Wiegner. Since neither of these children married, this family died out. A fourth Wiegner, Abraham, married Susanna Yeakel, and produced a long line of descendants. The Christopher Wiegner home in Towamencin seems to have been an early intellectual and religious center. George Weiss, Spangenberg and Zinzendorf all visited here; Whitefield preached here to 2,000; here Indians brought their squaws; and The Associated Brethren of Skippack met. Christopher Wiegner maintained a diary offering an intimate glimpse into the mind of a seriously thinking man buffeted by currents of radical religious thought and the strains of persecution and emigration. The original diary, extant in 1913, was then mysteriously lost, but a careful transcription prepared by Agnes Schultz in 1886 survives. Sections of the diary were written in a code which defied deciphering until 1973, when Dr. Peter Erb prepared an English translation of the entire diary, published by the Society of Descendants of the Schwenkfeldian Exiles as *The Spiritual Diary of Christopher Wiegner.*

No immigrants were buried in the Worcester Cemetery, initially set aside in 1836.

Looking forward a little, the final monument-unveiling ceremonies were held September 16 in the Yeakel Cemetery at Chestnut Hill. The monument in this cemetery listed ten immigrants buried here, six buried in the Hood Cemetery, 4900 Germantown Ave., Philadelphia, where erection of a monument could not be arranged, and four buried in Pilgrim Cemetery, the location of which is no longer known but thought to have been in the vicinity of the present Washington Square in Philadelphia. Besides the already-mentioned Ursula Anders Hoffmann and Anna Weiss, Anna Anders and David Schubert are buried here. Anna Reinwald Anders, a widow for nineteen years, migrated from Silesia to Saxony and, with her three children, to Philadelphia with the 1734 group where she died six days after arrival. David Schubert (Sr.), his wife and two children embarked for Philadelphia June 28, 1734. A son born two days later died August 18 and the mother died August 24, both being buried at sea. A two-year-old son, David, died four days after arrival and was the fourth member of this adventurous band buried in Pilgrim Cemetery.

A large crowd attended the Yeakel Cemetery ceremonies despite a steady light rain. Rev. Heebner offered prayer, Mr. Meschter read the historical statement, Mrs. Caroline Roberts Huber and William Yeakel unveiled the monument and Oscar S. Schultz read the biographical sketch, following which Dr. J. E. Burnett Buckenham delivered the address of the afternoon.

The erection and unveiling of the eight monuments had called forth interesting and valuable history out of the past. Descendants at the well attended ceremonies were inspired to reverence and appreciation for the faith, the character and the principles of their immigrant forbears, and to a desire for a better knowledge of their own roots and ancestry. It would have been hard to imagine a more effective launching for the summer-long Bicentennial Celebration.

Pilgrimage to Silesia

For the thirty-nine participants, no doubt the most memorable event of the bicentennial summer was the Pilgrimage to Silesia.

For some time after their arrival in America the Pennsylvania Schwenkfelders corresponded regularly with relatives and pre-emigration friends remaining in Europe. With the May 31, 1740 accession of Frederick the Great to the throne of Prussia and the October death of Emperor Charles VI, religious persecution in Silesia and Saxony subsided. Concerned over the loss of artisans and farmers, Frederick the Great on March 8, 1742 issued an edict inviting the Schwenkfelders specifically to return to their homes and promising restoration of abandoned property. While no individual or family accepted the offer, thereafter the compulsive incentive to emigrate ceased. A burst of correspondence with Carl Ehrenfried Heintze preceded the 1771 publication of the *Erläuterung.*

The 1726 migration to Saxony was eased somewhat by financial assistance from friendly sympathizers in Holland. When the eventual migration was undertaken, these same friends provided restful accommodations in Altona and later in Haarlem. Offering to return money not utilized at the time, the Schwenkfelders were urged to retain it for the benefit of the poor among them - the original Charity Fund. Furthermore, the three van Buyschanse brothers, proprietors of a mercantile house, arranged transportation at their own expense for the emigrants to Philadelphia aboard the good ship "St. Andrew," John Steadman, Captain. Around 1790 the Pennsylvania Schwenkfelders, hearing of reverses suffered by the van Buyschanse family, raised a not inconsequential fund and forwarded it to them. In 1816 the Pennsylvania Schwenkfelders sent a war relief fund to the Council of Görlitz. In 1860, correspondence flowed both ways across the ocean between the Pennsylvania Schwenkfelders and the Harpersdorf pastor, Oswald Kadelbach, as he was preparing his history of the Schwenkfelders.

Dr. Solomon Schultz visited Harpersdorf in 1860, Oscar Kriebel in 1893, and the *Corpus* editors on numerous occasions. Of the Pilgrimage group, Dr. Samuel K. Brecht had visited Silesia in 1911 in company with Dr. Johnson, and had talked with Major von Lucke, then owner of the old Schwenckfeld family homestead in Ossig. Lester Kriebel had visited the country during his year's study at the University of Giessen as an exchange student from Hartford Theological Seminary.

On his 1930 trip Rolland Johnson met Pastor Stock of the Lutheran Church at Ossig, Schwenckfeld's birthplace. Under date of February 21, 1934 Pastor Stock wrote Rolland, inquiring as to progress of the Pilgrimage plans and asking to be kept informed. In April Dr. Brecht, as Secretary of General Conference, received a letter from the Director of Land Traffic, Bureau of Silesia, extending a formal invitation "In the name and by the order of the President of

Upper and Lower Silesia." In May Pastor Stock acknowledged Rolland Johnson's letter and stated he had informed the local press, which requested more information suitable for publication. Kantor Siegfried Knörrlich of Harpersdorf wrote a warm welcome and offered assurance that the Viehweg plot would be in good shape for services there. Thus reassured, Pilgrimage plans proceeded.

Mr. Wayne C. Meschter organized the tour group. The North German Lloyd Steamship Co. provided ocean transportation, seven days over on the Columbus, tourist class, and six days return on the Europa, third class. Hotel accommodations and land transportation by train and bus in Europe were arranged by Amerop Travel Service. Leaving New York June 30 and returning August 3, following an itinerary carefully prepared with assistance from Selina Schultz, Dr. Johnson, Dr. Brecht and Lester Kriebel, the all-expenses per-person fee came to $434 (1934 dollars!).

When it became evident the Pilgrimage group would be disappointingly small, Mr. Meschter purchased a Bell and Howell 16 mm. movie camera, and his son Kyrel took almost 4,000 feet of motion pictures of the trip. Upon return these were shown some seventy-six times, before count was lost, to audiences large and small. In this way, by a carefully prepared "Official Report," the work of Lester Kriebel, assisted by extensive notes taken by Irma Schultz and by heavy coverage in the *Schwenkfeldian*, the inspiration of the trip was shared by a wide audience.

An entirely unanticipated consequence of the Pilgrimage was a post-World War II project providing relief for the Silesians exiled to West Germany, a humane undertaking in a sense repaying the assistance of theretofore unknown Dutch friends, who, by payment of the ocean fare, made it possible for our Schwenkfelder ancestors to enter America as free men rather than as redemptioners.

In the late afternoon of Friday, June 29, 1934 with the thermometer registering 102 degrees, thirty-four members of the Pilgrimage tour group, surrounded by an even larger group of friends and well-wishers, gathered on the eastbound platform of Pennsylvania Railroad's still elegant North Philadelphia station, to board a special car on the 5:13 New York express, newly electrified. Five members, completing the group of thirty-nine, joined the tour in New York. That evening the travelers were guests of the North German Lloyd Steamship Co. at dinner at the Hotel Pennsylvania, after which they went to the pier, where another large delegation of friends and well-wishers joined in the excitement of the midnight sailing.

Except for two or three of the group, the ocean trip was a new experience; for many a once-in-a-lifetime dream come true. Aside from some minor seasickness, the trip proved uneventful, and by 6:00 p.m. Friday, one week after leaving Philadelphia, the party disembarked by tender in the historic harbor of Plymouth, England, whence the Pilgrim Fathers had sailed in 1620 and where in 1734 the good ship "St. Andrew" with the main group of Schwenkfelder emigrants had remained for twelve days enroute to America. After a tedious boat train ride, the group settled into three neighboring London hotels at about 1:00 a.m. Mr. Max Brassel of Berlin, the German tour guide, joined the group on the boat train and continued with it until the return sailing from Bremen four weeks later. Saturday and Sunday were devoted to sightseeing in London. On Sunday evening the tour traveled by train to Harwich and by night boat across the channel to the Hook of Holland. Here they boarded motor buses for a ride through the Dutch countryside—bicycles, windmills, canals, tulip fields, wooden shoes and all—to visit the Peace Palace at The Hague and the delightful seaside resort of Scheveningen, where dikes protect Holland from the North Sea.

After lunch the buses continued to Haarlem, visiting the docks along the Spaarne river, which no doubt served as living quarters for the 1734 emigrants during their fifteen-day stopover. Then on to Amsterdam for the night, sightseeing the next morning, and an afternoon train for Cologne, the first stop in Germany. Most of the day Wednesday was spent on a Rhine steamer proceeding up the Rhine to Mainz, viewing the busy river barge traffic, turreted old castles, the Lorelei Rock, the Mouse Tower and other scenic landmarks. On Thursday the group proceeded by motor coach to Frankfurt am Main and on Friday to Strassburg, the tour's only stop in France.

The carefully prepared itinerary merged points of interest from two historical periods. Schwenckfeld lived during the period of intellectual, religious and political ferment we know as the Reformation. He was born in 1489, six years after Luther, five years after Zwingli, twenty years before Calvin - and three years before the voyage of Columbus to the New World. The itinerary included stops at Ossig, where Schwenckfeld was born and lived until 1529 when, at age forty, he thought it prudent to enter upon what proved to be life-long exile first in Strassburg (1529-33), then in Ulm (1534-39), in Justingen (1540-47), in Esslingen (1547-50) and other retreats until his death in Ulm in 1561. Visits to these towns evoked episodes during the life of Schwenckfeld.

The strongest nuclei of Schwenckfeld's followers survived in

Silesia, in southeast Germany, now a part of Poland. In the small towns of Harpersdorf, Deutmannsdorf, Langneundorf, Lauterseiffen, Probsthain and the surrounding area southwest of Liegnitz, Schwenkfelder families firmly resisted efforts to convert them and force their adoption at times of the Lutheran creed, at other times of the Catholic faith. Persecution reached a climax with the arrival in 1719 in Harpersdorf of a Jesuit mission charged in the name of the Emperor with their conversion. By 1726 conditions became intolerable, and Schwenkfelder families fled, often by night, with only the possessions they could carry, to refuge some fifty miles to the west to the area of Görlitz in Saxony. Here in such towns as Berthelsdorf and Herrnhut they lived peaceably for seven years beside Moravian settlers, under the protection of the Lutheran pietist, Count Zinzendorf. By 1734 their presence there became a political embarrassment to the Count and the Schwenkfelder families left on the long journey to America. Each of these points of historical interest from the period of the migration were included in the tour itinerary.

In Schwenckfeld's day Strassburg, its creaking timber bridge the only one across the Rhine, was a crossroads city of commerce, politics and religion. It was a principal seedbed of the so-called Radical Reformation. It entered the Reformation period with an already established reputation for religious vitality, variety and toleration. As early as 1524 the city magistrates took over entire responsibility for nomination, installation and remuneration of pastors of all seven of the city parishes, and in February 1529, by abolishing the mass, the city officially declared itself for the Magisterial Reformation. That reformation embraced the thought and followers of Luther, Zwingli and Calvin, and envisioned reform of conduct, morals and church practice by decrees of Christian magistrates (i.e., the secular government). In contrast, the Radical Reformers, disillusioned with lack of personal improvement within the Magisterial Reformation, sought salvation in separatist conventicles modelled on the very early church, preached New Testament scripture stripped of fourteen centuries' accretions of Catholic dogma and theology, and wished to be subject in religious matters only to their own self-supervision. In insisting on self-supervision they fractured the ancient and medieval conception of the corpus christianum going back to Constantine, which understood the church and civil community as virtually coterminus, and which hence construed schism as tantamount to sedition. The radicals accordingly invited persecution by Catholic, Lutheran and secular authorities, and generally they were not disappointed. Martyrdom featured significantly in the early

Radical Reformation.

When Schwenckfeld arrived in Strassburg, the first place of refuge in his long exile, he took up residence with the local Protestant preacher, Wolfgang Capito. During the following four years, as radical and magisterial reformers gradually separated, Strassburg became a center of religious ferment. Most of the principal figures of the Radical Reformation passed through or lived here, many, as Schwenckfeld, seeking refuge in its relatively tolerant environment. Here Schwenckfeld made the acquaintance of Martin Bucer, Matthew and Catherine Zell, Melchior Hoffmann, Sebastian Franck, Michael Servetus, Pilgram Marpeck and many others, later correspondence with whom would comprise a major portion of the *Corpus Schwenckfeldianorum*.

Here the twentieth-century pilgrims visited the old cathedral where Schwenckfeld attended worship services, standing beneath the pulpit with hand cupped to his ear because of impaired hearing, listening to the evangelical sermons of Matthew Zell. By 1533, once again drawing criticism in the complex religious politics of the city, Schwenckfeld found it prudent to move on.

On Saturday, July 15 the 1934 group journeyed by train from Strassburg through sections of the Black Forest and the Swabian Alps to the quite modern city of Stuttgart, and on Sunday proceeded by bus to Ulm via Esslingen and Justingen. In Esslingen the pilgrims drove by the site of the Franciscan convent where Schwenckfeld lived incognito from 1547 to 1550, continuing his vast correspondence and writing postils (scriptural commentaries) and religious treatises. It was here in 1547 that, overcome with weariness and sleep while writing late at night, he fell from his chair and dislocated his shoulder. In Justingen Schwenckfeld was a guest of George Ludwig von Freyberg from 1540 to 1547. In the Freyberg castle in 1541 Schwenckfeld wrote a large part of his *Confession,* the greatest work in his long controversy with the Swiss and Lutheran theologians. When the imperial armies entered Ulm in January 1547 Schwenckfeld was forced to flee; for harboring Schwenckfeld his host was punished by confiscation of his property, not to be recovered for several years. The castle was destroyed when Wallenstein invaded in 1626 during the Thirty Years' War

Arriving in Ulm, the tour group was hospitably received by an assistant clergyman at the great cathedral, the second largest in Germany (after Cologne), and with the highest steeple, 528 feet. During his stay in Ulm from 1534 to 1539 Schwenckfeld made many staunch friends, among them the Streicher family—the widow

Helena, her five daughters and one son, Hans, a physician. The great debate between Schwenckfeld and Pilgram Marpeck—spiritualism vs. Anabaptism—was initiated in correspondence between two well-placed ladies, Helena Streicher and Lady Magdalene von Pappenheim, with Schwenckfeld writing through Helena Streicher and Marpeck through Lady von Pappenheim. During his stay and on later visits, Schwenckfeld drew spiritual support from the Ulm conventicle and received increasingly necessary medical attention from one of the daughters, Agatha, also a physician of some note. It was in the Streicher home that Schwenckfeld died on December 10, 1561. The tour group visited the traditional Streicher house on Sattler Gasse, opposite the beautifully frescoed old Rathaus (town hall). In view of the customary excavation, desecration and burning of the bodies of so-called heretics, it may be presumed his close friends kept his death rigidly secret; they may have laid his body to rest beneath the house, the only spot of perfect safety. Schwenckfeld's final resting place is not known; indeed, the identity of the Streicher house is subject to some debate. Nevertheless, a brief service of remembrance in the neighborhood square was impressive, attracting a group of local people to witness the solemn ceremony. No monument was erected here since his birthplace in Ossig offered a more confidently identified location.

On Monday the tour proceeded to Munich by way of Augsburg, site of Schwenkfelder conventicles. After sightseeing the next morning, the tour journeyed by bus to Oberammergau, where the famous Passion Play was performed on this "off year" to mark the 300th anniversary of the 1634 performance, which fulfilled a vow made the previous year when plague was ravaging the country.

After viewing the Passion Play on Wednesday, the tour returned the next day by train to Munich and proceeded on to Nürnberg. During the afternoon the quaint and medieval city was explored, with visits to the house where Albrecht Dürer lived and painted, the home of Hans Sachs, the famous old Rathaus with its elaborate paintings and gilded halls, and the old fortress castle. Then on Friday an all-day train ride brought the group to Dresden, with an opportunity for sightseeing, including a visit to the Zwinger Gallery to see Raphael's "Sistine Madonna," Corregio's "Holy Night," and Hoffmann's "Christ in the Temple." The tour paused to take pictures of the Augustus-Brücke. When the 1734 Schwenkfelder emigrants fled from Saxony, they traveled by boat down the Elbe river from Pirna to Altona, of necessity passing beneath this bridge. They were terror-stricken lest some of the authorities should discover them at this point, arrest them, and prevent their journey to Altona.

On Saturday the tour visited Pirna, where the emigrants had embarked, and after spending the night at Bad Schandau, proceeded on Sunday to Görlitz. Here Dr. Kurt Ernesti of Braunschweig, for twenty-two years associated with the editorial work on the *Corpus*, joined the tour as the guest of Mr. Meschter. At Görlitz the pilgrims were overwhelmed by official receptions from church and state, including welcomes by Dr. Schmidt, superintendent of the Görlitz ministerium, and by the director of the German Welfare Agency for Foreign Travelers in Germany (Verein der Auslands Deutschen). Publicity furnished by Irma A. Schultz was used to advantage by the local newspapers.

On Sunday afternoon buses transported the group to Berthelsdorf, where many Schwenkfelder families lived from 1726 to 1734 under the protection of Count Zinzendorf. Here the emigrants settled, built houses, tilled the land and raised flax to weave their own linens. By previous arrangement with Gustav Schaeffer of Herrnhut, the Bicentennial Committee had ordered a granite marker erected in the local Lutheran Church cemetery, honoring those Schwenkfelders who died during their stay here. Appropriate unveiling and dedication ceremonies were held that afternoon, in which the local pastor Burkhart, Rev. Kriebel, Mr. Meschter, Dr. Brecht and Dr. Ernesti participated. The monument was unveiled by Mrs. Ellen Schultz and Irma A. Schultz, and was decorated with flowers placed by Patricia Mosser and Richard Cook. Elizabeth Burkhart, the pastor's sister, had also thoughtfully decorated the monument with purple and gold flowers, native Silesian colors. The German inscription on the monument may be translated: "In Memory of those faithful Schwenkfelder believers fleeing from Silesia buried here in the years 1725-34. Erected in loving and thankful memory by the Schwenkfelders of Pennsylvania 1934." Nearby tombstones bore familiar Schwenkfelder names, including Seipt, Heebner and Beyer.

The group then filed through the village to the old Gemeindehaus, a long, low, thatched-roof building originally erected by the emigrants during their stay here and used for private worship services. It was occupied in 1934 by August Miller and his niece, who greeted the group warmly. This house was occupied by Schwenkfelder Friedrich Wagner until his death at age 82 in 1771, the last Schwenkfelder death recorded in the local church records. It was later bought by August Miller's grandfather. Further up the street the group visited a house built by Caspar Kriebel in 1728 and, curiously, occupied in 1934 by a family with the name of Meschter. All enjoyed a refreshing drink from the spring beside the front walk.

The next day was spent in Görlitz, with a noon visit to Herrnhut, home of Count Zinzendorf and early center of the Moravian missionary movement. In the quaint Moravian cemetery here all gravestones lie flat. The men are buried on one side of a center walkway and the women on the other. Here are the graves of Count Zinzendorf and his two wives, and of Spangenberg, Zinzendorf's representative in America and controversial visitor to the Wiegner farmstead in Towamencin.

Noon the next day once again found the party warmly welcomed by local church and state officials, this time in Liegnitz, where Schwenckfeld had served as counselor at the ducal court of Frederick II. Highlights in Liegnitz were visits to the Sts. Peter and Paul Church and the Liebfrauenkirche. It was probably in the former that Valerius Rosenhayn initiated the Reformation in Silesia, and where Schwenkfelder preacher Johan Sigismund Werner early attracted capacity Reformation audiences. Local Pastor Bahlow explained how the church doors had to be opened so the overflow crowd in the square could see and hear the preacher in the pulpit. In the nearby Liebfrauenkirche Fabian Eckel was called as an early evangelical preacher. Here the local pastor pointed out a stained glass window dating from Reformation times, and portraying Eckel serving the Lord's Supper in both kinds to the congregation, the first such observance in Germany. In those days perhaps 3,000 to 4,000 Schwenkfelders lived here, including Schwenckfeld's faithful friend and advisor, Valentine Crautwald.

Early the next morning, Wednesday, July 25, buses set out for Harpersdorf, first ascending the Gröditzberg to see the ruins of the old dungeons so fraught with terror for the Schwenkfelders, many of whom experienced imprisonment there. From the summit the travelers enjoyed a magnificent view southwest to the Spitzberg, across the fertile valley once occupied and to a large extent owned by our Schwenkfelder ancestors. The landscape bore striking resemblance to Pennsylvania's Montgomery County, and one could readily realize why our ancestors, upon arrival in the new world, settled where they did, and so quickly felt at home. The route then led through Hockenau, home of Martin John, whose surviving correspondence preserves interesting and vivid details of trying Schwenkfelder days; through Deutmansdorf, original homeland of the Kriebel family; Zobten and Lauterseifen, each with its own "Viehweg"; and Armenruh, once the home of George Weiss, David Meschter, George Anders, George Yeakel and others; to Harpersdorf.

The visit to Harpersdorf may well have been the climactic afternoon of the whole pilgrimage, and deserves quotation in full of the following two paragraphs of Rev. Lester Kriebel's official pilgrimage report.

We reached Harpersdorf at noon, refreshed ourselves with a cup of coffee at the local hotel, and at 2:00 o'clock were cordially greeted in front of the hotel by almost the entire surrounding villages of Harpersdorf, Armenruh, Langneundorf and Lauterseifen. All the church organizations were represented, the Veteran's Association of the town and ministerial representatives from Goldberg and Probsthain. The Schwenkfelder party stood in front of the hotel and the various German groups in parallel line opposite. Here Pastor Nierlich of the Harpersdorf Lutheran Church made his official welcome, as did all the local town authorities. These were duly interpreted by the Schwenkfelder pastor, Rev. Lester K. Kriebel. The church choir and school children sang several German hymns under the direction of Kantor Siegfried Knörrlich accompanied by the town band. Rev. Lester K. Kriebel then introduced the moderator of the Schwenkfelder churches, Mr. Wayne C. Meschter, and the Secretary, Dr. S. K. Brecht, to the German citizens. They gave brief messages of thanks for this cordial greeting on the part of these German organizations. An invitation was then extended to Pastor Nierlich and his people to accompany the Schwenkfelders to the Schwenkfelder "Viehweg" and join in their services at that sacred spot.

One of the most impressive features of our entire pilgrimage abroad was the procession to the "Viehweg" and the services held there that afternoon. The school children and choir as well as the local band led the procession with music. The church dignitaries followed and then the officials of the Schwenkfelder church, the members of the Schwenkfelder pilgrimage, and the German friends and neighbors from the surrounding towns. The band very solemnly played as we marched nearly a half mile out of the village to the lofty heights of the "Viehweg" overlooking the village and the beautiful Silesian countryside as far as the Spitzberg and Groeditzberg. One could also hear the solemn tones of the church bells ringing from the old Lutheran church in Harpersdorf during the procession. One could not help but contrast this procession with mingled emotion of joy and sorrow to those sad processions during the period 1720 to 1740 when our beloved dead were brought out in shame and without Christian burial rights and interred in the so-called "dumping grounds" of Harpersdorf. In front of the Schwenkfelder "Viehweg" monument this procession paused and the members of the Schwenkfelder pilgrimage held a very impressive service after 200 years of separation from the homes of their ancestors in Harpersdorf. . . .

In the service that followed, Rev. Kriebel, Pastor Guhl, superintendent of the Goldberg district, Mr. Meschter, Dr. Brecht and Pastor Ernesti spoke, and the children's choir sang a hymn. Sherman and Spencer Meschter placed flowers on the Viehweg monument in the small plot which had indeed been spruced up for the occasion. It was an emotional moment for travelers and local residents alike. Among the Harpersdorf dignitaries, Mr. Wayne Meschter was particularly thrilled to make the acquaintance of a Paul Meschter, in whom the family resemblance with Wayne Meschter's grandfather, Rev. Jacob Meschter, was unmistakable. The 20th century pilgrims were reminded that only about half of the Schwenkfelders migrated to Pennsylvania. Those families remaining behind gradually merged with local groups and lost their separate identity. No doubt many of those participating in the afternoon ceremonies were also descendants from earlier Schwenkfelder families.

Following the service the group visited the local Lutheran church and in its cemetery the grave of Melchior Dorn, the last identifiable Schwenkfelder living in Europe, who died in 1826. Pastor Nierlich then conducted the party into the church, where a World War I memorial tablet listed among war dead the names of Meschter, Schultz and Anders. In the large church Pastor Nierlich showed the group the "Taufengel," and a painting of Pastor Johannes Samuel Neander. The "Taufengel," baptismal angel, was carved out of wood, and in a silver clam shell held baptismal water for infants. It originally hung by a rope in the old Lutheran church, destroyed by fire in 1726. A precious symbol in the religious struggles of the day, it had been rescued from the fire by then Pastor Neander at considerable risk to his own life. In the desecration of the church at the close of World War II the relic was smashed into bits, and by 1961 Andy Berky failed to find even a single piece he could remove as a memento for the Schwenkfelder Library. The 1972 pilgrimage found only overgrown ruins of the once-stately church. In 1963 Siegfried Knörrlich, son of Kantor Knörrlich, published an illustrated booklet detailing the eventful history of this church through the Reformation period and the sad times following World War II. A translation of Knörrlich's work by Sherman L. Gerhard was published in 1980 by the Society of Descendants of the Schwenkfeldian Exiles.

The final visit of the afternoon was to the old Meschter farmstead and the Catholic chapel erected thereon, dedicated in 1734. The chapel was built with money raised from fines collected from Schwenkfelders who refused to attend Catholic services and rites during the Jesuit Mission, 1719-1726. After bidding farewell at the Harpersdorf hotel to many friends and guests, the weary but satisfied pilgrims returned to Liegnitz. Truly a day to remember!

Once again turning back the clock to Reformation times, the pilgrims visited Ossig, where Schwenckfeld was born in 1489. The principal tribute to him necessarily took place here since his burial place is not known. After seeing the fine monument prepared by Gustav Schaeffer at Berthelsdorf, the tour leaders hastily commissioned him to prepare a marble tablet to be affixed to the wall of the Lutheran Church in Ossig. Between the Monday stop in Herrnhut and the Thursday visit to Ossig, Mr. Schaeffer completed his work. A moving service of unveiling and dedication climaxed the visit here.

On arrival in Ossig the visitors were again warmly welcomed. Perhaps 300 people, most of the population of the village, were gathered in front of the village church. Religious organizations were represented by no less than seven pastors. The Veterans' delegation of some thirty-five venerable elderly men was decked out in formal clothes and high black silk hats, lending a formal tone to the occasion. Young men's and women's agricultural organizations were represented. The town band played and the church choir sang hymns. Over the churchyard entrance had been erected a little wooden archway decorated with cedar boughs forming the words, "Herzlich Willkommen."

While the various organizations were assembling, Pastor Stock and several of the town officials conducted the twentieth century pilgrims to the estate at one time owned by the Schwenckfeld family, more recently by Major von Lucke, and in 1934 by an unidentified 26-year-old man who had begun repairs and cultivation to restore the productivity of the farm. They pointed out foundation stones of the original castle where the Schwenckfeld family lived and where Schwenckfeld was born, and in the garden in the rear, an old stone baptismal font taken from the original church in which the Schwenckfeld family worshiped. After a brief explanation, the visitors were conducted into the vestibule of the new castle with its huge fireplace and decorated mantel-piece, a huge stone which formerly ornamented the gateway to the old "schloss." Two little angel heads, a fine lion head, and the Schwenckfeld coat of arms carved into the stone remained in fine condition.

Returning to the church-yard, visitors and local citizens joined in the unveiling and dedication ceremony. The church choir sang. Rev. Kriebel, Mr. Meschter, Dr. Brecht and Pastor Ernesti spoke. Dr. Brecht and A. Lincoln Anson unveiled the tablet and Loretta Meschter and Marion Berky placed flowers. Pastor Stock opened the service with greetings, and church superintendent Treutler of Lüben, representing the German Evangelical Church, introduced the other pastors and offered appropriate remarks, accepting the tablet as a memorial which the local community would cherish. The German inscription on the tablet may be translated: "In reverent memory of Caspar Schwenckfeld von Ossig, 1489-1561, A gentle disciple of Christ, A true worshiper of God, A saint in self-denial, A scholar and a prince in the realm of truth and light—The Schwenkfelders of Pennsylvania 1934."

Bidding farewell to Pastor Stock and their new friends, the tour group returned to Liegnitz and proceeded the next day by bus to Breslau for a luncheon and greetings from Provost Jenetzky and the entire Breslau ministerium. Friday afternoon at leisure offered the pilgrims a chance to catch their breath after a strenuous, emotion-packed week—Sunday at Berthelsdorf, Monday at Herrnhut, Tuesday at Liegnitz, Wednesday at Harpersdorf and Thursday at Ossig.

After sightseeing in Breslau the tour proceeded by Saturday afternoon train to Berlin. Sunday offered a sightseeing bus and boat trip to Potsdam, with visits to the famous Sanssouci Palace built by Frederick the Great and to the royal palace of the Kaisers. Monday allowed some leisure and a very interesting evening with Bishop Henkel, bishop of Berlin-Charlottenburg and officials of the German travel agency. The bishop was a Bavarian and was entranced with the Pennsylvania Dutch dialect, which he insisted be spoken. He discussed the state of the church in Germany and pled for new ties of brotherhood spanning the ocean. As throughout the tour, echoes of new stirrings in the German nation could be detected, stirrings not yet fully developed at that time.

On Tuesday Mr. Meschter, Dr. Brecht and Pastor Ernesti detoured to Leipzig to meet with Breitkopf and Hartel, printers of the *Corpus*. They witnessed typesetting and a press run of a portion of Vol. XIII, to be completed by October. They also discussed cost and completion of the remaining volumes. They had time for a brief visit with Otto Harrassowitz, a book dealer who had been most helpful in locating and collecting relevant books and documents for the *Corpus* editors, and whose firm continues to this day to serve the Schwenkfelder Library.

The tour group entrained for Magdeburg, with a stop at Wittenberg to view the famous church door upon which Luther in 1517 nailed his ninety-five theses, precipitating the Protestant Reformation in Germany; the homes of Luther and Melanchthon; and the "Luther Oak," planted on the site where Luther burned the Papal Bull excommunicating him from the Roman church.

On Wednesday a train ride brought the group to Wolfenbüttel, the final visit to major points of Schwenkfelder interest. Brief services were held at the graves of Dr. and Mrs. Hartranft, where flowers were placed by Helen Schultz Cook and Miss Minnie Schultz. After pauses for pictures of the houses where Dr. Hartranft and where Dr. Johnson and family had lived during *Corpus* editorial days, the party was welcomed by Director Herse at the Ducal Library. Here at the very heart of *Corpus* research, the director had prepared an exhibit of Schwenckfeld prints. Of some 120 known Schwenckfeld books, this library holds copies of about sixty, of which twenty of the most interesting were on display. Unfortunately this library held no original Schwenckfeld manuscripts, although one copy with marginal annotations in Schwenckfeld's hand was exhibited. Also exhibited were a Gutenberg Bible, Luther's September Bible, another 15th century German Bible, and several rare manuscripts, including one by the German mystic, Johann Tauler (c1300-1361). From the Library the party went to the office of the Landeskirche of Braunschweig-Wolfenbüttel to receive greetings from Bishop Johnsen.

At Braunschweig Rev. Kriebel left the tour to extend his trip to Italy, and on arrival at Hamburg, Pastor Ernesti left to join his family on vacation. The latter was a great inspiration to the tour group, adding immensely to appreciation of Schwenkfelder sites. For him it was also a fitting reward for his years of tireless service to the *Corpus*.

While the tour group was in Hamburg on August 2, 1934, flags at half-mast marked the passing of German President von Hindenburg at 9:00 o'clock that morning, and by 11:00 o'clock special editions of newspapers announced that Adolf Hitler had taken over the presidential office. The war that eventually followed ravaged the old Schwenkfelder homelands. By 1961 when Andy Berky, with considerable courage, visited the area, it was a part of Poland, with all traces of former German inhabitation seemingly removed. Town and street names were in incomprehensible Polish and only with difficulty did Andy locate the bullet-scarred and neglected Viehweg monument, the once-beautiful surrounding grove overgrown with weeds and brambles. He could locate only one elderly lady with whom he could communicate through her smattering of German. Future tour groups would visit the Viehweg site, but the hospitable welcome and cordial reception by inhabitants with obviously similar roots could never be repeated.

The tour of the major Schwenkfelder points of interest from the sixteenth-century Reformation period and from the eighteenth-century migration period had now been completed. There remained only a visit to the Hamburg suburb of Altona to visit Vandersmissen Allee, named for the family that provided the 1734 emigrants shelter and assistance as they passed through this city. On Friday, August 3 the party proceeded by train to Bremen, and Bremerhaven to board the "Europa" for the return voyage home.

For the tour group, and for those back home for whom the story in words and pictures was told and retold, the pilgrimage represented the Schwenkfelder and Reformation history of Gedächtnis Tag sermons come vividly alive. The fall *Schwenkfeldian* for the year 1934 printed numerous letters testifying also to the deep impression made upon the local townspeople by the visit of the pilgrimage group and by the dedicatory services in which they participated so enthusiastically.

Faith of our Fathers

While the travelers were away a larger group of workers at home immersed themselves in the same history in preparation for the third Bicentennial event, the historical pageant "Faith of our Fathers," presented in Salford Grove, Sunday, August 26, 1934.

Among all the Schwenkfelder congregations, the most obvious choice to create and produce a drama was surely Mrs. Christine Schultz Shearer, an accomplished elocutionist herself, a lady with unbounded energy and great personal charm, a leader in Central District Church, Sunday School and Ladies Aid affairs, and a direct descendant of Rev. Christopher Schultz, notable immigrant leader and diarist, already introduced. At the second meeting of the Bicentennial Committee held October 24, 1933 Rev. Kriebel nominated her, and she was unanimously elected chairman of the Pageant Committee, a most fortuitous choice, as events proved. Dr. Brecht, Dr. Johnson, Rev. Hoffman, Rev. Kriebel and Selina Schultz completed the committee.

There is a wealth of source material relating to the migration of our Silesian ancestors to Pennsylvania. The sources are, however, diverse and widely scattered and it proved quite an undertaking to reduce the material to an effective drama and faithfully to recreate the character and speech of the immigrant family members. By her own admission, Mrs. Shearer did little else that winter other than read background material. Mrs. Schultz, with her profound knowledge and trained literary talents, actively collaborated, and many other Schwenkfelder historians offered suggestions of detail and atmosphere. By late spring the text of the drama was well in hand under the title, "Faith of our Fathers, A historical drama designed to represent in song, dialogue and pantomime, the leading events in the history of the Immigrant Schwenkfelders from 1726 to 1734." The text was copyrighted in 1934 by Christine Schultz Shearer, Selina Gerhard Schultz and Frances Leedom Hess. In 1955 it was printed by the Board of Publication of the Schwenkfelder Church as Vol. II, No. 5 of *Schwenkfeldiana*, preceded by a history prepared by Mrs. Schultz and followed by the text of Christopher Schultz's diary of the 1734 voyage on the "St. Andrew."

By June of 1934 attention had been turned to casting, costuming and producing the drama. Miss Frances Leedom Hess, a friend and teacher of Mrs. Shearer, was engaged as dramatic director. Mrs. Shearer's cousin, Amy Schultz Witham, undertook to research costumes appropriate to the times and circumstances. The cast included thirty-seven principal actors, whose costumes were rented for the occasion. About forty children and the chorus of 100 wore simple costumes provided either by themselves or by the several Ladies' Aid societies.

Particular efforts were made for persuasive casting, selecting individuals whose demeanor and personality fitted the role portrayed. So successful were these efforts that for years after the production individuals were remembered as the characters they portrayed. Malcolm Schweiker and the ushers erected a substantial stage in the Salford Grove, so situated that the gently sloping ground suggested a natural amphitheater. Carlotta Schultz Hoffman, another of Chrissie Shearer's numerous cousins, supervised the music. Palm chorister Milton Bieler led the chorus. Oscar Schultz undertook responsibility for acoustical arrangements, which allowed the entire open-air audience of some 3,000 people to hear every spoken word. Others too numerous to mention assisted in a hundred ways. A property committee undertook the delicate task of securing and returning period furniture and artifacts, lending an air of authenticity to the stage settings. And finally, Kyrel Meschter and Mr. Robbins of Williams, Brown and Earle, from a flatbed truck at the rear of the grove and using telephoto lenses, recorded the presentation on 800 feet of 16mm. movie film, now preserved in the Schwenkfelder Library.

Through June, July and early August, parts were memorized, participants were drilled individually and in small groups, and stage business was worked out to the minutest detail in non-stop rehearsals. The atmosphere of tension and expectation rose in a great crescendo as the drama took shape and the appointed day approached.

Sunday, August 26, dawned clear and pleasantly warm. The stage, decorated with natural greenery, blended into the woodland beauty of Salford Grove. A large and attentive audience turned out. The singing chorus, doing double duty as a curtain between the episodes, parted nine times for scenes portraying significant events in the story. The parts flowed evenly from one episode to the next. To the great relief and everlasting credit of those who worked so hard to produce it, the drama came off without a hitch. People unused to speaking in public outdid themselves. The entire production was pronounced an unqualified success. Persistent demands for its repetition, however, were resisted, for fear of anti-climax and in deference to the final events of the Bicentennial Celebration still to come in September.

In nine episodes the drama set forth the story of the migration of the Schwenkfelder immigrants from the 1726 decision to flee Harpersdorf, through the sojourn in Saxony and the ocean crossing, to the first Gedächtnis Tag celebration upon arrival in Philadelphia in 1734.

The Jesuit Mission established in Harpersdorf in 1719 had little success in persuading Schwenkfelder families to accept the Catholic faith. By the imperial Austrian edict of July 30, 1725 the Jesuits were empowered to use force to coerce the Schwenkfelders to convert to the Roman Catholic faith. When the news of this edict reached them, the little band of Schwenkfelders, numbering less than 800, realized that they stood at a crossroad.

Episode 1, "A Momentous Decision," was set in the Harpersdorf home of Melchior Schultz, Sr., on a spring evening in 1726. Adam Weigner, George Weiss, Caspar Kriebel, Melchior Kriebel, George Hoffmann, Otto Ernst and Gottfried Kindler are meeting in secret, since Schwenkfelders have been forbidden to congregate, to consider their plight. A messenger brings in the latest edict of Charles VI, empowering the missionaries to force conversion. Acceptance being impossible, after prayer and discussion plans are made to depart secretly that very night for Saxony. Portrayed is the scene of Melchior Schultz, Sr. and his wife Susanna posing the question of flight to their three sons, George, Melchior and Christopher. The decision made, father and sons go out to fill up the racks and troughs so the cattle will not suffer before someone finds them. The women left on stage gather together a few keepsakes and necessities and pack a basket of food. Father returns, reads from the large family Bible and offers prayer. The family is ready to depart, to meet the family of Melchior Kriebel before midnight so as to be as far away as possible by daybreak, when their absence might be discovered. They will cover the fifty miles to Berthelsdorf, Saxony, on foot, abandoning all belongings except those they are able to carry with them.

Episode 2, "Discomfiture in Harpersdorf," was set in the house of the Jesuit missionary, Pater Regent, in the spring of 1726. The discomfiture is on the part of Pater Regent, who is pacing the floor, considering his own plight and future with the church. A fire has just destroyed some thirty homes and the village church. Regent's associated missionary, Pater Milan, was attending festivities in one of the homes when the fire broke out; an agitated populace blames Milan for the fire. Milan has hastily departed. A knock on the door, and a messenger is speechless with fright upon seeing Pater Regent's frenzied state of fear. The messenger adds to the discomfiture by bringing news of the flight of the Schwenkfelders. Pater Regent, dreading royal displeasure over the failure of the mission, recovering, concludes the scene, "Shall I now admit utter failure and resign my position? No! I am determined to reap at least a part of the harvest that was about to fall into my garner. I will make haste to lay hold of the deserted Schwenkfelder homes, cattle and lands, for certainly they now belong to my cause. I may yet be able to overtake them and catch the precious game. Time and patience will win the victory. I shall cause Dresden to feel the power of Vienna. Then will Count Zinzendorf's protecting arm be paralyzed and the fugitives be returned to my hand. They shall yet adhere to my faith."

Episode 3, "More Discomfiture in Harpersdorf," portrays a scene in the Protestant parsonage in Harpersdorf about the same time. Lutheran Pastor Neander is pacing the floor of his study, mourning the fiery destruction of his church, which almost claimed his own life, when Baroness von Schweinichen bursts in with the news of the flight of the Schwenkfelders, several hundred of whom have now departed. Now without a church building, and with the town seriously depleted of workers, he and the Baroness consider the wisdom of the harsh measures which have brought this calamity upon them and finally begin to comprehend the power of the Schwenkfelders's faith.

Episode 4 portrayed in pantomime the trip by night from Harpersdorf to Saxony, as various family groups plodded slowly and laboriously across the stage, carrying such family goods as they were able.

The next episode, "A Haven in Saxony," takes place in the house of Balthasar Hoffmann in Berthelsdorf later that spring. While Hoffmann visits Count Zinzendorf, Hoffmann's brother and family, fugitives from Silesia, arrive and report on the miserable conditions they have left behind. Arrangements for temporary refuge for more Silesian Schwenkfelders are discussed.

Episode 6, "The Last Schwenkfelder Meeting in Berthelsdorf," takes place in April of 1734, in the "Gemeinde Haus"—the same as that visited on the Pilgrimage. The kindness of their Saxon protectors and their inability to dispose of their properties in Silesia impelled the Schwenkfelders to remain in Saxony temporarily, although they did not dismiss the idea of migrating to Pennsylvania. The delay provided opportunity for the families to regroup and later to proceed as a body. But the Harpersdorf Jesuits had not rested. This episode portrays the announcement to the Schwenkfelder meeting by Count Zinzendorf that a new decree would require their removal within a year. Preparing to leave, Grandmother Anna, too old to travel, presents each of the three Schultz brothers with a book, urging them to be faithful and courageous, as they always have been.

By episode 7, "Hospitality in Haarlem," the emigrant body has been granted respite from their journey in the home of Abraham van Buyschanse in June of 1734. The children of the group enter eating cakes and apples and play a game to the accompaniment of a German song. As they leave, Abraham, Isaac and Jaan van Buyschanse enter with George Weiss, Melchior Meschter, Balthasar Anders, Christopher Kriebel and others. The Schwenkfelders thank their hosts for their hospitality, dispatch a letter back to Saxony to assure those left behind of their safe passage to this point, and at van Buyschanse's urging retain 224 Rix dollars as a charity fund.

The eighth episode, "The Voyage," takes place aboard the "St. Andrew" June 28 to September 22, 1734. The young Christopher Schultz, realistically portrayed by Selina Schultz's son Eugene, is shown writing his diary of the trip and soliloquizing over his experiences.

The final episode portrays "The First Thanksgiving" in Philadelphia, on September 24, 1734. Having finally arrived in Philadelphia, the exiles gather in a service of thanksgiving—the first Gedächtnis Tag. Their elected spiritual leader, George Weiss, offers a prayer of thanks to God and entreats the exiles to remember the day in future years and repeatedly to thank God for the exiles' deliverance from the bondage of the oppressor. The chorus sings "Faith of Our Fathers" and George Weiss pronounces the benediction.

Once again Schwenkfelder history had been dramatically recalled to life, this time to a large audience and with widespread notice in the public press. Well over 200 people involved summer-long as cast, chorus, costumers, property custodians, researchers and reporters had absorbed their own rich cultural, social and spiritual heritage in a manner they would not forget for the rest of their lives.

The Two-hundredth Gedächtnis Tag Weekend

From the beginning the Bicentennial Committee had looked forward to the Gedächtnis Tag weekend, Saturday September 22, Sunday the 23rd and Monday the 24th, as the fitting climax of the summer-long celebration. The 1734 immigrants had landed on September 22, pledged allegiance to their new English Sovereign on the 23rd, and on the 24th gathered to give thanks to Almighty God. The 200th anniversary programs were planned appropriately for each of these days.

Saturday afternoon services were held on the shores of the Delaware River near the spot where the Schwenkfelder bands had landed. The program was a cooperative effort of the Bicentennial Committee and the "Society of the Descendants of the Schwenkfeldian Exiles," of which more later in its place. The Society president, Dr. James M. Anders presided, and a distinguished Tablet Committee with Dr. J. E. Burnett Buckenham as chairman included Dr. Anders, Dr. Brecht, Mrs. Mary Daub Farrell and Herbert Heebner Smith.

The audience first gathered, courtesy of the Pennsylvania Railroad, on Pier Ten, South Wharves, Delaware Ave. and Walnut St. at 2:00 p.m. After opening remarks by Dr. Anders, a hymn and invocation, Helen Schultz Cook recited incidents of the 1734 voyage, noting the nine exiles who did not survive the rigors of the ocean trip. At this point Edith Hoffman, niece of Helen Cook, boarded the city harbor inspection boat, "John Wanamaker," made available by the city director of wharves and docks, to cast nine memorial flower wreaths upon the swirling waters of the Delaware River.

The celebrants then crossed the street and assembled in front of the Webb Building on the northwest corner of Delaware Ave. and Walnut St., on the wall of which the Exile Society had erected a memorial tablet. At this point Dr. Anders introduced the Hon. J. Hampton Moore, Mayor of Philadelphia, who paid gracious tribute to Schwenkfelder contributions to the life of the city, mentioning by name Dr. Anders, "honored in the medical world for his fine spirit of citizenship." Selina Schultz's "family affair" had become a Philadelphia celebration.

The memorial tablet was then unveiled by Mrs. Mary Daub Farrell and Mrs. Irene Maxwell, Exile Society members and descendants respectively of immigrants John and David Heebner. The singing of "America" and a benediction by Rev. Heebner closed the 2:00 o'clock meeting.

The wording on the tablet reads as follows:

EXILES
FOR CONSCIENCE SAKE
To the memory of the followers of
CASPAR von SCHWENCKFELD
who fled from Silesia and found
in Pennsylvania a haven of religious toleration
They landed near this spot 1731-37
Erected by the Society of the Descendants of
the Schwenkfeldian Exiles September 22, 1934

This tablet had an eventful subsequent history, to be related in due course.

At 3:00 o'clock the meeting reconvened in the Friends' Meeting House at Fourth and Arch Streets. Dr. Anders thanked the Society of Friends for graciously making the meeting house available and for participating in the service. In commenting upon the exile journey to Philadelphia, Dr. Anders noted "...we should realize that it was on account of their material sacrifices, and their daring courage in braving the dangers of the sea, of the American Indians and the wilderness that awaited them, that their descendants during the intervening generations down to the present have been privileged to enjoy the fruits of a rich heritage."

After greetings by Howard W. Elkinton, a member of the Fourth and Arch Streets Meeting, Dr. Samuel Brecht gave the audience an intimate glimpse of the six groups of Schwenkfelders who emigrated to America during the years 1731-37. George Schultz, the first, arrived in Philadelphia October 14, 1731 and established a merchant business here. A group of eleven Schwenkfelders, arriving on September 18, 1733 on the "Pennsylvania Merchant," John Steadman Captain, included 16-year-old David Schultz, brother of George Schultz, whose fascinating diary of the voyage was recited by Dr. Brecht. David was a cousin of Christopher Schultz, diarist of the

1734 voyage—the third and largest migration.

David's elder brother Melchior had been a merchant in Haarlem and his business dealings with the Dutch Mennonites had no doubt paved the way for the assistance rendered by the van der Smissens in Altona and the van Buyschanse brothers in Haarlem. He was the sole Schwenkfelder on the fourth migration, arriving in Philadelphia June 28, 1735. Abraham Beyer and eight members of his family arrived October 19, 1736. The sixth and last group of fourteen Schwenkfelders, including members of the Wagner, Heebner and Krauss families, arrived September 26, 1737, again on the good ship "St. Andrew," John Steadman Captain. Altogether, counting births and deaths on the voyage, Dr. Brecht counted 219 persons figuring in the journeys, of whom nine died en voyage, leaving 210 actually to set foot in the new world on the six migrations. John Steadman no doubt docked his ship at Fishbourne's Wharf near the present location of Delaware Ave. and Walnut St., for he conducted a store on that wharf, offering for sale a wide variety of goods and seeking freight and passengers for his outgoing voyages, as witnessed by repeated advertisements in the *American Weekly Mercury,* samples of which Dr. Brecht presented.

Dr. Alexander Converse Purdy, professor of New Testament Exegesis at Hartford Theological Seminary, then addressed the gathering on the "Common Heritage of the Schwenkfelders and Quakers," noting in particular belief in the inwardness of religion, dedication to religious liberty, their fellowship of suffering for their faith, and the responsibilities inherent in a good name, shared by the two groups.

Sunday services, morning, afternoon and evening, were held in the Palm Schwenkfelder Church. At the morning worship service Rev. Levi Hoffman preached the sermon on the theme, "And there shall be one fold and one Shepherd," urging in the spirit of Schwenckfeld the brotherhood of Christians of all denominations. Dr. Elmer Johnson then unveiled a tablet on the wall of the sanctuary, memorializing Schwenkfelder ministers who had served the upper district churches, commenting briefly on each. We have already met the first three, sons of Silesian forbears, who had served the entire congregation of Schwenkfelders in America down to 1782: George Weiss, Balthasar Hoffmann and Christopher Schultz. These were followed by George Kriebel, 1787-1822; John Schultz, 1802-27; Christopher Schultz Jr., 1819-43; William Schultz, 1845-90; Joshua Schultz, 1845-92; Jacob Meschter, 1854-91; Oscar Kriebel, 1892-1932; and Lester K. Kriebel, then serving. The morning services concluded with the unveiling of two oil paintings by Adolph Pannash, "The Landing of the Schwenkfelders in Philadelphia, Pennsylvania, September, 1734," and an earlier portrait of Caspar Schwenckfeld, mirroring numerous extant prints.

That afternoon at 2:00 o'clock the United Schwenkfelder Chorus rendered a program of Handel's always inspiring and uplifting "Messiah," with Carlotta Schultz Hoffman as soprano soloist, Myrtle Beideman, alto, Daniel S. Snyder, tenor, Raymond K. Stong, bass, Marion Weber Glass, pianist, Helen Schultz Cook, organist, and Raymond Seeburger, chorister from the Philadelphia Church, director. Rev. Gottschall prefaced the musical program with a brief account of Handel's life and a tribute to his musical genius.

The Sunday evening service was under the supervision of the several Christian Endeavor Societies, with Paul Bieler opening with greetings as president of the host society. After a rousing rendition of Dudley Buck's "Festival Te Deum" by the United Schwenkfelder Chorus, which did yeoman service that day, a capacity audience was addressed by the nationally popular Dr. Daniel A. Poling, president of the International Society of Christian Endeavor. Dr. Poling had just returned from a fifty-seven day trip throughout Europe during which he had participated in seventy-three youth conferences and mass meetings. He presented first-hand glimpses of young people's work in the various countries which he visited.

Finally the climactic day arrived—Monday, September 24, 1934, the 200th Gedächtnis Tag. The Towamencin Meeting House was filled to overflowing. The program began at 9:30 a.m. and lasted well into the late afternoon. Without any intention of detracting from the significance of this solemn and moving occasion, our comments here will be quite abbreviated. On the morning program Rev. Lester Kriebel delivered the traditional Gedächtnis Tag historical sermon and Mr. Meschter spoke on "The Schwenkfelder Pilgrimage to Silesia and Saxony," both covering history we have already surveyed. Rev. Gottschall spoke on "The Schwenkfelder Renaissance," a principal subject of this history. After the traditional lunch of bread, apple butter and water, Dr. Johnson spoke on "The *Corpus Schwenckfeldianorum:* A Literary Movement," to which we will shortly direct our attention.

Rev. Hoffman delivered the inspirational address on "Mark the Perfect Man." In the afternoon Dr. Rockwell Harmon Potter, dean of Hartford Theological Seminary and president of the American Board of Commissioners for Foreign Missions, brought greetings on behalf of both organizations. He recalled Dr. Hartranft's work as initial editor of the *Corpus* and paid tribute to Dr. Johnson as a colleague and professor on the seminary staff. He also noted that over the past thirty years the Schwenkfelders had worked closely with the American Board, through which foreign missionary activity was conducted.

Selina Gerhard Schultz, associate and managing editor of the *Corpus* and, as we have so frequently noted, a wellspring of inspiration in all the Bicentennial Celebrations, gave a moving address on "Schwenckfeld's Supreme Message," concluding: "Caspar Schwenckfeld's supreme message to all Christendom today is this: The Kingdom of God is a spiritual kingdom apart from but within the kingdoms of this world. The one and only way to this kingdom is Christ, the narrow Way, the middle way between all other ways, and the only mediator between man and his maker. Follow Him! Follow Him!"

And finally, Rev. Harvey K. Heebner, supreme master of the felicitous phrase, brought the Bicentennial Celebration to a close with the words, "In the closing moments of this high day, let us all now bow in silent and earnest dedication of our lives, praying that He may pour out upon us the Holy Spirit of power. Then may we arise after the benediction and go forth to do His holy will, and moment by moment hear Him say to us: This is the way, walk ye in it. . . . Lo, I am with you always."

* * * * * *

The summer-long celebration had illuminated and inspired all who participated in or attended the ceremonies. It reflected great credit on all who planned and worked to complete the several projects. The general Bicentennial Committee held, in all, fourteen meetings. The comradery among committee members made them reluctant to terminate their activities, and they considered formally and informally steps to extend the enthusiasm so generated into the future—alas, an unlikely undertaking. A proposed printed centennial celebration book was referred to the Board of Publication, but considered too expensive an undertaking. In a January 1935 special supplement the *Schwenkfeldian* published proceedings of the meetings over the Gedächtnis Tag weekend. *Schwenckfeldiana* published over the years 1941 to 1952 were no doubt inspired at these sessions. Meticulous minutes of the proceedings of the Committee were prepared by the Secretary, Oscar S. Schultz, and are preserved in the Schwenkfelder Library in two carefully bound volumes, with frontispieces beautifully illuminated by Irwin P. Mensch, local artist and illuminator.

Having shared in the euphoria of the Bicentennial Celebration and absorbed some historical background, we must now settle down to the task before us: to recount the activities and achievements of Schwenkfelder descendants in our own twentieth century. The Schwenkfelders are an interesting religious body and at the same time an intriguing social phenomenon. How do we account for their survival as an identifiable community through 200 years in Europe and 250 years in America? What of the vigor and vitality of this community now, in the latter half of the twentieth century? And how will the present generation preserve the heritage of which we are the present beneficiaries for descendants into the twenty-first century? These are questions well worth our pondering as we approach the 250th Gedächtnis Tag in 1984, lacking but five years of 500 from the birth of Caspar Schwenckfeld.

We have already suggested the seminal role of the *Corpus Schwenckfeldianorum* project in our story, and this will engage our attention in the chapter that follows.

Chapter Two

Corpus Schwenckfeldianorum

As Schwenckfeld lay dying, his intimate friend, disciple and literary executor, Jacob Held von Tieffenau, records: "Finally, and in conclusion, he [Schwenckfeld] blessed and exhorted us to abide in divine truth, saying that his writings would serve us in his stead; he felt assurance that the doctrine he taught in his books was not his but that of his divine maker, and that after his death it would be brought more fully to light; God the Lord would call others who would carry forward the work begun by him, explain it more fully, and make it more widely known."

It was left to twentieth century Schwenkfelder descendants, their friends and supporters to fulfill Schwenckfeld's deathbed wish that his writings be brought "more fully to light," by editing and publishing the *Corpus Schwenckfeldianorum*. Its nineteen volumes and 18,000 pages present the texts of 1,252 surviving documents, together with bibliographical, philological, literary, historical and theological critical notes and comments. Projected in 1884, the first volume appeared in 1907, the last two in 1961, an even 400 years after Schwenckfeld's death. An initially projected biography of Schwenckfeld was published separately in 1946.

Caspar Schwenckfeld von Ossig was born in the principality of Liegnitz, Silesia in November or December, 1489. Of a noble and well-to-do family, he was university educated and entered into the life of a court counselor, from about 1518 serving Duke Frederick II of Liegnitz, a friend and protector. Aroused by the echoes of Luther's hammer on the door of the church at Wittenberg in 1517, Schwenckfeld entered upon a period of meditation and study, steeping himself in the literature of the Church Fathers, the scholastics and the humanists, and reading as they appeared from the press the works of Luther, Erasmus and others. Initially in sympathy with Luther, he became an early leader in the Reformation in Silesia. By 1525, however, the two reformers had become embroiled in vigorous theological controversy, particularly over the sacrament of the Lord's Supper. Schwenckfeld insisted that celebration of the Lord's Supper be suspended (Stillstand) until spiritual renewal became sufficiently evident that all Christians—Lutherans, Zwinglians, Anabaptists and others—could celebrate together in Christian brotherhood. A few years later, a booklet of Schwenckfeld's published in Zürich by Zwingli either deliberately or through misunderstanding aroused the Catholic authorities, who persuaded King Ferdinand to order Duke Frederick to eradicate Schwenkfeldianism in his realms. To save his Duke embarrassment, Schwenckfeld departed Ossig in 1529 at age 40 upon voluntary exile, which proved lifetime.

Schwenckfeld's writings, while temperate in tone, dealt with ideas which during his lifetime were the subjects of heated controversy. They excited vehement rebuttals and not infrequently vituperative personal attacks. Alienated alike from the Lutheran and Catholic camps, his works were suppressed, subjected to confiscation, and on occasion publicly burned by civil authorities prodded to action by Schwenckfeld's Lutheran and Catholic theological antagonists. Schwenckfeld insisted upon the essential unity of a Christian fellowship. Preaching a religion of spirit over form, defending religious liberty and individualism, insisting upon the rights of the laity and the freedom of the individual to worship in accordance with the dictates of his own conscience, Schwenckfeld collided head on with establishment theologians bent upon domination of emergent national churches and their civil protectors and supporters. During later life Schwenckfeld was forced to live and travel in secrecy, under threat of arrest and martyrdom. At one point this "Knight of Faith" was forced to spend a year and a half without once leaving the house of his protector. But true to his lifetime motto, "Whoever has received Christ can never be sad," he did not despair, but maintained his routine of study, writing, meditation and prayer. By the written word, in letters, tracts, treatises and books, Schwenckfeld and loyal disciples developed and expounded the theology of the "Middle Way" and defended their beliefs. Often printed and circulated clandestinely, these works were highly valued and assiduously studied in widespread conventicles of like-minded believers.

But outside the considerable circle of followers and supporters, defense of his doctrinal positions proved something of a losing battle. Schwenckfeld and his followers were condemned as heretics, and quite unjustly branded as mystics, enthusiasts, visionaries, or, a favorite term, as Schwärmer—fanatics. As Reformation history over the next 200 years was written by victorious Lutheran and Catholic scholars and theologians, the unflattering portrayal by his critics was largely preserved, while Schwenckfeld's seminal role in the movements for spirituality and for religious liberty and individual freedom was singularly ignored. More balanced accounts by church historians Gottfried Arnold (1666-1714), Christian August Salig (1692-1738) and others prepared the way for later revisionist scholarship but hardly stemmed the tide in their own day. It was a concern to set the record straight and rebut unfounded criticism that prompted Christopher Schultz to have printed the 1771 German edition of his *Erläuterung,* reprinted in 1942 in an English translation by Professor Elmer Gerhard as *A Vindication of Caspar Schwenckfeld von Ossig, An Elucidation of his Doctrine, and the Vicissitudes of his Followers.*

In the introduction to Vol. I of the *Corpus,* Dr. Hartranft, its initial editor, reflects the survival of unflattering criticism into the early twentieth century by relating the response of a small town archivist to a request for Schwenckfeld material: "Why do you want to revive such a dead issue? The heretic was laid out long ago; let him be buried undisturbed in his own dust." But Dr. Hartranft continues: "The clerics and politicians of Schwenckfeld's day did want to silence him the worst sort: they were immensely relieved when the tidings of his demise reached them. And most church historians continue to handle him reluctantly and to anatomize him with long and sharp instruments. They want to keep him in the old vaults, where they had consigned him three centuries and more ago, lest a spark of his enthusiasm might be smouldering in the ashes and might rise up to animate the Church with some glints of spirituality. But to oblivion heaven did not design him to be consigned."

After Schwenckfeld's death in 1561 in Ulm, Jacob Held von Tieffenau, assisted by Adam Reisner, Johann Heyd von Daum and others, continued to inspire his followers by printing his letters. Four folio volumes appeared in print between 1564 and 1570, and four more had been transcribed and ready for print, when the ever watchful persecutors broke up the little group in that city. In Strassburg and Speyer along the lower Rhine adherents remained until war destroyed their activity. Among these was Daniel Suderman, who reprinted a large number of Schwenckfeld's books during the years 1590 to 1630. The strongest nuclei of followers survived efforts to exterminate them in Lower Silesia, and from there the emigrants to Pennsylvania later issued. They met in conventicles, read, discussed and copied his books, and brought many manuscript and printed copies with them to America. Isolated tracts were soon printed in Allentown and Philadelphia, but none of these efforts approached a complete or even a representative collection, and copies of earlier printed editions became increasingly scarce. By the beginning of the twentieth century, perhaps half of Schwenckfeld's writings survived only in manuscript form, some in Schwenckfeld's own hand, more often by the hand of earlier copyists. Schwenckfeld volumes were widely scattered among European libraries, in a few private collections and in the homes of Schwenkfelders in Pennsylvania.

Beginning about 1860 a series of events quickened interest among Pennsylvania Schwenkfelders in their heritage and genealogy. Dr. Solomon Schultz's visit to Harpersdorf inspired purchase of the Viehweg plot and erection of the monument there in 1863. Oswald Kadelbach, Harpersdorf pastor and historian, published his *History of the Schwenckfelders.* And at the fall General Conference held in Worcester October 30, 1875 letters were read from Robert Barclay in England and from Judge Christopher Heydrick of Franklin, Venango County, Pennsylvania, both inquiring into Schwenkfelder history and beliefs. A committee was appointed to respond to both inquiries. Barclay was seeking support for his belief that Quaker doctrine and mode of worship may have had roots in the teachings of Schwenckfeld. Ensuing correspondence with Pennsylvania Schwenkfelder Daniel Schultz was incorporated, in part at least, in Barclay's 1876 *History of Religious Societies in the Commonwealth.* Judge Heydrick was interested in his own ancestry as a Schwenkfelder descendant, and his inquiries and continuing interest inspired publication of the 1879 Genealogical Record. Judge Heydrick's introductory "Historical Sketch" (reprinted in the 1923 *Genealogical Record*) vividly reminded the Schwenkfelders of the steadfast faith and character of their ancestors and the sacrifices by which they purchased for their descendants freedom and prosperity in the new world. They were heirs and stewards of a rich cultural and religious heritage, then over 300 years old.

Around 1835 August F. H. Schneider, a young student at the University of Berlin, read the non-partisan church historian Gottfried Arnold and turned his attention to the literature and study of Schwenckfeld. Over some thirty-five years Schneider accumulated the most comprehensive collection of *Schwenckfeldiana* assembled to that time. Early in his studies, by one of those improbable coincidences that so electrify the study of history, he became friendly with and acquired as a roommate Augustus C. Thompson, a graduate of the class of 1838 in the Theological Institute of Connecticut (soon to become Hartford Theological Seminary) and one of the first American theological students to enter the University of Berlin. To assist Schneider in his studies, already four years along, Thompson wrote to his brother at East Windsor Hill, asking him to contact the Schwenkfelders in Pennsylvania, and a close friendship developed. More than forty years later the Schneider collections were thrown on the market and largely through the generosity of Mr. Newton Case, many volumes, including Schneider's copious notebooks, were purchased for what shortly became the Case Memorial Library at Hartford Theological Seminary. There Thompson, a trustee of the seminary, recognized the handwriting of his former roommate, and proceeded to give Hartford professor, Dr. Hartranft, an enthusiastic exposition of Schwenckfeld as Schneider had taught him, thereby providentially preparing Dr. Hartranft for the call that was shortly to come his way.

Rev. Chester David Hartranft, D.D., was born in Montgomery County, Pennsylvania, October 15, 1839. His family having removed to Philadelphia, he graduated from Central High School and continued his studies in Rambo's School in Trappe, the Hill School in Pottstown and the University of Pennsylvania, where he graduated in 1861. After a brief military experience he entered the Reformed Theological Seminary at New Brunswick, N.J. After graduation and a brief term as pastor of the Dutch Reformed church at South Bushwick, N.Y, later a part of Brooklyn, he returned to serve for twelve years as pastor of the Reformed church in New Brunswick. In 1878, aged 39, he accepted an entirely unsolicited call to the Waldo Professorship of Ecclesiastical History at Hartford Theological Seminary. A man of broad intellectual and cultural interests, he entertained strong pedagogical convictions and for ten years labored quietly, persistently and in large measure successfully, to conform the seminary curriculum to his own visions. Contemplating resigning in 1888 to undertake full-time editorship of the *Corpus*, he was forced by circumstances to accept the presidency, in which capacity he served until 1902, when he took up residence in Wolfenbüttel, Germany, to pursue *Corpus* editorial work. He remained President Emeritus until his death.

From 1871 to 1879 Major General John Frederick Hartranft, a descendant of immigrant Tobias Hartranft of Lauterseiffen, Silesia, served as Governor of Pennsylvania. While Governor he learned of his Schwenkfelder ancestry, became interested in genealogy and participated actively in the preparation of the 1879 Genealogical Record. He located in the Pennsylvania archives the original ship list of the "St. Andrew," bearing the signatures of adult Schwenkfelder immigrants to the Oath of Allegiance. (The original is now in the Schwenkfelder Library. A facsimile appears in the 1923 *Genealogical Record.*) As the 150th Gedächtnis Tag in 1884 approached, Governor Hartranft, Judge Christopher Heydrick, State Senator William A. Yeakel, Dr. Solomon Schultz and others began to give thought to its proper observance. It was agreed they should seek an outstanding scholar, hopefully of Schwenkfelder descent, to prepare and deliver an elaborate historical address. Governor Hartranft mentioned his distant cousin, Dr. Chester D. Hartranft, then professor of ecclesiastical history at Hartford. Some discreet inquiries convinced Judge Heydrick that Dr. Hartranft was indeed a man of appropriate qualifications and stature, but he was concerned that Dr. Hartranft's name was not included in the 1879 *Genealogical Record.* When Governor Hartranft confirmed Dr. Hartranft's Schwenkfelder descent, Judge Heydrick took it upon himself, in a January 26, 1883 letter, to extend a tentative invitation. Interestingly enough, his letter concluded: "Governor Hartranft and I have recently had a conference on the subject and are agreed that the work can be better done by you than by any other Schwenkfelder—according to the flesh—of whom we have any knowledge. Neither of us adhere to the ancient faith, nor are we authorized to invite you to deliver such address, but we have great confidence that we can easily obtain such authority at the next anniversary, and desire in the meantime to interest you in the subject."

Dr. Hartranft accepted the invitation. The Society of Schwenkfelders approved the selection and appointed a Sesqui-Centennial Committee with Governor Hartranft as chairman. Governor Hartranft spoke at the Gedächtnis Tag service, and Judge Heydrick was included in the program. Due to the lateness of the hour, however, Judge Heydrick's paper could not be presented and had to await publication in the November 1914 *Schwenkfeldian* and a reprint under the title "The Schwenkfelders."

As already described, the invitation to Dr. Hartranft fell upon fertile soil. He was soon deeply absorbed in Schwenckfeld studies. Inspired by the noble character of Schwenckfeld and the power of his theology, Dr. Hartranft soon became intent, as others before him, upon securing for Schwenckfeld his rightful but long-denied place in Reformation scholarship. To a man of Dr. Hartranft's intellect and erudition, nothing short of an encyclopedic critical edition of his works would satisfactorily accomplish this end. "We owe it to the memory of the man. We owe it to the greatness of the movement, to bring into the light of day what was buried under such a mass of shameless obloquy. We owe it to the coming generations; how shall children know their faith—or that grand history of their sires? We owe it to Theological Science; it is busy re-editing, rewriting, readjusting; it has already lifted Schwenckfeld from the oblivion in which his persecutors sought to envelop him. Let us furnish the material for a true portraiture."

Accordingly, on August 27, 1884, less than a month before the sesquicentennial, he addressed a printed circular letter to the Schwenkfelder community, making an appeal to edit and publish the writings of Schwenckfeld as a literary monument. "Surely to bring this before the world would be a more suitable memorial of the greatness of our fathers, and of our gratitude to God, than to raise a shaft; nor could we make a nobler contribution to theological science and righteous living."

The circular letter and Dr. Hartranft's impassioned Gedächtnis Tag appeal evoked a burst of enthusiasm and matters proceeded with surprising dispatch. The fall General Conference on October 18, 1884 appointed a committee consisting of Joshua Schultz, Howard W. Kriebel, William S. Anders, George K. Meschter and Samuel K. Anders "to take into consideration the necessity of publishing the writings of Schwenckfeld." Dr. Hartranft offered to take a leave of absence from Hartford and spend an experimental year in Europe if the committee would provide him with $4,000 salary and $1,200 traveling expenses. Special District Conferences were held, the proposal accepted, and the money almost immediately subscribed. By January the leave of absence had been granted and on May 16, 1885 Dr. Hartranft, his wife and son sailed on the steamer "Belgenland" for Antwerp. Headquartered in Breslau, he began searching libraries and archives and shortly compiled a bibliography of over 900 documents.

Now the full dimensions of the undertaking began to emerge. It was anticipated the experimental year would permit preparation of a prospectus, on the basis of which legally binding subscriptions for the completed volumes would be solicited, with the sale proceeds reimbursing monies advanced during the editorial preparation. Not until May 1886 did Dr. Hartranft forward the first draft of a prospectus, explaining the delay by writing ". . . the literature of archives is a perfectly overwhelming mass. . . . I found it immeasurably more voluminous than my largest dreams."

Dr. Hartranft extended his stay in Europe through his summer vacation, but a decision on his return to Hartford could only briefly be delayed. With many details of the prospectus unresolved, the committee invited him to return for consultations and to report to the Schwenkfelder congregations at the Gedächtnis Tag services. In October he resumed his teaching post at Hartford. The fall General Conference relieved him of repayment of the money advanced, noting that while no concrete publishing project had resulted, he had indeed labored diligently and faithfully. The results of the experimental year were not encouraging.

By the spring General Conference of 1887 the committee reported a completed prospectus; that Breitkopf and Härtel of Leipzig, Germany, and Gustav E. Stechert of New York had agreed to announce the prospectus; that the price per volume had been fixed at $6.00, or $96.00 per set for the projected sixteen volumes; and that results of solicitation of subscriptions would determine whether or not the project seemed feasible. The sixteenth volume, a biography of Schwenckfeld, was included as an added incentive to subscribers. By the fall conference only 188 subscriptions had been secured, mostly from the Schwenkfelder group. Libraries, widely solicited, appeared content to await publication and then decide upon purchase.

At this point Dr. Hartranft volunteered to resign his position at Hartford and to devote the next four years to publishing Schwenckfeld's works and a fifth year to writing a biography and history of Schwenckfeld's place in the Reformation, if assured of $5,000 per year for the four years and $2,350 expense money. Propelled by a $5,000 pledge by Anthony H. Seipt, this fund was in fact raised and articles of agreement prepared. But Dr. Hartranft's letter of withdrawal called forth a deep reaction at Hartford. Two professors had just accepted calls to other institutions and a third had died. It was strongly feared Dr. Hartranft's withdrawal would hamper recruitment of faculty replacements, discourage student enrolment, threaten withdrawal of financial support and generally imperil the seminary and its leadership of the evangelical faith in New England. He was thereupon drafted as president of the seminary and the trustees appealed to the Schwenkfelders to acquiesce, which in good conscience they could hardly refuse. The resulting sharing of Dr. Hartranft's talents drew the Trustees of Hartford Theological Seminary into close association with the Schwenkfelders and the *Corpus Schwenckfeldianorum*—an apparent setback at the time which was to prove a providential association in the long run.

New articles of agreement solemnly obligated Dr. Hartranft to edit the writings of Schwenckfeld for publication, the first volume to be issued not later than September 24, 1890 and the whole to be completed in ten years. He was granted "by vote of the Trustees" the privilege of absence for as many years (not consecutive) as might be necessary to complete the work, and in addition he would utilize sixteen weeks of annual vacation for research in Europe. At the same time, he had on his hands Hartford Theological Seminary to be molded according to his ideas, the very existence of the seminary being at stake. It was a herculean task.

Dr. Hartranft did spend three months of the summer of 1888 in Europe, visiting libraries and archives in some sixty cities, engaging copyists, broadcasting circular letters of inquiry and generally establishing contacts and acquaintances through whom work could be carried on by correspondence. By fall, a perhaps predictable result, Dr. Hartranft was "suffering now very greatly from nervous exhaustion brought on by too much work," and was unable to attend the Gedächtnis Tag services. Family problems added to his distress and the press of work at Hartford and fragile health largely confined him to his home through most of 1889. No visit to Europe could be considered.

Meanwhile Professor Howard W. Kriebel stepped up his collecting efforts among families in Pennsylvania. A trunkload of manuscript material was forwarded to Hartford, to become part of the editorial materials later transferred to Wolfenbüttel, and in time returned to the Historical Library collections at Pennsburg. Collecting and copying continued in both Europe and America, but seminary demands and fragile health repeatedly postponed plans for a further visit to Europe. One encouraging event brightened the gloom when in February 1890 Schwenckfeld's Bible, with marginal notations in his own hand, was discovered and added to the collections. By January 1894 the committee and the contributors had lost patience, and advised Dr. Hartranft no further financial support was possible until a complete review of the project with him. A later meeting raised funds to permit limited copying to continue. By the summer of 1896 Dr. Hartranft again experienced severe nervous prostration. In 1897 a financial crisis at the seminary required his undivided attention. And so it went.

As the twentieth century dawned, sixteen years of effort and sacrifice had produced not a single volume. Indeed, despite intensive research, painstaking copying, and accumulation of a massive volume of materials, printer's copy for Vol. I was not even in any advanced stage of preparation. Thus did twentieth century Schwenkfelders inherit the *Corpus* project.

Early in 1900 the Pennsylvania Schwenkfelders appealed directly to the Hartford trustees. They reminded the trustees of Dr. Hartranft's solemn obligations under the so-far unfulfilled contract of 1888, of Schwenkfelder sacrifices at that time of crisis at the seminary and of the funds raised and expended over the years. Prodded by the aged Dr. Augustus Thompson, sympathetic trustees arranged Dr. Hartranft's return to Europe in March of 1902, and during a brief return visit to the United States in 1903, for his retirement as president, and election as president emeritus on half salary for life—a not inconsiderable contribution to the *Corpus* undertaking. Dr. Hartranft now removed his *Corpus* papers to Wolfenbüttel, Germany, whose library contained the largest collection of source material on the continent, and this town continued as headquarters for *Corpus* editorial work down to 1919.

Dr. Hartranft had devoted twenty-five years of his life to Hartford Theological Seminary. He had molded it to conform to his own inspired visions and had been the chief instrument for securing financial support. He had gathered around him a circle of influential friends, to whom more and more Dr. Hartranft personified together the interests of Hartford Theological Seminary and the *Corpus* publication effort. These devoted friends now increasingly involved themselves in the *Corpus* effort, arranging financial support duly noted in the prefaces of early volumes, and perhaps as importantly, lending their prestige to help persuade Dr. Hartranft to confine the manuscript format within practicable bounds. Among such friends were Dr. W. Douglas Mackenzie, who succeeded Dr. Hartranft as president of the seminary; Dr. Ernest C. Richardson, Hartford trustee and librarian at Princeton University; Hartford dean, Melancthon Williams Jacobus; Elbridge Torrey, esq., president of the Hartford trustees; and Professor Otto Bernhard Schlütter, who was sent independently to Germany to assist and who appears as Associate Editor of Vol. I of the *Corpus*. In the spring of 1903 H. W. Kriebel, dispatched to Wolfenbüttel to report to the Pennsylvania Schwenkfelders, found Dr. Hartranft and his copyists busily engaged in preparing a dictionary of Schwenckfeld's vocabulary. Dr. Richardson also visited Wolfenbüttel, coming away appalled at the lack of secretarial and clerical help while routine tasks sapped Dr. Hartranft's by-now quite limited physical and mental energies. The Schwenkfelders' $23,000 fund was being exhausted through copying and other editorial expenses, and with no volume even in sight, additional funds from subscribers were difficult to come by. Broader shoulders were now put to the wheel.

With Dr. Hartranft approaching 65 years of age and in uncertain health, and with his thorough but slow, plodding editorial methods, concern began to arise both in Pennsylvania and Hartford over the appearance of even one volume, to say nothing of the full sixteen. Help was clearly needed. In 1904 Hartford Theological Seminary granted to Mr. Elmer S. Johnson a one-year fellowship with a stipend of $750 to permit him to go to Germany and assist Dr. Hartranft. This fellowship was renewed annually, each year upon the expressed condition that Johnson devote his energies to bringing Vol. I to the press and to persuading Dr. Hartranft to conform to the original sixteen-volume program.

Elmer Ellsworth Schultz Johnson, a Schwenkfelder descendant on his mother's side, was born and raised on his father's farm near New Berlinville, Pa. Family friends arranged his enrolment at Perkiomen Seminary and then at Princeton University, from which he graduated in 1899. He then became a student at Hartford, studied under Dr. Hartranft, and after graduation served from 1902 to 1904 as the first regular minister of the First Schwenkfelder Church of Philadelphia.

In July 1904 Mr. Johnson, his wife and son arrived to take up residence in Wolfenbüttel. There he joined Dr. Hartranft, Dr. Hartranft's sister-in-law, Ida Berg, and Dr. Schlütter. He took with him a letter signed by Rev. William S. Anders as president and H. W. Kriebel as secretary of the Board of Publication of the Schwenkfelder Churches, which in 1898 had succeeded the original committee. The letter appointed Dr. Johnson Assistant Editor "through the joint action of the Hartford Theological Seminary and the General Conference of the Schwenkfelder Churches." Dr. Mackenzie addressed a letter of instructions to Dr. Hartranft, both letters charging the editors with the earliest possible printing of Vol. I and adherence to the original publishing program confined to sixteen volumes.

The next three years witnessed an intense struggle between the backers, working through Dr. Johnson, and the venerable editor, Dr. Hartranft. Correspondence across the ocean became increasingly strident in tone, Dr. Hartranft insisting upon his infinitely elaborate editorial program to the point of several threats to resign, a less likely occurrence than physical incapacity brought on by frustration of his designs. Vol. I came to print generally in accordance with Dr. Hartranft's plan, but in May 1906 a joint Publication Committee consisting of Dr. Hartranft, Rev. O. S. Kriebel representing the Schwenkfelders, and Dr. Mackenzie, later Dr. Richardson, representing the Hartford group took firm control of the editorial program. Dr. Hartranft reluctantly acceded, provided his acceptance not be interpreted as an infringement of his personal liberty or commit him to inward approval of the plan! The nature of this struggle can best be understood by a glance at Vol. I as it finally appeared in the fall of 1907.

Dr. Hartranft was enthralled with the rigor of German scholarship and determined that his work would compare favorably with other productions then under way, most notably the Weimar edition of Luther's works. He wanted not only to restore Schwenckfeld to his rightful historical and theological position but also to demonstrate Schwenckfeld's influence, comparable to that of Luther, on the development of modern German language. He accordingly insisted not only on reproducing original texts (he early wanted to photostat them all, but compromised by reproducing photographically only the title pages), but also on including for each document six critical analyses under the headings of Bibliography, Translation, Language, History, Theology and Vocabulary. As a result, the 730 pages of the first volume presented only seven documents, one actually a "lost" letter, one an oral address and only one a tract of any length. After 69 introductory pages, textual reproduction occupied only 53 pages, translations 36 pages, bibliographical notes 55 pages, language analysis 51 pages, historical notes 160 pages, comments on Schwenckfeld's theology 281 pages, and detailed vocabularies 75 pages. With over 1,000 documents to go, on this publishing program 100 volumes and several lifetimes could hardly have completed the work! Even Dr. Hartranft's warmest supporters were appalled.

In August 1907 Dr. Johnson returned to America, and until March 1909 was engaged primarily in securing new subscriptions. Advance sheets of Vol. I were presented to the fall General Conference, together with the word that finished volumes were on their way across the ocean, and a few weeks later the shipment of finished copies had been piled in the gymnasium of Perkiomen School, ready at last for distribution to subscribers. Sufficient new subscriptions were obtained to assure prosecution of the work for several more years. When the Johnson family returned to Germany they were accompanied by Dr. Johnson's sister-in-law, Selina Schultz Gerhard, then 28 years of age, duly appointed secretary to the editorial staff. In Dr. Johnson and Selina Gerhard, Dr. Hartranft now had youthful vigor and enthusiasm to ease his tasks and apt students to train for the future.

Early in 1911 the entire editorial staff returned to the United States, Dr. Hartranft bearing in his hand a finished copy of Vol. II. Dr. Hartranft delivered lectures to prompt additional subscriptions, and seemed to renew his health and vigor upon revisiting, after forty years, the scenes of his boyhood and youth in Pennsylvania and New Jersey. In November, having married his deceased wife's sister, Ida Berg, he returned to Wolfenbüttel, to be followed in January by the Johnson family and Miss Gerhard. Closely following a revised estimate of sixteen volumes, expanded to 950 pages per volume, Vol. III appeared in 1913, listing Dr. Hartranft as Editor, Dr. Johnson as Associate and Managing Editor, and Selina Schultz Gerhard as Assistant Editor. Vol. IV appeared in 1914, bringing the number of published documents to 153. Translations were by now abandoned, bibliographical notes confined to a page or two preceding each document, and historical, theological and language commentary more wisely left to the leisure of later scholars. They would benefit immeasurably from the ready availability of faithfully reproduced source texts, as well as the standard of Dr. Hartranft's scholarship set before them in Vol. I. Seventy years later it may be safely assumed that even Dr. Hartranft would not have been disappointed at the ongoing reconsideration of Schwenckfeld by students of Reformation history and theology. As he had predicted, Reformation history had to be largely rewritten.

In the summer of 1913 Dr. Hartranft's declining health prompted him, with his wife, to go to Switzerland for recuperation; however, he shortly became gravely ill. Dr. Johnson was called to bring him back to Wolfenbüttel, where he continued in a weak physical and mental condition. Suffering a paralytic stroke the next summer, he passed away on December 30, 1914, to be interred in the cemetery at Wolfenbüttel, where down to mid-twentieth century his grave was cared for by funds forwarded from America. On February 9, word of his death having reached America, Dean Jacobus delivered the address at a brief service of commemoration at Hartford, and on May 25, Professor Waldo Seldon Pratt gave the address at a formal memorial service.

During Dr. Hartranft's illness, Dr. Johnson and Miss Gerhard persevered in preparation of material for Vol. V, and it was shortly delivered to the printer. During an April 1914 trip through southern Germany they had successfully located missing manuscripts known to have been addressed by Schwenckfeld to the city of Ulm, and had also discovered an oil painting for which Schwenckfeld had posed in 1556. This painting, now in the Schwenkfelder Library, has served as the basis for most likenesses of Schwenckfeld reproduced in Schwenkfelder publications, and also for the modern painting by Adolph Pannash.

By 1914 Dr. Johnson had devoted ten years and Miss Gerhard five years to *Corpus* editorial work under Dr. Hartranft's direction. On the day following the February 9 commemoration service at Hartford, Doctors Mackenzie, Jacobus, Richardson and Paton of Hartford Theological Seminary met with members of the Schwenkfelder Board of Publication to initiate the obvious step of appointing Dr. Johnson to succeed Dr. Hartranft as Editor in Chief, with all the duties and responsibilities heretofore vested in Dr. Hartranft, including, importantly as it shortly developed, that of custodian of the editorial materials in Wolfenbüttel owned by the Board of Publication. He was also named to the Publication Committee, serving with Dr. Richardson and Rev. O. S. Kriebel. These appointments were subsequently confirmed by the Schwenkfelder Board of Publication meeting in Norristown, April 2, with E. K. Schultz, Oscar S. Kriebel, George H. Anders, Charles S. Anders and Samuel K. Brecht in attendance. In a May 19 letter Dr. Johnson formally accepted the appointment, assuring the Board of Publication, "I shall do all that within me lies to fulfill the obligations thus laid upon me."

But no sooner had the editors assumed their new responsibilities than new and potentially more dangerous uncertainties loomed before them. As they returned to Wolfenbüttel from their trip through southern Germany, war clouds over Europe began to darken. On June 28, 1914 the assassin's bullet at Sarajevo had ignited the spark; by the first week in August war had been declared and by fall the armies of the European powers were locked in the desperate struggle of World War I. With continued hospitality personally assured by the Mayor of Wolfenbüttel, the editors refused to join the homeward flight of American nationals from Germany, but continued quietly and persistently with their editorial work. Indeed, so highly were the *Corpus* undertaking and the integrity of the editors held by German neighbors and scholars that correspondents frequently appeared to go out of their way to accommodate requests for documents and information. Post-armistice removal of editorial offices to Pennsburg was compelled by reasons of economics, not politics.

By March 25, 1916 the printers, Breitkopf and Härtel, reported from Leipzig that Vol. V had been completed but that shipment to America could not be arranged. Only unbound sheets could be forwarded by mail. Printing of Vol. VI continued, although at a slower pace because of withdrawal of competent workers. After some 500 pages, printing was halted by inflated wage and material costs, and finally by an inability to secure further supplies of paper.

After the American declaration of war monthly remittances of funds from Hartford and from the Board of Publication became impossible. The faith of the printers continued work until the unpaid invoices totaled $1,327.36. To maintain his family and Miss Gerhard, Dr. Johnson borrowed from local friends, notably Dr. Karl Gerhard of Wolfenbüttel, who was most generous throughout the entire period. While of course handicapped, at no time during the final two years of the war were they in want of food or shelter, nor did they experience anything but courteous treatment from friends and neighbors. Contact with America was maintained through a friend in Switzerland, through the Red Cross, and briefly through embassy channels. Unable to renew their U.S. passports, they were forced to rely somewhat perilously on periodic renewals of an emergency passport issued by the German Government, and after the armistice on a passport issued by the Spanish embassy.

After the November 11, 1918 armistice, a return visit was necessary to preserve their American citizenship. In any event, German inflation made continued residence in Wolfenbüttel impractical. Efforts were initiated on both sides of the ocean to arrange return of staff and library to America. Dr. Johnson wrote that he required $4,000 to discharge debts he had incurred during the previous two years. The Board of Publication borrowed this sum and the State Department undertook to forward it to Germany, but only on the condition that Dr. Johnson and family return whether or not shipment of the library could be arranged. With the German residence permit about to expire and the money forwarded through the State Department not yet received, Dr. Johnson, through strenuous efforts and the aid of influential friends, arranged to mortgage the unshipped books to secure the debt to the printers, sold his household furniture to pay more insistent creditors, mortgaged the editorial materials to pay for passage of people and library, and arranged passage for both from Rotterdam to New York through the U.S. embassy at The Hague. During February the editors gave public notice of the removal of editorial offices to Pennsburg, Pennsylvania, effective March 1, that printing would continue in the hands of Breitkopf and Härtel, and that Pastor Kurt Ernesti of Braunschweig, who had assisted the editors in checking patristic references and other editorial details since preparation of Vol. III, would officially represent the editors in further historic researches in Germany.

To the intense relief of all concerned, Dr. and Mrs. Johnson, their son Rolland and Miss Gerhard arrived at the port of New York,

April 19, 1919 having been away from home for seven eventful years. One week later the editorial materials and library, packed in 146 boxes weighing twelve tons, were safely deposited on the second floor of the Carnegie Library on the campus of Perkiomen School in Pennsburg. Reporting their return to the spring General Conference, the Board of Publication noted: "This is an accomplishment of which any man might be proud and we take great pleasure in testifying to our admiration for the way the entire situation was handled, and for the excellent and gratifying results accomplished." The board further reported Vol. V ready for shipment as soon as conditions improved, 500 pages of Vol. VI in print and Vol. VII (bringing the total number of documents presented to 354) ready for the printers and deposited in the library at Wolfenbüttel to be called for when needed.

As the editors settled into their new quarters, they first had to see to the installation of shelving and cabinets, to unpack and organize the materials hastily packed for removal from Germany, and to store the rarest and most prized books and manuscripts in the "fireproof" vault running from the basement to the second floor of the Carnegie Library, originally designed with this purpose in mind. Then too, they had to readjust their personal lives. Dr. Johnson had been in Germany for most of the previous fifteen years; Miss Gerhard for most of the previous ten.

Selina Schultz Gerhard, the assistant editor, brought an end to a long-distance courtship by marrying, in December 1919, Eugene S. Schultz, a descendant of immigrant George Schultz. Mr. Schultz was a plant pathologist in the U.S. Department of Agriculture, and the couple took up residence in Washington, D.C. They summered in Presque Isle, Maine, where Mr. Schultz pursued his research into diseases of the potato plant. In January of 1922 a son, Eugene Arden, was born, to be followed six years later by a daughter, Alma.

Meanwhile Dr. Johnson, noting no vacancy in Schwenkfelder pulpits, requested of the Board of Publication, and was granted, permission to accept a call as minister of the Mennonite Church in Bally, a post he held for the remainder of his life. Shortly thereafter Hartford Theological Seminary requested him to deliver a course of lectures in church history, a call he could hardly refuse. Thus it came about that, while headquarters were maintained at Pennsburg, editorial work proceeded, albeit at a slow pace, in Washington, D.C., Presque Isle, Maine, and Hartford, Connecticut.

In January 1920 Miss Helen Schultz joined the staff, working on Vol. VII and appearing as associate editor of Vol. VIII. She, however, resigned in April 1921 to devote her full energies to preparation of material for the 1923 Genealogical Record. In June of 1921 Rev. Levi S. Hoffman was appointed associate editor, to devote to the *Corpus* work such time as his ministerial duties permitted. In 1922 H. W. Kriebel returned to Pennsburg and performed yeoman service as custodian of the Historical Library and assistant to the editors. Professor Kriebel had resigned as Secretary of the Board of Publication and from all church posts in 1906 as a result of a heated controversy with his cousin, Dr. O. S. Kriebel. Oscar S. Kriebel was desperately seeking, eventually with success, a grant from the Carnegie Foundation to construct the Carnegie Library on the campus of Perkiomen School. Howard W. Kriebel was outraged to think Schwenkfelders would accept, much less actively seek, such secular funds.

Amid such staff turmoil it is hardly surprising that editorial work slowed almost to a halt. With the excitement of original discovery largely over, the editorial task became a tedious and exhausting one. Moreover, it was a task toward which any newcomer could make only a very limited contribution. There was simply no substitute for the years of learning, first under Dr. Hartranft, later entirely on their own, which enlightened the work of Dr. Johnson and Mrs. Schultz. With Dr. Johnson's energies and interests now more widely dispersed, progress came to rest more and more upon the associate editor, Mrs. Schultz. It was she who persevered in reading and correcting proof sheets, permitting printing to continue. Vol. VI duly appeared in 1922 and Vol. VII in 1926. Dr. Johnson spent the summer of 1926 working on the biography of Schwenckfeld, always projected as a final volume to climax the series, but without visible results.

During 1925-26 the Board of Publication made impassioned entreaties to Mrs. Schultz to resume work and to take general charge of the publication effort. With the bicentennial year in view, a plan was developed to complete the work by 1934. A budget toward this end was prepared, reflecting the escalated costs of the post-war period. Many original subscribers and patrons were now deceased and collection of amounts due from their estates proved a delicate matter. Furthermore, most subscribers had paid in advance for Vols. VI, VII and VIII, and not a few their subscriptions for the whole series, so future proceeds from sale of volumes had to be substantially discounted. At the fall General Conference in 1927 it was announced that ten donors had pledged a total of $58,000, whereupon "the congregation burst spontaneously into the Doxology." Once again the publication effort was put on a fast track. With essential documents already assembled, Dr. Ernesti checking details in Europe, and Mrs. Schultz working diligently here, editorial work progressed and was in fact substantially completed by the 1934 target date. The most tedious task of all—transcription of the German and Latin notes in the margins of Schwenckfeld's Bible—occupied Mrs. Schultz for another year, but was completed for inclusion in Vol. XVIII.

Mrs. Schultz bore the brunt of reading and correcting proof sheets as they came off the press. Vol. VIII appeared in 1927, the preface duly noting that by reason of her marriage, the associate editor, Miss Selina Schultz Gerhard, had now become Mrs. Selina Gerhard Schultz. Vol. IX appeared in 1928 and Volume X, bringing the number of documents presented to 610, was received from the printers in 1929. Vol. X listed Dr. Johnson as Editor in Chief, Mrs. Schultz as Associate and Managing Editor, and Rev. Hoffman and Rev. Lester K. Kriebel as Associate Editors.

Rev. Lester K. Kriebel spent a year as a Hartford exchange student at the University of Giessen, Germany, during which time he visited the Schwenkfelder Silesian homelands. Upon his return in 1929, then age 31, he took up residence at Perkiomen School and assisted in the editorial work of the *Corpus.* Once again youthful energy had been recruited for the work. With Dr. Johnson as Editor, Mrs. Schultz as Associate and Managing Editor, and Rev. Lester K. Kriebel as Associate Editor, Vol. XI appeared in 1931, Vol. XII in 1932, Vol. XIII in 1935 and Vol. XIV in 1936. Altogether 984 documents had now been "brought more fully to light."

But the long and tortuous publication effort was fated for yet another extended delay, as for the second time the trials of a world war interrupted printing. Unfavorable exchange rates forced suspension of printing after 1936. In 1939 purchase of blocked German Marks at a substantial discount, and their transfer to the printers, permitted printing of Vol. XV. However, it could not be shipped and had to be stored in the printer's warehouse. Manuscripts for Vols. XVI to XVIII were forwarded to Dr. Ernesti, who passed away suddenly in January 1940. Dr. Theodore Sipple, engaged as Dr. Ernesti's successor, became seriously ill and could not continue. In 1941 Eberhard Teufel, pastor emeritus, scholar and historian of Stuttgart-Fellbach, Germany, was engaged, and when the United States joined the war against Germany, he took the unprinted manuscripts into his own home. Although an allied bomb grazed his home, and in a single week he lost two sons in the war, Teufel faithfully guarded the manuscripts entrusted to him through the remaining years of the war. At the conclusion of the war he sought the assistance of the U.S.

Army of Occupation to return the manuscripts to Pennsburg.

Meanwhile Allied bombing of Leipzig in December of 1943 heavily damaged the printing plant of Breitkopf and Härtel and the Schwenkfelder Board of Publication lost the 1,000 copies of Vol. XV as well as hundreds of copies of earlier volumes, together with other assets. Only five copies of Vol. XV had been mailed to European subscribers, one of which reached Pastor Teufel, who forwarded it to Pennsburg. When the Soviet Government subsequently confiscated the Breitkopf and Härtel firm and all its assets, the Board of Publication deemed it prudent to return all manuscripts to Pennsburg and await more settled conditions to resume printing.

In 1956 Mr. Wayne C. Meschter, Moderator of the Schwenkfelder General Conference and President of the Board of Publication, offered to donate funds for printing the remaining volumes and reproducing Vol. XV, provided arrangements could be made at reasonable cost, all in the hope of completing the work by 1961—the 400th anniversary of Schwenckfeld's death. In June of 1957 Andrew S. Berky, Director of the Schwenkfelder Library, personally carried the manuscript for Vol. XVI to Göttingen and contracted with Hubert and Co. of that city to print the remaining volumes. Vol. XVI appeared in 1959, Vol. XVII in 1960, and Vols. XVIII and XIX in 1961. Vol. XV, reproduced by photographic processes, also appeared in 1960. The last five volumes named Mrs. Schultz as Editor and Andrew S. Berky as Managing Editor. Thus by 1961, the 400th anniversary of Schwenckfeld's death, his deathbed wish had been magnificently fulfilled. All 1,252 known documents had been "brought more fully to light."

Publication of the earlier volumes of the *Corpus* alerted scholars, librarians and archivists to new interest in Schwenckfeld. In consequence, documents previously unknown and not included in the chronological presentation were brought to the attention of the editors, necessitating an increase in the number of volumes to nineteen. Vol. XVIII included sixty-five such documents as well as some undatable documents. Vol. XIX concluded the series, "including four very recently discovered documents of paramount importance."

The last 350 pages of Vol. XVIII present Schwenckfeld's annotations in the margins of his personal Bible, a copy of an edition printed by Peter Schöffer in Worms in 1529. The text of the Bible is in German, based on a Zurich translation; the annotations are primarily in abbreviated Latin, written with a fine pen in black or red ink. Textual references date most of the annotations during the years 1530-35, although those in the Song of Solomon are in handwriting resembling that of Schwenckfeld in later years. The most closely annotated is the book of Psalms, where the text is underlined and almost all available marginal space covered with closely worked script. Mrs. Schultz devoted the better part of a year, magnifying glass in hand, to transcribing the annotations, frequently struggling to understand abbreviations. From these annotations can be clearly deduced Schwenckfeld's intense study of the Bible in Greek, Latin and Hebrew versions, of the Septuagint, Vulgate and the Hebrew texts, as well as an intimate familiarity with the writings of the Church Fathers. Schwenckfeld must have purchased the Bible in 1529 shortly after his arrival in Strassburg. An autograph in Schwenckfeld's hand inside the front cover and dated 1555 bequeathes the Bible to Kathrina Streicher for many kindnesses to him. It then passed through several hands, including those of Daniel Suderman, who lived until 1632, after which it dropped out of sight for 250 years until it resurfaced at a London book auction in 1890. It was purchased by Otto Harrassowitz, a book dealer who supplied many volumes to Dr. Hartranft and whose firm still forwards appropriate items to the Schwenkfelder Library. He alerted Dr. Hartranft, who in turn alerted the Schwenkfelders in Pennsylvania. Anthony H. Seipt purchased it from Harrassowitz for $525. Six months later Mr. Seipt was reimbursed and the Bible added to the historical collection at Pennsburg. It is now perhaps the most prized possession of the Schwenkfelder Library.

Corpus Schwenckfeldianorum is an all embracing term. In Dr. Hartranft's idealistic vision the writings of Valentine Crautwald, whose theological and linguistic erudition so greatly assisted and influenced Schwenckfeld, were to be included along with relevant works of other contemporaries and correspondence among them. The climax of the series—indeed, the inspiration for the entire effort— was to be a biography of Schwenckfeld, a biography that would do justice to his noble character and life, and finally release it "from the reproach heaped upon it by those who established themselves the exclusive messengers of the Kingdom of God." With the *Corpus* series completed on the more modest scale dictated by practical considerations, this task also devolved upon Mrs. Schultz. A graduate of Perkiomen School, originally hired as secretary to the *Corpus* editors, for thirty years Mrs. Schultz had immersed herself in Reformation history and the literature of Schwenckfeld. It can safely be said no one, self-taught, before, nor likely following, will ever become more conversant with Schwenckfeld's writings or more intimately acquainted with his life and work. All of this laboriously acquired knowledge and understanding she now devotedly poured into the biography, providing at last a sympathetic portrait worthy of the reformer's noble character. The biography appeared independently of the *Corpus*, published in 1946 by the Board of Publication. Popular in lay and scholarly circles alike, it has issued forth in three subsequent editions. In an introduction to the 1977 edition, Dr. Peter Erb, Associate Director of the Schwenkfelder Library, surveys the current state of Schwenckfeld historiography, offering pregnant suggestions for areas meriting further study.

It would be impossible to sketch, even in outline, the full significance of the completed *Corpus Schwenckfeldianorum.* That it provided a major impetus to the study of Schwenckfeld there cannot be the slightest doubt. Because of it Paul Maier was able to write his important work on the person and work of Christ according to Schwenckfeld, E. J. Furcha and Reinhold Pietz to complete studies of Schwenckfeld's anthropology, and the renowned social theorist, Joachim Wach, to produce his widely noticed essay on the Silesian nobleman. Other works deserving of mention are Hans Urner's essay on Schwenckfeld's conception of baptism, Lashlee's dissertation on Schwenckfeld's view of reform, and most importantly for Schwenkfelders, Horst Weigelt's book on the Schwenkfelders in Silesia.

In 1973 Dr. Horst Weigelt, after two visits to and with some financial assistance from the Schwenkfelder Library, published in Berlin the German text of his *Spiritualistische Tradition im Protestantismus—Das Schwenkfeldertum In Schlesien.* With hundreds of citations from *Corpus* documents and Mrs. Schultz's biography, Dr. Weigelt traces the development of Schwenckfeld's thought during his lifetime, enlightening particularly the influence of Crautwald. He then traces the development of Schwenkfeldianism in Europe down through the 1734 migration and its gradual decline thereafter. In considering this decline, Dr. Weigelt notes that while first generation Schwenkfelders were nobles, theologians or physicians, and the second generation farmers, local officials or tradesmen, those remaining in Europe after 1734 were mostly house servants or gardeners, earning a living by spinning or other laboring tasks. Whereas many earlier Schwenkfelders knew Latin, Greek and Hebrew, many of these later people could hardly read or write. They lost the ethical passion of Schwenckfeld's concept of the "New Man." Carl Ehrenfried Heintze, controversial publisher of the 1771 German edition of Christopher Schultz's *Erläuterung,* stands forth as a Schwenkfelder pastor and theologian in the traditional mold, but after his death in

1775, Schwenkfeldianism in Silesia lost its significance. In 1984 the Schwenkfelder Library plans to publish an English translation of Dr. Weigelt's work by Peter Erb, enlightening a historic period of which little had previously been generally known.

But students of Schwenckfeld are all too prone to forget the importance of a work such as the *Corpus* for students of other areas of the Reformation. In 1962 George Huntston Williams, Winn Professor of Ecclesiastical History at Harvard University, published his *The Radical Reformation,* opening for the first time in a major way the scope and significance of the Radical Reformation and presenting Schwenckfeld's role in its historical and theological context. The book draws heavily on the *Corpus* and Mrs. Schultz's biography, with appropriate appreciation for Mrs. Schultz's assistance and cooperation. For the layman this book offers the most readable introduction to the Reformation and Schwenckfeld's seminal role in it.

The existence of the *Corpus* has been a great aid for the investigation of sixteenth-century Anabaptists, particularly Pilgram Marpeck (as reflected in William Klassen's study of Marpeck's hermeneutics and the Klassen-Klaassen edition and translation of Marpeck's works) and the Sabbatarian Anabaptists in eastern Europe. The works of Schwenckfeld also help us to understand the world of a revolutionary such as Thomas Müntzer, an apocalyptic prophet such as Melchior Hoffmann and a pacifist such as Menno Simons. A comparison of Schwenckfeld with men such as these not only illuminates the broader traditions of the Radical Reformation, but also helps us, in turn, to know Schwenckfeld better—how he was similar to his contemporaries and how he differed.

This mirror-like quality of Schwenckfeld's works as edited in the *Corpus,* reflecting the world around him and himself in that world, is clear as well when he is considered against the magisterial wing of the Reformation and the Reformation background, late medieval spirituality, the humanism of Erasmus, the early Luther's division of spiritual and physical church and sacrament, the sacramentalism of Zwingli and the reform endeavors of Bucer and Oecolampadius. Serving in this way to illuminate our understanding of the Reformation, the *Corpus* has fulfilled in a real sense the ecumenical hope which the dying Schwenckfeld placed in his writings transmitted through his descendants. These and other studies, in greater measure than he ever dared hope, are realizing Dr. Hartranft's vision of revisionist scholarship granting Schwenckfeld his rightful place in Reformation studies and portraying the noble character of the man in appropriate perspective.

It is eminently fitting that this chapter conclude by noting a singular honor bestowed upon Mrs. Schultz. On November 23, 1961 the ancient and prestigious University of Tübingen in West Germany awarded her an honorary Doctor's degree. Mrs. Schultz, then 81 years of age, accompanied by her husband and escorted by Andrew Berky, traveled by air to Germany under the sponsorship of the Schwenkfelder Library and was there entertained as a guest of the university. Before 150 persons Dr. Gerhard Rosenkranz, Dean of the Theological Faculty, conferred the degree, the citation reading in part: " . . . the Evangelical Theological Faculty of the Eberhard Karl University of Tübingen grants to the honorable Mrs. Selina Schultz, the learned editor and biographer of Caspar von Schwenckfeld, whose indefatigable lifework has disclosed anew to research, a venerable figure in the history of the German Reformation, and has thereby opened the approach to a source of deep Christian thoughts which have worked secretly but widely for a long time in the history of the spirit, the rights and privileges of a Doctor of Theology."

In response to a request by the faculty, Mrs. Schultz then addressed the assembly in German, simply and modestly reviewing her part in the *Corpus* publication and closing with a moving tribute to her husband, her son and her daughter, "for sympathetic cooperation and unqualified support" through her long years of labor. After visiting old friends and acquaintances in Germany the party returned to America. On July 19, 1969 Mrs. Schultz, at the ripe old age of 89, passed quietly to her eternal reward, to be followed three months later by her husband. Both were laid to rest in the family plot in the cemetery at Palm Church.

In all the annals of literary history it is doubtful that any work of this magnitude has been undertaken by so small a base of sponsorship, prosecuted through so much difficulty and frustration, and yet brought to such distinguished fruition. The *Corpus Schwenckfeldianorum* is indeed a fitting monument to Caspar Schwenckfeld von Ossig; a lasting testimony to the influence of the Schwenkfelder heritage.

Chapter Three

Schwenkfelder Library

Upon their arrival in Pennsylvania (1731-37) the Schwenkfelders brought with them highly prized books and manuscripts containing Schwenckfeld's works and other devotional literature. During the first fifty years in Pennsylvania they supplemented their collections by copying many volumes in their possession and making further purchases from Germany. Like other Pennsylvania-German groups, artists among them developed skills in penmanship and illuminated writing, producing beautiful "Fraktur" specimens and book plates.

With the decline in the knowledge of German among the Schwenkfelders in the mid-nineteenth century, study of these source materials seriously eroded, but with the publication of the 1879 *Genealogical Record,* the celebration of the 150th Gedächtnis Tag in 1884, and the launching of the *Corpus* project, interest was awakened and deliberate collection of materials undertaken.

At General Conference in 1885 church trustees were instructed to gather books and manuscripts remaining in Schwenkfelder possession, and Howard W. Kriebel was designated curator—a propitious choice. For over forty years Professor Kriebel pursued his studies of Schwenkfelder and local history as collector, genealogist, historian, writer and editor. Born in 1859 of a lineage including thirty-three immigrant Schwenkfelder ancestors, he studied at Kutztown State Normal School and Oberlin College, taught in local schools, preached in the meeting houses and married and settled on a farm near the Washington Meeting House. In this home he initiated the historical collections, by 1890 formally designated "Schwenkfelder Historical Library." When in 1892 he moved to East Greenville to take up his duties as an early teacher at Perkiomen School, which he helped his cousin, Rev. O. S. Kriebel organize, the library collections moved with him. He was a member of the Sesquicentennial Committee, and served as secretary of the Publishing Committee, in which capacity he carried on the initial correspondence with Dr. Hartranft to launch the *Corpus* project. In 1904 he prepared *The Schwenkfelders in Pennsylvania,* a historical sketch, published by the Pennsylvania German Society and still the most readable account of the Schwenkfelder movement in Pennsylvania. He was editor and publisher of *The Pennsylvania German* magazine of Lititz, Pa. Dr. Brecht pays gracious tribute to Mr. Kriebel as "the best informed man in the country today on the early history of the activities of the Schwenkfelders after their arrival in Pennsylvania," and gratefully acknowledges the contributions of Mr. Kriebel's research and fieldwork to the preparation of the 1923 *Genealogical Record.* We have already noted Howard Kriebel's active role in the identification and marking of immigrant graves, and in preparing historical sketches during the 1934 Bicentennial Celebration. In his *Schwenkfeldian* obituary following Mr. Kriebel's death in 1937, Dr. Brecht credits Mr. Kriebel with inspiring his own historical studies and, interestingly, Dr. Brecht in his turn was instrumental in prompting Wayne Meschter to provide the present home for the historical collections. Thus does a man's influence live after him.

The early Schwenkfeldiana were packed off to Hartford in 1890, and along with the Hartford collections, to Wolfenbüttel in 1903. When Howard Kriebel resigned his church offices in 1907, custodianship was transferred to Rev. O. S. Kriebel and the collections removed to a room in the Perkiomen School gymnasium.

When in 1906 Dr. Kriebel finally secured a $20,000 grant from Andrew Carnegie for a library building on the school campus, the grant was conditional upon raising locally a like amount as an endowment fund to provide for maintenance of the building and a debt-free school. By 1910 school debt had passed $38,000, requiring almost $60,000 to secure the Carnegie grant. In negotiations with Mr. Carnegie and local donors, express representations were made that "one purpose of the library building was to provide floor space and a fireproof section or vault for the housing, use and management of the collection of historical materials being formed by the Schwenkfelder Church." Schwenkfelder alumni, trustees and church members were instrumental in raising funds, Judge Heydrick making a key contribution of $9,000. Following the November 20, 1913 dedication, the historical materials were moved from the gymnasium to the second floor of the Carnegie Library, where in 1919 the twelve tons of *Corpus* editorial materials returned from Germany were unpacked and stored.

The second floor of the library served as home for the Schwenkfelder Historical Library for the next thirty years. Occupation of the space and a basement vault by the Schwenkfelder Board of Publication was legally formalized June 11, 1932 by filing with the Recorder of Deeds in the court house at Norristown a "Declaration and Assignment of Interest, Perkiomen School to the Board of Publication of the Schwenkfelder Church" wherein the school "grants, and assigns unto the Board of Publication of the Schwenkfelder Church, its successors and assigns, the free, absolute and unrestricted right, in perpetuity, to occupy and use the second floor of the Library Building and the vault in the basement thereof for the housing, care, use and management of the historical collections of the Schwenkfelder Church, together with the free right, liberty and privilege of ingress and egress to and from said Library Building." Income from endowment funds held by the Board of Publication as the Perkiomen School Library Endowment Fund is paid over to the school semi-annually as a contribution toward maintenance expenses of the building.

Besides the *Corpus* and Selina Schultz's biography of Schwenckfeld, three projects of the Board of Publication during the first half of the twentieth century require more than passing comment—the 1923 revision of the *Genealogical Record,* the 1942 translation of the *Erläuterung,* and two volumes (10 issues) of *Schwenkfeldiana* published between 1940 and 1955.

The 1879 *Genealogical Record* was a pioneering effort in that it undertook to trace genealogy of an entire religious sect. It reminded descendants of their unique heritage and awakened desire for further investigation and study. The ink was hardly dry before new births and deaths suggested the necessity for continually updating records. In 1899 General Conference resolved that registrars in each district be charged with maintaining a "Family Register." In 1905 a Kriebel Family Reunion Association was formed, with the object, as stated in their constitution, "To perpetuate the memory and foster the principles and virtues of the Kriebel ancestors of the members; to promote social intercourse among the latter, to preserve and disseminate historic information of the family." The meeting further resolved: "That the officers of this meeting appoint a committee of five to confer with representatives of other lines of descendants of Schwenkfelder Immigrants of 1734, with the purpose of devising ways and means of getting into print a new edition of *The Genealogical Record of the Descendants of the Schwenkfelders.*" A circular letter failed to elicit sufficient support, however, and nothing came of the movement.

In 1912 a self-appointed committee met in Norristown and discussed plans for collecting the material necessary to bring the record up to date. A circular request for genealogical information was addressed to heads of families, but no provision for editing or publishing the material was made. Just four days before his death in 1914, Judge Heydrick addressed a letter urging the compilation of a new genealogy and asking, "Can not something now be done to get the largest practical number of the now living descendants of the immigrant Schwenkfelders acquainted with one another, and with the history of their ancestors? I beg leave to suggest that the proposed revision of the *Genealogical Record* of the Schwenkfelders be made more historical than was heretofore thought of." As a direct result of this letter, the fall General Conference of 1914 referred the matter to the Board of Publication, "with power to act." The Board of Publication organized a *Genealogical Record* Revision Committee, which in turn appointed a Publishing Committee, of which Elmer K. Schultz was elected chairman, Samuel K. Brecht, secretary and editor, and Wayne C. Meschter, treasurer. Samuel Yeakel and Dr. J. E. Burnett Buckenham were shortly added to the committee.

By June 1917 individual guarantors had subscribed a fund totaling $2,500, shortly increased to $3,000—the then-estimated cost of collecting and editing the material. An office was opened in the Scheaff Building at 15th and Race Streets, Philadelphia, and a clerk was hired, then a second and finally a third, at the going rates of $7.00 to $9.00 per week. Dr. Brecht was a graduate of Haverford College, and had earned a Master's Degree from the University of Pennsylvania. Since 1905 he had been professor of mathematics at Boys' Central High School in Philadelphia. He initially undertook the editorship as an uncompensated spare-time project. Before it was completed, however, this proved impractical, and he was induced to secure a one-year leave of absence from his teaching job to devote full time to the project. To facilitate this arrangement the chairman and the treasurer of the committee made up a kitty of $2,500, the only remuneration Dr. Brecht received. They also advanced regular sums to maintain the office staff, and at one point Mr. Elmer Schultz advanced $5,000 to lend stability to the work and encourage Dr. Brecht. The treasurer's records and physical distribution of the books were handled in Mr. Meschter's American Preserve Co. office. Printed on 1,750 pages by Rand McNally and Co., proceeds of sales at $15.00 for the single-volume edition and $25.00 for the two-volume deluxe edition materially contributed toward out-of-pocket costs of preparation and printing, which costs approximated $34,000. Most guarantors accepted books in discharge of debts owed them, but no funds remained to repay advances by committee members and others, nor did Dr. Brecht receive any royalty payments.

The initial effort was to revise all data to July 1917, although information volunteered as late as December 1922 was incorporated where possible. While many helpful illustrations were included, the Publishing Committee, as a matter of policy, included no pictures of living individuals except for ministers of the respective churches. Dr. Johnson furnished photographs of old country scenes. Howard Kriebel traced family relationships and mapped original farmsteads. Dr. James M. Anders contributed an introduction, laying special stress on the spiritual heritage of the Schwenkfelders. Howard Kriebel's family numbering system, slightly modified, provided a convenient means of tracing lineage. Rev. O. S. Kriebel, Selina Schultz, Dr. Johnson and many others assisted. Helen Schultz supervised the codification of family records, read the proofs, and prepared the massive index.

The work had taken six years, including a difficult war period and post-war cost inflation. Almost fifty years had passed since the 1879 edition, adding two generations to the genealogy. Had the revision been further postponed, it is doubtful if it would have continued a feasible undertaking, since the number of descendants increased in geometric progression. The finished work was a credit to all who participated, particularly to Dr. Brecht, whose untiring labors were shortly recognized when Ursinus College conferred upon him an honorary degree of Doctor of Literature. Introductory pages and hundreds of mini-biographies scattered throughout the book provide a huge and valuable reservoir of historical information. Judge Heydrick would have been well pleased.

Christopher Schultz's *Erläuterung,* prepared with assistance from Caspar Kriebel, Christopher Kriebel and Balthazar Hoffmann, had been forwarded to Carl Ehrenfried Heintze, one of the few remaining adherents of the Schwenkfelder faith surviving in Silesia with whom the Pennsylvania Schwenkfelders had maintained correspondence. After some controversy over Heintze's editing of the text, it was printed in Germany in 1771. In 1830 a somewhat revised edition was printed in Sumneytown, Pennsylvania.

The book relates the history of the Schwenkfelders in Silesia and their trials and tribulations leading to the migration to Saxony and America. It then proceeds to a scholarly exposition and defense of

Schwenckfeld's teachings, dealing in difficult German and Latin with deep mysteries in theology, over which controversies of the Reformation raged.

Selina Schultz's brother, Elmer Schultz Gerhard, graduated from Perkiomen School and then earned Bachelor's and Master's degrees at Princeton University. He served for many years as professor in the department of languages at North East High School in Philadelphia, Pa. Working in his limited spare time, he struggled for several years with the difficult style and vocabulary of the original, striving to portray faithfully in English translation the author's thought as well as Schwenckfeld's exposition of the scriptures and Christian doctrine. His carefully prepared English text was published in 1942 by the Board of Publication under the title *A Vindication of Caspar Schwenckfeld von Ossig, An Elucidation of his Doctrine, and the Vicissitudes of His Followers,* thereby making available to present generations this valuable Schwenkfelder source book. Comments Professor Gerhard in his introduction: "In this book Christopher Schultz has brought us the essence, if not the quintessence, of Schwenckfeld's teaching and belief, as well as his amazing knowledge of the Bible and Christian doctrine from its very beginning. Surely one does find here what was never heard of before and never found in any other book, and topics of Christian faith for which one looks in vain elsewhere. It is the most concise, most comprehensive, and powerful vindication of Schwenckfeld, and of his doctrine and followers ever written."

The Schwenkfelder Historical Library contains voluminous source materials, including correspondence by early Pennsylvania Schwenkfelders, sermons and sermon outlines, devotional materials, diaries, account books, etc. Much of this is in manuscript form, written in a fine German script, some of it most minutely so. Deciphering and translating this material involves a lot of tedious and painstaking labor. It contains, however, a rich fund of literature and vivid insights into physical and spiritual conditions among the early Schwenkfelders in Pennsylvania.

Pursuing their purpose of making Schwenkfelder history and heritage available, particularly to the younger generations, the Board of Publication in 1940 started publishing *Schwenckfeldiana*, in issues appearing at roughly yearly intervals. Edited by Elmer Gerhard, who together with his sister Selina Schultz prepared most of the articles, the first two volumes developed biographies of early Schwenkfelder ministers in Pennsylvania. The third volume was a particularly informative survey of early Schwenkfelder schools and education. The

fourth issue presented the history of Moravian-Schwenkfelder relations, both in Saxony and in Pennsylvania, including quite controversial wrangling with Augustus Spangenberg (1704-1792), Zinzendorf's Moravian agent in America. Issue five, published in 1945,
described Schwenkfelder craftsmen, inventors and surveyors during
the colonial period. Issue six, the concluding issue of Vol. I, departed
somewhat from the previous format. Edited by Selina Schultz and
titled "Schwenkfelder Participation in Missionary, Welfare and
Foreign Missions supported by the Schwenkfelder Churches," it
included sketches of the Philadelphia, Norristown and Lansdale
missions—forerunners of the respective churches—and histories of
the Charity Fund and Relief Services over the years. Members of the
several churches contributed articles.

Vol. II was begun in 1949 with a "Biographical and Historical
Memorial for Flora K. Heebner (1874 - 1947)," for thirty-eight years
a missionary to China. A joint project of the Mission Board and the
Board of Publication, it was prepared by a committee with Rev.
Harvey K. Heebner serving as editor. It included articles by co-
workers in China, by representatives of the American Board of
Commissioners for Foreign Missions, with which the Schwenkfelder
Mission Board affiliated itself, and by various church representatives.
Vol. II, issue two, was devoted to relief activities on behalf of Silesian
refugees in West Germany following World War II. Issues three and
four presented, in English translation, excerpts from sermons
preached on the first 100 Schwenkfelder Memorial Days, 1734-1834.
Issue five, the last of the series, published in 1955, presented the text
of the historical drama, *Faith of our Fathers*, presented in the Salford
Grove, August 26, 1934 as part of the Bicentennial Celebration.

Taken together, *Schwenckfeldiana* ranks with Howard Kriebel's
The Schwenkfelders in Pennsylvania as readily available and readable
source materials on the Schwenkfelders in Pennsylvania. The time
may be ripe, however, for a modern study of Schwenkfelder individuals, activities and institutions during the formative period in this
country.

During the 1920s and 1930s, with interest in Schwenckfeldiana
running high, and with Howard Kriebel, Dr. Johnson, Selina
Schultz and Lester Kriebel actively acquiring new books, papers and
artifacts, the 2nd-floor vault in the Carnegie Library was soon filled
to overflowing. Cataloging and orderly shelf organization became
virtually impossible; working space was cramped to the point of
frustration. Furthermore, while the "fireproof vault" was a self-
sustaining masonry structure, it rose in the midst of a brick building

with wooden floor and roof structures and could hardly have preserved its irreplaceable collections in the event of a serious fire in the
building. A new fireproof building in which more adequately to
house and protect the collections became a serious concern of all those
involved and prompted Mr. Wayne C. Meschter to make possible the
present Schwenkfelder Library structure.

Mr. Meschter was born December 18, 1883 on the family farm
at Palm, Pa. He was one of six children of Charles Yeakel Meschter,
descendant of immigrant Melchior Meschter and Matilda Clemmer
Meschter, a lifelong member of the Hereford Mennonite Church at
Bally. When Wayne was a little over 5 years old his father died,
leaving his mother to raise the six children, to manage the 100-acre
farm and to struggle with some family debt. Two years later his
grandfather, Rev. Jacob Meschter, Schwenkfelder pastor for thirty-
seven years, who lived nearby, also died. At the early age of 13 Wayne
was hired out to a nearby farm for a seven-month term, April to
October, for $4.00 per month and board. From then on he worked
long summers on various farms and for one summer in the general
store of his uncle Levi Meschter in East Greenville while attending
Palm public schools during the winter months. At age 17 he attended
two winter terms at Perkiomen School, frequently hitching rides on
the local Perkiomen Railroad freight trains between school and home.
The entire family regularly attended church and Sunday school in the
upper district meeting houses.

On September 1, 1902, at the suggestion of his uncle, William
Y. Meschter, an officer in the Company, Wayne moved to Philadelphia to enter the employ of The American Preserve Co., then located
at 946-50 Beach St., just off Delaware Ave. By 1905 he had completed the commercial course at Temple University night school. On
Uncle William's death in 1909 Wayne acquired a stock interest in the
business and became Secretary Treasurer. From time to time he was
able to increase his stock holding, and when Company President Mr.
Lewis J. Link began to talk of retirement, Mr. Meschter sought
seriously to acquire control. Finally in 1916, after several abortive
discussions, Mr. Link granted Mr. Meschter a written option for
thirty days to buy the remaining stock for $156,000 cash! Mr. Link
was apparently confident the money could not be raised, and with but
$6,000 in his bank account, Mr. Meschter was not all that sure
himself!

At a local lunch counter Mr. Meschter had met Mr. Wilson H.
Lear, a well-to-do hardwood lumber dealer, whose yard adjoined the
American Preserve Co. plant. A common interest in Sunday school

work led the two into frequent discussions and a close friendship developed. Hearing of Mr. Link's offer and noting that the price went up each time the matter was discussed, Mr. Lear offered to help and arranged the necessary financing. On December 1, 1916 Mr. Meschter became the sole owner of the company. In 1920 the city condemned ninety feet from the front of the factory building, and the company was forced to seek new quarters. A lot at Third St. and Lehigh Ave. was purchased and the present structure erected. With the cost of building and equipment escalating to over $600,000 in the post-war inflation, and with sugar prices tumbling in the 1921 deflation, the company dangled on the brink of bankruptcy. Business recovered just in time, however, and operating profits slowly retired indebtedness to the building contractors. The company produced a line of preserves, jellies, apple butter, mince meat and some miscellaneous food products. By improving the quality of the products the company capitalized on the widening acceptance of prepared food products and business steadily expanded. By 1926 all debt to Mr. Lear had been repaid. The next decade, including the depression years of the early 1930s, proved the most profitable of Mr. Meschter's business career. With the corporate income tax set at 13 3/4% under the 1932 Revenue Act and the personal tax rate under 20%, these years afforded him the opportunity for accumulating a modest personal net worth.

Around 1937 Mr. Meschter suffered two years of poor health, including a serious neurosurgical operation at the Johns Hopkins Hospital in Baltimore. During this time also, company employees were organized as a local in the United Cannery and Allied Products Workers of America—CIO, and from April to September of 1940 engaged in a twenty-week strike, during which no plant operations were possible, producing a psychological blow from which Mr. Meschter never recovered. Fearing an illiquid estate in the event of his death, as of December 1, 1941 Mr. Meschter distributed some two-thirds of his company stock to his children, and formally retired as an officer of the corporation. Substantially recovered in health, he spent the wartime years as a "dollar-a-year" man in the Department of Agriculture in Washington. Following the end of the war Mr. Meschter entered upon perhaps the most satisfying decade of his life, devoting himself to personal interests, primary among which were the Schwenkfelder Church, of which he served as Vice-Moderator or Moderator from 1927 to 1957, and the Board of Publication, of which he was President from 1932 until his death, January 25, 1963.

Close association with Dr. Samuel K. Brecht in the

Schwenkfelder church at Philadelphia, particularly during the preparation of the *Genealogical Record,* and with Dr. Johnson, Selina Schultz and Rev. Lester Kriebel as the Board of Publication struggled with publication of the *Corpus,* served to impress upon Mr. Meschter the value and significance of the historical collections and the urgent need for more adequate facilities for housing and protecting them. When repeated efforts over the years toward this end failed to produce tangible results, Mr. Meschter took it upon himself to satisfy the need.

In December of 1944 Mr. Meschter delivered to the treasurer of the Board of Publication a check for $7,500, and at the April 26, 1945 meeting of the board indicated a willingness to furnish up to an additional $100,000 when and as needed to provide a suitable building to house the historical collections, provided the Board of Publication would assume responsibility for maintenance of the facility, that General Conference would approve separate incorporation of the library, and that the land on which the building would be erected would be owned by the corporation, all to the end that the library might be a perpetually independent institution. The Board of Publication accepted the offer, and the secretary of the board reported it to General Conference at its meeting in Lansdale, May 19, 1945. Conference approved the proposal in principle and authorized transfer of the historical materials to the Schwenkfelder Library when duly incorporated and ready to function.

At that time Mr. Meschter's personal and business attorney was Henry S. Borneman, Esq., an actively practicing lawyer in Philadelphia, a distinguished member of the Pennsylvania German Society and holder of a fine collection of rare books and Pennsylvania German Fraktur. Mr. Borneman took an active interest in the library project and was the principal advocate of a self-sustaining corporation. Appropriately on September 24, 1946 George K. Brecht, Esq., of Norristown, presented to the Honorable Judge Harold G. Knight in the Court of Common Pleas of Montgomery County, Norristown, Pennsylvania, the petition of twenty-five incorporators to form "Schwenkfelder Library" corporation. The purpose was stated as "the establishment and maintenance of a fully equipped library and activities allied thereto, as a Memorial to Caspar Schwenckfeld." The corporation sought perpetual existence, was to have no capital stock, and disclaimed contemplation of pecuniary gain or profit, incidental or otherwise, to its members. The twenty-five incorporators would be a self-perpetuating body, electing new members to fill vacancies, but with the charter provision that "at least two-thirds of the total

number of the members of the corporation shall always be descendants of the Schwenkfelder Immigrants into Pennsylvania before the
year 1750." The bylaws provide for a fifteen-member Board of
Directors to administer the affairs of the corporation. By a November
25, 1946 order of Judge Knight, Schwenkfelder Library was duly
chartered as a non-profit corporation in accordance with the petition
presented. Subsequently, in a July 8, 1955 ruling letter, the Internal
Revenue Service formally declared the corporation "an organization
described in Sec. 501 (c) (3) of the Internal Revenue Code of 1954 . . .
organized and operated exclusively for educational purposes." As
such the corporation pays no income taxes on contributions received
or on investment income, and contributions to the library are deduct-
ible as charitable contributions by the donor.

The members and directors listed in the Articles of Incorporation met at Perkiomen School informally on March 1, 1947 and
formally in the first stated annual meeting on May 3, 1947. The
articles of incorporation were approved and appropriate bylaws
adopted. Mr. Meschter was elected library president, Malcolm
Schweiker, vice-president, Wayne H. Rothenberger, treasurer, and
Lester K. Kriebel, secretary. The minutes of these meetings and
relevant exhibits were ordered permanently inscribed in a minute
book by Irwin P. Mensch, local calligrapher and artist. His library
"Treasure Book" remains an outstanding exhibit of the art of manuscript illumination.

Careful consideration had been given to the location of the new
building. There was some sentiment favoring a more rural setting in
the vicinity of the Palm church, but a consensus shortly developed
that a location adjacent to the campus of Perkiomen School would
prove mutually advantageous. The library would thus remain at the
Pennsburg address familiar to scholars around the world. The building would enhance the school campus and the library would be
readily accessible to the Perkiomen School community. After consideration over several meetings of school trustees and General Conference, the school offered to convey a plot 350 feet by 350 feet to the
library for the nominal consideration of $1.00. The library accepted,
and by the Fall board meeting, October 4, 1947, George Brecht, Esq.
reported that a deed to the land had been duly executed and recorded,
and title insurance in the name of the Library secured. The treasurer
reported initiation of a library endowment fund, with $4,210 re-
ceived in contributions from Gunard O. Carlson, Malcolm A.
Schweiker, Mrs. Ellen Schultz and Dr. Johnson, the latter making a
moving appeal for additional endowment funds to provide income

to carry on properly library activities.

An administrative committee composed of Wayne Meschter, Elmer Johnson, Lester Kriebel, Selina Schultz, Wayne Rothenberger and Henry Borneman, and a building committee made up of Malcolm Schweiker, chairman, Wayne Meschter, Gunard Carlson, Oscar Schultz and Kyrel Meschter were appointed. Committee members visited libraries at Franklin and Marshall, Princeton and other institutions, and consulted with a number of people, including Dr. Charles W. David of the University of Pennsylvania. Dr. Johnson drew up a list of floor space required for the various functions which totaled 10,310 square feet, including stack space for 30,000 volumes, an estimate that all too soon proved embarrassingly low. The administrative committee, largely under Mr. Borneman's leadership, interviewed a number of architects before choosing Sidney Martin of Philadelphia. Library directors approved this selection and Mr. Martin, in collaboration with the building committee, proceeded to draw up plans and specifications which were submitted to eight contractors for bids to be opened January 17, 1950. The bids ranged from a low of $237,000 to $276,000, and were rejected as too high. The library, as did the Central Schwenkfelder Church in similar circumstances, resisted the temptation to await lower building costs. Fortunately, in both instances a decision was made to persevere since continually rising building costs might well have made the projects impossible later. After further discussion, revised plans and specifications were approved and a contract negotiated with the John P. Hallahan Co. of Philadelphia. The building was duly completed at a cost in the neighborhood of $200,000. Mr. Meschter had meanwhile made additional contributions and finally made himself responsible for the funds required to complete the building, except that Malcolm Schweiker, president of American Encaustic Tile Co. in Lansdale donated all of the ceramic tile required in washrooms and service facilities.

The cornerstone was laid with appropriate ceremonies March 10, 1951 with the new Library Director, Andrew S. Berky, presiding and Malcolm Schweiker, Dr. Johnson, Mr. Borneman and Mr. Meschter speaking. The completed building was dedicated October 27, 1951 with an invocation by Rev. Harvey K. Heebner, presentation by Mr. Meschter, acceptance by Malcolm Schweiker, Library Vice-president, a dedicatory statement by Andrew Berky and benediction by Maurice Hohlfeld, professor, representing the Hartford Seminary Foundation.

As of May 1, 1951 title to the historical collections, certain endowment funds and rights of occupancy to designated areas of the Carnegie Library were formally transferred by the Board of Publication to Schwenkfelder Library. Contents of the vault were removed to the vault in the new building September 13, 14 and 15, 1951, thereby securing the heart of the collections in storage as fireproof as the technology of the day could provide. Removal of the remaining volumes followed at a more leisurely pace, while Andy and the board struggled with the structure, form and sources of financial support for new library activities.

The Library Board raised additional funds, and with the aid of Samuel Edgerton of Perkiomen School and Olive Zehner, a curator at Ephrata Cloisters, reconditioned the second floor of the Carnegie Library more properly to display valuable artifacts brought from Germany by the immigrants and antique pieces representative of their early life in Pennsylvania. This museum collection continues to grow and even in its cramped quarters to attract increasing numbers of scholars and visitors each year. It is a cultural resource of which the Schwenkfelder community and the entire Perkiomen region can be justifiably proud. Properly housed and staffed, the museum would take its deserved place along with those at Landis Valley, Ephrata, Peter Wentz Homestead and other similar collections as a center for the study of early Pennsylvania culture and history. Realization of the rich potential of this unique resource awaits an interested benefactor.

Staffing of the new library had been a subject of concern from the initiation of the project. Dr. Johnson and Selina Schultz were getting on in years and along with Lester Kriebel had primary activities elsewhere. A young person, preferably of Schwenkfelder descent, was clearly indicated. Andrew Schultz Berky was born September 5, 1922, a descendant on his mother's side from immigrant George Scholtze, a first cousin once removed of Dr. Johnson and of the same family line as Selina Schultz's husband Eugene. He attended Blair Academy and for a year and a half Williams College, where his education was interrupted by a four-year stint as a Navy pilot in World War II. In 1950 he completed his formal education by graduating from Franklin and Marshall with an A.B. degree in history. During the summer of 1948, before Andy's junior year at college, Mr. Meschter drove to Boyertown for a lengthy visit with him at his mother's home. Further discussions followed and at the May 7, 1949 board meeting, Andy was engaged as the initial "Director of the Schwenkfelder Library," at a salary of $250 per month. Continuing some graduate work at the University of Pennsylvania and with intensive orientation by Dr. Johnson and Lester Kriebel, he entered upon his new duties with all the enthusiasm of youth. For the next two decades Andy imprinted his own personality on the evolving library institution. He supported Board of Publication undertakings, and in the tradition of Howard W. Kriebel involved himself in local history activities. With a solid background in American history, a healthy curiosity and a facile and engaging writing style, he wrote a number of books and articles on local history, which were published by the Library. He became a popular lecturer, drawing attention to the library and its collections.

Mindful of the sacrifices of those who had collected and preserved the library materials, the new director felt under compulsion to engage the interest of qualified scholars trained in Reformation history and theology, and to make other holdings accessible to the general public through publication of manuscript materials of interest. He shortly translated and printed Christopher Schultz's *Account of the Circumstances Leading up to the American Revolution,* and then entered upon the more ambitious project of translating and editing the diaries of David Schultze. David Schultze, Schwenkfelder immigrant of 1733, poet, diarist, surveyor and legal consultant of Upper Hanover Township in the Perkiomen Valley, kept a detailed journal of his affairs for a period of more than sixty years. Of fifteen recovered diaries, all but one consisted of entries made in almanacs provided with blank spaces. Since recovered diaries did not run consecutively, Andy filled in the spaces, so far as possible, with editorial notes and explanations. A diary of the ocean voyage and of pioneer life in a foreign country, the story of David Schultze gives the general pattern endured by all German immigrants of the 18th century and "is a fascinating and compelling story, for it contains a quality which is not present in our own lives and in the world today." The translated and edited diaries were published by the library in two volumes during 1952 and 1953, under the title, *The Journals and Papers of David Schultze, 1726-1797.* In addition, during these years, library annual reports were printed in attractive booklets against a background of interesting historical vignettes.

Seeking to broaden the library audience, Andy conceived and arranged a series of lectures, subsequently published in 1956 under the title *The Challenge to American Life.* Five lectures, attracting enthusiastic audiences in the library auditorium, were delivered by distinguished leaders in their respective fields, as follows:

March 27, 1954, World Peace, by Dr. Joseph E. Johnson, President, Carnegie Endowment for International Peace
May 22, 1954, The Nature of American Freedom, by Dr. Henry Steele

Commager, Professor of History, Columbia University
April 9, 1955, Science and Industry, by Gaylord P. Harnwell, President, University of Pennsylvania
September 10, 1955, Spiritual Man, by Ralph Cooper Hutchinson, President, Lafayette College.
March 24, 1956, The Democratic Process, by James MacGregor Burns, Professor of Political Science, Williams College.

During the years 1953-1958 Andy authored and/or edited *The Passmore Pottery, 1828-1911*; *An Account of Dr. Benjamin Schultz of Pennsylvania...1722-1814*; *God Grants Liberty: A Collection of Fifteen Letters Written Between 1795 and 1846 by some prominent Americans*; Selina Schultz's translation of *The Mosquito Coast* and the *Story of the First Schwenkfelder Missionary Enterprise among the Indians of Honduras from 1768 to 1775*; *The Life and Times of Amos Schultz, 1809-1895*; *A Book of Days for 1954, A Sheet Calendar Enjoying Woodcuts from the Silesian Tagebuch of 1612*; *Practitioner in Physic: A Biography of Abraham Wagner, 1717-1763*; *The Schoolhouse Near the Old Spring* (published by the Pennsylvania German Society); *The Iron Collar*, a translation of Fedor Sommer's novel written in German in 1911 under the title *Die Schwenckfelder*; and *An Account of Some Hosensack Mills.*

Meanwhile the library had supported research by Dr. Joachim Seyppel while preparing his *Schwenckfeld, Knight of Faith,* and by Dr. John Joseph Stoudt in translating Schwenckfeld's *Passional* and *Prayerbook,* both published by the library in 1961 to mark the 400th anniversary of Schwenckfeld's death. The regular appearance of significant monographs and dissertations restudying Schwenckfeld's theology and his role in the Reformation were a steady source of satisfaction to all those who had labored to publish the *Corpus* and to gather and preserve the library collections.

During the latter years of the 1950s Andy's time and energies became increasingly absorbed in the completion of the *Corpus,* duly accomplished by 1961. By this time the funds turned over by the Board of Publication and contributions and bequests by interested individuals had increased the library's endowment to a little over $40,000. With an annual operating budget of some $20,000, the library was clearly dependent upon uncertain annual contributions to carry on its activities. Mr. Meschter desired, during his lifetime, to see an endowment fund providing enough income to assure maintenance of essential functions as a minimum. In a February 20, 1959 transmittal letter he delivered to the library a certificate for 1,830 shares of Wayne American Co. stock as a contribution toward this end. Mr. Meschter's letter to Director Berky read in part:

> We have drawn personal satisfaction from the accomplishments of the
> Library under your direction during the past eight years and are most
> anxious that such work continue and expand its influence over the years
> ahead.
>
> While the Library, to be truly effective, must attract interest and
> financial support from an ever widening group of individuals concerned
> with the preservation of our Schwenkfelder heritage, we have felt that
> our own part in this endeavor has not been properly complete without
> some basic provision for minimum operating funds.
>
> Mrs. Meschter and I would like during our lifetime, to complete
> our own part in the Library undertaking by a contribution for this
> purpose at this time. . . .
>
> We have entire confidence in the dedication and judgment of
> yourself and the present members of the Library Board of Directors,
> including their discretion and wisdom in selecting new members as
> vacancies occur who share an active interest in the purposes for which the
> Library has been erected. It is our hope that future Boards may continu-
> ally reinterpret the Schwenkfelder heritage to new generations through
> such activities as changing conditions may dictate, and no specific
> restriction is therefore attached to the management, application or use of
> this contribution.

During the early 1950s the American Preserve Company business suffered by reason of increasing domination of the market by
national and regional grocery chains, many of which drew their
supplies from captive manufacturing facilities. As of April 30, 1956
the company sold its inventory and equipment and then converted
the building at Third and Lehigh Ave. into a multi-tenanted income-
producing property. The name of the company was changed to
Wayne American Co. After receiving the contribution of Mr. Meschter's stock, the library accepted the offer of the remaining shareholders to sell their stock to the library in exchange for notes and the
library thereupon became the sole shareholder. The library then
brought about the dissolution of the corporation, utilized liquid
funds to pay off the stock purchase notes and became direct owner of
the Third and Lehigh Ave. building, a life insurance policy on Mr.
Meschter's life and some miscellaneous company assets. Two years
later the library sold the building for $465,000—$65,000 cash and
$400,000 in a 20-year 6% purchase-money mortgage. Level interest
and principal amortization payments provided the library with
$2,868 per month cash flow, the interest portion providing support
for library activities and the amortization portion regularly being
retained as endowment. During the last five years of the life of the

mortgage, payments were received but real estate taxes fell several years in arrears. As the neighborhood deteriorated, tenants found it impossible to conduct their business. Employees refused to travel to and from work and as leases expired vacancies occurred. Fortunately, a local appliance distributor whose warehouse had been destroyed by fire leased the first floor and, to improve building management and maintenance, purchased the building. To refinance his own mortgage, the balance of the library mortgage was paid off in full. Upon Mr. Meschter's death in 1963 the library collected the $100,000 face amount of the life insurance policy, thereby realizing a little more than $565,000 from the Wayne American Co. stock contribution.

By the early 1960s, with the library building in full operation, at least minimum activities endowed and the *Corpus* at long last completed, the library had seemed to complete an era, as noted by Mr. Berky in his Director's report to the Library Board October 7, 1961. "Interest in Schwenkfelder culture is shifting from that of deep personal involvement to a level of academic interests. The Schwenkfelder story just does not touch the lives of the people exposed to it as deeply as it once did. The tremendous mobility of society is fast changing our distinguishing characteristics and the Christian world is rapidly approaching a sameness and a oneness. All of this means that in the future, the Schwenkfelder Library will have to change its role to stay abreast of changing interests." He had previously suggested "the Board should begin to give consideration to the eventual development of a relationship with a top quality theological scholar, a person who can come in here, get at the heart of the Schwenkfelder movement, properly assess its intrinsic worth in relationship to Protestant development throughout the past four centuries, and relate its significance in terms of modern theological thought. I feel that only through this kind of an approach can the Schwenkfelder movement be given more vitality for the future and only through this kind of a person can the Library realize the full potential of its collection." With church membership growing through admission of non-descendant members, the role of the library as conservator of a spiritual heritage took on increasing urgency.

Perhaps spiritually drained by the exertions of the 1950s, Andy became restless and began to feel the attraction of new challenges. He increased his role as teacher and administrator at Perkiomen School and, beginning in 1962, the school and the library reached a time-sharing arrangement, each bearing one-half of Andy's salary. Problems facing the school administration required more and more of his time, until he became assistant headmaster, headmaster and then president of the school during a very trying time in its history. Finally in March 1973 he resigned his offices in both school and library, noting that he had completed two eleven-year terms of service. He felt it was time once again to move on to new challenges. He shortly was appointed director of the Peace Corps in Lesotho, southern Africa, and removed himself from direct contact with both school and library. He has, however, never lost interest in the ongoing progress of the institution he did so much to shape.

The 1960s were devoted in large measure to housekeeping chores. In 1965 Mr. Fred Grater, a member of the Palm church, was hired for the summer to undertake necessary cataloging work. With the assistance of the library he completed a course in library science at Drexel University and served the library as cataloger until 1975, when he resigned to undertake studies for a Master's degree in religion and culture at Wilfrid Laurier University in Waterloo, Ontario, Canada, all under the general oversight of Dr. Peter Erb, by that time associate director of the library. In October 1980, having completed his Master's thesis on Caspar Schwenckfeld's *Commentary on the Augsburg Confession,* Fred was employed by Emory University in Atlanta, Georgia, where he became engaged in organizing and cataloging a large part of the Case Memorial Library collections, which Emory acquired following a reorganization of Hartford Seminary.

During the years 1967-68 Miss Elke Arnold, master bookbinder, was employed to restore and organize the library collection of Frakturschriften. After the first thirty years getting settled in this country, Pennsylvania Schwenkfelders began to mark births, deaths and marriages with decorated and illuminated works of folk art, and also to produce remarkable specimens of book plates, house blessings and Vorschriften, treasured within families and eventually gravitating into the library collection of Fraktur. This collection over the years has attracted the interest of many scholars, cultural historians and authors in this field, and not a few specimens have been reproduced, with due credit to the library, in widely recognized books by Borneman, Shelley, Stoudt, Lichten and others, and have frequently been displayed in major folk art exhibits. Although some research into authorship and artistry has been done, a published study doing justice to this unique collection awaits the dedication of a qualified scholar and the financial support of an interested benefactor.

Library Member Fritz Eberhard rebound and restored more

valuable volumes in the Bible and manuscript collections and traveled to a seminar in Europe to learn of latest techniques in book preservation. Being printed in acid ink, the paper of old volumes is gradually being eaten away. Finally, the best advice suggested maintenance of constant temperature and humidity and the vault was specially equipped to this end. During 1981 special contributions enabled the library to purchase microfilming and read-print equipment and to undertake a long-term program of preserving documents on film. Not only would manuscripts be preserved in this manner, but once microfilmed they could be made available on duplicate films to distant scholars without the originals leaving the library premises. Disintegrating eighteenth- and nineteenth-century newspaper files could also be readily consulted by interested parties.

In the summer of 1970 the library was visited by Peter Erb, a doctoral candidate at the University of Toronto, Canada. A native of Canada and of Mennonite descent, Peter earned his Bachelor's degree at Waterloo Lutheran University in 1965, and a M.S.L. degree from the Pontifical Institute of Medieval Studies in 1970. He was seeking material for his Ph.D. dissertation, eventually completed in 1976, on The Role of Late Medieval Spirituality in the Work of Gottfried Arnold (1666-1714)—the same Gottfried Arnold who had aroused the interest of Friedrich Schneider, indirectly inspiring the *Corpus.* Here perhaps was the theological scholar Andy Berky sought, and in fact Peter's interest in the library collections brought on a third era of library activity.

Broadening his research in Reformation and Schwenckfeld theology, where the library possessed unduplicated resources, by June 1, 1973 Peter arranged clearance of his duties at Waterloo Lutheran University and moved his family to this area to undertake a fifteen-month consultantship at the library. Besides continuing his research, he would give thought and advice as to the general direction of library activities, oversee communications with interested scholars in the field and supervise a modest program of acquisition of new volumes as they became available to augment the library collections. As the fifteen-month consultantship drew to a close, Peter's continuing role in library affairs was the subject of serious deliberation. While his interest in the field continued unabated, had in fact been stimulated, he deemed it prudent to preserve his tenured position at Wilfrid Laurier University, where he enjoyed broader library facilities and stood in the mainstream of medieval and Reformation scholarship. He has served since that time as a corporation director and as Associate Director, regularly traveling to Pennsburg for library semi-annual meetings and on research missions. Within this role he has conceived and organized the Schwenkfelder Library Colloquium on Schwenckfeld and the Schwenkfelders to be held September 17-23, 1984 to mark the 250th anniversary of the arrival of the Schwenkfelders in Pennsylvania, the 100th anniversary of the initiation of the *Corpus* project and the 100th anniversary of the Schwenkfelder Historical Library.

On five consecutive Tuesday nights in October and November 1973 Peter delivered a series of lectures at the library, later published under the title *Schwenckfeld in His Reformation Setting,* the most readable sketch of Schwenckfeld's theology and participation in the Reformation available. It also contains a ready reference bibliography of Schwenkfelder-related publications. He contributed a perceptive and challenging introduction to the 1977 edition of Selina Schultz's biography of Schwenckfeld. In 1978 he deciphered the code in which much of it was originally written and translated and edited *The Spiritual Diary of Christopher Wiegner,* published and circulated by the Society of Descendants of the Schwenkfeldian Exiles. He has translated for publication by the Paulist Press works by Jacob Boehme and by Johann Arndt, and has published any number of articles in the *Mennonite Quarterly Review* and other scholarly magazines. He has served as managing editor of *Studies in Religion/Sciences religieuses,* a respected Canadian journal. He has served as advisor for many Master's theses and doctoral dissertations, and is currently professor of English and religion and culture at Wilfrid Laurier University, Waterloo, Ontario, Canada, where he lives with his wife Betty and two daughters. As Associate Director, Peter keeps the library abreast of ongoing Schwenckfeld scholarship, selects newly published or located books to augment the library collections, reviews manuscripts suitable for publication and suggests areas meriting further study and research.

In 1967 the Board of Publication printed Jack R. Rothenberger's Temple University Master's Thesis, *Caspar Schwenckfeld von Ossig and the Ecumenical Ideal,* and in 1968 Martha Kriebel's Lutheran Theological Seminary Master's Thesis, *Schwenkfelders and the Sacraments,* both with due acknowledgement to the Library staff and resources. In 1969 Ernest Lashlee submitted to the Harvard University Faculty his doctoral dissertation, *The Via Regia: A Study of Caspar Schwenckfeld's Ideas of Personal Renewal and Church Reform.* In 1970 the Board of Publication printed Edward J. Furcha's doctoral dissertation, *Schwenckfeld's Concept of the New Man.* Scholars were indeed being attracted by the *Corpus* and by the accessibility of materials at the library.

Interesting acquisitions continually come into possession of the library, of which, in closing this chapter, one illustration may suffice. In the 1930s Mr. Robert Billings of Vincentown, N.J., acquired a house organ believed to have been made circa 1830 in the organ works at Palm, Pa., founded by Schwenkfelder artisans John and Andrew Krauss. Mr. Billings frequently visited the Schwenkfelder Library, researching records to support his identification of the organ. In appreciation for attention paid to him during these visits, Mr. Billings donated the organ to the library. In 1975 the library engaged Mr. Thomas S. Eader to restore the organ to working order. It is displayed, playable, in the Silesian Room of the library. As a matter of policy, the library usually does not purchase items offered to it. Its acquisitions have been almost uniformly through donation. When particularly relevant items come up for sale, they usually are acquired by an interested benefactor and in turn donated to the library. Inflated market values of antiques make this policy a virtual necessity today, but it is to be hoped holders of items belonging in the library collections will recognize their debt to the past and to the sacrifices of those who have gone before, and assure the continued vitality and growth of the library and its collections.

Over the last thirty years library activities have assumed a routine and a momentum of their own. The library has become headquarters for the Society of Descendants of the Schwenkfeldian Exiles, which sponsors annual educational and inspirational meetings, attracting interested descendants from near and far who would otherwise have little contact with each other. It serves as publication office and Miss Conway as business manager for the *Schwenkfeldian*, periodic magazine of the General Conference. It is a clearing place for Board of Publication, church and library publications and literature. Initially employed in 1953, Miss Claire Conway serves as Secretary of the library corporation, greets visitors, answers mail and telephone inquiries, maintains mailing lists, organizes meetings and generally keeps the library functioning from day to day. Her retentive memory and helpful disposition have earned the gratitude of all who have sought materials from the library collections. In 1977 Mr. Dennis Moyer joined the staff and in 1983 he was designated Director. He has generally upgraded library and museum housekeeping, supports Peter Erb's research and publication efforts, supervises the microfilming program and organizes volunteer help. Notable among the latter is the work of Mrs. Elizabeth Gamon in restoring and preserving the library collection of textile materials, clothing, samplers, embroidery, etc. This work has been supported by a $5,000 grant from the Institute of Museum Sciences, Department of Education, Washington, D.C.

Officers of the corporation in 1984 are Dr. Claude A. Schultz, Jr., president, W. Kyrel Meschter, vice-president and treasurer, Claire E. Conway, secretary, Dennis Moyer, director and Dr. Peter Erb, associate director. Of the original incorporators only Wilbur Seipt, Ernest Heebner, and Kyrel Meschter survive. Ever mindful of Mr. Meschter's confidence in the discretion of future boards in selecting new members, interested younger descendants have been conscientiously sought out to observe the charter requirement that two-thirds of the members always be descendants of the Schwenkfelder immigrants into Pennsylvania before the year 1750. With changing times this task sometimes seems to the writer to become more difficult as the years go by, but hopefully this concern reflects only the veiled vision of age. The future belongs, as it must, to the next generations.

Chapter Four

The Palm Schwenkfelder Church

The first place of public worship erected by the Schwenkfelders following their arrival in America was a meeting house constructed in 1790 on a portion of the Hamilton tract in the Hosensack Valley. Additional meeting houses were erected in Washington Township, near Clayton, a year later, and in Kraussdale in 1825. Each of these three buildings was replaced and the replacements later remodeled, all during the nineteenth century.

At the turn of the century religious services ("Versammlung") were conducted at the three meeting houses every third Sunday, on a rotating basis. Preceded during the summer by a half-hour "Sing-Schule" or song service, the regular worship service began at 9:30 and was conducted in German. The service opened with the singing of a hymn and the reading of a gospel lesson, followed by lengthy prayers and one verse from a familiar hymn. The congregation stood for prayers and singing, and custom held that whenever the name of Jesus was spoken the worshipers bent their knee. The sermon, generally lengthy, was delivered by Reverend Jacob Meschter, Reverend Joshua Schultz, or Reverend William Schultz. All were usually in attendance, and no advance announcement was made as to which would be the preacher of the morning. Still another hymn was sung and the benediction pronounced. A regular offering was not part of the service but was called for whenever funds were needed. At such a time, two deacons were stationed at the door with hats in hand, receiving contributions as worshipers left the building.

Sunday school exercises likewise rotated among the three meeting houses. Hymnals and such few teaching helps as were available, usually individually owned, had to be carried from place to place. Individual classrooms were nonexistent. Sessions were suspended during the winter months of January, February, and March. Catechetical instruction consisted primarily of memorization work. The catechumens, led most often by a church layman, committed to memory the questions and answers found in the catechism. More advanced classes devoted a great deal of time to memorization of gospel lessons.

To provide the young people with an outlet for creative activity, a Young People's Society of Christian Endeavor was organized on March 25, 1894 with Elmer E. S. Johnson as president, Agnes Gerhard as recording secretary, Rev. E. B. Clemmer as secretary, and Nora Krauss as treasurer. During its early years the group met biweekly, most often in the Kraussdale meeting house, although meetings were sometimes held at Perkiomen Seminary or in private homes. Through their work in Christian Endeavor young people received education in commitment, dedication, and the sharing of time and talents. In the same year in which the local society was organized Rev. E. B. Clemmer became a delegate to the National Christian Endeavor convention in Cleveland, Ohio, inaugurating the group's participation in activities outside its own district.

On October 11, 1898, at the Kraussdale meeting house, the Ladies' Aid Society of the Schwenkfelder Church of the Upper District was organized "to assist the Church socially, financially, with active labor by its members as the case may require, and to take an active interest in caring for the needy." Miss Olivia Schultz was elected president, Mrs. Howard W. Kriebel, vice-president, Miss Selina Gerhard, secretary and Miss Lucina K. Schultz, treasurer. Early gatherings of the twenty-six members were held once each month on a Tuesday afternoon in the various meeting houses. From 1909 to 1911, however, members assembled in private homes. Sewing was done in the homes of those who were in need of additional help. The making of aprons, bonnets, and quilts was eventually added to the list of activities. Money was raised not only through membership dues, but later by the selling of useful household articles such as pin-trays, paperweights, thermometers, liniment, and soapflakes. Society members provided valuable assistance in visiting the sick and shut-in, serving meals for Conference and Gedächtnis Tag services, and participating in home and foreign mission relief projects. One early project involved assistance to Perkiomen Seminary. Members labored at the school to furnish a spare room and stitch and repair comforters, sheets, and pillow cases. The society dedicated itself to living out its motto, selected from Hebrews 13:16, "But to do good and to communicate forget not; for with such sacrifices God is well pleased."

A new era in the spiritual lives of those who worshiped in the Upper District, as indeed in the life of the entire Schwenkfelder denomination, began in 1892 when Oscar S. Kriebel undertook his dual responsibilities as pastor of the Upper District congregation and as principal of Perkiomen Seminary. Oscar Schultz Kriebel was born September 10, 1863 on a farm in Hereford Township, the son of Andrew and Christina Schultz Kriebel. On his paternal side he was descended from immigrant Christopher Kriebel. He was preceded in the Schwenkfelder ministry by his great-grandfather, John Schultz, a descendant of immigrant Susanna Dietrich Schultz. Upon the death of his father in 1876, Oscar Kriebel, then but 13 years of age, and his older brother only two years his senior had to assume responsibility for the management of the farm. His early education was received in the schools of Hereford Township. By age 17 he had passed the County's examination and was licensed to teach. Having excelled as a pupil in the Schwenkfelder Sunday school, he was elected its superintendent, to serve during its summer sessions. Following three years of teaching in a school near Corning, in the Hosensack Valley, Oscar Kriebel entered Oberlin Academy for two years of college preparatory studies, and then Oberlin College, from which he graduated with honors in 1889. To earn his way he taught in the schools of Ohio and Michigan.

His decision to enter the ministry came as a result of a visit paid to him at Oberlin by a committee of Schwenkfelders of the Upper District. On August 21, 1887 the Schwenkfelder church of the Upper District held an election for minister, choosing Mr. Kriebel as a "Lehr-Kandidat," or applicant for the duty and honor. This was followed by a second vote after the candidate proved his fitness for the calling.

After giving careful and prayerful consideration to the proposal of the Schwenkfelder committee, Mr. Kriebel entered Oberlin Theological Seminary, where he earned his A.M. degree. In 1891 he married an Oberlin alumna, Corinne Miller, of Castalia, Ohio. The couple spent a year abroad while Mr. Kriebel completed his theological studies at the University of Berlin. Upon their return they took up residence at the newly acquired Perkiomen Seminary. Mr. Kriebel was installed as pastor of the Upper District congregation and as principal of the school.

The consolidated Palm Schwenkfelder Church is a memorial to

the faith, enthusiasm, optimism, and leadership of Rev. Kriebel. Worshipers there remember him as an articulate and forceful speaker, impressive and inspiring in his sermon delivery. Through Perkiomen School he inspired an entire generation of Schwenkfelder ministers and many lay leaders. For the next forty years his spirit and enthusiasm permeated virtually every activity and organization of the Schwenkfelder denomination.

As an author, Reverend Kriebel published a number of treatises including *An Outline of the Study of the Acts, the Epistles, and Revelation; Sanctification versus Christian Perfection*; and *Conversion and Religious Experience*. For the writing of these works, Reverend Kriebel was awarded an honorary degree of Doctor of Divinity in 1907 by Franklin and Marshall College. He was addressed thereafter as Dr. O. S. Kriebel.

Dr. Kriebel took great interest in community affairs. He was a member of the Civil Service Reform Association of Pennsylvania, and campaigned to improve area roadways. He was a charter member of the Pennsburg-East Greenville Rotary Club, serving two terms as its president. He also held membership in several educational and historical societies, including the Headmasters' Association of Preparatory Schools in Pennsylvania, the Berks and Montgomery County Historical Societies, and the Pennsylvania German Society. For a number of years he served as president of the Private Secondary School Association of Pennsylvania.

During the first decade of the twentieth century Upper District Schwenkfelders began to feel that their meeting house facilities were inadequate, particularly for the Christian education program. Many children could attend Sunday school only when held at the meeting house near their home, and a different group of children attended at each meeting house. Departmentalization of classes and the transportation of teaching supplies from place to place presented difficulties.

Lack of space for the 1909 Sunday school convention and the Gedächtnis Tag services held in the Upper District seems to have emphasized to congregation members the limited capacity of their worship facilities. During the summer Dr. Kriebel visited a number of the district's Schwenkfelders, suggesting the necessity of adding to each of the meeting houses. This was considered to have been his method for generating some thought and discussion on the matter of expansion. As a result, a special District Conference was held on Saturday afternoon, October 9, 1909 in the Washington Meeting House. Good weather and interest in the proposal attracted a large attendance. Moderator Edwin K. Schultz and Dr. Kriebel outlined the object of the conference. Dr. Kriebel then moved to erect an addition to each of the meeting houses; following discussion, the motion was unanimously defeated. A second motion, made by Henry R. Seibert, called for the construction of a centrally located church building. After several hours of debate, this motion was adopted with only two negative votes. Adam S. Krauss, Josephus Gerhard, and Owen N. Schultz were appointed as a Finance and Purchasing Committee, and Henry Gerhard as a one-man Committee on Location. On the following day, in a letter to Elmer Johnson, Dr. Kriebel wrote: "The spirit was good, and the result almost unanimous. . . . The result has come about so suddenly as almost to take away my breath."

At a second special District Conference held December 4, 1909 the Finance Committee reported the purchase of almost three acres of land "at the turnpike above Palm" (now Penna. Route 29) from Thomas H. Gery, at a cost of $522.81. Subsequently an additional two acres were purchased from Mrs. Matilda Meschter at a cost of $341.25, and an adjoining lot from Henry G. Stauffer for $100. It was also resolved that the building should be constructed of native stone and have a level main floor, with the sanctuary toward the front and Sunday school rooms to the rear. A Building Committee was established to plan construction. Within two weeks the Finance Committee began to solicit subscriptions, using the following pledge:

> WE the undersigned hereby agree to pay to the Building Committee of the Schwenkfelder Church of the Upper District, on or before April 1st, 1910, the sum set opposite our names, for the erection of a house of worship, with ample room for the Sunday School at Palm, Montgomery County, Pennsylvania. For the faithful performance of this obligation we hereby bind ourselves, heirs, and assigns.

Although the exact amount needed was unknown at the time, estimates suggested that $18,000 should suffice. The committee, making many trips by horse and buggy to call on area Schwenkfelders, was able to compile a list of prospective contributions that exceeded the estimated amount. For this reason, many people assumed in later years that the church had been built debt-free. In fact, the building project ultimately cost more than the estimate, so that the congregation found itself with a deficit of over $5,000 when the building was completed. The first funds actually collected for the project came from Mrs. Oscar S. Kriebel, who contributed $500 for a pipe organ for the new church.

Much prayerful consideration went into the design of the

church so that it would meet not only the needs of the time but those of future generations as well. Excess ornamentation would be out of harmony with the customs and practices of the church, and would also be more costly. The building had to be plain, well planned, and above all, well built. The architectural firm of Savery-Sheetz and Savery of Philadelphia was hired to meet these challenges. As members of the Society of Friends, the Messrs. Savery and Sheetz understood the basic concept that the Building Committee envisioned and strove to hold costs within the estimated amount.

Having decided to use native stone, quarries located at Mill Hill, Zionsville and Siesholtzville were visited, after which the committee decided to purchase pink granite from the Walker Granite quarry in Siesholtzville, at a cost of $2.50 per ton. Moving the stone from the quarry to the building site presented quite a problem. Hauling by truck was unknown and railway transportation required travel to Alburtis, then to Emmaus Junction, and then down the Perkiomen Branch to Palm Station, where it would be loaded on wagons and brought to the building site. Learning of the cost of transportation at a District Conference, Allen S. Kriebel volunteered, "I'll make myself responsible to haul one-sixth of that amount of stone if it can all be hauled by team, and we can save the cost of the freight delivery." Mr. Kriebel and other members of the Upper District hauled all 536 tons (212 wagonloads) of stone used in the church building from the quarry to the church site, a distance of eight miles. Since all the members of the Building Committee possessed talent and experience in building operations, the committee believed the building task could be accomplished at less cost and more satisfactorily by supervising construction themselves; consequently no general contractor was engaged.

Actual excavation and construction of the church began on Monday, March 14, 1910. According to Owen K. Schultz:

> The first day, two promising boys dragged out the first scoopful of ground and jokingly remarked that they deserved to occupy the front seat after the church was finished.

Most of the excavation work was done by volunteer laborers who furnished picks, shovels, scoops, plows, wagons, and teams of horses.

As the excavation work was being completed, the Building Committee went about securing native lumber for the church. Joists were milled from trees located at the hitching post and shed areas of the Hosensack Meeting House grove. Additional lumber was obtained from woodlands owned by Henry K. Gerhard and from the

Kraussdale Meeting House grounds. Masons began their work in June. A datestone inscribed by the Walker Granite Company with the name of the church was added rather than a cornerstone. The first truss could not be raised until October because the stonemasons had not worked for eight weeks, but by November the last of ten trusses had been hoisted into place by derrick; by mid-January the church was under roof.

Throughout the spring and summer of 1911, the Building Committee worked out many details and appointments for the new church. One unique feature of the design was the oak-paneled ceiling, considered superior to the usual plastered ceilings of the day. Pews of oak were purchased from the Fleetwood Metal Body Company. The building was wired for electricity even though the Pennsburg Electric Light Company had not yet extended its lines from East Greenville to Palm. A special District Conference determined that no carpeting should cover the maple floors under the pews and that the sheds located at the meeting houses should be moved to the new site so that protection would be provided for horses and buggies.

Construction blueprints provided space for an organ but its installation was initially deferred because of the additional cost. Dr. and Mrs. O. S. Kriebel, however, felt strongly that organ music would make a valuable contribution to the spirit of worship services. They applied for and received from Mr. Andrew Carnegie the assurance of $875, with the provision that the church raise the $1,675 balance of the organ cost. Dr. Kriebel promised to raise the needed funds from people who had not subscribed to the building fund. Mr. Carnegie's offer was accepted by the congregation. The pipe organ was purchased from the C. S. Haskell Company of Philadelphia for $2,250.

Dedication of the new church was scheduled for September 24, 1911. Although the building was not completely finished, the members of the congregation proved equal to the task of preparation. Gedächtnis Tag and dedication services were held on the appointed days. Guest speakers at the dedication included:

Rev. Elmer E. S. Johnson, Wolfenbüttel, Germany
Rev. Levi S. Hoffman, Lansdale
Rev. Chester D. Hartranft
Rev. Eli Keller, former pastor, Zionsville Reformed Church of Allentown
Rev. O. F. Waage, St. Paul's Lutheran Church, Pennsburg
Rev. Edwin S. Anders, Towamencin Schwenkfelder Church

Rev. A. S. Shelly, Hereford Mennonite Church, Bally
Rev. C. M. DeLong, New Goshenhoppen Church, East Greenville
Rev. W. U. Kistler, St. Mark's Lutheran Church, Pennsburg
Mr. Robert J. Gottschall, Norristown Schwenkfelder Church
Rev. James L. Barton, Boston
Miss Flora K. Heebner, Taiku, Shansi, China
Rev. Harvey K. Heebner, First Schwenkfelder Church of Philadelphia

Several years later, Dr. O. S. Kriebel was to say:

When I looked upon the old church buildings a few days ago, still standing, small and unpretentious, with no effort or aim at architecture, and the inconveniences and disadvantages of meeting in these little churches on different Sundays in succession, and when I look upon this building, centrally located here . . . it seems to me nothing less than the grace of God in our hearts could have brought about such a change.

In the new building Sunday school classes were conducted the year round in facilities provided on the main floor and a balcony at the rear, in an area which could be separated from the sanctuary by large folding doors. Sunday school began at 9:00 a.m. with members seated in their respective classrooms, but with folding doors open so all could participate together in opening exercises. The folding doors were then closed, dividing the school into individual classes where attendance was recorded, a collection taken, and the day's lesson taught. At the end of the hour the folding doors were once again opened for the secretary's attendance report, announcements by the superintendent, and a closing hymn.

Leaders and teachers placed primary emphasis on rote memorization of Scripture and other matter, which they considered essential for the education of young Christians. To this end, in addition to *Cook's Comprehensive Quarterlies* and Herbert Moninger's *Training For Service*, memory booklets were used in study. Pupils received certificates for successful memorization of materials each month, and for their achievement of reading the Bible through in one year. Bible classes at Palm included the girls' Bible class, the young men's Bible class, the adult English Bible class, and the German Bible class.

Church services, which followed at 10:00 a.m., were conducted in German and English on alternate Sundays. By 1920, however, when English had replaced German as the language most familiar to younger members, German services were reduced to one per month. In keeping with tradition, a simple order of worship was adopted. The service began with a hymn, a reading from the Scriptures, the morning prayer, and another hymn. Worshipers remained seated during the hymn but stood for prayers. The sermon, usually forty-five minutes long, was followed by another prayer. While the congregation sang a hymn, collection was taken by two deacons. The term "Offering" did not become familiar to the Palm congregation until many years later. Following morning announcements, a closing hymn was sung. After 1925 the announcements were made before the sermon began and the church service closed with the singing of the Doxology and a benediction. Dr. O. S. Kriebel did not formally greet church worshipers after the service had ended, although his successors have made this a regular practice.

With the new church, and encouragement from Dr. Kriebel and his musically talented family, the role of music gradually expanded. The installation of the pipe organ had not been completed at the time of the church's dedication, and pending its installation congregational singing was accompanied by a small reed organ transported from the Washington Meeting House. When the pipe organ was installed, its console was located on a platform built on the left front of the sanctuary. There was no organ prelude, offertory, or postlude, and the organ was used exclusively to accompany congregational singing, led by "Vorsinger" (song leader) Henry R. Seibert, who was seated beside the organist throughout most of the service. On occasion, when congregational singing lacked sufficient zeal, Dr. Kriebel would stop the hymn in progress and inform Mr. Seibert and the congregation that he was not satisfied with their rendition of that particular hymn. Since hymns in the English language were used on alternate Sundays, *The New Manual of Praise* was chosen as the first English hymnal and placed in the pews alongside the German hymnals.

Members of the Palm congregation were not in favor of an organized choir. Some members deemed such a group unnecessary; others felt that once hymns were led by a choir, participation in singing by the rest of the worshipers would decline. Gradually, however, special music did become part of some special services. To provide choral music for these occasions, Dr. Kriebel's daughters, Mary and Frieda, organized the Palm Chorus, membership in which was open to all willing individuals of the congregation. Rehearsals were held only during the weeks prior to a special event. Later, under the direction of Milton S. Bieler, the Palm Chorus also provided musical programs of its own, including annual special programs given on the Sunday evening prior to Christmas Day.

New procedures for administering the sacrament of holy communion were instituted. While worshiping in the meeting houses, the women, seated on the side of the aisle opposite the men, were invited by the minister to come forward and receive the elements. Each received the bread and partook of the wine from a single chalice. After the female communicants returned to their pews, they were followed first by the older men and then by the younger men. During the communion service at Palm, the common chalice was replaced by individual cups for obvious sanitary reasons. Communicants remained seated in their pews to receive the elements so that meditation by individual participants would not be disrupted.

On January 1, 1912 Sunday school members met together for the first annual business meeting held in the new building. Enrolment reached 263 scholars. Officers for the term were elected as follows: E.K. Schultz, President; Adam S. Krauss, Vice-President; Daniel Y. Meschter, Superintendent; Oscar S. Schultz, Assistant Superintendent; Cora S. Schultz, Secretary; Milton Y. Krauss, Treasurer; Amos K. Schultz, Chorister; Milton S. Bieler, Assistant Chorister; Josephus S. Gerhard, Owen K. Schultz, and Allen S. Krauss, Managers; Rev. O.S. Kriebel, Superintendent of Home Department; Mrs. Jos. K. Schultz, Superintendent of Cradle Roll; Mrs. Calvin Kriebel, Superintendent of Primary Department.

The various departments of the Sunday school provided for the Christian education of all members of the school. The continuation of the Palm home department was still considered necessary even though the church was now centrally located. Through this department, Dr. Kriebel and several assistants worked to accommodate members of the school who were unable to attend services during the winter months. The cradle roll flourished under the leadership of Mrs. Joseph K. Schultz. Parents felt the importance of having their children included in the Sunday school organization at the earliest possible age. In addition to having their names entered on the roll, children were remembered with birthday, Christmas, and Easter cards.

Sunday school members contributed to the support of missionaries Flora K. Heebner, Mr. C. A. Nelson, and Miss Mary Ann Funk. They also supported the Lemon Hill Outing Association, enabling as many as 100 underprivileged Philadelphia children each year to participate in outings at Lemon Hill, Fairmount Park.

Creation of a library lent important support for the work of the Sunday school. Funds for the establishment of the library were received through subscription and through donations from the Bible classes. Dr. Kriebel headed a committee of four members responsible for acquiring books to complete the library. Other volumes were generously donated by church members. The position of librarian was most ably undertaken by Miss Minnie K. Schultz. By the end of the first year of the library's existence, Miss Schultz reported the acquisition of 265 books, including works on religion, missions, biography, pedagogy, travel, nature, literature, sociology, fiction, and reference. By 1915 the librarian's report listed 343 separate volumes, modest by later standards but a cherished resource for that day.

The spacious new sanctuary proved ideal for annual festivals and pageants sponsored by the Sunday school during the Christmas and Easter seasons, and on Children's Day, celebrated in June of each year. Under the leadership of the superintendent, members busily designed costumes and scenery and rehearsed the youth. The young people enthusiastically sang, recited, and acted out their parts on a large removable "stage," still in use, constructed in the front of the sanctuary by members of the church, including J. Willis Schultz, Oscar Schultz, Milton Schultz, Elmer Schultz, and Norman Kuhns. Many members fondly recall their participation in these exercises and pageants.

With renewed spirit and interest, the Young People's Society of Christian Endeavor held its first meeting in the new building on Sunday evening, October 8, 1911. On January 28 of the following year, their meeting became the first public gathering at which the church's lighting system was supplied with electricity from a public power company rather than by portable generators.

Prior to the building of the new church, organization of a Junior C.E. program was deemed virtually impossible due to the fact that younger members relied on others for transportation. With the new facilities now available, demand for a Junior C.E. program was finally met. The first regular meeting was held on Saturday, August 24, 1912, with thirty-four members present. The group's first officers included: Laura Moore, President; Ada Schultz, Vice-President; Edna Schultz, Secretary; Mae Kriebel, Treasurer. Several years later an Intermediate C.E. was also established. The expansion of Palm's C.E. program included a wider range of topics for discussion and a deeper interest in communicating with members outside the Upper District. These activities offered young people an outlet for expression not otherwise provided by the church. Here was an opportunity to strengthen character and to influence the lives of others through testimony and example. Speaking on the occasion of Palm church's twentieth-anniversary C.E. rally, Reverend Levi S. Hoffman related the following:

I remember very well Dr. Kriebel was the leader when I discussed my first topic and I remember later how I prepared my topics and the chickens and some of the horses and cows could tell you of the experiences that they and I had before I ever had courage enough to deliver my topics in the C. E. meetings. . . .

Almost a century after the start of the C.E. movement in the Upper District, former members still view C.E. experience as an invaluable part of their education.

After September of 1911 the Ladies' Aid Society met in the basement of the new church and their Tuesday meetings became day-long sessions of quilting, sewing, and planning for monthly activities. Their programs and outreach steadily grew. Home and foreign mission projects were deemed especially important. Material and financial support were provided to Flora K. Heebner and later to Mabel H. Reiff in the foreign mission field. Following her marriage, Olivia K. Schultz, first society president, moved to Philadelphia. There her work and interests were transferred to the Schwenkfelder mission of that city. At her suggestion, the women at Palm sent contributions of money, materials, and clothing. This made it possible for neighborhood children and adults who lacked proper clothing to attend Sunday school and church services. Some of these individuals later became active members of the First Schwenkfelder Church of Philadelphia. To support these endeavors, fund-raising projects continued. These were supplemented by dues and donations from the members, as well as by the planning of socials and entertainment.

The success of these socials has been attributed to the efforts of President Mrs. Joseph K. Schultz and to Corinne Kriebel, wife of the pastor. Both of these women shared a talent for music and the ability to procure interesting and inspiring individuals who offered readings, recitations, piano and organ recitals, and lectures. Dr. Kriebel also contributed to some social functions featuring lantern slides taken during his extensive travels. The August 1912 issue of the *Schwenkfeldian* reported:

> The entertainment given in the Palm Church on Saturday evening, July 27, under the auspices of the Ladies' Aid Society was largely attended and very much enjoyed by all. The entertainment consisted of some of the finest selections of Victor records given on Mrs. O. S. Kriebel's new machine.

The variety of events served members of both the church and the community as a valuable source of fellowship and cultural growth.

The growth of the church and the expansion of its program

continually made new demands upon the time and energy of its pastor. By 1928 Dr. Kriebel was 65 years of age and his incessant activity over the years on behalf of church and school began to take its toll on his health. The Palm congregation came to realize the need for additional pastoral leadership. At a special District Conference held May 4. 1929 a call was extended to Rev. Lester K. Kriebel to serve as assistant pastor.

Lester K. Kriebel, descended on his mother's side from immigrant Melchior Kriebel, Sr., was born November 22, 1898 at the homestead of Caspar Kriebel in Towamencin Township. He received his early public school education in Gwynedd Township, graduating from West Point High School in 1916 and from Lansdale High School in 1917. He then attended Perkiomen School, during which time he began his years of affiliation as a worshiper and worker in the Palm church. Following graduation and a year working as a clerk in the freight claims department of the Reading Railway at Philadelphia's Reading Terminal, he went on to earn an A.B. degree from Brown University in June of 1923. Having decided to enter the ministry, he enrolled at Hartford Theological Seminary and while there served for over two years as a student pastor for the Salem Congregational Church in Connecticut. Following graduation from Hartford Theological Seminary with a Bachelor of Divinity degree, he returned to Pennsylvania and was ordained at the Towamencin church on July 4, 1926. During the same year, Rev. Kriebel was called into service as supply pastor for five months at the Palm church. During that autumn he taught English and ancient history at Perkiomen School and supplied the pulpit of the First Schwenkfelder Church in Philadelphia while Rev. Heebner traveled in China. Early in 1927 he once again was called to the Upper District to supply the pulpit in the absence of Dr. O. S. Kriebel.

In 1927 Rev. Kriebel accepted the privilege and challenge of traveling abroad as an exchange student from Hartford Theological Seminary, his trip financed in part by the Palm congregation. His studies included a year's attendance at the University of Giessen, Germany, and travels through England, Holland, France, Egypt, and the Holy Land, preparing him for his later activities as scholar and historian, for which he was held in great respect. He also was able to visit the Schwenkfelder homelands in Silesia, Germany. The members of the Palm congregation welcomed him upon his return with a formal reception held September 26, 1928. Not long thereafter he was appointed associate editor of the *Corpus Schwenckfeldianorum*. In this assignment he made weekly trips to Washington,

D.C., to work with Selina Gerhard Schultz, and returned to spend weekends in the Upper District.

From the beginning of his affiliation with the Palm congregation Lester Kriebel enjoyed a special rapport with the young people. In January of 1927 he was instrumental in the organization of an Ushers' League, whose ten charter members included young men from the Palm congregation and from neighboring churches. Church deacons had been responsible for what little ushering was done, but as the number of special activities increased the need arose for a group specially trained to usher and receive the offering. Under the leadership of Rev. Kriebel, President Paul Bieler, Vice-President Norman Kriebel, Secretary Leon Long, and Treasurer Raymond Kriebel, the Ushers' League held regular monthly meetings and training sessions, supplemented by evening entertainments for the congregation. These social events included plays and musicals often highlighted with selections rendered by the Ushers' League quartet composed of vocalists John Moyer, Lester Schultz, Paul Bieler, and Foster Schultz. Ushers' League members also formed the Palm church's first softball team. Over the years, as the organization's membership tripled, the Ushers' League became one of the more valuable social and service groups in the Upper District.

In addition to his work with the Y.M.C.A., Rev. Kriebel promoted a Boy Scouts of America program. On March 11, 1929 the fathers of potential scouts held a meeting at the Palm Schwenkfelder Church to discuss the boy scout movement. Permission was then secured from the church's Board of Trustees for the use of the church basement as a meeting place. Boys interested in the scouting program were invited to meet at Palm and a committee headed by Warren G. Schultz was organized to sponsor a scout troop for the Palm community. Rev. Lester Kriebel was appointed scoutmaster, assisted by Abner K. Schultz and Rolland Johnson. Thus began an affiliation between the Palm church and the Boy Scouts of America which has existed until the present time.

The tradition of an annual Advent Party was brought to the Upper District following Rev. Kriebel's travels in Germany. It is held in the evening on the first Sunday in Advent in accordance with a custom based on ancient traditions originating in central and southern Germany. Shortly after sunset, German families gathered with their friends to light three candles on the altar and those placed among the evergreens of an Advent wreath suspended from the ceiling. Using candlelight as the only illumination, the celebration continued with an informal secular and religious program, after which refreshments were served. The first Schwenkfelder Advent Party was held at Perkiomen School, where a few friends met to light the candles of their wreath, pray, and hear the Advent story along with stories of Christmas traditions in other lands. Following the celebration, apple tart and coffee were offered as refreshments. During the following years, this inspiring event was held in the church basement at Palm and was sponsored by the Ushers' League and Christian Endeavor societies, each with their invited guests. A more elaborate program was offered, including recitations, carols, prayer, and instrumental and vocal selections rendered by many talented members of the community. Three traditional varieties of German cookies were added as refreshments. These "pfeffernusse," "buderstollen," and "springerle" were, at first, prepared by a baker living in Lansdale, Pa. Today, the Advent Party has become a celebration by the entire congregation, viewed as a meaningful way in which to welcome the Advent season and recalling to Schwenkfelders of the Upper District the traditions of their homeland and the coming of the Christchild.

An uninterrupted ministry of nearly forty years in the Upper District was broken on February 16, 1932 by the sudden death of Dr. O. S. Kriebel. A sense of sorrow and inexpressible loss was felt by those whose lives had been touched by this accomplished leader and loyal friend. Funeral and memorial services held at Perkiomen School and the Palm Schwenkfelder Church were attended by over 2,000 of Dr. Kriebel's friends and associates, attesting to the respect in which he was held by all. Rev. Harvey K. Heebner, in his editorial in the *Schwenkfeldian* of March, 1932 offered the following charge to the church members of the Upper District:

> . . . We have for forty years been looking to a mountain of character and power and today we look up and the mountain is removed. How can we carry on without him? is asked by many. The answer is—carry on and accomplish in his spirit the unfinished tasks that were first with him. God still lives, God's grace is sufficient for every time of need. . . .

With Dr. Kriebel's death pastoral responsibilities fell naturally upon Rev. Lester Kriebel. After careful deliberation, a formal call was extended to him and accepted at a special church service Sunday morning, September 18. He was duly installed as pastor on October 16, 1932.

As we have seen, members of the Palm congregation worked hard in preparation for, and were active participants in, the events of the 1934 Bicentennial Celebration, marking the 200th anniversary of the arrival of their forefathers in this country. A bronze tablet in honor and memory of the pastors who had served the Upper District during the preceding 200 years was placed on the inside wall at the rear of the church and unveiled as part of the services of the celebration on Sunday, September 23, 1934.

Seven members of the Palm congregation joined the tour group to the Schwenkfelder homelands in Silesia. Rev. Kriebel was granted a leave of absence to serve as a guide and interpreter for the pilgrimage. The tour group benefited immensely from his store of knowledge gained during his previous travels there and his abiding interest in the history of the Schwenkfelder movement.

Rev. Kriebel was also instrumental in arranging a special feature of the Bicentennial service at Palm on Sunday morning, September 23—the unveiling of the oil painting "The Landing of the Schwenkfelders in Philadelphia, Pennsylvania, September 1734" by Adolph Pannash. A desire for such a painting had been expressed frequently. Rev. C. Z. Weiser, in an article on Schwenckfeld, had written, "I have often, when looking at the landing of the Pilgrims, asked myself why some one of our Pennsylvania artists has not long ago taken the landing of the Schwenkfelders under his pencil. Such a picture would help to perpetuate an historical event which transpired within the career and limits of Pennsylvania, which ought not to be forgotten and over which any of the New England States would grow proud."

Mr. Pannash, a portrait painter living in Flushing, Long Island, was born in Brandenburg, Germany, not far north of the province of Silesia. In October of 1932, during a brief vacation at the Mountain Inn, Scot Run, Pennsylvania, Rev. Kriebel made the acquaintance of Mr. Pannash and his wife. With a common ancestral background and interest in Reformation history, Mr. Pannash soon became interested in the Schwenkfelders and their history, and a sincere friendship developed. Mr. Pannash presented Rev. Kriebel with a 16 x 20 inch oil portrait of Schwenckfeld, mirroring numerous extant prints. During further visits and correspondence Rev. Kriebel persuaded Mr. Pannash to undertake a painting of the landing of the Schwenkfelders. A trial sketch tinted with water color was presented to the Palm church. Finding it "a remarkable representation created by a very cultured, sympathetic mind," a group from Palm's congregation pledged their support for the completion of the project. In May of 1934 the completed painting was taken to the Franklin Printing Company of Philadelphia for the purpose of making colored lithographs available for individuals. The first supply of these prints sold out, but a second printing in 1977 keeps this popular item available.

Mr. Pannash, accompanied by four generations of his family, journeyed to Palm to take part in the unveiling ceremony. In his remarks Rev. Kriebel expressed the thought,

> I feel convinced that the historical painting, "The Landing of the Schwenkfelders" will be a valuable factor to impress upon our young people, at least in part, some of the sacrifices that our forefathers have made and I should like to see a print of this painting in every home represented in this church. It will also help to familiarize them with the history of our people.

The painting now hangs in the Schwenkfelder Library.

In September of 1930 Mrs. Chester Schultz, who had served the church as organist for many years, resigned. She was succeeded by Miss Florence Schultz, who would serve the church for the next thirty years. During the summer of 1937 the organ was reconditioned and upgraded at a cost of $1,300, and a dedication service was held November 12, 1937. After some eight years of discussion the Board of Trustees authorized the purchase of 250 copies of the *Pilgrim Hymnal* at a cost of $1.00 per copy. These hymnals were used during the Sunday morning worship services down into the 1960s. Mr. Willis Schultz arranged construction of suitable pew racks for the new hymnals.

Since the basement coal storage space was no longer needed, the kitchen area was enlarged and improved in 1935. In 1938 the English Bible class purchased curtains to replace the window shades in the sanctuary, and over 100 azaleas were planted in front of the church, greatly enhancing the appearance of the church grounds.

As the church's thirtieth anniversary approached, new electric lights were installed in the sanctuary, the sanctuary was painted, new carpeting was installed, and the pews were re-varnished. The anniversary celebration was initially planned for the week of September 28, 1941. However, an infantile paralysis epidemic swept through Montgomery and nine other counties at that time. As children under the age of 16 were excluded from all public gatherings, the anniversary festivities had to be postponed until November.

The celebration included a regular worship service on November 9, 1941, followed that afternoon by a special musical program presented by the Palm Chorus under the direction of Milton Bieler. On November 16, the sermon during the morning worship service was given by Dr. Elmer E. S. Johnson. That afternoon, ministers of the denomination and the community took part in an historical program. In the evening, the Christian Endeavor societies sponsored a young people's evangelistic service.

The Board of Trustees did not ignore the need for improvement of the church's outlying properties. In the summer of 1930 extensive work was done at Hosensack, including the painting and plastering of the meeting house and the installation of two iron gates in the stone fence surrounding the property. The trustees reported at the 1934 annual District Conference that "1300 trees, plants, shrubs, and evergreens" had been donated and planted at Kraussdale and that permission had been given to the Ushers' League to build a log footbridge across the creek at the Hosensack Meeting House so that the tract on the other side of the creek could be used for outdoor meetings of the league, Christian Endeavor, and other groups. Eight years later, the upkeep of the "Grove" at Hosensack became the exclusive responsibility of the Ushers' League, until the group's disbandment during the early 1960s. Throughout this period special care was given to these properties. The mowing of grass and the trimming, feeding, and spraying of shrubbery are mentioned annually in reports given by the Board of Trustees.

America's entry into World War II, and particularly the resulting gasoline rationing, disrupted many church programs. To save gas and tires the Sunday school picnic, the Advent Party, and the parents' supper were cancelled, and plans for a Daily Vacation Bible School deferred. District Conferences were held on Sundays, and the Memorial Day services were held at the Palm church rather than at the outlying cemeteries. Rev. Kriebel tried to adapt the worship services and messages to "the needs of war," and encouraged the church members to keep in close contact with servicemen. The Christian Endeavor societies kept an accurate record of the names and addresses of church members serving in the armed forces.

The adult Bible class drew up a resolution opposing the adoption of Daylight Saving Time, which in addition to War Time would have meant a two-hour advance over Standard Time, seriously disrupting the schedules of farmers in the congregation. The trustees took out war damage insurance. In January of 1943 the Office of Price Administration requested the Palm church to re-convert its heating system to coal. In spite of the plea that there was no longer a storage space for coal, the O.P.A. threatened to withdraw the church's ration of oil coupons, thus forcing the change back to coal heat.

Various organizations of the church offered assistance where it was needed. The trustees granted the Red Cross permission to use the church basement for first aid courses. Responding to a request from

Holland for clothing, the Ladies' Aid Society packed sixty-two boxes, amounting to over 500 pounds of the items needed, and sent them directly to Holland. In return, the church received a shipment of tulip, crocus, and hyacinth bulbs from the children of Holland. These were planted in the grove on the south side of the church. Church members joined in the denomination-wide project of forwarding food and clothing packages to Harpersdorf refugee families expelled from their homelands and resettled in West Germany. In response to another appeal, second-hand clothing, new material, thread, buttons, needles, and medicines were collected and sent to Mindinao with Mr. Frank Woodward, a missionary, when he returned to the Philippines.

Thirty-seven men and three women from the Palm congregation served in the armed forces, and in 1943 the congregation purchased a service flag in their honor. At their request the pamphlet entitled *Who are the Schwenkfelders?* was prepared for distribution.

All those who served returned home shortly after the end of the war, and an appreciation dinner in their honor was held in the church basement on January 18, 1947. Approximately 250 servicemen and their families attended. Because the response to this affair was so great, space for preparation of the meal became a problem. Turkeys for the dinner were roasted in the ovens of Brunner's Bakery in nearby East Greenville and transported to the church. The program following the meal included the singing of patriotic songs and short messages by Rev. Lester Kriebel, Moderator Amos K. Schultz, and Sunday School Superintendent Wayne Rothenberger. Mrs. Adam S. Schultz and Mr. Edwin Fox spoke, respectively, for the mothers and fathers of service personnel. An electric clock was presented to each veteran as a token of remembrance from the members of the church.

At the 1944 annual District Conference, on motion of Rev. Lester Kriebel, the church bylaws were amended to add the position of vice-moderator; at the following conference Mr. Paul Bieler was elected to this new office.

With the end of the war in 1945, activities at Palm began to return to pre-war levels. Meetings were again held at their normal times and dates. Special activities such as the Sunday school picnic, parents' supper, and the Advent Party were resumed, and planning for a Daily Vacation Bible School was renewed.

The idea for a Daily Vacation Bible School originated at the annual business meeting of the Sunday school, January 15, 1942. Prior to that time, many children of the Upper District attended and several adults taught in such a school conducted by the Hereford

Mennonite Church in Bally, Pennsylvania. A committee chaired by Mrs. Ralph Bieler was formed to organize a Bible school at Palm. After the war-time interruption, planning was resumed and the first Bible school at Palm was held in 1947. Sessions were held Monday through Friday from 9:00 a.m. to 11:30 a.m. Each session began and ended with a worship program. Class periods consisted of memory work, Bible stories, workbooks, and handwork. Music and recreation periods were also a part of each session. The closing day of the school featured a picnic on the church lawn. On Sunday evening following the school's two-week session, a closing program was presented in the church. At this time songs were sung and group presentations given demonstrating some of the lessons students had learned during the Bible school sessions.

Inspired by oratorio music he had heard at Oberlin, Dr. Kriebel resolved to give the people of the Upper Perkiomen Valley the opportunity to learn to enjoy this music. In 1905 he and Charles and Eleanor Weirich of the Perkiomen School music department obtained the services of J. Henry Kowalski of Philadelphia to direct a chorus of community singers in a performance of Handel's "Messiah." Twenty members of the Upper District churches participated. The following spring the same group, again under the direction of Mr. Kowalski, presented Hayden's "The Creation." This marked the first time that these compositions had been performed in the Upper Perkiomen Valley. Subsequently, the "Messiah," or choruses selected from it, have been performed in the Palm church during the Christmas or Easter seasons.

For the next twenty years an informal group of members with an interest in singing rendered special music for various occasions. On May 14, 1925 this group was formally organized as the Palm Chorus, with Mrs. Israel Adams as director and Milton S. Bieler as president. In 1930, through the efforts of the choral groups, two Steinway grand pianos were purchased, one for the church sanctuary and one for the Sunday school room.

During the 1930s and 1940s, with the exception of the war years, the forty-member chorus, directed by Milton S. Bieler, presented anthems during the regular worship service several times a year. They also performed cantatas, including the "Messiah," during the Easter and Christmas seasons. The chorus supplied music for community activities and many members took an active part in singing with the United Schwenkfelder Choir, formed in 1928.

In 1950, after many years of service, Mr. Bieler handed down his duties as chorister and director of the Palm Chorus to his son Paul, who served in both capacities until 1969. In 1954 the Palm Chorus became known as the senior choir and rendered anthems bi-weekly during the Sunday worship services, alternating with the junior choir, reorganized in 1950 under the direction of Mrs. Waldo Johnson. In February of 1954 the Sunday morning order of worship was adjusted to accommodate the choir participation, but with due care for preserving the basic dignity and simplicity of the service.

In 1948 a committee was appointed by Moderator Claude A. Schultz to prepare a church manual. After two years of work this committee presented to District Conference a manual which included a historical statement regarding the Schwenkfelders, a revised constitution and bylaws of the Palm Schwenkfelder Church, and the constitutions of the Sunday school, Ladies' Aid Society, Young People's Schwenkfelder Christian Endeavor, Intermediate Schwenkfelder Christian Endeavor, Junior Schwenkfelder Christian Endeavor, and the Ushers' League. This manual was printed and distributed to church members in 1951.

This same year interest was expressed in the idea of distributing a weekly church bulletin. A committee was appointed to publish the weekly pamphlet. After overcoming some problems, the Board of Trustees purchased a typewriter and mimeograph machine to aid in the preparation of the bulletin. In 1952 a part-time secretary was hired to edit the bulletin at a salary of $2.00 per week.

At the annual District Conference on January 18, 1955 a proposal was made by Church Secretary Andrew Berky to engage Jack Rothenberger as an associate pastor. In his presentation, Mr. Berky expressed concern that Mr. Rothenberger was the first ministerial candidate from the Schwenkfelder Church in fifty years and that at this time there were no apparent openings in the Schwenkfelder ministry. Mr. Berky's proposal suggested that Mr. Rothenberger be engaged as an associate pastor at Palm and also as a part-time counselor at Perkiomen School. This idea was endorsed by Perkiomen School Headmaster Stephen Roberts. After much positive comment a special District Conference on February 8, 1955 resolved that a call be issued for a one-year period, at the end of which time the plan "could be renewed or abandoned at the option of the candidate or the Church, or both." Mr. Rothenberger was ordained June 26, 1955 and served as associate pastor until July 1, 1956, when he accepted a call as pastor of the Lansdale Schwenkfelder Church.

In January 1957 Conference discussed the advisability of expanding the Diaconate to include three deaconesses in addition to the three deacons. A motion was passed by Conference to appoint three deaconesses for a one-year trial period. The following month, Moderator Claude A. Schultz appointed Mrs. Mae Kuhns, Mrs. Sara Bieler, and Mrs. Arlene Kriebel as the first deaconesses at the Palm church. The experiment proved successful and the Diaconate was permanently expanded in 1958.

In 1946 a new interior wall was installed in the church basement and the area provided with heat so that additional space could be made available for the growing primary department. Moveable partitions were installed to separate the various "classrooms." In addition, at the request of the Ladies' Aid Society, the kitchen was expanded and improved.

Prior to 1948, the money needed to meet the church budget had been raised by the annual solicitation of each church member by one of the deacons. However, in that year the Board of Trustees recommended the rebuilding of the top part of the church tower and the repointing of portions of the church's outer walls. Since the cost of these projects doubled the budget for 1949, the congregation decided to establish a Finance Committee to solicit the money to meet future budget obligations. Also, upon the recommendation of the Finance Committee, an envelope system of offerings was established to allow members to distribute their giving throughout the year.

Until the 1950s the pastors of the Palm church were responsible for securing their own living quarters. In December of 1950 the property immediately adjoining the church on the north side became available. Following approval at a special District Conference the church purchased this property from the estate of Ida B. Stauffer for $23,000. However, the home, which was labeled "The Annex," was not immediately made available for the pastor's residency, since there was some feeling that the property might be converted into nursing home facilities. This proved impractical and the Board of Trustees used the annex for its meetings and gave the Boy Scouts the use of the garage for their meetings. In June 1951 the Board of Trustees decided not to "make available for living quarters any part or portions of the church annex to anyone, for the present time. . . . Should the pastor desire to occupy one or more rooms as a study . . . this desire and request should be so granted." In 1952 the trustees changed their minds and allowed Rev. Kriebel to occupy the second floor of the annex.

In the meantime, the Ladies' Aid Society had been given permission by the trustees to use the annex for their meetings, for their weekly quilting sessions, and in 1951 for their first Fall Festival. This annual event, which grew out of hobby shows held in the church basement, has become not only a highlight of the church year at Palm, but also one of the most widely attended activities in the Upper Perkiomen Valley. Today, the Festival, held the last Wednesday in August, features the display and sale of items by area hobbyists and craftsmen, the sale of plants, baked and canned goods, needlework, a light lunch, and an open-air concert by the Red Hill Band.

An ongoing debate was revived at the 1952 District Conference when J. Willis Schultz proposed "That the antiquated church sheds (erected at the meeting houses as horse sheds and moved to Palm after the completion of the church), be removed to make place for adequate parking facilities." After a heated discussion it was decided to authorize the removal of the sheds and the trustees advertised for bids for the project. Contractor Joseph Cianfelice offered to remove the sheds and pay the church $300. Cianfelice, however, ran into difficulties and asked the trustees to let him out of the contract with only a portion of the work completed. Members of the church completed the project and Wilmer Schultz supervised the grading and installation of a new gravel parking lot.

During 1955 the sanctuary's pipe organ was thoroughly renovated and a set of twenty-one chimes added. On Sunday evening, November 20, 1955 approximately 700 people were present for the dedication of the chimes and a new pulpit Bible. The guest organist for the evening was Mr. Larry Ferrari of Philadelphia.

In November of 1957 the Palm congregation, along with the Upper Perkiomen Valley community and co-workers and associates throughout the Schwenkfelder denomination, was shocked and saddened when personal problems made further service by their pastor out of the question. On November 26, 1957 the Board of Trustees and the Diaconate accepted the resignation of Rev. Lester Kriebel, abruptly terminating the thirty-year pastorate of an educated, dedicated, and popular pastor, at the untimely age of 59.

The resignation of Rev. Lester Kriebel posed a particular problem to the Palm church since there were no ministers of the Schwenkfelder tradition available to fill the pulpit, nor were there any ministerial students of the Schwenkfelder tradition in training at the time. The church officers appointed a Pastoral Committee, co-chaired by Paul S. Kriebel and Mrs. Sara Bieler and comprised of deacons, members of the Board of Trustees, and members of the congregation, charged with responsibility for locating a suitable candidate. During the interim, pastoral services were performed by a number of friends of the congregation, including Rev. Jack Rothenberger, Rev. Fred A. Trimble, Rev. Philip R. Hoh, Rev. Arthur F.

Wagner, and Dr. E. E. S. Johnson.

After twelve months of diligent searching, the Pastoral Committee reported to a special District Conference on February 3, 1959 that in attempting to find a pastor they were faced with several problems:

> Our main problem was to be how to find enough good reasons to persuade a minister to leave his denomination and join ours. . . . A second problem faced was the fact that in our small denomination we do not have any of the pastors' retreats, conferences, seminars and meetings that mean a great deal to individual ministers. . . . A third basic problem came through traditional differences of worship and belief.

The committee, however, was able to propose that a call be extended to Mr. and Mrs. Howard Kriebel, who were then students at Lancaster Theological Seminary. The proposed call was to become effective on July 1, 1959 for Martha Kriebel and on June 1, 1960 for Howard Kriebel, who would serve as a student pastor until that time. The proposal was overwhelmingly accepted by the congregation. The service of ordination for Martha Kriebel was held at the Palm church on June 28, 1959.

Rev. Martha Bean Kriebel was born in Philadelphia, Pennsylvania, on May 22, 1935, the daughter of Mr. and Mrs. Claude H. Bean. She received her elementary education in the public schools of that city and was graduated by the Philadelphia High School for Girls in February 1953. She entered Ursinus College, where she pursued the pre-medical course leading to a Bachelor of Science degree, which she received "cum laude" in June 1956. During her final year at Ursinus, at the suggestion of one of her professors, her plans to attend medical school to become a medical missionary were changed when she felt a call to the Christian ministry. She decided to seek a Bachelor of Divinity degree from the Lancaster Theological Seminary and graduated from that institution in June of 1959. During her years in the seminary she did fieldwork in Trinity Evangelical and Reformed Church, Pottstown, Pa., and in the Reformed Church at Falkner Swamp, Pa. Together with her husband Howard, she spent the summer of 1957 as a student worker in the Pioneer parish near Clarington, Ohio, and the summer of 1958 as a student worker in Grace church, West Point, Pa.

Howard L. Kriebel is a native of Norristown, the son of Mr. and Mrs. Howard W. Kriebel. He was graduated from Norristown High School and Millersville State Teachers' College. On June 7, 1960 he was graduated from the Lancaster Theological Seminary.

Shortly after the call was extended to the Reverends Kriebel, they requested of the church officers that an affiliated relationship with the Lehigh Synod of the United Church of Christ be established in order that they might have a dual standing as ministers of the Schwenkfelder and United Church of Christ denominations. It was the sense of a special District Conference held April 2, 1959 "That the ministry of Howard and Martha Kriebel could be enhanced and strengthened if they were enabled to maintain a relationship with the United Church of Christ and potential benefits from this proposed "dual standing" could accrue to the congregation." The following June another special District Conference approved the affiliation of the Palm church with the Lehigh Synod of the United Church of Christ.

The Reverends Kriebel requested that the church house, as the annex had been called since it became living quarters, be remodeled to make it available for family living. Upon completion of these renovations the Kriebels moved into what was now officially called the "parsonage."

With the new ministers came a number of innovative ideas. In the Schwenkfelder tradition infants had been consecrated or dedicated, and children, upon reaching the age of discretion and receiving catechetical instruction, were baptized upon joining church. Children of new families from other traditions were, upon request, baptized in an informal service. The new pastors, upon request, introduced the sacrament of infant baptism into the regular Sunday worship service, and a preparatory service prior to the celebration of holy communion was reinstituted. New hymnals were purchased and dedicated and several pamphlets on such subjects as infant consecration, the church year, and the cross were prepared. In order to provide more intensive study for the catechumens, catechetical class instruction was expanded from ten to thirty sessions, with confirmation taking place on Palm Sunday. To impart additional information and inspiration to the people at Palm, a monthly newsletter, called "The Palm Leaves," was begun, Rev. Martha Kriebel designing its letterhead.

In July 1961 Rev. Howard Kriebel tendered his resignation to the Board of Trustees and the Diaconate. He had been given permission by the Board of Trustees in 1960 to serve as a part-time industrial arts teacher in the Upper Perkiomen School District, and he came to prefer the teaching profession over the ministry. He did, however, remain active in church youth group activities, particularly the Boy Scout program.

The fiftieth anniversary of the dedication of the Palm Schwenkfelder Church was celebrated with an historical program presented on Sunday evening, September 17, 1961. Mrs. H. William Martin read a paper on the history of the building of the church, old photographs taken during its construction were presented, and members recalled incidents from the time of construction and dedication of the building. The congregation also received three oil paintings of the Schwenkfelder meeting houses at Kraussdale, Hosensack, and Washington, painted by local artist and member of the Palm church, Wayne H. Rothenberger. The following Sunday, ministerial sons of the congregation, Rev. Jack Rothenberger and Rev. Levi S. Hoffman, participated in the service and Rev. Martha Kriebel delivered the anniversary sermon.

During the 1960s the inactive segment of the church membership prompted concern. Several different visitation programs were instituted, including an "Undershepherd Plan," to bring these members back into active church involvement. A laity Sunday service was instituted, and children's sermons reinstated. In 1963 mid-week Lenten services were started, and in the following year, upon the request of the senior choir, the first Easter dawn service was held. In 1967 the church was joined in this service by the Pennsburg United Church of Christ. In 1968 Upper Perkiomen Valley churches initiated joint Thanksgiving Eve services. The first service was held at the St. Philip Neri Roman Catholic Church with Rev. Kriebel taking part in the liturgy and the senior choir joining in a massed choir from participating churches. The annual Sunday school Christmas program was moved to the Sunday before Christmas, and a Christmas Eve candlelight service instituted.

In 1962 the Ushers' League formed a group for the older men of the church and held its first annual pancake and sausage supper. The two groups operated jointly until they officially merged and became known as "The Men of Palm" in 1964. In addition to the pancake and sausage supper, the Men of Palm initiated a chicken barbeque in 1965 to serve as a fund-raiser as well as to provide fellowship. In 1966 they reinstituted the congregation's annual Advent Party, which had not been held since the late 1950s.

During the late 1950s the question of space utilization once again became a major issue, with the adequacy of the Sunday school facilities the focus of concern. In June 1960 the Board of Trustees invited the Rev. Dr. John Scotford, an experienced church building consultant, to survey the facilities and suggest future steps. In the fall of that year ten committees, involving every member of the congregation, were appointed to draw up specific needs and recommendations. District Conference in 1961 authorized the Board of Trustees to "engage the services of an architect to assist in the development of such plans as could . . . provide such additional facilities and improvements" as the study group deemed necessary. Several months later Buchart Associates of Lancaster, Pa., were engaged and building and finance committees were appointed by Moderator William Schultz.

The Building Committee presented its basic plans for the renovation of the present building and development of an addition for larger and better Sunday school facilities to the congregation on October 9, 1962. The Finance Committee also presented its plans for raising funds to meet the costs for this construction. The congregation decided on a program to be carried out in three phases: church basement, new Christian education building, and sanctuary. Primarily through volunteer labor of the men of the church, the basement was renovated during the spring and summer months of 1963.

Work on the second phase began when ground was broken for a new Christian education building on April 26, 1964. On Thanksgiving Sunday, November 22, 1964, more than 300 members of the church witnessed the placing of the datestone in the back wall of the new building. After a brief service, the following articles were placed in an inner box sealed in the stone: a Bible presented by Rev. Martha Kriebel, brochures of the building program presented by Moderator William Schultz, the names of the young people of the church presented by Doreen Kriebel, an announcement of the service, a newspaper article, and a bulletin from the service presented by Sunday School President Willard Schultz. The new building was dedicated on September 12, 1965.

During Rev. Martha Kriebel's pastorate a renewed emphasis was placed on Christian education. Throughout 1961 and 1962 the Sunday school evaluated and introduced a completely new curriculum. The youth programs were re-evaluated and changed as the Christian Endeavor was gradually replaced by participation in the United Schwenkfelder Youth Fellowship. In 1965 Moderator William N. Schultz appointed a Christian Education Committee to oversee the education program of the church.

In February 1965 the Christian Education Committee formed a study group to investigate the feasibility of establishing a weekday nursery school. Noting the excellent facilities provided by the new Christian education building, the group proposed a non-denominational, non-profit school to provide a wholesome pre-school educational program for three- and four-year-olds following guidelines established by the State. At a special District Conference in March the congregation adopted a resolution defining the relationship between the church and the nursery school, to be called the "Palm Country Day School." Later that year the Board of Trustees added the salary of the teacher to the church payroll and the school opened its doors in September with twenty-one children registered. Teachers and assistants attempt to instill in their students the characteristics of independence in personal needs, cooperation, obedience, politeness, self-control, confidence, broader vocabularies, and appreciation of music, art, and nature. Activities, designed to be enjoyable as well as educational, include painting, singing and rhythm, conversation, stories and games, dramatic plays, science activities, holiday projects, and counting and reading readiness activities. By 1983 the program had expanded to three sessions per day, with an enrolment of eighty-eight students.

At this point the building rehabilitation program as initially planned was interrupted for several years when it was discovered that the church's slate roof needed extensive repairs. After contacting several contractors, the Board of Trustees recommended to District Conference in 1969 that the roof be replaced and that insulation be installed where necessary. The Conference approved the $20,000 needed for the project and the new slate roof was completed later that year.

While the roof project was in progress, the priority committee continued with its evaluation of the sanctuary and decided to give preferential treatment to the organ. In early 1971, upon the recommendation of a special study sub-committee, the old pipe organ was replaced with a new Allen electronic organ and carillon purchased at a cost of $23,500. The new organ was dedicated during the morning worship service on May 23, 1971. A special evening service was arranged for the community and every pew and chair in the sanctuary was filled. The program was highlighted by a concert performed by the Upper Perkiomen High School choir under the direction of Richard Lampe and an organ recital by Carl Gearhart of the Allen Organ Co.

The renovations to the sanctuary were completed in 1972 when the Board of Trustees decided to install new carpeting and lighting, completely refinish all the pews, and have the draperies professionally dry cleaned.

On March 18, 1972 Rev. Martha Kriebel was elected one of three assistant conference ministers of the Pennsylvania Southeast

Conference of the United Church of Christ. This high honor resulted in her resignation as pastor of the Palm church, effective in August of 1972.

In addition to the many changes at the Palm church instituted during her pastorate, Rev. Martha Kriebel was instrumental in organizing the Upper Perkiomen Valley Community Council's thrift shop, tutorial services for the middle school branch of the Mental Health Center, and a senior citizens' activity center. Rev. Kriebel was elected to "Who's Who Among Young Women in America" and also was a recipient of the Distinguished Service Award of the Junior Chamber of Commerce of the Upper Perkiomen Valley. She earned her master's degree from the Lutheran Theological Seminary in Philadelphia. Her thesis, "Schwenkfelders and the Sacraments," was published by the Board of Publication in 1968, and has become a standard reference source in Schwenkfelder theology. Although expressing a reluctance to leave the only parish she had thus far served, she said quite simply, "God has called us to a new challenge." The Reverends Kriebel, along with sons Jonathan and David, planned to take up residence in Sumneytown, Pa.

The moderator, Stanley Kurtz, appointed a Pastoral Committee, chaired by Ray L. Rothenberger, to recommend a replacement for Rev. Kriebel. On Sunday morning, November 26, 1972, at a special District Conference held after the morning worship service, which he conducted, a call was extended to Rev. Ronald Krick to serve the Palm church.

Rev. Ronald Krick is a native of Berks County and graduated from Hamburg High School in 1950. Being influenced by his family's strong ties with the church and by his church camping experiences at Camp Mensch Mill in Berks County, Ronald made the decision while in high school to enter the Christian ministry. He entered Franklin and Marshall College and went on to graduate from Lancaster Theological Seminary and to complete graduate studies at Michigan State University and at the Lancaster Theological Seminary. In 1957 he became pastor of the St. John's United Church of Christ in Denver, Pa., where he served 480 parishioners.

In addition to his parish duties, Rev. Krick was active in church conference and community affairs. He was chairman of the Town and Country Department of the Penn Central Conference of the United Church of Christ and served as president of the Denver Federation of Churches. He was elected president and secretary of the Commission on Welfare of the Union church. Rev. Krick also served as vice-president of the Lancaster Association of the Penn Central Conference. He was a member of the Board of Directors of the Ephrata Area Social Services and served as a counselor in the County Telephone Ministry, and a part-time chaplain at Ephrata Hospital.

The new pastor, his wife Joyce, and their two sons Kevin and Daniel moved into the parsonage in January 1972 and Rev. Krick was installed as pastor at Palm on February 2, 1972.

Early in Rev. Krick's pastorate, the constitution and bylaws of the church were reviewed and revised by a special committee. An elected Board of Christian Education was established, charged with general oversight of the entire educational program of the church, the Sunday school, and other educational programs affiliated with the church, including the youth groups and the scouting programs. Responsibility for the music program was vested in a new Music Committee, appointed by the moderator. And finally, the expanded nine-member Diaconate was formally recognized.

In 1977 a set of twelve antique handbells was donated for use in the church. With the help of the new Music Committee, Katherine Engle organized the church's first youth bell choir, introducing a musical form not formerly experienced in the Palm church. Later, in 1982, the committee was able to acquire a set of twenty-eight handbells. Today, in addition to the senior choir, worship services are enhanced by the participation of a junior choir, a bell choir, and a brass choir. These groups present a monthly musical offering during the worship service in addition to performing at special services.

On Sunday, May 13, 1979, members and friends at Palm celebrated the ordination of Sharon Solt into the ministries of both the United Church of Christ and the Schwenkfelder church. A member of the Palm congregation, Rev. Solt graduated from Upper Perkiomen High School, Catawba College, and Drew Theological School of Madison, New Jersey, and earned a certificate from the United Theological College located in Bangalore, India. Rev. Solt has stated that her special concerns for the ministry include missions, ecumenism, and interfaith relations. Following her ordination, she accepted a call to serve as the director of Christian education and parish development for the Broadway United Church of Christ in New York City.

During the summer and early fall of the same year, Pastor Krick was granted a sabbatical leave in order to continue studies at Eastern Baptist and Lancaster seminaries. In his absence pastoral duties were carried out by Dr. John B. Frantz, retired pastor of the Trinity U. C. C. Church in Pottstown.

Rev. Krick's ministry has focused particular concern on

strengthening Christian fellowship and caring not only within the church but also in closer relationships with other community groups. In 1977 the practice of recording worship services on cassette tapes was begun, so that replaying of the tapes could add a greater sense of participation and sharing among the elderly and disabled who could not attend church services in person. The organizing of an annual all-church picnic gave an opportunity for members to meet in an informal atmosphere. "Prayer and Share" and Bible study groups were formed to assist in guidance, discussion, and awareness, and to enhance understanding and interpretation of the Scriptures. The pastor and Mrs. Krick, an educator, initiated a Marriage Encounter program, designed to promote growth in the marital relationship by offering couples a chance to explore their relationship to one another in a private and loving atmosphere.

Members have offered of themselves for the well-being of the community through an annual Harvest Home service, the C.R.O.P Hunger Walk, and blood donations to the Red Cross. Pastor Krick has stated, "We cannot stop at being a society for the preservation of church buildings, our ethnic background, or our denominational organization. These things are not good, bad, or indifferent in and of themselves. In fact they can be our inspiration and guide for future reformation. . . . We need to be servants in the service of mankind." Rev. Krick, as Rev. Kriebel before him, has been called upon to devote ever-increasing time and energy to individual guidance and counseling.

In 1980 the church decided to participate in a pastoral intern program, hoping thereby to enhance the youth activities program and provide experience for a student of the participating seminary. David Luz, a member of the Central Schwenkfelder Church and a student at Eastern Baptist Theological Seminary, began his internship at Palm in July of 1981. David graduated from North Penn High School in 1974 and continued his education, majoring in music, at Mansfield State College. Before attending seminary he worked at the American Olean Tile Company and as a houseparent, along with his wife, Joanne, at the Northern Home for Children. During illness and an extended hospital stay, David was moved and greatly influenced by visits made to him by the Reverends Rothenberger and Byron of the Central Schwenkfelder Church. Their discussions and encouragement led to his enrolment at the Eastern Baptist Theological Seminary, Philadelphia. While at the seminary, David favored both biblical studies and psychology courses in counseling. His own fond experiences in C. E. groups, Sunday school, and youth choir helped him to recognize the value of church youth activities.

Following his arrival at Palm, David and Pastor Krick began to work as a team to rebuild an interest in activities for the youth group and young adults. A young married couples group was organized in 1981 to provide fellowship for that segment of the congregation. Additional adult advisors were recruited and the young people encouraged to participate in existing activities, service projects, awareness projects and in Sunday worship services. Interaction between Palm's young people and other youth groups throughout the Upper Perkiomen Valley was encouraged. Palm's first youth musical, "And There Was Light . . . ," was presented to the public in the fall of 1981.

Recognizing the benefits of the work that Pastor Krick and David Luz had been able to accomplish together, church members met on October 14, 1981 to discuss hiring an assistant pastor. In December an Assistant Pastor Study Committee chaired by Ralph Bieler proposed to District Conference that a call be extended to David Luz to become Palm's assistant pastor. Upon completion of his Master of Divinity degree, Rev. Luz was ordained into the Schwenkfelder ministry at the Central church on June 13 and installed as assistant minister at Palm on June 27, 1982.

As the twentieth century has unfolded, the Upper District has undergone great changes in the physical structure of the church and in the expansion of its programs as it has attempted to meet the spiritual needs of its membership and residents of the surrounding community. As Pastor Krick stated in his 1981 annual report to the congregation:

> Just as a building is built by using many bricks, so a Christian community is built by many people working together to serve those who are of the household of faith, those who have not yet heard of Jesus Christ, and those who have special needs such as food, shelter, clothing, and know-how to care for themselves.

It has been this spirit of community which has made the Palm Schwenkfelder Church effective in helping to build God's Kingdom here on earth over the last eight decades.

Chapter Five

The Central Schwenkfelder Church

The Central Schwenkfelder Church is attractively situated on high ground along Valley Forge Road (Pennsylvania Route 363), between Skippack Pike and Sumneytown Pike, in Montgomery County. Its colonial stone church edifice with stately white ionic columns and cross-crowned steeple draws the attention of all who pass by. "Central Schwenkfelder Church," set across the white portico in black letters readily legible from the roadway, quickly affirms its identity. Glimpses of its 131-foot-high steeple, illuminated at night, attract attention from miles around.

The Central congregation today numbers some 1,400 members. The surrounding countryside, once principally the preserve of Schwenkfelder farmsteads settled following the 1734 migration and passed along for almost 200 years from generation to generation in the same family, has more recently been built up into a semi-suburban community within easy commuting distance of Lansdale, Norristown, Collegeville, and even Philadelphia. Rising land values have increasingly discouraged family farming although outstanding exceptions may be noted.

The changing nature of the surrounding community has been reflected in the church congregation. Less than half of the current members trace their ancestry to Schwenkfelder immigrants. In contrast to the stiffly traditional, somewhat withdrawn, congregations of the so-called "Lower District" ("Middle District" or "Central" after the establishment of the Philadelphia church) churches of the nineteenth century, the modern church has truly become a community church, warmly extending the right hand of fellowship to all neighbors of Christian profession. The strong Schwenkfelder tradition of past generations has eroded and the sense of denomination weakened, but the appeal of the church has been broadened and its outreach strengthened with the greater diversity of membership.

Neither Schwenckfeld during his lifetime nor his followers in Europe following his death contemplated any formal church organization. Indeed, in the political and religious conditions of the times any attempt at organization would almost certainly have been quickly crushed. Worship and catechetical instruction of children were carried on in the homes under the natural leadership of the parents, assisted and encouraged by early leaders who visited from home to home. The more forceful leaders were designated to perform marriage rites, conduct funerals, etc.

During the first twenty-five years in this country the establishment of homesteads largely absorbed the energy and attention of the immigrants and, along with the difficulties of travel and communication, tended to weaken the close ties that had bound them together through the years of persecution in Silesia. The faith for which they had made so many sacrifices began to lose its hold on them, especially on the children and young people growing up in their new homeland. On October 9, 1762 they assembled in special conference at the home of Christopher Kriebel to consider the situation. The conferees addressed themselves to three questions, questions which have not lost their pertinence even down to the present day: "(1) Will we be able to bear with one another if a closer union is formed so that what is undertaken may not be ended in strife and works of evil? (2) Will we be willing to grant to each other the liberty of reading authors other than those commonly accepted by us? (3) Will we be ready to bear with one another if in some point of doctrine we cannot agree in our views?"

Since affirmative answers emerged, plans for a closer union were taken under advisement and Christopher Schultz was instructed to prepare his catechism for the press. It was printed the following year. The immediate practical result was a more formal plan for regular rotation of Sunday meetings from house to house, with worship services in the morning and "Kinderlehr"—catechetical instruction of children—in the afternoon. The "Haus-Vater"—head of the household—was responsible for arrangements, including a midday meal. By the end of the eighteenth century worship services were being held in school houses and meeting houses.

In 1782 a loose "Society" was formed. Forty-one "Haus-Väter" subscribed to a statement of seventeen principles prepared by Christopher Schultz. This statement was revised several times and in 1851, as rewritten by Rev. Joshua Schultz, published under the title "Constitution and Bylaws of the Schwenkfelder Society." Further revised in 1898 and 1902, it became the "Formula for the Government and Discipline of the Schwenkfelder Church," usage of the word "church" then being of quite recent origin.

In 1838 one Edmund Flinn, husband of descendant Maria Weigner, having earlier benefited from Schwenkfelder charity, provided in his will a bequest to the "Sociey of Schwenkfelders." Relatives contested the will (ultimately unsuccessfully) on the grounds that no such organization enjoyed legal existence. As a result, the "Managers of the Literary and Charitable Funds of the Society of Schwenkfelders" was duly incorporated to receive and administer funds and property. Not until 1909, however, did a further revision of the Formula of Government provide for the legal incorporation of The Schwenkfelder Church.

The Society was democratic, although patriarchal. Its business was conducted at General Conferences held spring and fall, where all members participated without distinction between ministers and the laity. Local affairs were arranged in district conferences, one in the Upper District and one in the Lower District. Ministers of the Society were elected, or on occasion selected by lot, from candidates deemed of suitable moral character and disposition. They were not paid but were expected to obtain their living from their daily occupation, usually farming. Dr. O. S. Kriebel, installed as pastor in the Upper District in 1892, was the first Schwenkfelder specifically educated and compensated as a minister. In the Middle District, the first pastor entering the ministry as a vocation rather than an avocation was Rev. Levi S. Hoffman, ordained and installed in 1910.

Middle District Meeting Houses

At the beginning of the present century Schwenkfelders of the Middle District worshiped in three Meeting Houses—Towamencin, Worcester, and Salford.

The Towamencin Meeting House, off Valley Forge Road south of Sumneytown Pike, was the first established in the district. Probably preceded by a log school house built in 1765 in the same general location, a log meeting house was erected in 1793, joining the Hosensack (1790) and Washington (1791) meeting houses of the Upper District as early Schwenkfelder places of worship. The first services were held there on July 21, 1793. In 1854 this building was replaced by a stone structure which did service until 1893, when a handsome brick edifice was erected a short distance from the older building on the opposite side of the road. The new building contained a commodious basement with room for divisions for Sunday school purposes—a facility pioneered eleven years earlier at the Worcester building to the great consternation of traditionalists, whose fears seem to have been laid to rest in the meantime. This building served the Middle District congregation until the erection of the present Central Schwenkfelder Church facility.

The first Worcester Meeting House, on the corner of Township Line and Church Road (now Trooper Rd.) in Worcester Township, was built in 1836, to be replaced in 1882 by the larger structure with basement which served the southern end of the district down to the merger of the Central congregations.

The Salford Meeting House was the last to be established, dating only from 1869. It serves as a reminder of travel difficulties before the advent of paved roads and the automobile, when a meeting house within walking distance—or at least easy carriage distance—was a necessity, particularly in winter when drifting snow frequently forced travelers to detour over open fields or in spring when mud made dirt roads equally impassable. Services in the Salford Meeting House were regularly conducted in the German language. By 1900, with roads improved and the other meeting houses more accessible, services at Salford were reduced to every third Sunday and to a union Harvest Home service each fall in conjunction with neighboring churches. In time services were confined to special observances and an annual pilgrimage on the first Sunday of August.

Middle District Lay Ministers

During the early years of the twentieth century the Middle District congregation was served by three ministers, Rev. William Schultz Anders, Rev. George K. Meschter, and Rev. Edwin S. Anders. Rev. Elmer A. Yeakel served only briefly during 1908. The ministers all appear to have served as associate ministers with, however, a well defined deference to seniority.

The three ministers were an impressive lot, held in high esteem by their congregation and exerting great influence by force of character and dint of dedication. They were the last of the lay pastors, performing their church duties as an avocation, without pay. Their passing marked the end of an era, although a tradition of strong lay leadership in the churches and denomination survives to this day.

William S. Anders and Edwin S. Anders were both descended from immigrant Anna Reinwald Anders but not more closely related. George K. Meschter was descended from immigrant Melchior Meschter. The forbears of all three, and of their wives as well, were a continuous line of immigrant descendants. William Anders and George Meschter were contemporaries, both having been born in 1840, William dying in 1907 and George in 1910. Edwin Anders was born in 1857 and lived to a ripe old age of 80, dying in 1937. He survived the election of his successor, Rev. Levi Hoffman, by twenty-seven years, during which veneration for the older man's seniority cast something of a shadow over the young pastor. For the first twenty-five years of his pastorate Rev. Hoffman deferred to his elder predecessor, allowing him to conduct communion and baptism services. Rev. Hoffman lived to be 95, witnessing the installation of three successors.

Rev. William S. Anders received his education in the public schools of Worcester Township and then spent two years as a student at Mount Kirk Seminary, Providence Township, Montgomery County, which was conducted for many years by the Rev. Henry Rodenbaugh, who served also as pastor of the Lower Providence Presbyterian Church. He thereupon engaged in school teaching in Towamencin, Worcester, and Norriton Townships for eight years. On February 1, 1868 Mr. Anders married Susan H. Krauss of Worcester Township and at about the same time relinquished his school post to work his father's farm, also in Worcester Township. He farmed successfully for some twenty-five years, retiring to a house on an adjoining plot where he lived the rest of his life.

William S. Anders was called to the Schwenkfelder ministry in 1871, served a brief probationary period, and was then fully installed. These duties were not undertaken lightly. A co-worker on the Anders farm recalled:

> On a Saturday afternoon in the early summer of 1871 he returned from a congregational meeting held in the Worcester church. Sad in countenance he passed me in the yard without recognizing me and walked to the house. Not wishing to obtrude myself upon him, I remained at a distance and wondered what might be the cause of his anxiety. My suspense was ended when, at the evening meal from which he was absent, Mrs. Anders told me what had happened—William had been chosen a minister. . . . For weeks and months the battle of decision raged in his mind but he finally surrendered unconditionally to the Divine call.

The last decades of the nineteenth century were years of growth and development of the Middle District congregation, as well as of the Schwenkfelder denomination. The new, greatly enlarged Worcester and Towamencin Meeting Houses were built and the variety of congregational activities gradually expanded. Rev. William Anders courageously faced up to a perennially contentious problem. During the years in Europe and the early years in Pennsylvania the Schwenkfelders honored Schwenckfeld's "Still-Stand," refraining from celebrating the sacraments of the Lord's Supper and Baptism. This was not out of any unbelief but out of consideration by Schwenckfeld that violent dissensions within the family of God made celebration of the sacraments an affront to the God they all worshiped. Pressure slowly built up to overcome this reluctance to celebrate the sacraments. The following letter from Rev. William S. Anders to Rev. Howard W. Kriebel of the Upper District, dated Worcester, March 16, 1882 suggests the difficult position in which Rev. Anders found himself.

Dear Bro:

Your letter of the 13th inst. is at hand, and will endeavor to answer the questions you ask in regard to the institution of the Sacraments in our congregation. From the contents of your letter I infer that there are some who still criticise the way by which they were instituted. I at that time heard such criticisms myself, but they came either from highly ritualistic or from such persons who regarded the Lord's dying commands as of no account, and might be neglected or observed at pleasure.

Such were not consulted, but the opinions of Christian men of the Presbyterian, Mennonites and other churches were obtained and duly weighed, and the Aufsatz, made in the year 1858 by bro. Joshua Schultz and subscribed to by all the ministers of the congregation at that time were taken as a guide. But above all it was made the subject of our prayers to Almighty God, that He should direct our steps in wisdom, grant his counsel, help, and grace that our actions might be consistent with His will so that we might be benefited and His great name glorified. Bro. Joshua Schultz at a special conference held, I think in the spring of '75 agreed to take a leading part, with a view to their institution in the near future, when the time came he refused, the consequence was a further delay of 2 1/2 years. When in the autumn of 1877 finding that no aid or participation could be expected from the brethren of the U.D., we concluded to go on, and accordingly met in pursuance to a previous announcement at the house of A. K. Heebner whose wife was an invalid and for years desired to be baptized. I suppose about 25 were baptized. I first baptized bro. Meschter; then Meschter myself; I the others.

I hope this mode will meet your approval. You will remember that all beginnings are difficult, and this because of its importance was especially so, and pressed heavily upon my mind at the time, but I trust the good Lord of the fullness of His grace has, and will in the future supply that of which we are deficient. And in regard to the other questions the time is not set for the celebration of the Lord's Supper. Preparatory services are always held the day previous, on which day members of the congregation, as well as others who desire it, are baptized. None however but those who have some time before notified the ministers or elders of their wish. If already members, or such who have received catechetical instruction a further instruction is not considered necessary. If, however, the applicant is thought to be wanting in such knowledge, he is taken through a short course of instruction. A more definite plan will undoubtedly be adopted in the near future.

Dear Bro. write again telling me what are some of the criticisms you hear and by whom made. Come down soon and preach English for me. Bro. J. B. Kriebel has been unwell all winter, and I am nearly always alone in Worcester. Yours in grace, W. S. Anders.

A wave of earnest discussion, argument, and recrimination followed, which occasioned the appointment of a compromise committee in 1888, whose report was adopted and printed in 1894. By virtue of the committee report, opportunity was given in the Upper District for baptism and communion, which have been continued regularly since. It was the abuse of the sacraments, celebrated by contentious factions, not the sacraments themselves, to which Schwenckfeld and his followers took exception.

A few years before his death Rev. William Anders presented his resignation. While the congregation agreed to relieve him of regular duties, it refused to accept his resignation. Faithful to the end, Rev. Anders met his death while performing his ministerial duty. The Anders brothers spent the coldest parts of the winter in Florida, where they owned a productive orange grove. On February 18, 1907 Rev. Anders was walking to the home of Hon. William D. Heebner in Orange City, Florida to rehearse for a wedding ceremony which Rev. Anders was to perform two days later, when he fell over and expired in a few minutes, having been a sufferer from heart disease for several years.

Rev. Anders regularly conducted the German language services in the Salford Meeting House and was actively engaged in Sunday school work for more than forty years. He served as superintendent of the Towamencin Sunday school and as German language teacher of an adult Bible class. He was president of the Schwenkfelder Board of Publication during the early years of the *Corpus* undertaking and a faithful supporter of the *Schwenkfeldian*. He served as a school director of Worcester Township, as a director of Ursinus college, and for many years as a director of Montgomery National Bank of Norristown, as did his father before him. He was an organizer and treasurer of the Souderton, Skippack and Fairview Electric Railway Company.

George K. Meschter attended local schools and then graduated from the University of Pennsylvania Medical School in 1867, pursuing post-graduate work there and in Philadelphia hospitals. He purchased the practice of his preceptor, Dr. Joel H. Krauss, of Worcester, Montgomery County, Pa. and here practised medicine for twenty-five years. He acquired one of the most extensive practices in the county, becoming one of its busiest physicians. Doctors B. T. Kohler, E. K. Blank, James M. Anders, David D. Custer, and Josiah K. Gerhard studied under him as preceptor, the last becoming his professional partner. Upon Dr. Gerhard's death in 1886 Dr. James R. Care became associated with Dr. Meschter and in 1919 the practice passed into the hands of Dr. Herbert B. Shearer. In 1893, partly because of failing health, Dr. Meschter gave up the active practise of medicine.

Rev. George K. Meschter assumed the duties of a second calling while still a practising physician. He was elected minister of the Schwenkfelder congregation of the Middle District on March 23, 1883 to succeed the Rev. John B. Kriebel, deceased. He pondered until fall whether he should accept this election, after which he took up his added duties. After the death of Rev. William S. Anders in 1907 Dr. Meschter became the senior minister of the Middle District. He was also active in the Schwenkfelder Mission in Norristown, Pa., and was consequently invited to assume full charge of services there in 1905, continuing until forced by failing health to retire in 1908.

Rev. Meschter was identified with every movement of the Schwenkfelder church. In 1882 he was a member of the Building Committee of the Worcester Schwenkfelder Church. He was secretary of the Board of Foreign Missions of the Schwenkfelder Church from 1904 to 1910, and was a trustee of Perkiomen School.

Edwin S. Anders received only a local public school education. He lived his entire life on the family farm in Towamencin Township, one of the best cultivated in the area. He was elected a minister in 1886 and gave unstintingly of his time and energy in performing his ministerial duties. Both Rev. and Mrs. Anders were noted for their genuine hospitality and were frequently called upon for advice and assistance. The "latch string was always out" for neighbors and friends, and many families were blessed by the generous and unostentatious benefits of the Anders family.

A successful farmer, Rev. Anders participated actively in secular affairs, although he was averse to entering politics and never sought public office. He served as a trustee of Perkiomen School. As a member of the Board of Publication he was one of the most active supporters of the *Corpus* movement and of the Schwenkfelder Historical Library. By diligent and persistent search of garrets, closets, and storerooms of many homes, Rev. Anders discovered hundreds of books, papers, and artifacts that now repose in the Schwenkfelder Library. He was such an enthusiastic collector of historical documents and examples of early folk art that he frequently delved into his own purse to obtain articles that would not be gifted to the library. After the installation of Rev. Hoffman, he served as senior pastor, or pastor emeritus, until his death in 1937.

From the beginning of worship in the early meeting houses men and women traditionally sat on opposite sides of the central aisle. The women occupied the left side of the sanctuary, with a foot rest underneath the pews. The men sat on the right side, with a shelf underneath the benches, upon which they could place their hats, song books, etc. This practice continued until 1893 when Mr. and Mrs. Amos Schultz (parents of Mrs. Malcolm Schweiker) were married. They and five or six other newly-wed couples decided to worship as a family unit, much to the consternation of the traditionalists. Family worship slowly gained support, however, and a Worcester district note in the November 1910 issue of the *Schwenkfeldian* read: "At this point allow us to congratulate the members in engaging in family worship in the church. Can any one imagine a more pleasant sight than fathers, mothers, brothers and sisters occupying the same pew in the services in the house of God." But tradition died slowly and it is said that some couples persisted in sitting on opposite sides of the aisle even in the new Central church. It was left to Rev. Hoffman's new bride to initiate the participation of women in the business sessions of the Conference. Her attendance at the first District Conference following the Hoffmans' arrival (fall of 1910) was a bold innovation which more progressive ladies of the congregation gradually emulated.

There was but one church congregation in the Middle District, with worship services held Sunday mornings alternately at Worcester and Towamencin. There were, however, two Sunday school organizations, with Sunday school held every Sunday in both churches—in the afternoon when there was morning church, in the morning when there was no morning worship service. After the advent of the automobile Sunday school was held every Sunday morning, with church services scheduled to allow a half hour for families to travel from one meeting house to the other. Sunday school classes were suspended from the end of November to the beginning of April. To heat the church auditorium for Sunday worship the heater had to be started on Saturday and it was not easy to heat the basement Sunday school rooms. The Ladies' Aid Society held its meetings on Monday following church services in Towamencin, as it was easier to maintain the furnace in operation an extra day than to fire it up a second time. Both Sunday schools had orchestras to accompany singing.

Down to 1907 weddings were held in the parsonage or in the home of the bride rather than in the church. Likewise Christian Endeavor or Sunday school class socials were not permitted in the church basement but had to be held in members' homes. An active Christian Endeavor Society embracing members of all ages was organized in 1905 and met regularly on Sunday evenings at Towamencin. Not until after the building of the new Central church was this society divided into junior, junior high, and senior high societies. A Women's Christian Temperance Union was organized June 14, 1905 at the home of Mrs. Amos Anders. It rendered active service in meeting charitable and relief needs, as well as promoting the cause of temperance. The congregation-wide Ladies' Aid Society, later to become such a creative force, was not organized until 1912. Mrs. Hiram K. Kriebel was elected its first president.

Reminiscing later, Rev. Hoffman described the funeral practice at the turn of the century:

Before the days of Morticians, the Undertakers had no funeral homes. There were no Viewings the evening before the Funerals. There were no telephones, no mail deliveries; messengers were sent to inform the relatives in case of a funeral. The bodies were kept in the homes. For the most part the funerals were held in the morning. The first part of the service was held in the home, the distant relatives came and ate before the ceremony began. At the house, the service began with a prayer, a Scripture Lesson, some comments, and a few hymns. Then a regular service in the Meeting House; at the grave a few Scripture Passages, hymns, a prayer, interment, and the benediction. The relatives returned back to the house for condolences and a meal. Some of the chosen neighbors dug the grave, served as pall bearers, and closed the grave. The young men took care of the horses, and the neighboring women set the house in order, and prepared and served the meals.

New members were baptized and confirmed at preparatory services held Saturday afternoon preceding the Sunday of the communion service. In the communion service as conducted by Rev. Edwin Anders communicants proceeded to the front of the sanctuary to receive the bread and wine (grape juice), the latter from a common cup, or chalice. Rev. Anders would raise his hand when there were enough members standing there without crowding. Because men were seated on one side of the sanctuary and women on the other, family members did not commune together. No invitations were extended to visitors. There was no reception for new members or procedure for acquainting them with the activities of the church and no certificates of confirmation were issued.

The January 1906 issue of the *Schwenkfeldian* included an article by Schwenkfelder Howard S. Anders, A.M., M.D., professor of physical diagnosis at the Medico-Chirurgical College in Philadelphia, in which he decried the use of the common cup in serving communion on health grounds and called attention to the rapidly expanding use of individual communion cups among many denominations and its use at the First Schwenkfelder Church in Philadelphia. He noted:

> It was a bold but not sacrilegious thing for sanitary science to invade the sacred precincts of the administration of a church ordinance so profoundly, spiritually, meaningly memorial as the Lord's Supper is to the Christian believer. In its boldness it demonstrated the newer and better conception of Christian liberty, philosophy and ethics that there is no real separation between the sacred and secular; and that as the spirit of the former should daily pervade the latter, so should the modern, rational methods of the latter influence and aid the former. The innovation did not and does not attack the significance, symbolism or solemnity of the ordinance; its effort was directed solely to modifying the method of administering the communion wine so that the participants might be protected against all possible contamination, . . . for it is not the cup, essentially, but the wine in the cup which, after all, Jesus designated to represent His blood.

Within the first year of Rev. Hoffman's pastorate the question came before a special District Conference called to consider the matter. Rev. Hoffman stated his position, "For efficiency, dignity, agility and for sanity, that (in individual cups) is the only way to serve communion." The conference agreed and the new practice was adopted.

Rev. Levi S. Hoffman

With the death of Rev. William S. Anders in February 1907 and the retirement of Rev. George Meschter in 1908 the congregation was clearly in need of a new minister. Almost as if preordained, the selection pointed to Schwenkfelder descendant Levi S. Hoffman. A complex personality, deeply spiritual, a profound scholar, and a rigid dogmatist, he was in many respects cast in the traditional mold of Schwenkfelder ministers, capable of preaching stern sermons, in the German or English language as the occasion required. Yet he was destined to serve the Middle District congregation for fifty and more years and to preside over a period of great change, witnessing the rise of the Lansdale church, in which he played a leading role, and culminating in the establishment of the Central Schwenkfelder Church, with facilities finally permitting the entire Middle District congregation to participate together in all activities.

Levi Samuel Hoffman was born at Topton, Berks County, October 9, 1875. Through his mother his Schwenkfelder lineage traced back over six generations, embracing 126 Schwenkfelder ancestors, including four ministers, among whom were immigrant ministers Balthasar Hoffmann and Christopher Schultz. His father was engaged as a wheelwright but six years later moved to a farm near Kraussdale, Pa., where Levi lived the typical life of a farm boy at the time. Even as a child he persuaded his young friends to "play church," with himself as preacher. He attended the local schools and was a faithful attendant at the meetings of the local literary society, where he became one of the leaders in debates conducted by the society. Attending the Kraussdale C. E. Society meetings he came into contact with students and professors from Perkiomen School and, encouraged by his pastor, Rev. O. S. Kriebel, he enrolled at the school, walking back and forth from the Kraussdale farm to Pennsburg. Having obtained his teacher's certificate he spent three years teaching in the public schools while continuing his studies at night and at summer sessions. He graduated from Perkiomen in 1903.

At this time the brightest graduates of Perkiomen generally chose Princeton to pursue college studies. With limited financial resources, however, Levi turned to smaller New England colleges where the small town prospects of part-time employment seemed more promising. His Perkiomen mathematics teacher, Professor Elmer Jacoby, had passed along to him a catalog from Brown University at Providence, Rhode Island. On a visit with Dean Alexander Meikeljohn he discovered he could enter Brown by registering for a Ph.B. degree, and by taking some extra work could switch over and graduate as an A.B. Furthermore, the dean informed him that Providence offered probably as many opportunities for part-time employment as any of the college towns of New England. Thus he decided to enter Brown in the fall of 1903, learning only later that three of his Perkiomen classmates, Horace Funk, Herbert B. Shearer, and Vernon K. Kriebel would travel with him and continue as classmates in college.

While Levi was home for vacation following his freshman year at Brown, Dr. Kriebel approached him at the close of a Kraussdale C. E. meeting to say, "Many of our members think that you ought to preach and I feel the same way." Levi responded, "But I don't want to preach. I want to teach." The pastor responded, "It isn't a question whether you want to preach but whether you ought to." Shortly thereafter, while Hoffman was working in the field harvesting grain, Professor Jacoby drove up in a carriage to deliver a message from Dr. Kriebel. The following Sunday Dr. Kriebel would be in New York City to see the Johnsons off for Europe and Levi was to preach the morning sermon at the Hosensack Meeting House. At the close of the Sunday school session the congregation was concerned to note the absence of their pastor. To their great surprise Mr. Hoffman mounted the pulpit and conducted the morning worship service. Hearing favorable reports, Dr. Kriebel insisted he wanted to hear Mr. Hoffman preach and a few Sundays later Levi preached in German at the Kraussdale Meeting House with Dr. Kriebel in the congregation. Thereafter he was pressed into service on numerous occasions when in the neighborhood.

At the close of his sophomore year he was asked to become acting pastor of the Hope Congregational Church in East Providence, Rhode Island. Learning that many boys in the church did not attend Sunday school, Mr. Hoffman obtained a list of their names and made a personal call on each in his home, thus gathering together his first Sunday school class. He continued preaching and teaching in this church throughout his final two years at Brown.

The members of this church and friends at home urged young Hoffman to consider seriously the ministry but still desiring to teach and feeling unworthy to become a minister, he held back. The dictates of his own conscience, which he had managed to ignore until this time, prevailed however, and in his sermon one night at the end of his senior year he announced, "I have now decided to become a minister or to die in the attempt." He graduated in the spring of 1907 with the liberal education he had sought and an A.B. degree.

In the fall of the same year he entered Hartford Theological Seminary, influenced in the choice by Dr. Chester Hartranft and the Hartford-Schwenkfelder association in the *Corpus* publication effort. President Dr. William D. Mackenzie, Riley Professor of Christian Theology, Dean Dr. Melancton W. Jacobus, professor of New Testament exegesis and criticism, Dr. Merriam, professor of homeletics, and Dr. Geer, professor of church history, made deep and lasting impressions upon their apt pupil, imbuing his later sermons with scholarly theological insights and developing in him a dramatic style of sermon delivery.

During his first year at Hartford he became teacher of the "Friendly Class," an organized class of ladies and young men in the Weatherfield Avenue Congregational Church. During the summer of that year, upon the recommendation of the Weatherfield pastor, Mr. Hoffman was employed as acting pastor of the South Doxbury Congregational Church in Vermont where his efforts earned a fervent plea to return the following year. Having in mind to go west and obtain some experience in the work on the frontier, he declined to make such a promise but did agree that if he decided to work in New England, he would accept their offer.

While serving this church Rev. Hoffman boarded weekends at the home of Mr. and Mrs. Walter Turner. Mrs. Turner was superintendent of the Sunday school and before her marriage had been a deaconess in the Fall River, Massachusetts, Methodist Deaconess Home. That summer Mrs. Turner received into her household Miss Adelaide Mattox, also of the Fall River home, ordered by her doctor to spend a summer in Vermont to recuperate from an illness. Mr. Hoffman soon learned of the existence of deaconesses, and to his surprise one Sunday attended church in Fall River to hear a deaconess preach the sermon. His association with Miss Mattox ripened into a close friendship and following his graduation, they were united in marriage on June 29, 1910 at the Deaconess Home in Fall River.

During his second year at the seminary, Mr. Hoffman was visited by a committee of the Schwenkfelder Church of the Middle District, who entreated him to spend the following summer in their district, as they were in need of a pastor. Mr. Hoffman could not resist this call and instead of staying in New England or going west he came to the Middle District as supply pastor for the summer. Upon graduation the next spring, having been duly elected in the meantime, he returned to the Schwenkfelder Church of the Middle District, bringing his new bride with him. He was formally ordained and installed September 18, 1910.

Early Moves Toward Consolidation

In 1910 the Middle District had a church membership of some 450 persons, about twice that of the Upper District. The Worcester

Sunday school reported an enrolment of around 200 and Towamencin around 300. The alternation of Sunday worship services between Worcester and Towamencin continued to be at best an inconvenience, at worst a severe handicap to congregational activities, particularly Sunday school and young people's activities. With Sunday school conducted immediately preceding the church hour in each church on the off Sundays, families with children in Sunday school almost inevitably became alternate Sunday worshipers. Members living near Fairview, Norritonville, and DeKalb Street Pike could hardly journey by horse and buggy to church in Towamencin and get home in time to care for their farm animals. Likewise, the Worcester Meeting House required a lengthy journey for families living in the Kulpsville, Lansdale, and North Wales area. Young people's activities and the congregation-wide Ladies' Aid Society suffered from ambiguity of meeting places.

In 1910 automobiles were just coming into general use and at that time only a few members of the congregation owned one. In all Worcester Township there were said to be only five autos and there was considerable discussion as to whether automobiles should be allowed to drive on the church grounds and possibly scare the horses tied there at the time of service. In 1910 a meeting was held at the home of Mr. and Mrs. Emmanuel Heebner on Valley Forge Road. Here it was suggested that services in Worcester be arranged for every Sunday but since it was soon realized this would require securing another minister and the congregation would probably divide into two, this thought was abandoned. Mr. Amos Schultz proposed that a new church be built at a more convenient central location but this suggestion was ahead of its time by forty years.

Mr. Schultz lived almost equidistant from the two meeting houses, and was one of the early owners of an automobile. One of the most successful farmers in the area, Mr. Schultz was a progressive member of the Worcester School Board, treasurer, and with John H. Schultz a co-founder of the Reading Bone Fertilizer Co., a director of the Lansdale National Bank, and a leader in the Farmers' Union, which built the Farmers' Hall at Center Point. Not surprisingly he had a vision of the improved roads of the future and was a persistent advocate of a central church. The September 1911 dedication of the new central church building at Palm kept the issue alive. A Worcester district note in the December 1913 issue of the *Schwenkfeldian* declared,

> A suggestion has been made that the Worcester and Towamencin churches should also unite and centralize their activities in one building

> but it is doubtful if this is a wise suggestion. Still we think there is ample justification for the separate churches in Worcester and Towamencin and that it would be a mistake to unite the activities in one locality. It seems to us that a better plan would be to have preaching services in each church every Sunday if it could be arranged in any way. As a matter of fact we believe that two good sized church organizations could be sustained in the Middle District. Beginning with next spring we are told that we will have an occasional evening service in the church here.

This drew a vigorous rebuttal from Rev. Hoffman in the following issue, in which he pleaded the case for unification.

No action was taken, however, and the disruptions of World War I shortly directed attention to other matters. At a congregational meeting in 1923 Mr. Schultz suggested that members subscribe to Building and Loan shares and during the next few months a total of 134 shares were so subscribed. These would mature principally between 1935 and 1937, providing some $26,800 as a nucleus of the eventual building fund.

In 1920 Mr. Amos Schultz's daughter, Blanche, married Mr. Malcolm Alderfer Schweiker and the Middle District church acquired an adopted son who would gradually come to share his father-in-law's vision and become a prime mover in the establishment of the present Central Schwenkfelder Church. Mr. Schweiker graduated from the Williamson Trade School near Media, Pa., in 1914 and entered into the construction business. In 1923, after his discharge from World War I service, he and his brother, Roy, founded the Franklin Tile Co. at Lansdale, Pa., later to be known as the American-Olean Tile Co. The business grew, struggled somewhat during the depression years of the early 1930s, and then entered upon a period of phenomenal growth. The Lansdale plant was repeatedly expanded and plants at other locations were acquired. By the building boom that followed World War II the company's products enjoyed wide acceptance and the company became the clear leader in its field, pioneering new uses of ceramic tile in washrooms, food service facilities, heavy traffic areas, and similar applications in schools, public buildings, and manufacturing plants. The mushrooming growth of the company accelerated until it outgrew single family ownership and in 1958 it was merged into National Gypsum Co., with the Schweiker brothers continuing in management of the tile company and Malcolm serving until 1967 as a highly-regarded director, and for the rest of his life a respected consultant to the public company.

By 1930 Mr. Schweiker had been elected president of the Middle District Board of Trustees, a post in which he would serve for the next thirty-five years. As the time for maturity of the Building and Loan shares approached the matter of a new church building naturally became a priority item on the trustees' agenda. Those members who had been paying into the building and loan fund for the past twelve years wanted to see some result from their sacrifice. But as to just how, when, or where the building fund was to be applied there were a multitude of suggestions but nothing approaching a consensus.

The Building and Loan Fund Committee recommended to the fall District Conference held October 28, 1937 that a new church building be built "as soon in the future as it can be satisfactorily planned, financed and completed." The Conference thereupon directed that the name of the Building and Loan Fund be changed to "Building Fund of the Central Schwenkfelder Church" and that a building committee be established to "study such things as church location, design, size, capacity, prospective cost, time of building, method of financing, and all other related questions," and to solicit additional Building and Loan subscriptions and other gifts. The committee, to serve until relieved of its duties by the congregation, was broadly based, consisting of "The Board of Trustees currently in office; two deacons chosen by the Deacons each year; the presidents currently in office of the Ladies' Aid Society, the Christian Endeavor Society, the Towamencin and Worcester Ushers' Leagues; and the superintendents of the primary and main rooms of each the Worcester and Towamencin Sunday schools; and, in addition thereto, the moderator shall appoint each year, to serve for the current year, six members at large from the congregation." As president of the trustees Mr. Schweiker became chairman pro tem and then chairman for the life of the committee. Mr. Wilbur Seipt was elected vice chairman, Melvin Kratz secretary, and Lester Heebner treasurer. Rev. Hoffman as pastor, and Ernest Heebner as moderator, served ex officio.

The committee diligently and methodically approached its task and with Mr. Schweiker's talent for administrative leadership and penchant for meticulous staff work between meetings, a building program began to crystalize. More importantly, a consensus gradually began to develop in the congregation. After a year and a half of study the committee presented its recommendations in a twelve-page printed report, mailed to each member along with a call for a special District Conference to be held in the Towamencin Church on April 12, 1939.

The committee concluded that only a new church building at a new location would meet the needs of the congregation and supported this decision with a detailed review of the factors prompting their conclusion. Alternative Sunday worship services were patently unsatisfactory, especially for those members of the congregation with Sunday school age children. The music program did not unite the best talent in single worship services. Schwenkfelder children were increasingly scattering and Schwenkfelder families, giving up farming, were moving away. At the same time, new families moving into the community tended to be discouraged by the alternate Sunday worship program and consequently to select a new church home elsewhere. Gradual erosion of church membership seemed inevitable.

Even more serious were the problems in the Sunday school. The Worcester and Towamencin basement Sunday school rooms were overcrowded and clearly inadequate. One case of contagious illness could quickly spread through the overcrowded beginners' and primary departments. So serious was the problem that many parents were reluctant to bring their children during the heavy cold season—a condition not at all helped by the idiosyncrasies of the fifty-year-old heating systems. As for young people, no classroom privacy was afforded. Noise and confusion could overwhelm even the most conscientious teacher and classroom discussion was severely handicapped. As health standards improved and advanced teaching methods were introduced, both in the public schools and in new Sunday schools in the area, the Schwenkfelder Sunday schools increasingly suffered by comparison. Young people attending Sunday school and C. E. conferences were exposed to the more adequate facilities where they visited and, suffering discouragement upon their return, tended to drift away.

While embracing two Sunday school organizations and not totally homogeneous, the Middle District congregation was served by a single minister, transacted business in a single District Conference, and met together in communion and special services. Yet neither the Worcester nor the Towamencin facilities could accommodate all those wishing to participate in such services. No one knew how many people, having to travel some distance, stayed away out of uncertainty of finding a seat. Allowing for modest future growth, an auditorium seating at least 550 persons seemed necessary.

Having defined the need—and in the preceding paragraphs can be discerned the scale and design of the later Central church building, particularly the spacious Sunday school wing—the committee considered meeting the need by improvements to either the Worcester or Towamencin properties. The Worcester location was quickly ruled out as the meeting house required major expenditures for a new roof and heating system.

The somewhat larger Towamencin building was in better shape but a makeshift addition of a new church building and renovation of the old building for Sunday school classroom purposes may well have cost as much as a building at a new location. Major additions at either location would have required acquisition of additional land. The desirability of an entirely new location, after a year and a half of intensive study and discussion, seemed manifest to all.

The committee than made a careful survey of possible building sites. The geographical distribution of member homes, plotted on a map, pointed to Center Point as the most centrally located site. It was noted that a new church on Skippack Pike, if east of Center Point would encroach upon the neighborhood of the Bethel church or if west, on the neighborhood of Wentz's Church, but there was at the time no church along Valley Forge Road between Lansdale and Fairview Village. With farmers reluctant to sell off portions of their farms, not that many available sites could be identified, particularly with desirable elevation, drainage, exposure, and outlook. The committee finally selected a tract of about ten acres of land on the west side of Valley Forge Road about a half mile north of Center Point and secured from the owners, Mr. and Mrs. J. Lyndale Hileman, an option to purchase the property for $300 per acre.

The committee then submitted the following recommendations, which the District Conference approved:

(1) That a new Church and Sunday school building be built and that all church and Sunday school and other services now held in the Worcester and Towamencin Churches be held in the new building;

(2) That the start of actual construction of a new church and Sunday school building should be made only after sufficient money is on hand or pledged and after recommendations in respect to probable cost, size, method of financing, and time of building are made to the congregation and the congregation approves such recommendations;

(3) That a tract of land of approximately ten acres on Valley Forge Road, Route No. 363, owned by Mr. and Mrs. J. Lyndale Hileman, be purchased at this time so that a suitable location for a future church and Sunday school building will be available when needed; and

(4) That the building committee continue its work by making a study of the estimated size, cost, method of financing, and time of building, and present its recommendations to the congregation at such future time or times as the committee develops its recommendations.

The committee had deferred new solicitation for funds, feeling that such a solicitation would be more effective once a decision to build a central church at a specific location had been made. They now proceeded to solicit new Building and Loan subscriptions, gifts and pledges, bringing the total of available funds to almost $66,000, including the Building and Loan shares which would be due to mature in 1951.

Hopes ran high as a new church and Sunday school building was finally coming into sight. These hopes were dashed, however, by the outbreak of World War II, during which neither materials nor labor for construction were available. The principal activity during this period was the effort of the indefatigable Ladies' Aid to raise an organ fund which by 1948 amounted to something over $10,000.

The Central Schwenkfelder Church Building

The Schwenkfelder congregation, however, included leaders who were not easily discouraged and who pushed doggedly ahead despite the wartime escalation of building costs, which required a total reappraisal of building fund requirements. A special meeting of the congregation on February 17, 1945 authorized the Building Committee to employ an architect and to prepare plans for presentation to the congregation for consideration. The Building Committee engaged Mr. Charles M. Talley of Telford, Pa., as architect for the new church building. Mr. Talley prepared plans which were presented to a meeting of the congregation July 7, 1948. The plans called for three units, consisting of a Sunday school section, a church section, and a social hall section which would be available for Sunday school assemblies, social gatherings, church entertainments, and similar functions. The congregation authorized the Building Committee to proceed with construction to the extent they deemed advisable.

The Building Committee realized that all three units of this church would ultimately be needed but it felt that the combined cost of the three units at the time would be beyond the means immediately available. They therefore decided to build the Sunday school and church units and leave the social hall unit for completion at a later date. Largely capitalizing on Mr. Schweiker's knowledge of construction practice, the committee acted as its own general contractor, contracting out the individual craft work, with the architect exercising general supervision.

Ground was broken on Wednesday, September 15, 1948 for construction of the first two sections. Plans called for all excavating

work, installation of foundations, rough grading and rough stoning
of roadway, installation of water drainage and a sewage system, and
drilling of a well to be completed in the fall of 1948. Then during
1949 the steel work would be erected, the stone work completed, and
the roof, windows, etc., installed, so as to enclose the building before
the winter of 1949-1950, with the mechanical and interior finish
work to be completed in 1950. The committee felt the leisurely plan
of construction would result in cost economies and in addition give
the congregation time to seek and arrange for additional funds. The
cornerstone was laid August 14, 1949.

During 1947 the third solicitation for the building fund was
made for cash gifts and pledges payable over a three-year period. The
response was most heartening, raising funds on hand and in prospect,
together with interest earned, to $226,912.08, to which should be
added the Ladies' Aid organ fund of $10,035. As construction pro-
ceeded, however, cost estimates steadily escalated. By December 31,
1950 funds available from the three solicitations together with interest earned and the organ fund totaled about $264,000. During 1951,
with the structure nearing completion, another $47,000 in new gifts
and collection of old pledges was raised. The committee arranged two
temporary bank loans to provide $240,000 and Mr. Schweiker ad-
vanced $36,000, later forgiven as a gift, to pay bills as they became
due and to complete the church and Sunday school portion of the
building, bringing the total of funds raised to $583,000. The two
temporary loans were then to be funded by the issuance and sale of
mortgage bonds.

Mr. Schweiker had meanwhile purchased and gifted to the
church three parcels of land to protect the boundaries of the church
property from encroachments which might spoil its attractive outlook: The "Kennedy" property to the south across Steelman Road, a
triangular "Geyer" plot to the rear, and some additional land on the
north from the Steelmans. The ushers razed the Kennedy building,
storing the lumber in the sheds at Towamencin for possible future
use. Contemplating the additional costs and time wasted by construction in two bites and the psychological problems of raising
additional funds while servicing a bond issue, Mr. Schweiker determined to complete the entire project by making the Schweiker family
responsible for the costs of constructing and furnishing the Fellowship Hall wing. The Schweikers' oldest son, Malcolm Jr., was raised
in the Worcester church and Sunday school and was a popular
participant in its young peoples' activities and scouting. In 1945 the
Schweiker family and the entire congregation were saddened to learn

that he had been killed in action in the invasion of Okinawa during the Second World War. The gift of Fellowship Hall was made by Mr. and Mrs. Schweiker, Richard and Sylvia, in memory of Malcolm Jr. Construction proceeded apace with all construction bills attributable to the Fellowship Hall wing, and not infrequently bills for amenities added to the church and Sunday school building, processed through the same channels as those of the church building but paid by Lester Heebner from a separate Fellowship Hall Trust Fund, supplied by contributions from the Schweiker family. Such payments totaled approximately $200,000, covering not only the building but furnishings and equipment necessary to make the Hall fully usable.

While inclusion of Fellowship Hall extended the construction timetable, by the early spring of 1951 interior work clearly began to reveal the appearance of the completed structure. From the initial groundbreaking, interest in the progress of construction had lured to the site a steady stream of visitors—members, friends, and just plain curious passers-by. As the building approached completion this procession rose to as many as 200 on Sunday afternoons and members of the ushers' organization had to be called upon to control parking, to direct visitors throughout the building, and to answer questions. With a dedication target date of June 10 announced, contractors worked feverishly to complete the inside trim, to adjust the mechanical equipment, to install the organ, and to attend to a multitude of last-minute details. Carpet was laid, venetian blinds were hung, windows were washed, and volunteer workers cleaned up, and then cleaned up again.

Meanwhile, the final worship service at the Towamencin Meeting House was held on May 27. Special music was provided and Fred Seipt read the "Last Call for Chores," a poem written by Rev. Hoffman, retelling the trauma of the last evening the Schwenkfelder forefathers spent on their farms in Silesia before setting out for Saxony, and in time for the New World. Rev. Lester Kriebel, raised in the Towamencin church and at the time pastor of the Palm church, preached the sermon on Acts 2:17, "And it shall come to pass in the last days saith God that I will pour out my Spirit on all flesh; and your young men shall see visions, your old men dream dreams." In order to dream in old age one must have vision in youth. In developing character as we carry out the vision we shall be filled with power and courage. But let me give you a word of warning. "After every great experience comes a time of temptation and trial. Then you will need to hold firm to your purposes, visions and responsibilities. What a challenge you have! Think of the ministry of evangelism, education, recreation."

The following Sunday saw the final services in the Worcester Meeting House. Past pastors, moderators, and Sunday school superintendents spoke. In the Sunday school session Mrs. Shearer noted historic events which had taken place there over the years. Dr. E. E. S. Johnson preached the final sermon, concluding with a tribute to Rev. Hoffman, pastor of the church for forty years.

The dedication itself was held on Sunday, June 10, with two identical worship services, one at 10:00 a.m. and the second at 2:30, which permitted members of the other Schwenkfelder churches to attend their home churches in the morning and the dedication service in the afternoon. Despite a steadily falling rain, the audience at both services filled the sanctuary, narthex and Fellowship Hall, and overflowed into Sunday school classrooms, where the building-wide public address system permitted them to hear the proceedings and to participate in the spirit of the event. In the ritual of dedication the presentation for dedication was made by Ernest A. Heebner, moderator of the church, and was accepted by Malcolm A. Schweiker, president of the Board of Trustees. Robert Krauss had charge of the music and moved the congregation with his solo, "Bless this House." Rev. Hoffman preached on the text from Jeremiah 6:16, "Thus saith the Lord, Stand ye at the crossroads, and see, and ask for the old paths, where is the good way, and walk therein, and so shall ye be safe and prosper":

> This building is beautifully situated and has been acclaimed marvelous in its design. All of which bespeaks the fact that here was loftiness in vision, the exceptional in venture, and grandeur in construction. . . . Greater than this edifice is the personnel that produced it; the personnel that is, and that is to become, through the use of it. Up to now this church was in buildings divided. But through this venture we are helping to answer one of Christ's unanswered prayers. . . . Problems many loomed up like mountains. Impressions faulty, opinions varied, suggestions manifold, solutions inaccurate, minds startled. 'Alas, what shall we do?' . . . Then the question was asked, 'Wouldn't this be a good time to pray?' On at least four different occasions when we were at the crossroads, after prayer for light and guidance, in every case when a written vote was taken the decision was unanimous.

Recollections vary as to whether the question so resolved in the spirit of prayer pertained to the wisdom of proceeding in the face of escalating costs, whether the top of the sanctuary windows should be round or square, or whether there should be a cross on top of the steeple. More likely all these and many other decisions were reached after heart-searching prayer.

All who attended were delighted with the result of the many years of planning and dedicated effort. The building itself seemed just the right blend of colonial architectural motifs and modern functional engineering. Its plan is in the form of a cross, the main sanctuary portion 212 feet from front to rear, and the Sunday school-narthex-Fellowship Hall wing 278 feet from left to right as one faces the church from the highway. The ample narthex, joining sanctuary, Sunday school wing, and Fellowship Hall was deliberately designed as a meeting place to encourage informal fellowship as people entered the church, or passed from Sunday school to sanctuary to Fellowship Hall. Seating about 650 people, the sanctuary tastefully echoes the simple white walls and woodwork of the early colonial meeting houses, but in impressive modern execution. Ample clear glass windows are shaded by white venetian blinds. Hanging lanterns of colonial design light the white barrel-vaulted ceiling which rises at its dome thirty-six feet above the floor of the sanctuary. The wood-paneled chancel accommodates the divided choir and organ, as well as the religious appointments. The chancel and church aisles are carpeted in deep red. The Sunday school wing provides individual classrooms of varying capacities, accommodating together about 700 infant, beginner, primary, intermediate, and adult scholars. Fellowship Hall accommodates approximately 600 people during Sunday school assemblies or about 350 persons seated at dining tables. Fellowship Hall is equipped with a fully operational stage, film projector, and amplification system, together with a large kitchen, with stainless steel institutional equipment readily capable of serving capacity seating in the hall. A public address system permits any service in the sanctuary or Fellowship Hall to be broadcast throughout the building.

There followed an entire week of special services. A prayer and praise service was held on Sunday evening, with Dr. Moses Bailey, Nettleton Professor of the Old Testament at the Hartford Seminary Foundation, speaking on the theme, "The Song for the Dedication of the House," using the Thirteenth Psalm as his text. On Monday evening the Ladies' Aid welcomed Miss Marjorie Penney, director of Fellowship House, Philadelphia, as guest speaker. Tuesday evening was devoted to a musical service and Wednesday evening to a missionary meeting, with Miss Mabel Reiff among the speakers. A union community church service was held on Thursday evening, at which neighboring churches were invited to participate. Finally on Saturday evening the young people conducted the service with Norman W.

Paulin, minister of Grace Baptist Temple, Philadelphia and popular in young people's work as the speaker. On Sunday evening, June 17, the Christian Endeavor held their first meeting in the new church with all the Christian Endeavor Societies of Montgomery County invited to attend as guests. During the following week 103 pupils were enrolled in the Daily Vacation Bible School.

Thus was brought to fruition the forty-year dream of a Central Schwenkfelder Church, at a cost of some $850,000, more than thirty times the amount pledged in the initial subscription of Building and Loan shares some twenty-eight years before. For a congregation numbering only 600 members even in 1950 it was a tremendous achievement. Malcolm Schweiker, as president of the trustees and chairman of the Building Committee, was unquestionably the prime moving spirit. His talents and position lent credibility to both the financial planning and the design and construction of the building. The new church, nevertheless, reflected in hundreds of ways credit upon the entire congregation. The original Building and Loan sub-scribers had set the process in motion. Over the years individuals contributed according to their means. Sunday school classes, the C. E. Society, the Ushers' Association and the Ladies' Aid did their part. Ladies baked, sewed, and contributed handicrafts for sale at "Country Fairs," auctions, and similar events. Literally hundreds worked long hours to prepare and serve the annual turkey suppers which became a steady support of the building fund and later of the "Mortgage Payoff Fund." Not an insignificant amount of volunteer labor contributed to the progress of construction. Abe Reiff supervised volunteer workers and stood guard over the uncompleted structure and materials on the site during the early days of construction. Wilbur Seipt served as chairman of the trustees' committee dealing with the sub-contractors. The Ladies' Aid Society, led by Mrs. Christine Shearer, supplied many amenities besides the organ. Amos K. Rothenberger, treasurer of the church, served as chairman of the solicitation com-mittee, and Lester Heebner presided over Building Committee funds.

Sunday school services were omitted during the Sunday of dedication and the first exercises in the new building were held the following Sunday. The church congregation had always been a single organization but two separate Sunday school organizations had to be merged and this proved not a simple matter. Questionnaires were sent to each person enrolled seeking their preference as to class assignment. Then cards were mailed, even to those who did not return the questionnaire, assigning each member to a class where it was felt they belonged, even though such assignments were not considered final. On Sunday, June 17, all teachers and scholars gathered in Fellowship Hall for opening exercises and then were guided to their assigned classrooms where the time was devoted to getting acquainted and organizing for regular class work the following Sunday. The Sunday school building had been laid out to accommodate the Sunday school as it was then structured and it was not long before it was functioning smoothly. Indeed the basic structure then set up has been maintained to the present day.

The trustees turned their attention to two basic tasks. Arrangements had been made with the Philadelphia National Bank as trustee to offer $250,000 first-mortgage 4 1/2% twenty-year bonds, dated March 15, 1951, the proceeds to be used to repay the temporary bank loans negotiated to complete construction. During April and May bond subscriptions were solicited. Approximately half the issue was placed among members, friends, organizations, building suppliers, and others in the denomination and community. Bond Number 1 was subscribed for and issued to Mr. Wayne Meschter, moderator of General Conference. By November all of the bonds had been placed except for a small balance of $11,400. Ernest Heebner's Sunday school class agreed to serve as a special committee to resolicit members to place the remainder of the bonds by year end, which they were successful in accomplishing. Attention then concentrated on a drive to reduce the mortgage, in which the first years are critical, as the interest factor, initially $11,250, looms large and must first be provided for.

The second major task facing the trustees involved the Worcester Meeting House. At the spring District Conference of 1951 it was explained that it would cost nearly $15,000 to put the Worcester Meeting House in good repair and that afterward the cost of painting and maintaining the structure would amount to $300 to $400 per year. On this basis the church council authorized the trustees to remove the church when the trustees thought it advisable. The trustees solicited bids from various concerns who made a business of removing buildings. The most favorable bid was from R. W. Scholl of Hatfield who offered to remove the buildings for the materials and to hold the church harmless in event of an accident. Warned the September 1951 church letter: "Wrecking buildings is a dangerous operation and when the work of removal starts our members and their children should stay away from the church site. We had no serious accidents in building our new church. Let us try to keep the same record in removing the Worcester church."

By May of 1953 it was reported that the site of the Worcester church had been graded and seeded. A committee was appointed appropriately to mark the site and on Sunday afternoon, September 20, the granite marker now standing at the location of the old Worcester pulpit was unveiled by Moderator Warren S. Kriebel and Allen K. Kriebel, vice-president of the Board of Trustees. On the rear of the monument, carved in the stone, were noted:

> Notable events which took place here: The one hundred fiftieth anniversary of the arrival of the Schwenkfelders in Pennsylvania and of their Gedächtniss Tag was observed Wednesday, September 24, 1884, following which the Schwenkfelders, under the leadership of Dr. Chester D. Hartranft, projected the *Corpus Schwenckfeldianorum*; General Conference appointed a committee October 17, 1891, which led to the purchase of Perkiomen Seminary. The first Schwenkfelder Missionary, Flora K. Heebner, was commissioned here. Worship services were inaugurated in 1836, and the last was held June 3, 1951.

Meanwhile the Towamencin church, in better shape physically, was put to constructive use. For six months it served the congregation of the Brethren church on Cowpath Road near Hatfield while their own church was extensively remodeled. Then for eight months the building served for similar reasons the congregation of the Indian Creek Brethren Church as a meeting place for church and Sunday school services. In 1957 the first floor of the building was renovated principally by the young people of the C. E. Society. The walls and ceiling were painted and the floor sanded and finished. New electric wiring was installed from the pole to the entrance switch and a new entrance switch installed, since the old wiring was considered unsafe. It was planned that the room be available for special programs, meetings, and activities by various organizations of the church.

Working Together

To raise money for the building fund several Sunday school classes joined together in 1947 to serve a turkey supper in the Kulpsville High School building and the event soon became a popular annual undertaking. With the pervasive excitement of the church dedication year and the attractive facilities of the new Fellowship Hall and its splendidly equipped kitchen, popular interest turned the 1951 turkey supper into an extraordinary event. Supported by the men and women of the Sunday school, the supper committee, co-chaired by Mrs. Amos K. Rothenberger and Mrs. Irma Stong, planned on serving 3,000 dinners, with the doors open from 3:00 to 8:00 o'clock p.m. Twenty-five hundred tickets were sold ahead of time and 500 reserved for sale at the door. The 500 tickets for sale at the door were all spoken for by 4:30 and before the evening was over an estimated 2,000 persons had been turned away unserved. Others waited long hours for their turn at the tables. Twenty-three men relieved each other in carving 130 turkeys totalling 3,016 pounds. Sixty young women, assisted by a dozen men, served as waitresses. By the 10:00 o'clock closing, as the happy but exhausted workers, after seven hours of uninterrupted pressure, finally sat down to eat for themselves, spirits were just a little low. They revived with great alacrity, however, when it was announced that Mr. and Mrs. Edwin H. Rosenberry had just presented a receipted bill for the $1,508.00 cost of the turkeys, thereby swelling the receipts from the supper to $3,870.40. This year proceeds were turned over to the church treasurer to assist in meeting the extraordinary operating expenses of the year. In subsequent years supper proceeds were applied to reduction of the mortgage.

The next year, profiting from experience, the supper committee arranged to sell only 2,000 tickets, all beforehand, with tickets available at the door only for adult accompanied children. While avoiding the congestion of the previous year, this arrangement left such a large number of people disappointed at their inability to secure tickets that the committee hastily arranged an overflow supper a month later. The two suppers raised $3,624.47 for the mortgage reduction fund. By 1953 two suppers were scheduled from the beginning and the sale of tickets regulated accordingly. It was not long before the ticket sale was regulated down to an assigned time of sitting. Besides their regular contribution to the mortgage reduction fund, these events generated widespread publicity and attracted favorable attention to the Central Schwenkfelder Church. As much as any activity, they contributed to the successful merging of the two congregations. The food was widely acclaimed and the social fellowship warm and stimulating despite the long wait in the sanctuary before being served.

In January of 1952 the Building Committee held its last meeting. At the District Conference meeting on February 19, 1952 it was formally discharged, with an overwhelming vote of thanks for a job well done.

The year 1951 had indeed been a year of dramatic events. It was almost as though the nineteenth century had been left behind and a giant leap taken into the middle of the twentieth century. The psychological and social adjustments forced upon the congregation finding itself united in single services and sharing other activities in the spacious new accommodations were softened by the euphoria of the events of the dedication year. As the year drew to a close, however, new problems demanded attention. New members were attracted, activities proliferated, and as their scale expanded in step with the larger facilities, new demands were made upon staff and new operating and maintenance costs had to be provided for. The mortgage loomed before them and many wondered if they would ever be able to pay it off. Now would be put to the test the concern of the "Haus Väter" meeting in 1762, "Will we be able to bear with one another if a closer union is formed so that what is undertaken may not be ended in strife and works of evil?" And as Rev. Kriebel had warned at the final Towamencin service, "After every great experience comes a time of temptation and trial. Then you will need to hold firm to your purpose, visions and responsibilities."

In December of 1951, as the eventful year drew to its close, Rev. Hoffman, then 76 years of age, was hospitalized for surgery. There was neither associate nor assistant minister and supply pastors had to be secured to fill the pulpit until Rev. Hoffman returned on February 16, 1952. The twin matters of assistance and pension began to receive attention from the Committee on the Ministry and the trustees.

When the Schwenkfelder churches turned to full-time ministers, salaries were something new and over the years they had not been particularly generous. No one had thought to look ahead and make provision for the ministers' declining years. They were not eligible for Social Security. Many members of the congregation, church officers, and trustees, felt it only proper that some declaration of intention as to a pension for Rev. Hoffman should be made so that he would have the opportunity to think about and plan ahead for retirement and the activities he might desire to carry on after retirement. The trustees accordingly on December 5, 1955 passed a resolution authorizing payment of a pension to Rev. Hoffman at the time of his retirement, whenever that should occur. Rev. Hoffman was so informed by the moderator of the church, Mr. Warren Kriebel, and the president of the trustees, Malcolm Schweiker.

It will be recalled that upon graduation from Hartford Theological Seminary Rev. Hoffman had married Adelaide Mattox, a deaconess at the Fall River Deaconess Home. Mrs. Hoffman had entered enthusiastically into the work of the church. She served as president of the Worcester W.C.T.U. and was active in the Christian Endeavor Society and in most of the activities of the Lansdale church. About

1925, however, her health began to fail and for the next twenty years she was increasingly unable to take an active part in the affairs of either church. She died in March of 1945. Throughout their marriage the Hoffmans had remained in friendly contact with another deaconess of the Fall River Home, Mrs. Eva Christine Frields. Mrs. Frields moved on to serve until her retirement as superintendent of the Chaddock Boys' School, later Chaddock College, in Quincy, Illinois. Mrs. Friield, now retired and a widow, was united in marriage to Rev. Hoffman in September of 1946. She was a forceful member of the Building Committee until completion of the church, and until handicapped as the result of a stroke, ably supported her husband in the work of the church.

The Diaconate and trustees thought that Rev. Hoffman, who had shunned regular vacations during most of his ministry, should have an opportunity to visit some of the interesting places in the United States. They made arrangements for an extended vacation for Rev. Hoffman with an appropriate gift from the funds of the church for that purpose. He and his wife left on July 19, 1955, drove to Chicago to visit friends, and then took the train for the Pacific northwest to visit friends and relatives and to see the natural wonders of the west. Despite the necessity of pushing Eva Christine in a wheelchair through the national parks, the couple enjoyed the pleasant and refreshing change. They returned to Lansdale on Thursday, September 15 and the following Sunday afternoon were feted at a reception in the Central church attended by over 600 people. The Sunday was forty-five years to the day from his Sunday, September 18, 1910 ordination in the Worcester Meeting House.

Meanwhile the Committee on the Ministry had begun consideration of hiring a second minister. Realizing that housing would be required, they appealed to the trustees, who arranged purchase of a lot at 1061 Hillside Ave., Lansdale, and for the construction of a manse. Their choice of a minister fell to Rev. William Brandt Bradshaw. Rev. Bradshaw had graduated from the Yale School of Divinity in June of 1958 and had been ordained into the Christian ministry at the First Congregational Church in Lebanon, Mo., his home town, on June 15. He was installed as associate minister of the Central church on July 27, 1958. Rev. Bradshaw possessed a pleasant, outgoing personality, which soon won him many friends and seemed to offer him a promising career at Central. He was also a man of outspoken convictions, which he did not hesitate to press upon the members of his new congregation, not infrequently to the embarrassment of the senior minister, Rev. Hoffman.

The original turkey suppers had been launched to raise funds for the erection of the new church building. After 1951 they continued with proceeds applied to the mortgage reduction fund. By the time Rev. Bradshaw appeared on the scene money so raised, together with gifts and funds from other sources, had reduced the original $250,000 mortgage to $125,000 and the annual interest charge from $11,250 to $5,625. The suppers represented a substantial drain on the interest and energies of the congregation. To Rev. Bradshaw they appeared as a commercial venture for which use of the church facilities was inappropriate. He urged their discontinuance. In October of 1959, after two years of deliberation, the trustees recommended to Church Council that the November 14, 1959 supper be the final one, thus discontinuing the series at the peak of their success rather than permitting them to run into increasing criticism. Coupled with a resolution of profound thanks to Mrs. Rothenberger and her committee and to all congregation members who had participated, the Council concurred and the suppers were discontinued.

The implied criticism of past activity was not lost upon Rev. Hoffman, then approaching his 80th birthday. Asked to preach the Thanksgiving sermon for 1959, Rev. Hoffman described the first Thanksgiving meal, the blessings of family gatherings, and the merits of holiday celebrations. He then went on to discuss the turkey suppers and observed that if you work in a restaurant like Howard Johnsons and give one tenth of what you earn to the church, you are an angel. But if you serve in the kitchen of Fellowship Hall when we have our turkey suppers and give of your time, a long day, your energy, your ingenuity, your good will, your uplifts and all to the church, then it now appears you are considered by some to be a sinner. At this point Rev. Bradshaw and a number of his supporters left the sanctuary. Rev. Hoffman completed his sermon, and immediately thereafter, in a December 1, 1959 letter, offered his resignation as minister of the church.

The trustees saw no alternative to accepting Rev. Hoffman's withdrawal from active service but, mindful of his fifty years of service to the congregation and unwilling to see it terminate on such a sad note, they voted to continue his then current salary for life, to offer him the use of the church facilities whenever mutually convenient, and to welcome his participation in any and all activities of the church. When he took out a bank loan to purchase a new home more convenient for Mrs. Hoffman, and was unable promptly to sell his old house, the trustees arranged to come to his temporary assistance. Members of the congregation helped him in the discharge of his bank loan. Rev. Hoffman was to live another fifteen years, passing away July 17, 1970 at the ripe old age of 95. The great changes in which he had so actively participated and the accompanying strife and turmoil were not without effect upon his personality. With seemingly more than his share of family difficulties, frustrated and embittered, his last years seemed a poor reward for a lifetime of service to God and church, following always the dictates of his own strong and clear conscience.

The Ladies' Aid Society

Throughout the years the ladies of the Central Schwenkfelder Church have maintained an active and influential Ladies' Aid Society, responsible for many constructive contributions to the life of the church.

The society traces its beginnings to the evening of March 9, 1912, when, at the request of the ladies of the Lower District, Mrs. Joseph Schultz, president of the Palm Ladies' Aid Society, came down to talk about the activities of the Palm society. After considerable discussion, she chaired the election of officers for the local society, electing Mrs. Hiram K. Kriebel president, Mrs. A. K. Dresher vice-president, Miss Ada Rothenberger secretary, and Miss Kate Schultz treasurer. During the early years quilting was perhaps the principal activity, with the ladies meeting Mondays following Sunday church services at Towamencin, taking advantage of the heater already fired up for Sunday. Besides quilts, they made a variety of items such as sunbonnets, aprons, iron covers, pillow cases, etc. Mr. Allen Kriebel took these items to be sold at his market in Philadelphia, with money realized being contributed to the support of the church or of Miss Flora Heebner in China.

Mrs. William Shelly succeeded Mrs. Kriebel as president, but when Mrs. Shelly moved out of the community the office fell to Mrs. Herbert Shearer, who continued as the dynamic leader of the society for the next twenty-five years. Under her leadership the society steadfastly supported the movement for the building of the Central church, accumulating an organ fund even before construction of the church became a certainty.

In May of 1951 the first Country Fair was held at the Harris Gramm Farm on Water Street, Worcester, with Miss Catherine Gramm as the first general chairman. The Fair was so successful it became an annual event. Through the years it has been held in the Fairview Hall, Fairview Village, the Farmers' Hall, Center Point, and the Worcester School, Center Point. Mr. George Williams, caretaker of the Variety Club Camp and member of the Central Schwenkfelder Church, saw a need for larger facilities and beginning in 1966 arranged for the Ladies' Aid to have the Country Fair at the Variety Club Camp in Worcester, where it has been held annually ever since on the third Saturday in September. Organized by the society, but enlisting the support of many church organizations, the Fair has become the chief fund raising activity of the society. The society s budget in recent years has hovered around $20,000, with principal distributions going to the church operating fund and a variety of mission projects. They have supported visits by the Red Cross Bloodmobile, golden age and senior adult activities, the Happy Days Pre-School program, the Daily Vacation Bible School, and other projects.

When Mrs. Shearer retired in 1959, no one wanted to become obligated to serve for so long a period; the bylaws were changed to limit the term of office to five years. Mrs. Lawrence Siddons, Mrs. Merrill King, Mrs. John W. Clemens, Miss Ruth Kriebel, Mrs. Hilbert Keisker and Mrs. Oliver Smith have in turn served as president.

Years of Turmoil

Following Rev. Hoffman's withdrawal from active ministry, Rev. Bradshaw was elevated to minister, which position seemed to offer him the fullest possible scope for constructive application of his youthful energies and widely recognized talents. He, however, proved impatient and seemed rather to stir up controversy than to blend the elements of the new united congregation into a harmonious and productive unity. His term of service proved disappointingly short. In the fall of 1960 personal problems precipitated his resignation, following which he removed with his family to Scotland to pursue theological studies and research. Several years later he returned to this country to become pastor of the First Congregational Church, Norfolk, Nebraska, and still later to lead a church in California.

In May of Rev. Bradshaw's last year Mr. George S. Toth Jr. of Bethlehem, a student at Lancaster Theological Seminary, was retained as student assistant in the ministry during his summer vacation. In welcoming Mr. Toth, Rev. Bradshaw described the church ministry in the June church letter as follows:

There are two reasons for his coming, to help with the ministerial work here at the church and to help him receive training for the Christian ministry. This church now is over 850 in membership and our members are located throughout a wide geographical area of many miles. It is impossible in a church of this size for any one minister to be a real "pastor," one who visits with the members in their homes, visits them in the hospitals, helps them solve problems, talks with them about spiritual matters, and in general one who becomes more than just a "preacher" on Sunday. There are just not enough hours in the day or days in the week to do this much work. I often feel I neglect many of our present members, and there are over twenty-five new families in the area who have visited our church in the last two months whom I have not yet had time to visit. Secondly, it is not easy to learn the work of the minister. One can spend many years in school but nothing takes the place of actual experience. Every Christian church should try, if at all possible, to help train ministerial students. Our church will be doing this kind of mission work when Mr. Toth is here with us this summer.

The use of student assistants thus initiated soon became a more or less regular practice.

In his letter advising the congregation of his resignation, Rev. Bradshaw further summed up problems beneath the surface of the united congregation ready at any time to burst into destructive flames.

There are four areas in which I feel our church needs to be strengthened. All of us must put Jesus Christ and the work of the Father first, above all other, in our lives. Second, we must be deeply concerned about the lost souls of the world and must do all we can to strengthen our mission efforts, both at home and abroad. Third, we must learn to have true Christian love (See I Corinthians 13) for each other; the work of the Christian church cannot be effective when we are at odds with each other. Fourth, we must be receptive to new ideas and new people.

The Committee on the Ministry announced that it would carefully deliberate the choice of a successor, and that in the meantime Rev. Arthur F. Wagner would serve as interim minister while also carrying on his duties as a teacher in Springfield Township High School in Montgomery County. It was almost a year later that a new minister was installed. The committee once again turned to a graduate of the Yale Divinity School, but this time to a man of more mature years. Rev. Eric T. Braund was installed Sunday afternoon, September 17, 1961 with appropriate exercises during which John K. Snyder, chairman of the committee, presented the candidate. Rev. William D. Powell, general secretary of the Greater Philadelphia Council of Churches, described Rev. Braund's ecclesiastical credentials, Moderator Warren S. Kriebel gave the charge to the minister, Rev. Martha B. Kriebel of the Palm church gave the charge to the congregation, and Rev. Jack Rothenberger, chairman of the Schwenkfelder ministerium and pastor of the Lansdale church, extended the right hand of fellowship. All the Schwenkfelder ministers, including Rev. Hoffman, participated in the ceremonies.

Rev. Braund earned his B.D. degree at Yale in 1939, served as director of the Methodist Student Federation, as associate secretary of the YMCA at Northwestern University, and as a Navy chaplain during World War II. He then was called as pastor of the Greenbelt Community Congregational Church in Maryland, which he served for eleven years to January 1957. During this pastorate he served in several church association posts. In 1957 he was designated director of the Philadelphia-South Jersey area of the National Conference of Christians and Jews. When called to the Central church he was, with Rev. William D. Powell, associate general secretary of the Greater Philadelphia Council of Churches.

Rev. Braund has been described by his friend, assistant, and later successor, Dr. Berthold Jacksteit, as an unusually able and devoted servant of Christ, a faithful pastor, a delightful person, a man of cheerful and beautiful spirit, a friend who blessed the lives of all who had the privilege of knowing him. Still mindful of the magnitude of the task assigned a single minister, the Committee on the Ministry arranged during 1962 for Dr. Jacksteit, while still continuing his work in the education and publication activities of the American Baptist Convention at Valley Forge, to act as a part-time consultant in Christian education work and in the direction of youth activities, and to participate in the religious services. At a special congregational meeting, Sunday, May 19, 1963 this arrangement was formalized. It was from this vantage point of a subordinate part-time position that Dr. Jacksteit watched with increasing concern and dismay the gradual breakdown of his respected friend, Rev. Braund, as he struggled against the strife and tension now rampant in the congregation. In the spring of 1966 he was ordered by his doctor to take a six-month leave of absence. Finally he tendered his resignation, effective October 1 of that year.

In May of 1961, pursuant to a resolution of General Conference, Mr. Herbert Weber, General Conference moderator, appointed a broadly based committee to study the future of the five Schwenkfelder churches, with particular reference to the question of possible affiliation with a larger denominational body. This committee, chaired by Mr. Wilbur Seipt, was influenced by the long missionary

connection with the Congregational Church, by this time a part of
the United Church of Christ, by the similarity in local church
governance, and by the provisions of the United Church Constitution
for associate membership, which presumably would not jeopardize
the Schwenkfelder tradition. After two years of study and discussion,
this committee on September 23, 1963 unanimously voted to recommend to the individual churches associate membership in the
United Church of Christ. It was hoped that such affiliation would put
the local churches in touch with a seminary source of trained ministers and with professionally-developed Sunday school curriculum
materials, and would extend the witness of the church across the
nation. Two congregational meetings were held at Central to inform
the congregation and a local committee chaired by Mr. G. William
Meschter was appointed to summarize the discussions so held. Notwithstanding favorable action by District Conferences at Norristown,
Palm, and Lansdale, at its congregational meeting February 9, 1965
the membership voted against affiliation. The majority of the congregation preferred to preserve the church's independence and existing Schwenkfelder denominational status.

A second source of hard feelings manifested itself in professed
differences of theological opinion along lines which had caused difficulties on several occasions down through the years and which had
been exacerbated by the Fundamentalist-Modernist controversy of
the 1920s. The *Corpus* effort induced in the editors and others
possessed of intellectual curiosity a profound respect for the person
and teachings of Schwenckfeld, which indeed is now widely shared.
Schwenckfeld contributed relevant and helpful spiritual insights and
rightfully takes his place among the church fathers and Reformation
scholars in the development of theological thought. Schwenkfelders
saw themselves as spiritual descendants of Schwenckfeld, much as
Lutherans looked to their origins in Luther, Reformed churches to
Zwingli and Calvin, or Presbyterians to John Knox. They did not in
any sense, however, worship Schwenckfeld to the derogation of
Christ, as was sometimes charged. Indeed, quite the contrary.
Perhaps in natural reaction to the intercessory claims of the Roman
church, Protestants generally taught a more direct relationship between the individual and God through Christ. Schwenckfeld laid
particular emphasis on individual worth and liberty of conscience. He
taught, moreover, that it is God who saves, not people who save
themselves or others. He emphasized Christian concern for one's
neighbors, as well as visible conversion and new birth. The individual's duty was of a more personal nature, to live so that he would more

and more come to a knowledge of the living Christ—"Erkenntnis Christi."

This theological strain in particular was uncongenial to persons of a fundamentalist persuasion, of which there was an active group in the congregation. Controversy seemed to reach a climax in 1965 when formal request was made that those of differing theological persuasion be granted the use of the Towamencin Meeting House to meet as a separate congregation and worship in their own way. This, of course, would have defeated the long standing effort at creation of one Central church. This proposal became moot, however, when during the winter of 1965-1966 vandals set fire to the interior of the Towamencin church. Although a settlement was made with the insurance company, it was not deemed worthwhile to restore the interior. In the spring of 1966 an auction was held and removable items were sold for sufficient proceeds to defray the net costs of demolition. The building was razed. Dissension surfaced at the February 1966 annual congregational meeting, when for the only time the election of Mr. Harold Kerper, choice of the nominating committee as moderator, was challenged by a nomination from the floor.

After the Towamencin Meeting House had been razed and the site leveled and seeded, a memorial marker was also erected there. It was dedicated at noon on Sunday, October 22, 1967 with Rev. Arthur Wagner delivering the memorial message. As with the marker at the Worcester site, the rear of the marker noted significant events which had taken place there:

> First Schwenkfelder secular school, which was non-sectarian but owned and controlled by the Schwenkfeldian Exiles, was erected here in 1765. First Schwenkfelder Sunday School to preserve the German language and increase religious instruction of youth established here 1861. At General Conferences held here the following decisions were made. April 2, 1917—to build church in Lansdale. May 19, 1917—Norristown Mission established as a Church under General Conference. May 18, 1929—Churches of Middle District, Norristown, Palm and Philadelphia given permission to incorporate separately. Perkiomen School Library incorporated. Last Church Service held here May 27, 1951.

In June of 1965 Rev. Braund was hospitalized with a heart condition and took an extended summer vacation to visit his son in Iowa. Rev. Jacksteit and Rev. Wagner shared ministerial duties during the summer. The Committee on the Ministry now more than ever recognized the need for pastoral assistance. From about 600 in 1951. church membership had steadily increased until it passed 1,000 in 1964. Church school enrolment had increased from around 600 to 800. Church families were widely spread geographically, with ministers making calls in homes and hospitals from Norristown to Souderton and from Harleysville and Lederach to Ambler and beyond. The committee saw tremendous opportunities, not only to bring the gospel of Christ to more and more persons, but also to strengthen the commitment of each one and to hasten the growth of the church family. With Rev. Braund's hearty endorsement, the committee therefore proposed, and the congregation meeting in February 1966 agreed, to extend a call to Dr. Jacksteit as full-time associate minister of the church. A date of May 1, 1966 was set for his installation, but as Rev. Braund's health deteriorated and he was granted a leave of absence, Rev. Jacksteit was reluctant to seem, in any way, to be moving into Rev. Braund's place. He therefore insisted that his installation be deferred, although he and Rev. Wagner again agreed to carry on during Rev. Braund's absence.

With ample time for reflection, Rev. Braund during the summer of 1966 reluctantly decided he would have to give up his pastorate at Central. He arranged instead to return to his former position in the administrative work of the National Conference of Christians and Jews. In his friendly letter of resignation, Rev. Braund, in order to bring them fully into focus before the congregation, cited four sources of frustration which bore on his decision. First, "The failure of the church to act favorably on the unanimous recommendation of the Conference Committee that our several churches definitely become 'associates' of the United Church of Christ. This was and is a 'wound' that runs counter to my best judgement and conviction, . . ."Secondly, frustrations concerning the lack of a coordinated curriculum in the church school which would, in his view, be impossible until the church affiliated as part of a larger denomination. Third, he was depressed by the "lack of a vital concept of stewardship which puts the claims of Christ and His Church to young and old, rich and poor, through the challenge of a definite financial commitment via a definite pledge card system." And finally, "the apparent disinterest and unwillingness to grapple creatively with controversy on the pressing social issues and public concerns so vital to the health of the church and all free institutions in America." It was a sobering and challenging indictment.

With Rev. Braund's resignation received and accepted, Rev. Jacksteit's reluctance to accept a larger role receded. A special congregational meeting was called by Mr. Harold Kerper as moderator, and Mr. Andrew C. Anders, chairman of the Committee on the

Ministry, for Sunday, October 23, 1966, when a call was extended to Dr. Jacksteit as minister. He accepted and was installed with appropriate ceremonies on Sunday afternoon, February 5, 1967. All of the Schwenkfelder ministers, including Rev. Hoffman, participated. Rev. Dr. Glenn H. Asquith of the American Baptist Board of Education and Publication, where Dr. Jacksteit had served for the past nine years, preached the sermon, Rev. Dr. Paul T. Slinghoff, Conference Minister of the Pennsylvania Southeast Conference, United Church of Christ, gave the charge to the pastor, Dr. Maurice Hohlfeld gave the charge to the congregation, and Rev. Jack R. Rothenberger, then chaplain at Perkiomen School, performed the formal installation.

It is a tribute to the traditionally strong lay leadership of the church under moderators Warren S. Kriebel, Lester S. Heebner, and Harold G. Kerper, that throughout these years of turmoil the regular day to day business of the church was carried on, and membership and congregational giving steadily increased. On January 15, 1965 the final payment was made to the trustees and all remaining outstanding mortgage bonds were called for redemption.

The Garden of Memories

The year 1965 also saw the Garden of Memories cemetery project brought to fruition. When land for the new Central church was purchased in 1937, no provision for a cemetery adjoining the church was included. The Salford burial ground was full and the Towamencin and Worcester cemeteries nearly so, but additional land adjoining the new church was not immediately available.

Then came World War II to take a great toll of the gallant youths of America, including the life of Malcolm Alderfer Schweiker Jr., killed in action on Okinawa. The Schweiker family, as an enduring tribute to him and to the ideals reflected in his life, created The Garden of Memories for his burial place and as a memorial to fulfill the future cemetery needs of the congregation of the Central Schwenkfelder Church. In 1959 they caused the Malcolm A. Schweiker Jr. Foundation, a family charitable trust, to purchase the Lyndale Hileman farm adjoining the church as a cemetery site. The farm buildings, except for the home, were removed and an office with adjoining service building for equipment was built. Roads, curbs, and parking areas were also constructed. After deeding sufficient land to expand the parking area in the rear of the church, twenty acres of farm lands were graded, seeded, and landscaped with more than

3,000 trees and shrubs, to provide for more than 10,000 graves, expected to meet the needs of the church for some 200 years—about the length of time the Salford and Towamencin cemeteries had served the congregation.

The Garden of Memories was dedicated Easter morning, April 22, 1962, and Malcolm Alderfer Schweiker Jr. was interred there April 29, 1962. On January 31, 1964 "The Garden of Memories of Worcester" was chartered pursuant to petition to the Montgomery County Court of Common Pleas as a self-perpetuating non-profit corporation. The original incorporators were Malcolm Schweiker, Richard Schweiker, and William Strasburg, representing the founders, and Ellis Anders and Ellis W. Kriebel, representing the church. The bylaws provided that the family would continue to designate three members of the Board of Managers and to elect two members subject to approval by the church, with any expansion of the board to include equal additions representing the family and the church. In default of family representation, the church would elect the board.

The founders and the family foundation deeded the property to The Garden of Memories of Worcester corporation, and undertook to develop the property at a cost of some $225,000, to provide the legally required initial endowment of $25,000, and to make up operating deficits during the early years of operation. Burial space is provided for members of the congregation, regular attenders of its services, other persons residing in the community within a radius of two miles, and such other persons as the Board of Managers may approve from time to time. No charge is made for a burial lot, but each applicant is required to make a contribution, originally $200, to an endowment fund to provide for perpetual care. A plot was reserved for donor family members, and for burial without contribution of ministers of the congregation or others similarly deserving of special consideration. Before his own death Rev. Hoffman arranged to have the remains of his first wife, Adelaide, transferred from the Washington Schwenkfelder Burial Ground, and reinterred in the Garden of Memories, where he in turn was buried. Rev. Eric Braund was interred in the reserved plot in 1968 and Dr. J. Maurice Hohlfeld in 1973.

The Garden of Memories of Worcester was formed as an independent non-profit corporation, legally separate from the church. This arrangement avoided any confusion with some $70,000 of endowment funds held by the church, the income from which is dedicated to perpetual maintenance of graves in the Worcester, Towamencin, and Salford cemeteries, with any excess available for general church operating expenses. It further permitted the founders to develop the property without requiring approval of expenditures by any church body. At its February 9, 1965 congregational meeting the church accepted and agreed to cooperate in the arrangements set forth in the Garden of Memories bylaws, to appoint or approve two members of the Board of Managers annually, and to distribute or publish with its Annual Report the Annual Report of the Garden of Memories. Mr. Schweiker had now seen to the completion of the basic Central Schwenkfelder Church project.

Dr. Berthold Jacksteit

As Dr. Jacksteit undertook his now full-time duties he was, of course, no stranger to the congregation, nor was he unacquainted with the circumstances that so distressed Rev. Braund. Events would prove, however, his was a most propitious choice, as during the following nine years of his pastorate the spiritual life of the church would be quickened, its mission outreach greatly expanded, the pastoral and administrative staffs strengthened, and the problems of merger largely outgrown.

Dr. Jacksteit possessed a deeply spiritual Christian faith, born out of severe adversity endured by his family during his early years. He was born February 3, 1910 in a small town then in western Russia but since World War I a part of Poland. His father, of German background, gave up a small business to become pastor to a congregation of German speaking residents, of whom there were a large number in that general region. Upon the outbreak of World War I the German-speaking pastor was immediately taken into custody, to spend the next five years in Russian prison and concentration camps. His family was driven as refugees to wander deep into Russia. After about a year of rootless existence they came into Austria-Hungary, and finally into Germany. At the close of the war they found themselves in Germany, where the family was almost miraculously united and where Berthold received his first formal education, albeit a thoroughly disagreeable experience for the poverty stricken, alien refugee.

A parishioner of his father's church who had migrated to the United States before the war learned of the family's whereabouts and was instrumental in arranging emigration to America, first of two older sisters, and then about 1922 of the rest of the family. They settled in Rochester, N.Y. In 1928 his father was called by the Baptist church to go to northwestern Canada to minister to a group of recently-arrived immigrants, the last group of Russian origin to be permitted to emigrate to America. Young Bert remained in Rochester, completed his elementary education, and then graduated from Westminister College and the North American Baptist Seminary, at that time located in Rochester, later removed to Sioux Falls, South Dakota. He pursued further studies at the University of Pittsburgh, where he earned a Master of Arts degree in education and did further work toward a doctorate in the field of philosophy. He was later awarded an honorary Doctor of Divinity degree from North American Baptist Seminary. He then served terms as pastor at two Pittsburgh area churches, and at the Bethel Baptist Church of Anaheim, California. He came east to work for nine and a half years with the Board of Education and Publication of the American Baptist Convention at Valley Forge. A specialist in Christian education, he wrote and edited Sunday school curriculum materials and served as consultant and advisor at many youth camps and conferences throughout the United States. A personal friend of Rev. Braund, Dr. Jacksteit first came into contact with Central in 1963 as a consultant on the Christian education and youth programs.

Dr. Jacksteit assumed his new responsibilities as of January 1, 1967, and in the January church letter issued the following challenge to the congregation:

> . . .I promise not to be easy on you. I shall expect of you the best you are capable of giving—not because of me, personally, but because we are engaged in God's work, and he deserves our best. Playing at religion does not please God. Neither does it win the respect and support of responsible men and women. For that reason, I believe that it is my duty to be continually challenging you to your utmost and highest even as I must steadfastly hold myself to that standard.
>
> There is no limit to what a dedicated congregation can do for God and for the community in which it has been placed. Our primary concern is not to build an organization but to serve persons in the name of Jesus Christ. Yet if we are not strong and united as a congregation and fully dedicated to the task before us, we shall not be able to minister to people in the most effective way. Therefore your cooperation and your commitment to the work of the church are so very important.
>
> Ask yourself these questions: How faithful am I in attending the services of the church? How regularly am I attending Sunday church school in order to learn more about the faith I profess? How generously am I supporting the work of God in and through my church? How often do I pray for my church, my pastor, my fellow-members? How willing am I to give leadership and to participate in activities in which my abilities and help are needed?

By the answers you give to these questions, you help to determine what this new chapter in the history of your church will bring forth. Let us covenant together to give God our highest and best that with his help the history we shall be writing in the years ahead will make challenging and exciting reading.

In the July 1967 church letter, the challenge became more specific:

I would like to share with you a deep concern. It has to do with our financial support of our church's ministry and mission in the world. . . . As your minister it is not my business to raise money or to hound you for it. But it is my God-given duty to see that we are faithful in our financial stewardship—and the simple fact is that we are not faithful. Anything but! And frankly, I'm appalled. A church of our size and of our financial standing ought to be giving at least twice as much—in fact, at least three times as much for missions. In a world that is desperately in need of Christ, how can we be satisfied with the small investment we are making in Christ's mission in the world. . . . For your own sake and for the sake of our church I plead with you, therefore, to open your heart and to share more generously the treasure that God entrusts to you. Give generously—as God so generously gives to you; give regularly; give as unto the Lord. You will find that richer blessings and greater joy will be yours as a result. Best of all, you will make it possible for your church to share more fully and widely in Christ's mission in the world.

During 1966 disbursements for missions were $11,051, an average of $10.59 per member. Considering the generally affluent community in which it is located, and the sacrifices of those who made possible the attractive church building, church giving may well, as the pastor pointed out, have "come very near the bottom in giving when compared to what the vast majority of Christians in our country give to the work of Christ's Kingdom."

The influence of the pastor's personality and his firm conviction of Christian faith was reinforced by his sermons. He was an unusually effective and impressive preacher. He expounded the gospel message in a simple and straightforward manner, but reflected in his sermons his philosophical education and varied lifetime experiences. He lived life to the full. He and his wife, Jane, raised four daughters, yet found it in their hearts to take into their home a fifth adopted daughter. He preached from the depth of his own experience, giving fully of himself, yet relating his messages to events in the congregation, the community, and the world around. Initially a stranger to the Schwenkfelder tradition, he came to have a deep appreciation for the character and theological insights of Schwenckfeld, and he and his wife came to feel quite at home in the Central congregation. He kept the congregation members aware of their special heritage, their abundant temporal wealth, and their duty to their God and their fellowmen.

Perhaps his most memorable sermons were those preached on seven Sunday mornings during the Winter of 1970-1971, on the theme, "What America Means to Me." In a voice frequently breaking down from emotion, he related in some detail the experiences of his father and his family in Europe during World War I. They had experienced first hand privation and hunger, the almost unbelievable inhumanity of man to man when aroused by nationalistic enthusiasms, persecution because of religious affiliation, and indignities heaped upon them as refugee strangers in an alien land. When, in 1940, Rev. Jacksteit was threatened with deportation because of his father's earlier travel out of the country (to Canada) while still an alien, he went to Washington to plead his case. One rainy January evening he stood on the steps of the Capitol gazing out at the Washington Monument, in deep depression, and considered all that he might be forced to give up. America meant to him, said the pastor, freedom from hunger and fear of physical violence, and the greatest freedom of all, simply to be considered a human being. All who heard this moving personal testimony came away with a new sense of pride in their country and of appreciation for the blessings of freedom which are all too often taken for granted. American naturalization finally realized to him was not a matter to be taken lightly. He reminded the congregation that millions of people around the world would gladly sacrifice their own lives if they could but secure for their children the heritage of freedom Americans enjoy.

The congregation responded to the quiet, but firm, prodding by the pastor and new vitality gradually coursed through the programs and activities of the church. Talented new members from the surrounding community were drawn into the church and filtered into leadership positions. By the end of 1968 Dr. Jacksteit was able to sound a more optimistic note, expressing his pleasure with "the spirit of harmony that prevails. While we have our problems, I cannot but feel that we are learning to trust one another a little more, to accept our differences, and to work together as one people in Christ."

In 1966, the year before Rev. Jacksteit became senior pastor, the church's operating and mission budgets totaled $84,158, of which mission disbursements of $11,051 accounted for 13 percent. Of total mission disbursements, $3,800, or 34 percent represented the Central church's allotment of the Conference Mission Board budget, and $4,022, or 36 percent went directly to support the Philadelphia church. The remainder was allocated among a large number of mission projects. Over the years such projects included support for the work of Rev. and Mrs. Chester Ranck in the Kentucky Highlands, Miss Joan Hunsberger in Brazil, Dr. Norval and Rev. Wilbur Christy in Pakistan, Joy Ranch, Inc. in Virginia, Elsie Pfister in Kentucky, New Life Boys' Ranch near Harleysville, the Glenn Matt Campus Crusade, the Migrant Workers Mission project of the Pennsylvania Council of Churches, the Mennonite Mission to the Navajo Indians, the North African Mission, the American Bible Society, the Wyclif Bible Translators (J. Ruth), and various other mission projects. Many of these projects were also receiving support from the Conference Mission Board and from the other churches. The program seemed to lack a central focus essential to exciting interest and support.

In 1968 the Mission Committee, under the chairmanship of Kenneth W. Clemens, searched for a project that the Central church could call its own. They undertook a five- or six-year commitment to contribute $6,000 annually for the construction of a Christian high school in Nagaland, northern India. The American Baptist Foreign Mission Society had sent an evaluation team into the area, and Rev. Richard Beers, a member of the team, described the needs of the people there to the Mission Committee and the congregation. The school would serve the Christian population comprising 40-50 percent of the people. Besides meeting the need for education, it was hoped the school would serve their spiritual needs as well, exerting a Christian influence on students, faculty, and administration, and through them on the entire community. A $6,000 contribution was made each year 1969 through 1973. Rev. Beers returned in July of 1970 to give a progress report and in 1971 the headmistress of the school wrote that the first unit had been completed and work started on the second unit. Her letter and accompanying pictures were placed in a special display in the narthex.

In January of 1969 the members of the Philadelphia congregation requested the resignations of Rev. James Serdy and his associate, Barry Wally, and set up their own search committee to secure a minister attuned to their needs. Since it was felt that the church needed a spiritual leader of a higher caliber than could be obtained at a salary the local congregation could support, the Central Mission committee made an allocation of $5,000 to supplement the salary provided by the congregation. The Strawberry Mansion co-op was supported, and a "Fresh Air Program" instituted to bring groups of black children out into the country during the summer.

As a result of these allocations, the mission budget for 1969 was double that of 1968 and in his report to the congregation Ken Clemens echoed the pastor's challenge, "Attempt great things for God and expect great things in return." The 1969 budget was raised and a $2,000 payment against the 1970 Nagaland pledge paid in advance. The 1970 budget was increased another $5,000 to cover an increased $13,000 allocation to the General Conference Mission Board and other increases. Expansion of mission giving continued as Betty Jean Rothenberger, Curtis Weigner, and Lois Rothenberger in turn succeeded Kenneth Clemens as Mission Committee chairperson.

During 1972 the church responded generously to the appeal for flood relief funds following the flood at Wilkes-Barre. Rev. Rothenberger organized several work crews which were sent from the church to the Wilkes-Barre area to help with the difficult cleanup operation. In addition a large amount of clothing and household furniture was donated and sent to this area after some of the cleanup work was done. A Mission Emphasis Sunday was held on December 10, 1972, when the entire day's services were devoted to missions. New Life Boys' Ranch, both staff and some of the boys, took part in the Sunday school session, representatives from Campus Crusade spoke during the worship service, and the Philadelphia Schwenkfelder Choir presented "The Messiah" at the evening service. Rev. Arnold Brooker, the new pastor of the Philadelphia church, spoke briefly.

The Mission Committee laid particular emphasis on efforts to spread participation among more members of the church. In 1974 only 429 members out of a total membership of 1,183 contributed to the mission budget. In an effort to broaden participation questionnaires were distributed with the church bulletin, giving the congregation an opportunity to express specific opinions on all the budget items. The results were tabulated, published, and used by the committee as a guide in setting up the proposed budget.

By 1975, the last full year of Rev. Jacksteit's pastorate, the combined operating and mission budgets of the church reached $199,059, with disbursements per member more than doubling from $80.61 in 1966 to $162.36. The mission budget had increased from $11,051 to $47,216, or from an average of $10.59 to $38.51 per member. The mission budget accounted for 23 percent of combined budgets, up from 13 percent. Moreover, the momentum built up carried over as Rev. Rothenberger succeeded Rev. Jacksteit as minister.

During Rev. Jacksteit's pastorate, as indeed throughout Central's history, a great many people gave generously of their time and talents to serve on the boards and committees through which the work of the church is carried on. The Diaconate, chaired successively by Norman Weigner, Harold Beyer, Lloyd Radcliff, Glenn Kriebel, Jack Graham, and Norman Nyce, worked through regular committees charged with arranging receptions for new members, Homecoming Dinners, Love Feast Communions, and receptions for special occasions. The Special Services Committee arranged Easter Dawn, Salford Pilgrimage, and Song Services in Salford Grove, and other special events. A committee visited the sick and another the bereaved. A Benevolence Committee provided financial aid where needed. and an Outreach Committee campaigned for new members and strove to make them feel at home once they joined.

The Board of Trustees, with John W. Clemens as president, discharged the numerous housekeeping responsibilities with which it is charged, as well as completing the planting of shrubbery around the church. In addition it was responsible for maintenance of the Worcester, Towamencin, and Salford properties and cemeteries, funding for which was provided from special endowment funds in the care of the board.

It was early considered desirable that a parsonage be provided so that Rev. Jacksteit could reside closer to the church than at his home near Valley Forge. A committee under the chairmanship of G. William Meschter undertook to secure a site and build a suitable parsonage. This was held in abeyance, however, when in 1969 Jack Rothenberger was elected minister of Christian education and moved into the Hillside Ave. parsonage, lending less urgency to Dr. Jacksteit's residency within the confines of the parish. It was not until 1971 that the parsonage in the Hunter Hill development, 1095 Crossbow Way, Lansdale, Pa., was built and the Jacksteit family moved into the vicinity of the church.

In February of 1968 the Board of Trustees, upon the recommendation of the Diaconate, established the Memorial Fund, with G. William Meschter as its first secretary. Memorial contributions, principally contributions in lieu of flowers in connection with funerals, are held in a separate fund to be expended in a relatively short period of time for such purposes as the trustees may from time to time designate. They have been principally designated to accumulate an organ renewal fund, anticipating the day when the perennially faltering church organ will require major overhaul. Contributions made to the church for endowment purposes, income only to be used, are held in the Endowment Fund.

The 1960s and 1970s were decades of ferment and change. Traditional manners and attitudes gave way to conspicuous new lifestyles; there was widespread unrest among the youth of the land. Dr. Jacksteit and church and Sunday school leaders were seriously concerned over the effects of these changes and the encroachment of the affluent society upon the youth of the church. Special attention was paid to the Christian education program, both in the Sunday school and through collateral study groups. Efforts were made to involve as many young people as possible in a wide variety of special activities. And finally, in what Dr. Jacksteit regarded as a significant force in the spiritual growth of the church, the young people themselves transformed the musical program of the church.

Under the leadership of Dolores Meschter, Richard L. Nyce, Abram R. Kulp, Nancy Krauss, Frances Witte, and David Hamme, the Music Committee saw to the regular employment of choir director, organist, and assistants to supply appropriate music for regular and special worship services. Director Stanley Clattenberg and organist John Gottschall resigned during 1970. Mr. Donald Eby was employed as organist and Professor Joel Anderson as choir director. Senior, Dorian, and Junior choirs rehearsed regularly and offered selections at the various services. Meanwhile Robert Krauss served as Sunday school chorister and frequent tenor soloist with the choir, Arlayne Clemens as Sunday school pianist, and Randall Kriebel, Leila Anders, Eva Mae Witte, Esther Allebach, and Richard Nyce as Sunday school organists. In 1972 Dr. Joel Anderson resigned without prior warning. In what would prove a fortuitous move, Dottie Mayes, Jane Jacksteit, and Robert Krauss substituted as directors of the choirs until a permanent director could be obtained. Dottie Mayes, soon to become Mrs. Sherman Heebner, was employed to direct the Junior choir and Robert Upton the Senior and Dorian choirs. Mrs. Heebner initiated a "Cherub Choir" for children in kindergarten, first and second grade, which grew steadily and channeled children into the Junior and older choirs.

In no area were the changes of the times more far-reaching than in the field of music. A new beat, a new tone, a new lifestyle became the rage of the day. Before long the influence of these changes was felt in the field of religious music. The new beat and new tone entered the church and a new instrument—the guitar—became the vehicle by which it made its entrance. One of the choice contributions of Rev. Eric Braund to the church had been an unusually beautiful and dignified worship service. To many more traditionally inclined, the new beat and the guitar had no place in such a service and the first efforts to introduce them did not meet with much success, to say the least.

But then the young people of the church entered the scene. In the summer of 1971 they wanted to present the Christian musical "Tell It Like It Is." They asked the pastor's wife, Jane Jacksteit, an active choir member, to direct it. They were extremely apprehensive of the reaction of the congregation when they decided to do this. But when at the performance the congregation gave them a standing ovation, the ice was broken. A new music, and even more importantly, a new spirit was in. The young people began to play a more and more significant role in the spiritual growth of the church. Their musical presentations enriched their own lives and enabled them to grow in Christian grace, and this in turn was passed on to the entire congregation. In a real sense the young people now became the spiritual dynamo of the church and set a strong example of dedicated Christian discipleship. Thus by the time Dottie Heebner appeared on the scene the foundations had already been laid for the outstanding musical ministry with children and youth that the church has enjoyed ever since. Too much credit cannot be given Mrs. Heebner, not only for her untiring labor with the Cherub, Junior, and Dorian choirs, but for her talented direction of musical presentations involving the combined choirs of the church, which celebrate the Christmas and Easter seasons and other special occasions. Her seemingly effortless virtuosity on the piano lends an air of confidence to all who participate, and carries off vocal and instrumental effects of unusual complexity and difficulty for a volunteer choir and instrumentalists. The discipline of the children and the dedication of their parents in bringing them to rehearsals is little short of unbelievable in a day of loose discipline in schools and multiple outside diversions. It is, furthermore, no accident that when the children perform, church attendance is noticeably higher as parents and grandparents turn out to hear the children perform. Not infrequently their presentations are greeted with spontaneous applause, a reaction unthinkable in the church sanctuary ten years earlier.

During the summer of 1968 Ronald Krauss, a member of the church and a student at the Yale School of Divinity, was hired to assist in planning and carrying out the summer youth program. His work during the short summer of his employment proved so successful that pressure immediately built for the hiring of a full-time director of Christian education. The Committee on the Ministry issued a call to Rev. Jack Rothenberger, who took up his duties in September of 1969. Jack came to Central after serving as chaplain, dean of admissions, and headmaster of Perkiomen School. It was felt his experience with young people there, and with their problems particularly associated with the times, would prove valuable in the Central program. With Rev. Arthur Wagner as associate minister and Jack as minister of Christian education, Fred Seipt, reporting for the Committee on the Ministry, judged, "With his addition to our already excellent staff of Rev. Jacksteit and Rev. Wagner, we believe that our church will have the finest, most well-balanced ministerial staff it has ever had, and will insure the continued success of our church in filling the needs of our people and of the people of this community."

In consultation with Rev. Jacksteit, the Board of Christian Education, with Wilbur Seipt as chairman, focused special attention on the Sunday school curriculum. In 1969 the "Christian Faith and Work Plan" was adopted. It was hoped this unified curriculum from cradle roll to adult departments would bring deeper meaning and greater understanding of the Christian faith to the Sunday school scholars. At the same time a greatly expanded program of adult elective courses, each dealing with a timely Christian concern, was introduced to attract the interest and increase the participation of young married couples and older individuals in the Sunday school program. Under general superintendents Ruth Kriebel and Robert Krauss the Sunday school flourished. Junior, Junior High and Senior High Christian Endeavor Societies were active. An infant nursery to care for small children during the church service was established, along with an extended session to which smaller children, including the Cherub choir, adjourned from the church service prior to the sermon and following a special children's talk. A Flower Committee was established to arrange placement of flowers on the altar for worship services and their delivery after the service to sick or bereaved members of the church. Boy Scout Troop 133 and Scout Explorer Post 200 participated in the God and Country program, Camp Delmont, and February pilgrimages to Valley Forge. Four dens of Cub Pack 200 were active with the younger boys. Viola Anders kept careful watch over the growing church library.

Under the general supervision of Rev. Rothenberger as director of Christian education and the Board of Christian Education, a large group of young people, particularly those of high school age, were engaged in a wide variety of Sunday school, Christian Endeavor, and social and athletic activities, with Roger Heebner as perhaps the most energetic advisor. During 1972 a Youth Activities Committee (later Activities Committee) designated a portion of the basement floor of the Sunday school building as a Youth Activities Center. The area was furnished as a lounge, two ping pong tables and an electric bowling machine were installed, and a shuffle board was marked off in the hall. Movies were shown and social gatherings, both formal and informal, encouraged. Outdoor facilities for softball and volleyball were also made available. The same Activities Committee was responsible for initiating a Senior Adults Group, which met Wednesdays during the day in the Youth Activities Center facilities, with Ruth Kriebel as its first president. The Activities Committee also initiated the Happy Days Pre-School Learning Center, which evolved as a major community tuition-supported program for children ages three to five. The original two classes, each meeting twice weekly, have now expanded into four classes, involving ten sessions throughout the week. The classes are designed to give the small children a social experience to smooth their entrance into kindergarten and school, together with limited learning assistance.

In perhaps the most significant effort to upgrade the quality of religious instruction at Central, in 1972 Rev. Rothenberger introduced the Bethel Bible Study Program. This graduate level Bible study course was authored by Rev. Harley Swiggum, a Lutheran minister in Madison, Wisconsin. Some eighteen denominations participated in using the course of study, which was later extended worldwide. Jack and Jean Rothenberger spent two weeks in Madison in intensive study of the course materials, then returned to teach a class of fifteen carefully selected teachers or leaders in weekly two and one half hour sessions, with ten or twelve hours of homework in between, over a two-year period. Five participants in this class thereupon volunteered to enlist their own classes of thirty persons each, who in turn engaged in a two-year study course. In this way some 150 people initially benefited from the study, a number which over the years was multiplied approximately three times as the courses were repeated with new groups. Then Jack and Jean, Helen Keyser, and Fran Witte journeyed to Madison to be introduced into four new programs, as a result of which Fran Witte taught a course on the Ten Commandments, Helen Keyser a course on Proverbs, and Jack and Jean a course on the family. Jack Graham led a group in study of the course material on the church. In 1975 when Tom and Nancy Byron joined the church staff they also journeyed to Madison for the intensive course, as did Lynn Vanderhoof when she was appointed minister of Christian education. The overview provided in this study made individual Bible passages more meaningful and generally raised the level of teaching in the Sunday school.

As he approached retirement in early 1975, Rev. Jacksteit

looked back on forty-one years of service in the Christian ministry, having been ordained when still a seminary student and serving a little country parish. He had served the Central church for thirteen years, first as a part-time consultant in Christian education, and after January 1, 1967 as pastor. The church was hardly recognizable as the same church as the one he had then taken charge of. His spirit and dedication had permeated the church body and enhanced its service to members, community, and the church universal. Giving for church support and for missions had increased dramatically. While Sunday school enrolment and average attendance had declined over the period, there seems little doubt that the quality and effectiveness of the program had been enhanced. Four hundred and forty-one new members had been received into the church, and church membership had increased from 1,044 to 1,226.

A recognition and appreciation dinner was planned for Dr. and Mrs. Jacksteit on the occasion of his retirement, but characteristically he asked that it be canceled. Instead, a reception was held in their honor in Fellowship Hall following the 10:30 worship service on Sunday, February 29, 1976. At the request of the Committee on the Ministry, John W. Clemens chaired a committee which raised a retirement purse presented to Dr. Jacksteit at this reception. The Jacksteit family made an extended visit to old friends from the Anaheim congregation in California and then settled into a new home in Havre De Grace, Maryland. Dr. Jacksteit, as Pastor Emeritus, occasionally returns to the Central pulpit and to participate in other activities. He and his family continue to enjoy the warm affection of their friends and co-workers of their eventful pastorate at Central.

Dr. Jack R. Rothenberger

Rev. Rothenberger and Rev. Jacksteit had enjoyed a congenial relationship, including a year during which Jack was the formally designated successor. The transition upon Rev. Jacksteit's retirement at the beginning of 1976 caused hardly a ripple in the life of the church. At 46 years of age Rev. Rothenberger was in the prime of life and enjoyed splendid physical health. He entered enthusiastically upon his new responsibilities, for which all his training and experience down to that time seemed uniquely to have prepared him. The church also seemed poised to enter upon perhaps its period of greatest prosperity. The expansion of the church continued and the effectiveness of its mission gathered strength as the 1970s turned into the 1980s.

Rev. Rothenberger seemed naturally to belong in the Central pulpit. A descendant of immigrant Anna Krauss, he attended the Palm Schwenkfelder Church where during their high school years he met Jean D. Schultz, whom he later married. Jean is one of eight children of Willis and Jennie Schultz, a family tracing descent from immigrant Christopher Schultz and one long active in Schwenkfelder affairs. Jack had earned a B.S. degree in psychology at Juniata College, a B.D. degree from Hartford Theological Seminary, where he was steeped in Schwenkfelder history under Dr. Elmer E. S. Johnson, and a Master of Sacred Theology degree from the Temple School of Theology. He had been licensed as a Schwenkfelder minister by General Conference in 1954 and ordained by the Conference in 1955. In 1964 he also received ministerial standing in the United Church of Christ. He had served as associate pastor of the Palm church, pastor of the Lansdale Schwenkfelder Church, and as chaplain, dean of admissions, and headmaster of Perkiomen School. As minister of religious education at Central beginning in 1969, as co-pastor and senior pastor designate, Jack was already thoroughly at home in the Central congregation.

Seeking further training, in the spring of 1974 Jack began work on a Doctor of Ministry program at the U.C.C. Lancaster Theological Seminary. He undertook a project in the area of the educational ministry of the church, exploring the relevance of present-day experiential education to some of the teachings of Schwenckfeld, particularly his concept of "Erkenntnis Christi"—the experiential knowledge of Christ—and his reference to the "School of Christ." In May of 1977 he received his degree. Out of this project grew the annual "Schwenkfelder School of Christ," during which keynote speakers and seminars explore contemporary issues, with the object of making Christ really known in the sense that Schwenckfeld used the term "Erkenntnis Christi."

The tenth annual School of Christ on March 11, 1984 considered the theme, "Living Your Christianity." Since Caspar Schwenckfeld was an advisor to his Duke it seemed appropriate to invite as a keynote speaker a member of Central church who had served in high positions in the federal government. Richard Schultz Schweiker, son of Malcolm and Blanche Schweiker, four-time U.S. Representative, two-time U.S. Senator, and recently Secretary of Health and Human Services in the cabinet of President Ronald Reagan, joined with Dr. Rothenberger as keynote speakers. They were followed by a panel of six laypersons from the several churches chaired by John Hewett, headmaster of Perkiomen School, which addressed the general question, "How do I apply the Christian faith in my job." This initial event of the Schwenkfelder Anniversary Year celebration excited widespread interest and attracted an overflow audience.

Rev. Rothenberger has been ably assisted and supported in his ministry by Rev. Thomas R. Byron, who was installed as assistant minister, December 28, 1975 and designated associate minister in 1979. Tom had graduated from Eastern Baptist College with a B.A. degree in social work in 1971 and gone on to earn an M.A.R. degree from Eastern Baptist Theological Seminary in 1973. He was ordained by the Philadelphia Baptist Association in his native North Wales Baptist Church on April 6, 1975.

During 1975 the Committee on the Ministry considered some forty-nine candidates for assistant minister. Chairman Lloyd Radcliff was acquainted with Tom and urged him to apply. Tom was at first little inclined to do so as he had been trained for a career as urban missionary in Philadelphia and lacked some of the normal courses of training for a parish ministry. At the time he was serving as Coordinator for Services for the People's Emergency Center in Philadelphia. This weekend agency, operating in conjunction with the United Methodist Church, concentrated on providing food and shelter for the homeless. Furthermore, he was about to marry Nancy MacQueen and had his mind on his coming July honeymoon. When funding for his job at the Center expired at the end of June, however, he took a little more interest in Central and promised Lloyd to come in for an interview upon his return. There was shortly a meeting of the minds and a call was extended to Tom. He undertook to make up the parish ministry courses he had missed and, with the benefit of a three-month introduction under Dr. Jacksteit, soon felt quite at home in the parish ministry. Tom and Jack developed a mutually stimulating relationship and the church has been richly blessed by their finely tuned and effective ministry, drawing the large and diverse Central congregation into a more closely-knit Christian family.

In line with his missionary concern, Tom had served as a counselor for a state-wide delegation of youth that journeyed to Managua, Nicaragua in 1973 to assist missionaries there in recovering from an earthquake that had destroyed many aspects of their work. He was the director of a similar mission to El Salvador and Nicaragua in 1974 and had been involved in two other similar missions. This interest carried over into his ministry at Central and became an effective instrument of his ministry to the high school youth of the church. Believing that faith must have life, he led groups of young people during the summers of 1976 and 1977 into the hill country of Kentucky to work on renovating a church, and the second summer a community center, in Presbyterian missions there. The young people got a taste of life in more primitive communities and learned valuable lessons in getting to know and get along with people of quite different lifestyles. During the summer of 1978 a similar mission performed rehabilitation work after a flood in Johnstown, Pa. The young people learned the patience, cooperation, sensitivity, and love so necessary to a genuine caring community. Then during the first week of July in 1979 he and Nancy led a group of twenty-three young people to the International Christian Endeavor convention in Hawaii. And finally, although surely not the last, in 1981 he and Nancy led a group of young people on a wilderness trip, during which they climbed New Hampshire's Mt. Washington.

Moderator John H. Graham worked diligently and with admirable success to assure that the governing boards of the church performed their assigned tasks and coordinated their activities. While sometimes taking a while, the decision-making process seemed to work surprisingly well, allowing a full hearing for all opinions.

The Board of Trustees, with Oliver Smith as president, maintained the church property and the properties of the three meeting houses in excellent condition. The operating budget by 1982 rose to $274,297, equivalent to $195.23 per member. Combined mission and operating budgets totaled $364,289, equivalent to $259.28 per member, more than three times that of 1966. Endowment funds of some $500,000 were consolidated in a trust fund at Philadelphia National Bank, with the annual income making a significant contribution toward operating expenses. The trustees also maintained a building reserve fund to provide for prospective nonrecurring expenses such as major repairs to the heating system or a new roof, and established a pension reserve fund. When the energy crisis of the early 1980s struck, a committee surveyed the use of energy throughout the property and implemented a number of improvements to control this rapidly escalating cost. In 1982, after several years of study and discussion, an entrance ramp and other conveniences were installed to make the church property more readily accessible to handicapped persons.

At the annual congregational meeting on February 28, 1978 the Mission Committee was formally organized as an elected board. Under Mr. Robert Ingram as its first president the board strove to bring a better sense of order into the mission program of the church. It developed guidelines allocating 75 percent of available funds to the support of home missions and 25 percent to foreign, with each category broken down into 75 percent for educational and 25 percent for human need projects. A mission representative system was set up whereby one member was assigned to develop correspondence and communication with each mission project and in turn to relay such communications to the congregation. Regular mission programs were presented throughout the church year. Giving for missions maintained a steady increase, reaching $89,992, equivalent to $64.05 per member, in 1982.

In 1971 Ronald Krauss of the congregation was ordained into the Christian ministry in joint services of the Schwenkfelder Conference and the United Church of Christ. His brother, Robert, was ordained on June 27, 1976 and served at a number of posts as chaplain in the U.S. Air Force. In 1983 Chaplain Krauss was appointed a Major and assigned to the Pentagon. In 1982 David Luz, raised in the Central congregation and having graduated from Eastern Baptist Theological Seminary, was ordained, serving first as student pastor and then as assistant pastor of the Palm church. In 1983 Karen Kriebel Gallagher graduated from Eastern Baptist Theological Seminary and awaited a church call precedent to ordination. In early 1984 she worked as interim part-time youth advisor on the Central staff.

In connection with the national Bicentennial celebration in 1976, it seemed appropriate for the Schwenkfelders to repeat the historical drama "Faith of our Fathers," originally presented in Salford Grove during the Schwenkfelder Bicentennial in 1934. Jean Rothenberger and Emily Clemens co-chaired a general committee which arranged the presentation Thursday evening August 12, Sunday afternoon August 15, and Tuesday evening August 17, 1976 in the large auditorium of the North Penn High School in Lansdale. Mr. David C. Hofman of the Perkiomen School faculty directed the drama and Donald C. Eby, choir director and organist at Central, directed the music. A large cast labored diligently during the early summer and was rewarded by splendid performances attended by capacity audiences.

The Diaconate, with Richard Read and Robert Wrigley as chairmen, maintained its usual services. In 1980 they proposed that the church sponsor a refugee family and, receiving congregational approval, organized volunteers into numerous committees to handle the multitude of details involved. The chairpersons of these committees formed a CORE Committee chaired by Mrs. Drake (Sandy) Williams to exercise overall supervision. Originally modest farmers in the Cambodian countryside, Khimma Tha, his wife, and six children fled first to Thailand and then to the Philippines, where the Lutheran Children and Family Service became interested in their plight and sought sponsors required for immigration into the U.S. The Central church arranged to sponsor this family while the Gwynedd Square Presbyterian Church arranged to sponsor two additional children of the same family, then married and with families of their own, so that the entire family group would be resettled in the same locality.

A house was rented in Lansdale and readied for its new occupants. Clothes were collected and sorted, cupboards were stocked, and donated furniture was moved into the house. With everything in readiness to the extent possible, a curious and expectant welcoming committee journeyed to the Philadelphia Airport on the evening of October 22, 1982 to await the 10:52 p.m. arrival of the family group. They arrived wearing brightly-colored ski jackets from the cold weather depot for refugees at the Chicago Airport, but with bare feet! They had flown from the Philippines to Japan, Alaska, Chicago, and finally to Philadelphia, carrying three small but heavy bundles, their only possessions. Fortunately the girls had picked up a few words of English in the Philippines and a refugee previously resettled by the Gwynedd Square church made himself available as an interpreter.

Then came the long process of getting to know the Thas, ascertaining their sizes, food preferences, and skills. Social Security numbers were applied for, the children, ranging from 5 to 18 years of age, were enrolled in the North Penn School District, and a job lead opened up employment for Mr. Tha. The language committee began simple tutoring. The CORE Committee discovered anew the complexities of our system as it tried to impart in a short time the things that had taken them an entire lifetime to learn. The CORE Committee, the subcommittees, and many members of the congregation and community earned the appreciation of all involved for their extraordinary Christian service in the successful resettlement of this family.

The Board of Christian Education under Ken Clemens, Drake Williams, and William Black as chairmen, encouraged and supervised the Daily Vacation Bible School, the Happy Days Pre-School Learning Center, and a wide variety of social and athletic activities. The Bethel Bible Study Program was continued and adult elective courses in the Sunday school were expanded until by 1982 there were eight elective courses from which to choose. These two programs served to stimulate interest in the Sunday school program, particularly among young adults, who frequently became involved in active and serious discussion of timely topics. In 1978 Helen Keyser succeeded Robert Krauss as general Sunday school superintendent.

In March of 1979 Linda M. Vanderhoof, then completing her studies at Eastern Baptist Theological Seminary, began part-time work at the church as student youth director. Upon completion of her studies in the spring of 1980 she was called as minister of Christian education, in which capacity she served until the latter part of 1983. Beginning in September 1983 Robert Burns and Steve Drobot, students at Eastern College, undertook part-time work with the young people under the seminary's field extension cooperative program, affording them practical experience as part of their college training.

In September of 1972 Jack and Jean Rothenberger conducted a group of eighteen travelers on a twenty-one-day pilgrimage to the Schwenkfelder Silesian homelands, retracing the steps of the early Schwenkfelder immigrants. In 1977 Rev. Byron led a tour of the same area. In 1979 Rev. Rothenberger led a tour of the Holy Lands with stops at Rome, Athens, Cairo, and Ephesus, and a week in Israel. Each such experience expanded the understanding and intellectual horizons not only of those who participated but of those at home who benefited from their reports and more lively teaching and preaching.

In 1976 Dr. Rothenberger inaugurated a series of leadership planning retreats during which beginnings were made at strategic planning, sorting out goals to be accomplished during the coming year or in a more appropriate time frame. The church had become a complex organization requiring meticulous attention to a host of administrative details. By 1984 membership had increased to 1,446 and attendance at services frequently reached the capacity of the auditorium, prompting discussion of structural modifications to expand seating capacity. Taping of worship services and their broadcast over station WNPV extended the ministry of the church to those unable to get to services and to the broader community.

By 1984 an even more significant expansion of the church's ministry appeared in prospect with the establishment of the 265-unit Meadowood Total Life Care Community project on the Schweiker homestead property close by the church. Sponsored by the Schweiker family, William E. Strasburg is the prime moving spirit and serves as chairman of the Meadowood board. Dr. Rothenberger serves as vice-chairman and nine of the ten board members are drawn from the Schwenkfelder church membership. Residents of the retirement community will have only a short walk to the church facilities, and the church ministry will naturally reach out to serve their needs in a multitude of ways.

A staggering range of responsibilities lay claim upon Dr. Rothenberger's time and seemingly boundless energy. The Central congregation embraces people from differing backgrounds and circumstances. They look to the church and its pastors to serve a broad variety of interests and needs, from the presentation of infants for consecration to an active program specifically for senior citizens. While lay leadership carries formal responsibility for church program and activities, the pastors' responsibility for the spiritual unity and vigor of the congregation requires them to be continuously alert to currents of thinking and endlessly patient in dealing with members. In his sermons Dr. Rothenberger seeks faithfully to expound the scriptures, frequently drawing insights from the thought of Caspar Schwenckfeld. He exercises a high degree of diplomacy in addressing the spiritual concerns of all the elements of the congregation while at the same time being careful to avoid themes which might unnecessarily give offense to some. He shares the pulpit on a regular basis with Rev. Byron and on special occasions welcomes guest preachers, the young people of the church, and others to participate in worship services. Special Sunday morning services are devoted to mission presentations and musical programs.

Dr. Rothenberger carries a second weighty responsibility. As the sole Schwenkfelder minister of his day tracing descent from Schwenkfelder immigrants and the only one whose academic education includes in-depth study of Schwenkfelder history and theology, he is conscientiously sensitive to maintenance of denominational institutions and to preservation of the Schwenkfelder heritage. He serves as editor of the *Schwenkfeldian*, a demanding task in itself, has served as chairman of the Perkiomen School Executive Committee subject to considerable tension and conflict, and as an active member of the Schwenkfelder Library Board, the Mission Board, and the Board of Advanced Living. His influence is constructive and so pervasive that it is difficult to envision the conduct of denominational activities without his leadership. Indeed the very thought should prompt urgent consideration of identification and encouragement of denominational leadership for the succeeding generation.

Arising in some degree from his study of Schwenckfeld's thought, Jack is furthermore actively concerned with interdenominational and ecumenical activities. He has represented the denomination in the Montgomery County Sunday School Association and as president of several ministerial associations within the county. Since 1957 he has represented the Schwenkfelders in the Pennsylvania State

Sunday School Association and in the Pennsylvania Council of Churches, where he has served in a variety of positions, including participant in the Conference of Interchurch Cooperation, embracing Protestant and Roman Catholic church leaders. He has represented General Conference on the Division of Overseas Ministries of the National Council of Churches.

Throughout the twentieth century the Schwenkfelder congregations have been active in the Christian Endeavor movement. Rev. Rothenberger has served the county, state, and national Christian Endeavor federations in official capacities. In 1982 Jack led a tour group to England and took a side trip to attend the International Christian Endeavor convention in Edinburgh, Scotland. There he was elected president of the International Christian Endeavor Society. The following year during the annual convention in Seattle, Washington, he was installed to serve a two-year term. A group of eighteen people accompanied Jack to the convention and continued on with an interesting tour of Alaska. Jack's service in these activities, not the least as president of International Christian Endeavor, has generated widespread publicity and reflected great credit on the local church and denomination.

As Dr. Rothenberger, on the eve of the Schwenkfelder Anniversary Year in 1984 contemplates the future, the opportunities for service have never seemed more challenging. Central church's congregation includes people ready and willing to devote a great variety of talents to the mission of the church. It includes also people desperately in need of spiritual guidance and the support of a caring Christian community. The church is at once rich in tradition and alive to the needs of the time. Congregation and ministers alike have much for which to be thankful. Looking to God for leadership of His church, the Christian ministry of the Central Schwenkfelder Church is continuing to make an effective difference in the lives of people, not only in Montgomery County but around the world. In every respect of its ministry the Central church seeks to make the living Christ really known and provides opportunities to make that knowledge show in practical living.

Chapter Six

Schwenkfelder Missions

The Schwenkfelder renaissance around the turn of the century which saw the initiation of the *Corpus* project and the acquisition of Perkiomen School witnessed also a new burst of interest in missions, both home and foreign.

Ever mindful of Schwenckfeld's concern for the people of the world and of the generosity of Moravian and Mennonite friends during their own period of persecution, the Schwenkfelders in Pennsylvania had not been insensitive to the needs of their fellow men. They were interested in and supported Moravian missionary Christian Frederick Post, who worked with the Indians in western Pennsylvania and Ohio and then established a pioneer mission on the Mosquito Coast of Honduras. Intriguing correspondence during the years 1768-1775 between the Schultz brothers in Goshenhoppen and missionary Post in Honduras has been translated and printed by the Schwenkfelder Library. In 1790 they had forwarded assistance to the von Buyschanse family, and in 1816 they had raised a war-relief fund sent to the Council of Görlitz. In 1844 General Conference had voted a contribution in support of Benjamin Schneider, a native of Montgomery County and for fifteen years a missionary in Brusa, Turkey. Beginning in 1853 they had periodically contributed to the American Tract Society in New York for the purchase and distribution of Bibles.

It was only in 1894, however, that mission interests became a central concern of the Schwenkfelder community. In that year Dr. James M. Anders and Mr. William Y. Meschter undertook to "establish a Schwenkfelder Church in Philadelphia, in order that those belonging to this faith who were from time to time removing from the country to the city, should have a suitable home." They reported their desire to Rev. O. S. Kriebel, who in turn laid the matter before General Conference on October 20, 1894, with the result that a Missionary Committee was appointed. At the spring General Conference May 25, 1895 this committee recommended that a Board of Missions be constituted, and the members of the Missionary Committee were appointed to the new board—Rev. O. S. Kriebel, Elmer E. S. Johnson, Dr. James M. Anders, Joseph K. Schultz, Rev. George K. Meschter, Joseph S. Anders, and William K. Heebner. A charter was granted December 24, 1895 and the Board of Home and Foreign Missions of the Schwenkfelder Church in the United States of America was launched.

The board proceeded immediately with the organization first of a Sunday school, and then of a church, to become by May 1899 The First Schwenkfelder Church of Philadelphia. A mission begun in 1904 in Norristown and one in 1916 in Lansdale were forerunners of the respective churches.

In 1900 Rev. H. S. Jenanyan, a missionary in Tarsus and Iconium visited Pennsylvania, presenting the needs of Armenian Christians then suffering persecution under Turkish rule. His plea was referred to the Mission Board, and pledges of $300 annually for a period of three years were made to support his work, thereby formally initiating the foreign missionary work of the board.

The enterprise, however, that captured the imagination and enlisted the support of the Pennsylvania Schwenkfelders, dispelling any latent tendencies toward parochialism in the Schwenkfelder community, was the mission in Taiku, Shansi, China. To this mission one of their very own, a girl born and raised on a Worcester Township Schwenkfelder farmstead, reared in the Worcester Sunday school and educated at Perkiomen School, devoted thirty-eight years of her life. Returning home on four furloughs, she regaled church and Sunday school audiences with her experiences, visited in the homes of family and friends, and scattered Chinese souvenirs and mementos, as well as more substantial Chinese artifacts, long decorating mantle-pieces, or later exhibited in the Schwenkfelder Library. In hundreds of letters to family and friends, regularly reprinted in the *Schwenkfeldian*, and in more formal reports to the Mission Board and Conference, she vividly pictured travel and living conditions in a remote and backward province, among people of an old and totally alien culture and religion, speaking and writing an obscure and difficult language, the people ravaged by opium and the women crippled by bound feet. With her devoted brother, Rev. Harvey K. Heebner, the popular pastor of the Philadelphia church, serving as secretary of the Mission

Board and editor of the *Schwenkfeldian*, Flora K. Heebner never seemed far removed from the thoughts of Schwenkfelder adults and children alike. She became for them the living embodiment of Christ's last commandment, "Go ye into all the world and preach the Gospel to every creature," in an age that confidently anticipated the entire world to be won for Christ through missionary enterprise.

Taiku, Shansi, China

During most of the nineteenth century China, and interior China in particular, remained largely shut off from the outside world. The Manchus had conquered China in the seventeenth century, but had accepted Chinese culture and ruled according to traditions which had evolved in China during the course of two millenia. At the apex of its power in the eighteenth century, the Manchu dynasty ruled China virtually as one nation, its 400,000,000 people strongly bound together by cultural, religious (Confucianism) and political (the Manchu empire) ties. Looking upon all foreigners as inferior suppliants, it recognized no other sovereign power, refusing even normal diplomatic intercourse or exchange of ambassadors. Under these conditions China remained relatively impervious to Western ideas in general and to Christianity in particular.

While after the Opium War (1842) missionaries could live and work in the treaty ports, and after the Arrow War (1856-60) could go into the interior, they faced the opposition of entrenched traditions and culture, and progress came only with great difficulty. The Manchu dynasty did not surrender power until 1912, but for two generations before that time it had been declining amid political corruption and moral degeneration. In the Sino-Japanese war of 1894-1895 the Japanese roundly defeated the Chinese defense forces and forced their way into northern China. Noting the Japanese success, Russia challenged their intrusion into Manchuria, and in its turn was defeated in the Russo-Japanese war of 1904-1905, a war, to the great chagrin of the Chinese, fought mostly on Chinese soil. Her political independence and territorial integrity imminently threatened, China set about adopting many phases of Western culture, opening the way for Western medicine, education, and missionary activity.

Shansi is a province of north China, somewhat larger than the state of Pennsylvania. While rich in coal, iron and oil, 85 percent of its 11,000,000 population depends on farming for a precarious livelihood, perennially threatened by temperature extremes, drought, flood or famine. Taiku ("Great Vale"), about 250 miles southwest of Peking, a walled city with four suburbs and a population at the turn of the century of perhaps 25,000 people, lies on a plain 100 miles long and 70 miles wide, at an altitude of 2,200 feet, surrounded and virtually isolated by mountains rising to heights over a mile above the plain.

In 1877 this entire region suffered severely from a great famine, and relief workers entered Shansi, until then rarely visited by foreigners. In the spring of 1882 Rev. Martin Luther Stimson, sent to north China, made an exploratory trip into Shansi and shortly settled with his wife in Taiyuan. Before the year was out they were joined by Rev. and Mrs. I. J. Atwood, Rev. and Mrs. C. D. Tenney, and Rev. C. M. Cady. Some time later Rev. Atwood rented a "haunted house," the only property available, in nearby Taiku, and all the missionaries except for the Stimsons eventually settled there. The Taiku mission and one in Fenchou became the principal scenes of American Board missionary activity in Shansi.

These workers were members of the "China Band" from Oberlin College, founded in 1833. From 1851 to 1866 the president of the college was Rev. Charles Finney, a powerful teacher, evangelist and abolitionist, whose home served as a "station" on the underground railway spiriting runaway slaves to Canada. Under his leadership Oberlin assumed a deeply religious character, which persisted following his death. During the latter part of the nineteenth century Dr. Judson Smith, a teacher in the Oberlin Theological Seminary, delivered stirring lectures on the history of the expansion of Christianity and interested his students and faculty associates in the great need of the Chinese people, and in carrying the gospel message to them. Over the years a steady stream of workers from the Oberlin community would be inspired to serve in the mission field, and from this source came the principal workers supporting the Shansi, China, missions. Dr. Smith shortly became executive secretary of the American Board of Commissioners for Foreign Missions, which administered the mission activity from headquarters in Boston.

The American Board had its origin in August 1806 in the storied "Haystack Meeting," when five young men of Williams College met one day to consider their Christian obligation and their life work. In a heavy thunderstorm they took refuge under a haystack, where they pledged to devote their lives to missionary endeavor in foreign lands. This pledge led to the organization in 1810 of the American Board of Commissioners for Foreign Missions. In 1812 the board sent out its first missionaries, and others followed to all parts of the earth, establishing churches, schools, hospitals, printing presses, and industrial institutions. The first foreign missionary organization in America, it became the mission arm of the Congregational Churches, eventually (1925) directing the efforts of some 800 missionaries with about 5,000 native associates working under fifteen different flags.

Facing the appalling physical suffering of the people around him, and feeling the great need for medical services, Rev. Atwood and his wife returned to Chicago where he studied for a medical degree, but by 1889 he had returned to the mission to establish rudimentary hospital services there. In 1891 Rev. and Mrs. George E. Williams joined the mission. Three daughters were born to the Williams family, of which the oldest was named Gladys for the joy she brought into the stark living conditions. A school for boys was established, irregular classes and seminars for adults undertaken, opium refuges maintained, preaching missions into the surrounding countryside organized and local church members recruited. In 1894, in a truly pioneering effort, Mrs. Lydia Lord Davis started the girls' school, later called the Precious Dew Girls' School, Pei Lu, in memory of the two martyred teachers, Miss Bird (Pei) and Miss Partridge (Lu). Chinese tradition had regarded girl babies as a burden, "one more mouth to feed," and many were exposed and allowed to die. Education of women was looked upon as sheer nonsense. One of the most conspicuous accomplishments of Christian Missions in China would be improvement of the lot of women, and particularly the eradication of the practice of foot binding—folding a baby's tender toes beneath the sole of the foot and binding them there to keep the feet tiny, dainty, painful, and useless. In 1894 sixteen adults and eight schoolboys were organized into the Taiku Church, which slowly attracted new members. Progress became visible and enthusiasm in Taiku and back in Oberlin ran high.

Then in 1900 disaster struck. The Boxers, dedicated to driving from China all "foreign devils," and encouraged by the Empress Dowager, fearful of Western inroads into her degenerating "monarchy," rose in a short, but extremely violent, uprising. All of the ten adult missionaries then in the Shansi field, along with five children, were massacred, as were some eighty of the 100 church members. The rest were scattered, to seek refuge in the surrounding mountain fastnesses.

Dr. Atwood was on furlough in the United States. Mr. and Mrs. Davis had returned to the United States on furlough in 1897. Mr. Davis had gone back to China in 1899, but Mrs. Davis's return had been delayed because of ill health, and she remained at Oberlin. Their furlough due, Rev. Williams had escorted his wife to the coast but was detained himself in China by concern over an ailing fellow worker. The wife of Rev. J. B. Thompson had died, leaving two small children which Mrs. Williams undertook to take with her to America, to be cared for by relatives. Together with Gladys and her two other daughters she sailed in 1899 with five children, ages two months to 6 years, under her care, and settled in Oberlin to await the arrival of her husband. But it was not to be. Both Mr. Davis and Rev. Williams were martyred in the uprising.

The Boxer uprising was put down by foreign military intervention, and died out almost as suddenly as it had flared up, although the emotions which had inspired it were hardly extinguished. When shock and bewilderment abated, new workers volunteered and undertook reopening and staffing of the mission stations. Dr. Atwood returned to China, interceded with the American Board not to give up the work, gathered and encouraged the remnants of the church in China, and called for new volunteers to carry on the work. Back in Oberlin, Mrs. Williams and Mrs. Davis, despite the martyrdom of their husbands, lent their support to resumption of the work in Shansi.

Five people responded to the call for help from Dr. Atwood: Dr. and Mrs. Willoughby Hemingway, Rev. and Mrs. Paul Leaton Corbin, and Miss Flora K. Heebner.

Flora K. Heebner

Miss Flora Krauss Heebner was born in 1874, one of seven children of Henry H. and Susanna Krauss Heebner, both of immigrant descent, on the family farmstead in Worcester Township, Montgomery County, Pennsylvania. After graduating from Stump Hall school she attended the State Normal School in West Chester, but on the invitation of Rev. O. S. Kriebel left before graduating to become a student-teacher at Perkiomen School, from which she graduated with the class of 1896. As so many others of that era, she came under the spell of Rev. O. S. Kriebel, became active in the Upper District churches, and helped foster the first Christian Endeavor Society there. For three years following graduation she taught in the local public schools, in the Worcester Sunday school in which she had been raised, and in the newly formed Sunday school in Philadelphia. Then in 1899, along with her brother Harvey, she entered Oberlin College, thirty-five miles west of Cleveland, Ohio, from which both graduated in 1903.

Venturesome and energetic by nature, at Oberlin Miss Heebner soon fell under the spell of the "China Band" and Dr. Judson Smith. She attended meetings of the China Volunteer Organization and made the acquaintance of the two martyr widows. Indeed, when her Lord Cottage dormitory was destroyed by fire, Flora lived for a time with Mrs. Williams, who also accompanied Flora on visits to the Worcester farm, where she came to know Rev. Harvey Heebner and the Schwenkfelders. The threefold appeal of foreign missions, offering adventure, sacrifice, and outpouring of energy, met in Miss Heebner a hearty response.

But the Schwenkfelder Mission Board had other priorities. While at Oberlin Miss Heebner was visited first by Rev. O. S. Kriebel, placing before her the need for her services at Perkiomen School and at the new Philadelphia church, and then in December of her senior year by Elmer E. S. Johnson, secretary of the Schwenkfelder Mission Board, who conveyed the official "call" signed by every member of the board, asking her to serve as "Home Missionary of the Philadelphia Church." After graduating and spending the summer in evangelistic work under the auspices of the American Sunday School Union at a lumbering camp in the highlands of Tennessee, she dutifully reported for work as parish visitor in Philadelphia, where by now Rev. Elmer Johnson was serving as minister.

The fires stoked at Oberlin, however, had been but temporarily banked, by no means extinguished. Her heart had been given to the foreign mission fields, the frontiers of the world's greater needs. Thither she must go. And so once again she spoke to the secretary of the Mission Board. At its meeting in Norristown called January 18, 1904 to organize a mission there, the board acquiesced in Miss Heebner's appeal and instructed the secretary to forward her application to The American Board of Commissioners for Foreign Missions in Boston. In sponsoring Miss Heebner's mission, the Schwenkfelder Mission Board fell into natural alliance with the American Board, which had a highly developed worldwide organization, skilled at facilitating travel, currency exchange, funds transfer etc., as well as a network of workers supplying religious, political and economic intelligence for the guidance of missionary activities. A January 22, 1904 letter to Dr. Judson Smith, secretary of the American Board, elicited a favorable response the very next day. Subsequently, on June 8, 1904, Dr. Smith wrote Miss Heebner, "It gives me great pleasure to report to you that yesterday the Prudential Committee appointed you a Missionary of the American Board and designated you to the Shansi

Mission with expectation that you will go to the field late in the summer in company with Mr. and Mrs. Corbin. This brings you into the list of my correspondents and I hasten to welcome you most heartily to the ranks of the Missionaries of the Board and to the choice company of the men and women who are to compose the Shansi Mission. . . . "

On June 29, 1904 a farewell service was held at the First Schwenkfelder Church of Philadelphia for Pastor and Mrs. Elmer Johnson, and for Miss Heebner. The Johnsons were departing for Wolfenbüttel, Germany, to join Dr. Hartranft in *Corpus* editorial work, and Miss Heebner for Taiku, Shansi, China, as a missionary jointly supported by the Schwenkfelder Mission Board and the Women's Board of the Interior—the women's auxiliary of the American Board. The infant city church bravely gave up these leaders in view of their wider fields of service for Christ and Kingdom, thereby immensely widening their own horizons for years ahead.

The commissioning and farewell service in the home church, Worcester on August 14, 1904 brought together large delegations from all the Schwenkfelder districts. The edifice was crowded. The Sunday School Convention the previous day, at which Miss Heebner spoke, helped to pave the way for this memorable event—the sending forth of the first Schwenkfelder foreign missionary. Her family physician and pastor, Dr. George K. Meschter, expressed the spirit of the occasion in a poem, "The Guiding Hand," the first verse of which was read:

> My Savior, Lord of all,
> I hear Thy loving call,
> Thy call for me.
> What wilt Thou have me do
> All, all life's journey through?
> I consecrate anew
> My all to Thee.

The following Wednesday Miss Heebner departed for San Francisco, and then, in the company of Rev. and Mrs. Paul L. Corbin, Oberlin collegemates, for Tung Chou, near Peking, for a year of language study. Finally, on June 17, 1905, after a long overland journey by mule litter—a corrugated iron shelter fastened on two poles, suspended over a mule in front and one in back—on June 17, 1905, she arrived in Taiku, to be her home away from home until forced by the exigencies of foreign invasion to give it up on June 9, 1942—including travel time, a thirty-eight-year stint, punctuated by four furloughs, in 1910, 1918, 1926 and 1936.

The Taiku Mission

Thus did Miss Heebner arrive on the China mission scene following a period of disastrous destruction, but at the dawn of the period of most striking growth which Christianity enjoyed at any time in China. Within the succeeding ten years Sun Yat Sen, a mission school-educated and -baptized revolutionary leader even before the Boxer uprising, would become provisional president of the emerging Chinese republic and patron saint of the new order in China. A professing Christian, Charles Jones Soong would become the financial head of the revolutionary movement and founder of the influential "Soong Dynasty." His son would follow him as financial head of the nationalist government, and his three daughters would marry, respectively, Sun Yat Sen, H. H. Kung, long a Christian member of the cabinet, and Chiang Kai-shek, who followed Sun Yat Sen as leader of the Kuomintang.

Upon arrival on the scene following the destruction of the Boxer uprising, the new "China Band" faced almost overwhelming difficulties. All the mission buildings had been razed to the ground, and the few remaining church members, who had escaped martyrdom by hiding out in the rugged mountain fastnesses of the province, were understandably hesitant about coming back to the "Jesus Church." For five years rainfall had been meager, and the Christians were blamed for the drought. In the ten years preceding 1904 the population of the province had suffered a severe decline as a result of famine, opium smoking, footbinding, needling by native doctors, tuberculosis, still births from primitive maternity care, and infanticide, especially of girl babies. Shansi province, near the cradle of the Chinese race and rich in natural resources, sorely needed schools, churches, hospitals, and Christ.

Dr. and Mrs. Atwood had returned almost immediately to "hold the fort" until the second China Band could be recruited and arrive on the scene. In 1903 Dr. and Mrs. Willoughby Hemingway arrived, to carry on the medical work initiated by Dr. Atwood before the uprising. Dr. Hemingway opened a dispensary and clinic in the "Flower Garden." Supported by a steady stream of staff personnel from the United States, principally Oberlin-inspired, the clinic steadily grew into a 100-bed regional hospital, with a school of nursing, only later to be overshadowed by the medical center at Fenchowfu. Its service area was limited only by the difficulties of travel, for heading westward a traveler would not encounter another hospital until arrival in Persia!

Mission work was initially resumed in the "Flower Garden," about a mile to the east of the city. At one time the estate of a wealthy Chinese gentleman, it was given by the Chinese government as indemnity for the loss of life and property in 1900. Here were the graves of the martyrs lost in the Boxer uprising, and here in time would rise Ming Hsien, the Oberlin-In-Shansi Memorial Academy. Here Miss Heebner began her work, first organizing a kindergarten for the little children. As the children began to feel at home with her, she gradually came to know and befriend their parents and to recruit them into the church. Here in the kindergarten Miss Heebner was "in her glory." On her first furlough home she reported, "The children, they are such dears and so responsive, reminding me of that roomfull in the Worcester Sunday school. When the meeting was in progress, several of them forgot themselves and climbed into my lap."

Carrying on the work pioneered by Mrs. Lydia Lord Davis, Miss Heebner also began teaching in the girls' school, and with characteristic energy, to assume administrative duties as well. "Land was bought, funds collected, more girls gathered, the school transferred to the mission compound, and a fine modern building erected." Writing in 1910, Mrs. Hemingway described the beginning of the girls' school:

> In Taiku the small beginning of a Girls School has in five years been raised to a grade equal to any in the province. Miss Heebner has herself taught a good share of the classes, led prayers, and superintended every detail of school management, beside planning, and supervising the erection of two school buildings; one in 1906 in the Flower Garden, and one in 1909 in the Suburb. Every spring and fall, a month was reserved for Bible classes in Fenchowfu, and the women lived between times on the impetus and encouragement of those classes. In all, Miss Heebner has conducted nineteen classes. . . . One would not expect to do much touring in the country, while so busy with teaching, but Miss Heebner carried the country stations on her heart and when a few days could be spared anywhere, she took advantage of them to go around the circle of Taiku country work. . . . So it has come about that Miss Heebner knows the whole field of our Shansi Mission as perhaps no other worker will ever have need to know it.

Laws prohibiting the sale of opium and the growing of the opium poppy in China were passed at the turn of the century. Breaking the scourge of opium smoking, however, required intensive person-to-person care. Opium refuges, where lessening doses of opium eased the pain and terror of withdrawal, offered hope for breaking the habit, once thought by the Chinese to be impossible. In

Miss Heebner's words, "Our opium work is like this: Women come and live from two weeks to two months while they take the cure. During this time the Bible Woman has daily and nightly opportunity to comfort and instruct them. She has prayers with them and teaches them the fundamentals of Christian doctrine. We have two women's refuges in the country. We come into contact with such pathetic suffering, but many learn to know Jesus during those weeks. There is a call for another refuge for women to be opened to the east of Taiku—but that means another Bible Woman, with a court to be prepared." In another letter Miss Heebner related that, at the then favorable rate of exchange, $62.50 forwarded to her was enough to pay the rent of a court of buildings for a refuge. The opium refuges, along with the hospital, reclaimed desperately sick individuals, many of whom expressed their thanks by opening their hearts and minds to the gospel message.

On her first furlough in 1910 Miss Heebner traveled for two weeks across Asia on the still primitive Trans-Siberian Railway, to visit Dr. and Mrs. Johnson in Wolfenbüttel, Germany, before sailing for New York, thereby becoming not only the first Schwenkfelder foreign missionary but the first Schwenkfelder to encircle the globe. On her arrival in America, the home churches sponsored two vacations—to Asbury Park, N.J., and to Mount Pocono, Pa. Her depleted energies revived, she addressed the home churches and was then asked by the American Board, as she would be in following furloughs, to speak among the Congregational churches of the central west. From Peoria, Illinois, on May 16, 1911 she wrote: "I've spoken ninety times during the year so far, and forty four times on this western trip. This has been an unparalleled chance of telling of the work in Shansi and of how the world is all one neighborhood and only the stars are foreign lands. My prayer is that God may transform this message into usable material for building the Kingdom in our martyr mission of Shansi." The Elgin (Illinois) Congregational Church, "that supports the other half of me," was especially kind. This church built the companion wing of the city church in Taiku, another wing of which was built by the Schwenkfelders.

Returning to the Orient after her furlough, Miss Heebner was detained in Peking by the revolution that ended the rule of the old order and ushered in a republican form of government. After more language study at Tungchou, by the end of May she was back "home" in Taiku. On the final leg of her trip the cart was late in starting. On orders of the local magistrate, policemen had held up the driver and required him to have his queue cut off. She saw several men going home sadly holding their precious pigtails in their hand. Most people, however, seemed to be glad to be free from this ancient sign of subjection to the Manchu rulers.

The second decade of the century witnessed rapid expansion of the work in Shansi province. In 1909 a revival of the city church was led by Mr. H. H. Kung. A native of Taiku, he was a classmate of Flora and Harvey Heebner at Oberlin, studied further at Yale, and returned to play an instrumental role in the establishment of Ming Hsien. He continued as honorary president of this institution even after going on to a larger role in Chinese affairs. The physical plant was improved with new buildings and all activities were reorganized. The medical, evangelistic, and women's work were concentrated in the south suburb compound, leaving the Flower Garden free for the expansion of Ming Hsien. The mission staff drew recruits from America, and perhaps more importantly, mission school-educated Chinese began to assume important administrative and teaching positions.

In 1910 when the girls at the Taiku Mission were without a school home, the Schwenkfelders in Pennsylvania responded to the call and funds came from the Sunday schools, ladies' aid societies, Christian Endeavor Societies, from the churches, and from individuals and groups forwarding gifts ranging from $1.00 to $50.00. The sum total made possible the construction of the Woman's Building and the purchase of land for both this and the future Girls' School site. Miss Heebner then started a building fund.

It was decided at the annual meeting of the Schwenkfelder Board of Missions in 1913 that the $1,000 bequeathed by William Y. Meschter to the Mission Board of the Schwenkfelder Church be used for the erection of a house in Taiku for Miss Heebner and the ladies of the mission associated with her, "said house to be her permanent home while in this station." This Meschter Memorial, the second Schwenkfelder-assisted building in Taiku, had space enough for five ladies, each to have her own study and bedroom, and it soon became known as the Taiku Ladies' House.

Dr. Hemingway continued in charge of the Taiku hospital in its new and larger quarters and with its expanded staff. In 1912, with his wife and two daughters, Isabel and Adelaide, he spent a year and a half on furlough in the United States. Interestingly, after their return to China, Adelaide and Isabel, who were born in China and learned Chinese before English, found it necessary to return to school to learn the language all over again to greet their old playmates. A third daughter, Winifred, was born to the Hemingways in 1916.

Schwenkfelder Daisy Gehman Fairfield, a graduate of Perkiomen School and along with her husband, a graduate of Oberlin, served the mission from 1910 to 1928, following which Wynn Fairfield kept in active touch with the work as secretary of the Foreign Mission Conference of North America. In 1919 Rev. Philip Dutton, a specialist in rural evangelization, and his wife arrived; in 1921 trained nurse Helen Dizney reinforced the hospital staff and supervised the training of Chinese nurses. Later, in 1927, Raymond Moyer, of Lansdale, Pa., one of the Oberlin representatives upon whom Flora lavished special hospitality, thereby keeping in touch with new programs and plans, arrived to join the Ming Hsien staff. An English teacher, but also a trained agriculturalist, he established a model farm to demonstrate improved crop cultivation and livestock breeding techniques, offering relief from chronic famine.

When home on her second furlough in 1918, Miss Heebner reported that special funds received from the home folks amounted to $3,795.07. The Women's School, the kindergartens, the outstations, the opium refuges, and the Bible women in the refuges were all assisted by these special funds. At this time, she also voiced her desperate need for assistance in the Taiku Mission. The Schwenkfelder Mission Board responded by sending Gladys Williams, who by this time had graduated from Oberlin, to become the second foreign missionary adopted by the Schwenkfelder denomination. Miss Williams left her home in Oberlin with a glad heart, for at last her hopes were to be realized. She arrived in Peking the first week of October ready for language study, and in March 1919 boarded the train for Shansi. Miss Heebner escorted her to the mission. The reception was an emotional one.

> There were the old friends of her father and mother, her own childhood friends and playmates waiting for her outside the Taiku gate, to do honor to this one who was willing to come back and suffer with them for the sake of helping them, and to take up the work laid down by her father. Tears were in the eyes of many as they gave her welcome. Lined up on either side of the road were the school-girls singing a song of welcome in her honor, which was written by one of her playmates, now a teacher in the girls' school. Her old nurse, who had become a Bible woman and matron of Dr. Hemingway's hospital, and she walked arm in arm about the place renewing the memories of long ago.

Flora Heebner welcomed her in the Ladies' House of the mission where she took residence, to continue as Flora's closest associate during the remainder of her service in Taiku.

In 1920 Gladys Williams had the joy of attending the dedication of the "Alice Williams School for Married Women," named for her mother. This school, built with monies received from the Schwenkfelders, was started by Miss Heebner as her new project. In September of the same year Gladys wrote, "The Women's School opens Friday and it is going to be running over. We can only take in thirty women and over forty have applied."

The year 1921 witnessed the worst famine since that of 1877. Hungry and destitute people knocked on the mission doors seeking help. The staff of the *Schwenkfeldian* decided to make an appeal to their subscribers, friends, and organizations, and the sum of $300 was sent to Miss Heebner, which she used to look after old women and children who had been left stranded. Famine relief on the part of the International Red Cross included extensive work-relief programs. Roads were built down through Shansi province. The missionaries were on the spot and doled out the grain at the end of each day's work. The people of Taiku long remembered Dr. Hemingway's and the missionaries' part in this program. When the famine was broken President Li Yuan Hung sent to the Taiku mission station a "very proper" banner of thanks for the mercy of the mission, and the magistrate (mayor) of Taiku gave $3,000 towards the erection of a new city church. In 1921, following the famine, there was a small unexpended balance. At her request, Miss Heebner was told to purchase new plots of ground upon which to erect new mission schools. The model farm of the Ming Hsien School, later started by Raymond Moyer, pointed the way out of famine. New drought-resisting grains, American fruit trees, field and sweet corn, potatoes and tomatoes, foreign pigs, cows, sheep, and poultry, through higher yields brought more food from the good earth.

The Taiku church built in 1910 was outside the city walls, about a mile from the center of city life. By 1923 Rev. Philip Dutton, treasurer of the project, wrote a stirring appeal for funds to erect a new city church in the central area to replace the old church, now completely outgrown. The Schwenkfelders responded generously, the Congregational Church of Elgin, Illinois, did their part, the local Taiku government helped, and the Chinese neighbors contributed, so that the approximately $27,000 required was substantially raised. A suitable site was purchased and the existing buildings carefully razed to supply bricks, tiles, and lumber for the new edifice. By the end of 1924 the new Taiku City Church, built on the site of the stoning of the martyrs in 1900, was dedicated. A tasteful blend of Chinese architecture on the outside and foreign utilitarian layout inside, the church consisted of three buildings. The central auditorium, with balconies around the sides, was capable of seating 1,000 people, so as to accommodate the students of Ming Hsien, who were required to attend. On the left there was a two-story women's wing, the gift of the Schwenkfelders, and on the right a two-story men's wing, the gift of the mid-western churches.

For festivities of the Christmas holidays, Miss Heebner made candy, for which she was famous throughout the province. Her visits to the outstations were special at this time. She would take with her boxes of little things such as pencils, erasers, pens, washcloths, towels, aprons, pin cushions, handkerchiefs, and soap to be distributed to the boys and girls, in many cases the only gifts they would receive. These gifts were sent by the Schwenkfelder Sunday school classes and church organizations in Pennsylvania. In her big, flat, square muff made of fur she carried the gifts to homes and schools, brightening many lives and spreading the gospel message.

Throughout her lifetime Flora Heebner kept in intimate touch with a legion of friends and supporters, of whom none was more devoted to her well-being and to the work she personified than her brother, Rev. Harvey K. Heebner, pastor of the First Schwenkfelder Church in Philadelphia, editor of the *Schwenkfeldian* and secretary of the Mission Board. As the time for Miss Heebner's third furlough in 1926 approached, the Philadelphia church granted their pastor a five-month leave of absence and subscribed a fund to defray traveling expenses so that he could join his sister in Taiku, observe the work there and accompany her on her trip home. Leaving Philadelphia July 12, 1926 he sailed July 21 from Seattle on the S.S. "McKinley" in the company of Rev. and Mrs. Wynn Fairfield, who were returning from furlough and would show him the way almost to Taiku. Mr. Wayne Meschter was in the northwest on a business trip and he and his wife bade the party Godspeed from the pier as they sailed. By way of Shanghai, Tientsin, Peking, and then through the rugged and scenic mountains, they came to Shansi. Flora met them at Yeutze, about thirty miles from Taiku, where the Fairfields said their good-byes. Having recklessly expressed his curiosity, the missionaries at Fenchoufu arranged for their visitor an extemporaneous trip to a mountain outstation, whereupon the Philadelphia pastor had a taste of mountain travel, walking, pushing, and occasionally riding on top of a cartload of matches, up precipitous trails, around hairpin bends, to a mountain pass, where they were soaked to the skin in a sudden downpour. The party returned to Fenchoufu, "tamed, toughened and taught." On their way they had passed three groups of evangelists. "Through such as these the Kingdom comes."

After a month in Taiku, "bicycling with Corbin," visiting the schools, speaking in the church with Corbin as interpreter, and generally observing the work there, Rev. Heebner and Flora traveled to meet with Perkiomen graduate Dr. Frank Laubach and his wife in Manila. They then traveled by way of Singapore, Sumatra, Ceylon, Palestine, and Egypt, before returning to New York December 7 on the S.S. "Majestic," and to an enthusiastic "Welcome Home" service at the Philadelphia church. Rev. Heebner had lantern slides made of his trip pictures, which he used to lecture widely on the missionary enterprise. The slides are extant in the Schwenkfelder Library.

By the time Miss Heebner returned to China, military activity, which was to plague north China during the remainder of her service there, had gotten underway. Two contending armies had the road blocked 100 miles west of Peiping. Avoiding cities and railroad junctions, Miss Heebner, together with six China Inland missionaries, hired mules and drivers, and boring through the two armies arrived in Taiku March 13, 1928 to the astonishment of the mission staff, who thought she was still in America. Even when in sight of the plain, the warning hurled at them constantly was: "You can't get through." Luckily, a soldier from Taiku, hearing the debate, said, "This is one of our Taiku teachers, let her proceed," and the party did.

Education of, and assistance to, Chinese students now began to bear fruit as the work of church, school and hospital was carried on more and more by Chinese staff. Aster, for twenty-five years a ward of the Aster Circle of Miss Heebner's American friends, taught for several years in the girls' school and in the women's Bible school, and later became the wife of Dr. Wen of Taiku Hospital, continuing her teaching until 1936. Lan Hua Liu Yui, "Blue Flower," aided in her education at Oberlin and Columbia University, became dean of women in Shantung Christian University. Stephen Meng, a recipient of scholarship aid, became first a student and then a teacher in Peking Union Medical School. Chauncey Young became secretary of the Taiku churches. Wang Hsueh Jen, supported by missionary funds, became teacher in the Oberlin-In-Shansi Academy, and then loyal pastor of the Taiku church. After 1951 Wang served as superintendent of the Tungchow Hospital for several years. His son, Wang Fu Pan, as a boy the ward of Schwenkfelder Sunday schools, is only now winding up thirty years of service as professor and chief surgeon in the first teaching hospital of Suzhou. Wu Yue Lan, supported almost entirely by Miss Heebner's "specials," taught for many years in the women's Bible school, and served as director of religious education in the Station Association, carrying special responsibility for the village churches.

As others undertook the burdens of teaching, Miss Heebner's time and energies became increasingly absorbed in administrative duties. But she always reserved time for evangelistic work in the mountain outstations. In a 1935 letter she described one of these journeys.

Two and a half years ago I was in this place, one of our fartherest outstations. It is a tiny village of forty families located in a pocket of our southern mountains. We skirt the highest peak we can see to the east from Taiku and cut into the mountains along the Wu Ma River—the first river crossed in going north from Taiku. We go to its entrance in carts, then transfer to pack-animals, and then go about ten miles more up the river bed into a narrow gorge. This goes up and down and in and out of gullies in a most wonderful way. The last mile is one stiff climb. But somehow it did not seem near so far or so hard as the first time I negotiated it. Around this gully is almost a circular bastion of rock mountains.

This mountain is surrounded by deep, precipitous gullies and the very top is a flat tableland, and the sides are terraced from top to bottom for crops. At one place on the top I could look around and count twenty five terraced fields. . . . It is a precious experience to go in and out of these homes—meeting our sisters of another race where they live and talking to them of things near to their lives and lifting their thoughts above their narrow surroundings to the great things of the Spirit.

This morning we are having church with the sky as our roof and the everlasting hills as witnesses. Twenty joined the church! Paths leading up and down the gullies—there are no roads—lead to other hamlets and people come up and down them, converging here before our little cave room, with dirt floor, and dirt-arched roof, and a "bed" made of suncried brick.

On returning from her fourth furlough in 1936-1937, Flora found the mission compound crowded with refugees. On the night of November 8, 1937 victorious Japanese soldiers were billeted in every home in Taiku city and the surrounding suburbs. Suddenly women, girls, and children began to be dropped over the twelve foot wall that enclosed the compound, seeking refuge from the invaders. There were 600 in the mission compound and another 500 on the hospital grounds. These had their own food, clothing, and bedding. All they wanted was a safe place to stay. They returned home only when it was time for spring planting. It was a wonderful chance for Christian living and witness, everyone enclosed together within the same walls. The Ladies' House and the Hemingway House sheltered families of Christians whose fathers had gone west with Ming Hsien while the women and children stayed in the compound. The hospital had the families of its local employees as well as a number of richer family groups who could pay for hospitality. In this way the hospital kept its core of students, workers, and staff along with the patients who were too sick to go home before the Japanese arrived. The compound was a little island of peace in a land at war. After the fall of 1941, when relations were strained between Japan and the USA, the tables were turned. People who had gone home but left precious parcels for safekeeping in the mission houses, came to take them home for safety.

In September of 1937 Ming Hsien moved southward and westward rather than accept Japanese domination. The staff that remained in Taiku by 1941 included Isabel and Winifred Hemingway, Flora, and "Bob" Mueller. On July 11, 1941 the local magistrate, puppet of the Japanese authority, ordered the mission schools closed, including the large coeducational primary school and the women's Bible training school. The hospital was to carry on, which it did, becoming the Taiku County Hospital as soon as the missionaries left. On and after December 8, 1941 the missionaries were under guard since, unknown to them, war had been declared between Japan and the United States. All mail was stopped. At this time Flora had the heart-wrenching duty of burning the valuable records of the mission compiled through the years. In the hands of the invaders they would have identified the leaders of the mission and its outstations, possibly to their peril. For a whole day the chimney of the Ladies' House belched out the smoke of these valuable records, membership lists, rosters of officials, diaries, etc.

Notice was received that the missionaries were to leave Taiku. After several false starts they were whisked away on June 9, 1942 by train en route to Peking and Shanghai, to be joined along the way by missionaries of different denominations. At Shanghai they boarded the "Conte Verde," a diplomatic exchange ship, which took them past Singapore and on to Africa. The "Asama-Muru" carried Americans from Japan, Hong Kong and Korea. At Lorenzo Marques, Mozambique, the repatriation ship "Gripsholm" took on board the passengers from both ships, and only then did the Taiku missionaries find out that Raymond Moyer had been picked up on the "Asama-Muru." On July 27 they sailed for New York by way of Rio de Janeiro, Brazil. Lifebelts were kept handy throughout the trip, as the waters were infested by German submarines. On arriving in New

York August 25, they received a royal welcome by relatives and friends who crowded the wharf. Miss Heebner went directly to the ancestral farm in Worcester.

In the summer of 1943 Miss Heebner was on the staff of the Pine Mountain Settlement School in Kentucky, to which a number of American Board Missionaries were assigned for part-time service. During October and November she was on her old beat in the midwestern states. The Iowa scenery with its corn, pigs, and cattle rested her tired nerves. She was back on the old farm in Worcester by December. From January 3 to 7, 1944 she was sent as the delegate of the Schwenkfelder Mission Board to the fiftieth anniversary of the North American Missions Conference in Chicago. Her summer itinerary, made up by the American Board, took her through the southern states, then west again. On October 19, 1944 she wrote: "Surely, I am on the trek again, north central Iowa. Where will these winged feet go next? What a time in which to live!" At the Toronto convention, where she was a delegate of the American Board, Flora met her old friends, Rev. Laubach and Rev. Fairfield. The summer of 1945 again found her at the Pine Mountain school, her last assignment.

In the fall of 1945 Miss Heebner returned to the home farm, and soon there were indications of slight paralysis. The years of active service in China, especially the last hard years of invasion and repatriation, were taking their inevitable toll. Growing increasingly helpless and silent due to loss of speech, she uttered no complaint, and her last intelligible words were, "It's all right. He knows." For two years she remained helpless in the old home on the hill. She passed quietly to her reward on December 21, 1947, five days before her seventy-third birthday. Three days later she was buried in the Worcester Schwenkfelder Cemetery, Rev. Levi Hoffman preaching the funeral sermon on the theme, "I have fought the good fight, I have finished my course. I have kept the faith."

For a short period following the close of World War II, with the Nationalist government nominally in control in China, there was a resumption of missionary activity in Shansi. Gladys Williams had come home on furlough in 1940 and had then been unable to return. In 1947, however, she was permitted back, along with Isabel Hemingway, Dr. Alma Cooke, and a new Schwenkfelder recruit, Miss Mabel Reiff. They lived in the Dutton House, which was in the best repair.

Miss Mabel Heebner Reiff, the daughter of Mr. and Mrs. Abram Reiff, was raised on a Worcester farmstead and nurtured in the

Schwenkfelder Sunday schools of the Middle District. Inspired by the example of Flora Heebner, she applied to the American Board and was accepted. In preparation for her work on the mission field, she studied at the Kennedy School of Missions in Hartford, Connecticut, and in the Chinese language department of Yale University. In December of 1946 she set sail from San Francisco to the strains of "God Be With You 'Till We Meet Again," along with some 700 missionaries heading for the far east. She disembarked in Shanghai, but weather conditions and military activity delayed her arrival in Taiku until August.

Oberlin-In-Shansi was still in west China, where it had fled for the duration of the war. The women's school and Pei Lu, the elementary school, were open. The church in the city was open. Mabel taught English in the Pei Lu grade school, served on the Pei Lu board, and worked with women evangelists. Sometimes she accompanied them to the country for home meetings with women who could not get in to the city church.

Economic conditions were very poor. Some of the Chinese were using the bark from trees in their soup for added nutrition. The Kuomintang, Chiang Kai-shek's government, was very hard on the people, demanding ever more taxes in grain. One summer evening Mabel walked with Isabel Hemingway out into the fields where they were winnowing grain. A soldier with a gun over his shoulder was watching how much grain they were getting so that the government would not be cheated. A lady in the field whispered to Izzy (Isabel), "Harvest-time used to be a happy time, but not anymore."

The government schools were of poor quality, so when students finished Pei Lu some of them went out to Peking and T'ungchou to the mission schools there. In June 1948 Mabel took eight students and two children out to Peking, where the children's parents awaited them. The train ride from Taiku to Taiyuan, which usually took about two hours, took over six hours and they arrived in Taiyuan after dark. The train had been sidetracked frequently to allow troop trains carrying soldiers wounded on the battlefields to pass through to the hospital in Taiyuan. It took Mabel and her group several days in Taiyuan to get air passage to Peking. A few days after they left Taiku the Red Army took it over, and Mabel was never able to return there. When the school year began she was sent to the mission junior high school at T'ungchou, about ten miles from Peking, where she taught English and held Bible classes. In December 1948, with the advance of the Red Army, the school was closed and the staff evacuated to Peiping, where Mabel taught in Bridgman Academy (a high school).

In a June 10, 1950 letter, Helen Dizney wrote from Peiping:

> You will be glad to know how busy and cheerful Mabel Reiff is these days. It was a severe blow to her to have to give up plans to go back to Taiku, but after she accepted it she did a good job of finding lots to do here. Laura Cross, with whom she lives, says she is doing a fine piece of work in her teaching of English. . . . I am always so glad to see her in the choir at church, the only foreigner there.

The Red Army took over Peking in January 1949, and the Peoples' Republic of China was set up in October, with Peking as its capital. The missionaries continued to teach, but by December 1950 Mr. Galt, the general secretary, urged withdrawal of all American missionaries as soon as possible. Miss Reiff had steerage passage dated February 4, 1951. This gave them four weeks to finish classes, give exams, get marks in, pack, and "empty out the house." Mabel traveled on the first all-woman "manned" train from Peking to Tientsin, sailing south from there to Hong Kong on a British freighter and then on to America on the U.S.S. "Cleveland."

By April 1951, Mary Dewar, Don Farley and Gladys Williams were ordered to leave Taiku for Taiyuan Fu, where they met Louise Meebold from Fenchow. Ten days later they were notified that their travel and exit permits were ready and they were to report at the Foreign Office, prepared to leave that evening for Tientsin. In Peking there was much red tape of checking in, checking out, and a visit to the Foreign Office, after which Mary Dewar and Gladys had a very short time to go through their trunks, which had been left in Peking three years before. They had to cull out what they could take with them and pack the rest to be left in China. All baggage had to be inspected and so they had to leave it behind in care of the travel transfer agency. This baggage never caught up with them. Gladys traveled all the way in her Chinese clothes with no change of clothes available. After visiting friends in California she reached her home in Oberlin.

In 1951 Miss Williams took the position as matron of the Walker missionary home in Auburndale, Massachusetts, and remained there until her retirement in 1963. On January 30, 1964 she took up residence in Pilgrim Place, Claremont, California, where she died on January 8, 1981.

Mabel Reiff worked part time in the New York City mission among the Puerto Ricans in the Bronx and studied theology and Christian education at Union Theological Seminary in New York City. She was director of Christian education in the Presbyterian churches in Mineola, Long Island, and Rye, New York, until 1963, at which time she applied and was accepted by the United Church Board for World Ministries, successor to the American Board, and served for a short term in Japan. Mabel had six months of Japanese language study in Tokyo and then taught in the Shinonome school in Matsuyana on Shikoku Island, Japan, until March 1967. After returning to the States, Miss Reiff again worked in the field of Christian education until 1971. She then accepted the position as teacher in the children's centers of the Los Angeles United School District in California where she remained until her retirement in 1978. In 1981 Mabel took up residence in Pilgrim Place, Claremont, California.

After 1950 strained relations between the People's Republic of China and the United States made contact with inland China difficult once again. Then the "Cultural Revolution" of 1966-1976 spread fear and caused disruption of church and social organization staffs. After the death of Mao Zedong in 1976 and the purge of the "Gang of Four," contact once again became practical and numerous church groups, including several Oberlin-related groups, visited China. Isabel Hemingway, as a member of such a group, visited Taiku in the summer of 1981. Both hospital and school continued to serve the people of the area, although both were operated as government institutions. She met with a number of people who had at one time been her students, who were then near retirement and turning responsibilities over to a new generation. Reports suggest that, as has happened so often before, the Christian church has emerged from the period of persecution with a burst of new energy and enthusiasm. It is now a Chinese church, determined to be self-governing, self-supporting, and self-propagating. The future will not be like the past. The past did its work, which is now beginning to bear fruit.

While the Taiku mission provided the primary focus for Schwenkfelder mission activity during the first half of the twentieth century, interest in this field understandably declined after Flora Heebner's return to America in 1942, and particularly following Mabel Reiff's withdrawal from China in 1951. Moreover, China was by no means the sole area of missionary interest. Throughout this same period there was a multitude of missionary and relief activities supported by the Mission Board and by the individual churches, Sunday schools, Sunday school classes, ladies' aid organizations, Christian Endeavor Societies and other groups. In its fiftieth anniversary review in 1945, the Mission Board noted support for The American Bible Society; Pocket Testament League; Scripture Gift Mission; American Friends Service; American Red Cross; American

Mission to the Greeks; Salvation Army; American Sunday School Union; the American Mission to the Lepers; Anti-Saloon League; the Gideons; the Fifth Street Community Center, Philadelphia; Royer Greaves School for the Blind; and help for Mrs. Archibald Campbell in Korea, and Dr. and Mrs. Carl Becker in the Congo, Africa.

After 1945 the field widened. Schwenkfelder support flowed through the American Board to work in India, Africa, and the Caroline Islands. Registered Nurse Helen Dizney, for fourteen years associated with the Taiku Hospital, was commissioned to Chikore, Rhodesia, where Schwenkfelder contributions assisted in building a nurses' home named the Flora K. Heebner Memorial. Louise Meebold of the Shansi mission, after two years' imprisonment by the Japanese military following Pearl Harbor and rescue by an air-borne humanitarian mission, was commissioned to Truk in the Caroline Islands. Registered Nurse Hazel Atwood, for twenty years director of nursing services at Foochow in south China, was sent to Wai, Satara District, India. In addition the Schwenkfelder Mission Board contributed to the support of Mr. and Mrs. Maxwell Welch at the American Board mission station in Bilundo, Angola, Africa.

The Southern Highlands

Nestled in a small valley where the two forks of Troublesome Creek join lies the little village of Hindman, county seat of Knott County in eastern Kentucky, in the heartland of the "Southern Highlands" of Appalachia. Once a haven for settlers coming off the wilderness trail westward from the eastern seaboard, the area had been chosen for settlement due to its abundance of game and heavy timber. Settled by almost pure Anglo Saxon stock, the area had been bypassed by later waves of European immigrants, and the settlers preserved their Anglo Saxon culture to an amazing degree. By 1900 the game and timber resources had been largely exhausted and the population was forced to eke out a precarious existence by farming the unbelievably inhospitable terrain, dependent upon the whims of nature and subject to heavy rains and intermittent floods. Travel was by foot, muleback, or "jolt wagon," a muledrawn vehicle traveling rocky creek beds for want of roads. Shut in and isolated, the people lacked the amenities of twentieth century civilization, perhaps most conspicuously opportunity for even a rudimentary education.

Here in 1902 two Kentucky ladies, Miss May Stone and Miss Katherine Pettit, having visited the area and been implored by the local women to return, established the Hindman Settlement School, with 162 pupils enrolled. Buildings erected by the men of the community were twice destroyed by fire, but each time reestablished on a larger scale. Eleven years later, Miss Pettit started another school in a lonely valley at Pine Mountain, forty miles from Hindman as the crow flies but over 100 miles by the devious roads through the narrow valleys and over the mountain itself. During the 1920s Mr. and Mrs. Chester Ranck of Philadelphia, Pa., established a community center, "Faith Hill," at Lucky Fork, Kentucky, which during their twenty-five of years service grew to include a grade school, church, dispensary, and a number of outstations.

Flora Heebner spent the summer of 1903, following her graduation from Oberlin, working in this field under the auspices of the American Sunday School Union. She found primitive conditions but great eagerness in learning the scriptures. Upon her return as parish visitor to Philadelphia she aroused interest in the southern highlands field. Miss Stone and members of her staff visited several Schwenkfelder churches, and a steadily increasing volume of help in money, goods, and personal missionary service followed. The Philadelphia men's Bible class adopted a "ward" at the Hindman school, and in 1929 Rev. Heebner, accompanied by Charles Seibert of the men's class, made the first of his several journeys to Kentucky to see the work at first hand. Rev. Heebner was particularly impressed by the inhospitable terrain.

Near Hindman we saw where twenty-six of these cabins were swept over the new concrete bridge, forty feet and more above the normal flow of the river. How steep these hills! Corn is about the only crop that is raised. Grain is practically out of the question. It seems to plant this corn one must use a shot gun! There is great peril in falling from one's farm. . . . We had a fine time with Elmer, the ward of our Bible Class. A giant of a lad, he came far to the School and told Miss Stone that his father had run away again with another woman, and that he simply would sit on the door step of the School till something turned up, and it did, very luckily. He milks eight Guernsey cows each day, helps mine coal in the School Campus mine, and in summer in lieu of base ball, football and tennis, because there is no flat ground for these games, he breaks colts. Hindman School has entirely changed the spirit and attitude of the people of that community. Stills and feuds have gone, and White Gold instead of White Mule is the product most in demand now. Trying to assay this White Gold of rich mountain personality being mined at Hindman, I made the following partial analysis:—Self-reliance, downright hospitality, religious fervor, thirst for knowledge, mental keenness, uncanny ability to read human nature and get your number, the ability of "going without," sense of justice, long memories, love for home and hill. It is good to have a stake in the hills.

In 1939 Mrs. Eleanor Dobelbower of the Philadelphia church visited the Rancks and attended Sunday services in the Community House at Lucky Fork, while fifty-one little children gathered for religious instruction. Miss Heebner spent two summers—1943 and 1945—after her return from China on the staff of the Pine Mountain school, and Mabel Reiff, during the summer of 1944, taught school in nearby Harlan County, Kentucky. In 1942 and again in 1955 floods devastated the Hindman school campus; each time the churches and church organizations responded with assistance. In 1960 Mr. and Mrs. John W. Clemens of the Central church visited with Mr. and Mrs. Chester Ranck in Kentucky, Mrs. Ranck spoke at the Central Sunday school "Christmas in August" service on Sunday morning, August 7, and the next day Rev. Ranck addressed the Central Ladies' Aid Society. In 1966 Mr. and Mrs. Kenneth Clemens visited the mission in Mistletoe, Kentucky, taking with them the funds, food and clothing donated by friends and members of the church. All of the churches and a number of church organizations at one time or another took an interest in and supported the work in this area.

The World Literacy Campaign

The World Literacy Campaign owed its inspiration and initiation to Dr. Frank C. Laubach. While a student in the class of 1905 at Perkiomen School, he decided to dedicate his life to mission activity. Returning fifty years later to his class reunion, he described his Perkiomen experience in an address to the graduating class.

> Young men of the class of 1955, some of you will help save the world for 2005. You are in the valley of decision just as we were in 1905. I offer you my advice. When we were here in Perkiomen under the influence of great Dr. Kriebel, and the fine professors he had gathered around him, I formulated a fixed purpose to live to serve, not myself, but the world. Under Roy Strock, our football coach, we studied the lives of the great missionaries. Then I decided to go out where the need was greatest and to spend my life helping make a better world. It was the best decision I ever made. Whenever I followed need, not asking whether it was either pleasant or safe, that was wise. So, young men, I recommend to you to make that basic decision. You are choosing whether to spend life trying to get all you can out of the world or to give all you can to help the world. My advice is, forget your own little self and bury yourself in the world's

great problem. You are just as big as your thoughts and your love and your interest.

Dr. Laubach pursued his education at Princeton University, where he majored in sociology, graduating in 1909. He received his M.A. degree in sociology from Columbia in 1911 and graduated from Union Theological Seminary in 1913. He was ordained as a Congregational minister in 1914 and served briefly as secretary of the Charity Organization Society of New York. A year later, having completed his thesis, "Why there are Vagrants," he received his Ph.D. in sociology from Columbia University.

In 1912 he married Effa Seely, a registered nurse and school teacher from his home town of Benton, Pa., about fifteen miles north of Bloomsburg. Then in 1915 he accepted the call of the American Board to go to the Philippines. Correspondence with friends who had been among the first teachers to go to the southern island of Mindanao had interested the couple in the Mohammedan Moros of the province of Lanao, on Mindanao island, but on arrival in the Philippines the American authorities refused them passage to this province, since conditions among the fierce Moro tribesmen at the time were deemed especially unfavorable for missionary endeavor. The couple therefore had to be content with going to Cagayan, in the province of Misamis Oriental. In 1922 they were transferred to Manila, where Dr. Laubach became dean of Union College, a position he held until 1927.

In 1929 Dr. Laubach went to Lanao alone, leaving his wife and son, Robert, in Manila. The Moros were at first implacably hostile to the would-be Christian proselytizer, remaining undeviatingly loyal to their Moslem priests. One day, he reported later, "My prayers were answered in an utterly humiliating flash of truth." He discovered that he had not accepted the Moros' brown skins and he needed to be more color blind. He immediately began to study the Koran, which pleased the Moro priests, and to learn the Maranaw dialect, until that time never reduced to writing. He found it a simple language, with but sixteen basic sounds, and with the help of a Filipino educator, Donato Galia, he was able to represent these in a modified Roman alphabet of four vowels and twelve consonants. To teach the Moros, 95 percent of whom were illiterate, to read their own language, he devised picture-word-syllable charts, the letter S, for instance, superimposed upon a picture of a snake. In six weeks he had compiled 1,300 Maranaw words, which he started teaching with such success that a Moro of average intelligence could learn to read in a period of about a week. With staff cutbacks during the depression, help was scarce, and the Moro chieftains initiated the plan of "each one teach one," whereby each person learning to read undertook to teach another in the family or community. Some of the natives accepted the new opportunity with unexpected enthusiasm. One Moro assassin thanked him by offering to kill anyone whom the missionary disliked! A Moro chieftain ordered the death penalty for anyone who broke the "each one teach one" chain.

The reading classes in time developed into the Maranaw Folk Schools, with Dr. Laubach as director. The schools, credited with teaching 70 percent of the Moros to read, were so successful that Dr. Laubach was asked to prepare lessons in other Filipino dialects. Reading matter for the new literates was provided in a newspaper, *Lanao Progress,* founded by Laubach and printed biweekly. The newspaper carried world news items and discussions of local problems in such fields as law, sanitation, and agriculture. To keep peace with the Moslem priests, Moro epic poems were set in print and articles stressing the common Old Testament heritage of the Moslem and Christian faiths prepared.

By this time the world was in the grip of the great depression, bringing a decline in missionary giving and forcing the American Board to remove some 200 workers from their rolls. Secretarial help, so desperately needed in the school and teaching work, was simply beyond the board's capacity to supply. Laubach's letters to his father in Benton bewailed his frustrations at the desperate lack of help in his activities. One of these letters, published in the *Benton Argus,* included the following appeal: "There is a chance for somebody with a sympathetic heart and plenty of push to be of large service here. I need a young man or woman who can take dictation by shorthand or on the typewriter, who can attend to all sorts of details, who is friendly and knows how to keep people happy. Is there not somebody who would like to get this experience and who could come without receiving a large salary?"

Miss Minnie K. Schultz, a worker in the Palm church and employed in the Perkiomen School office, had heard Dr. Laubach talk in the Palm church on Conference Sunday in 1928. Along with a number of Palm young people, she had taken up a suggestion by Mrs. Laubach that they correspond with young people in the Philippines. Upon reading Dr. Laubach's appeal in the *Argus,* she consulted with her uncle, Dr. Kriebel, and no doubt encouraged by him decided to offer her services. When Dr. Laubach wrote that he could not offer her a salary, nor even furnish travel and living expenses, Minnie raised travel money from friends, relatives, and church and Sunday school organizations. With a fitting farewell service, she sped on her way. The long trip was eased at many stops by hospitality arranged by the American Board and in January 1933, Minnie arrived at the home of Dr. and Mrs. Laubach at Dansalan, Lanao, Mindanao, where by this time Dr. Laubach had at last succeeded in establishing his family. She fell to work with typewriter and mimeograph machine, preparing lesson materials, assisting with the newspaper, organizing the library, and perhaps most fortuitously, facilitating Dr. Laubach's expanding worldwide correspondence.

Word of the success of the picture-word-syllable charts and the "each one teach one" campaign gradually spread beyond the Philippines. It began to assume the proportions of a worldwide campaign during Dr. Laubach's journey to the United States on his 1935-1936 furlough. Writing later, Dr. Laubach described the sequence of events.

> It was our irrepressibly enthusiastic secretary, Minnie Schultz, who really pushed us over the brink into world literacy tours. She persuaded me to prepare a letter for persons along our route to America via India and Suez, which we would be taking when we left on furlough. Before I realized it, over a period of several weeks 200 personalized two page letters had been typed for me to sign. Many of those who received these letters sent us most urgent invitations to visit them. We wrote accepting invitations from Singapore, Ceylon, parts of India, Cairo, Palestine, Syria and Turkey. I was half frightened at my own audacity.

Minnie accompanied Dr. and Mrs. Laubach and Bob on most of their journey to the United States. Although she was unable to arrange a visit to Flora Heebner in Taiku, as she dearly yearned to do, she did visit Cairo, where the party spent hours in the Museum of Antiquities; Jerusalem, where they joined a Franciscan procession to the fourteen stations of the cross; Beirut, Constantinople, and Europe. Minnie returned to Dansalan in November of 1936, continuing to work there until May of 1939 when news of her mother's failing health prompted her return home to Palm.

At each stop on the journey home Dr. Laubach helped local educators and missionaries prepare literacy charts in the local languages. In India he met Mohandas Gandhi, who was skeptical about teaching illiterates, believing India's economic problems more pressing. Four years later, however, Gandhi wrote, "I am converted, and now believe that literacy should be required for the franchise." Before the end of his furlough, the World Literacy Committee (later incorporated into the Committee on World Literacy and Christian Literature of the Foreign Missions Conference of North America) had been formed in New York to make funds available to Dr. Laubach to further his work. Some fifty missionary societies in the U.S. and Britain collaborated to arrange Dr. Laubach's literacy tours, to pool information on teaching illiterates, to publish charts, primers, and lessons, and to create reading material for new literates. After all, what is the profit in learning to read if it is not put to constructive use? Rev. Heebner described the effort as "one of the most successful and practical ways of introducing the Kingdom of Heaven to those who sit in darkness. It is a dynamic way of opening the eyes of the blind."

Dr. Laubach returned to the Philippines after his furlough in 1936, but for the next fifteen years was mostly engaged in world travels, visiting Asian and African countries, spending about two weeks in each language area to assist local leaders find key words for their languages and to prepare picture-word-syllable charts so that they could carry on the teaching after his departure. The year 1941 found him in Mexico, and when the attack on Pearl Harbor prevented his return to the Philippines, he devoted the next several years to working in Central and South American countries. In 1946 he drafted recommendations for a world plan of fundamental education at the request of the United Nations Educational, Scientific and Cultural Organization (UNESCO). In 1950 World Literacy, Inc. was organized to serve nonreligious clients. Through it Dr. Laubach served as consultant for the United States' Point Four Program, for 185 foreign missions, and for more than 100 national, provincial, and municipal governments.

In 1955 Dr. Laubach organized Laubach Literacy Inc., a nonprofit organization subsequently directed by his son, Dr. Robert Laubach, of Syracuse, N.Y. In 1980 this organization organized the Laubach Golden Jubilee Assembly held at LeMoyne College, Syracuse, N.Y. Dr. Bob, who was 14 years old when Minnie Schultz joined the Laubachs in Dansalan, invited her to attend, as he and she were virtually the only persons still living who were there in Lanao when his father started his literacy program. He awarded Minnie Certificate Number One, since she was the first volunteer to offer her services to his father. The certificate read: "Minnie K. Schultz, In this fiftieth year of Each One Teach One, I am grateful to you. Two decades or more ago, you helped Frank and Effa Laubach build their vision of world literacy. Literacy challenges loom ever greater. Your pioneering efforts then help us meet today's challenges. My friend, I thank you." (Signed) Dr. Bob Laubach.

Beginning about 1924, correspondence between Dr. Laubach and Dr. O. S. Kriebel led the Mission Board and church organizations to support Matias Cuadra. Cuadra's father and mother were both Moros living on the small island of Siasi, southwest of Mindanao. His mother was quite religious and had hopes her son would dedicate his life to work as a Mohammedan priest. In 1904, without the knowledge of his parents, he was taken by a Jesuit priest to Borneo. Three years later he was baptized as a Roman Catholic and became a sacristan or helper in the performance of the mass. For eight years he lived with the priest, but with World War I looming, the priest left for Germany. Returning to the Philippines, he was befriended by Rev. and Mrs. D. S. Lund, missionaries with whom he lived for three years. They arranged his enrolment at the seminary in Manila, where Dr. Laubach supervised his studies and financial support from the Schwenkfelder Mission Board assisted him in completing his seminary course. On Rev. Heebner's return trip after visiting Taiku in 1926, he and Flora visited the Laubachs in Manila, met Mr. Cuadra, and reported in a letter home, "He told us about his struggles for an education, of the great need for evangelists in his native Mindanao, the largest island of the group, the home of the war-like and America-loving Moros (Mohammedans). He is aching to go back to them when he finishes his studies. He has already been instrumental in starting two churches down there. I am so glad that our Mission Board is helping this young man, who embodies true prophetic zeal and spirit." Upon graduation he became the first Moro to be ordained into the Christian ministry. He shortly married a Filipino girl, and together they went down to Siasi to proclaim the gospel of Christ in the midst of Islam.

During the early 1930s the Mission Board provided assistance for Mr. Cuadra to come to America for study at the Berkley Theological Seminary, Columbia University, and Union Seminary, and then paid his fare to return to the Philippines by way of Jerusalem. He then assumed the responsibilities of executive secretary of the Philippine Committee of Christian Education. "I spend only a week in the office to answer letters and perform other details of office work. Most of my time is spent in a series of evangelistic services and conferences, in the different provinces."

When World War II broke out, Rev. Cuadra was a chaplain in the Philippine Army. When America declared war, he was inducted into the U.S. Army, fought side by side with American soldiers at Corregidor and suffered the "Death March" to the concentration camp, where he was appointed chaplain of the camp. Following the war he became bishop of the Evangelical Church in the Philippines and head of the Balintawak Conference of Greater Manila, engaged in rebuilding and restaffing the churches destroyed during the war. In 1957 Bishop Cuadra and his daughter were guests of Jack and Jean Rothenberger, and the bishop preached in the Lansdale church. For years thereafter the Lansdale church sent their used Sunday school materials to him for use in the Philippines.

Dr. J. Maurice Hohlfeld

After receiving his Th.M. degree from Princeton Theological Seminary in 1942, and wishing to pursue his growing interest in language pedagogy and linguistics, Rev. Hohlfeld made inquiries at the University of Pennsylvania. He was introduced to the Army Specialized Training Program, where he served as an instructor, teaching army personnel to learn Arabic using the new science of "linguistics." This led to research in teaching Spanish and German in the department of modern languages at Ursinus College during 1945-1948, using two experimental groups learning Spanish—one in the traditional method, the other using linguistic science. He earned his Ph.D. from the University of Pennsylvania, submitting as his doctoral dissertation, "An Experiment Employing Two Methods of Teaching Spanish to College Freshmen."

Maurice had first met Dr. Frank Laubach at a Student Volunteer Movement convention in 1935, and had continued correspondence with him during the interim. In 1945 Maurice became a consultant for the Committee on World Literacy and Christian Literature of the National Council of Churches of Christ in the U.S.A., commonly referred to as the "Laubach Committee," and two years later assisted Dr. Laubach in the preparation of his "Adult Literacy Education As A Means Of Social Reconstruction" for the UNESCO publication, *Fundamental Education*.

The committee then suggested that Maurice teach a course on literacy education, emphasizing the Laubach "Each One Teach One" method, to missionaries preparing to go into foreign countries. Arrangements were made in cooperation with the Kennedy School of Missions, one of the four schools of the Hartford Seminary Foundation specifically endowed to train prospective missionaries, to offer such a course, with the Laubach Committee and the Schwenkfelder Mission Board supplementing Maurice's salary as a part-time lecturer at the seminary. In the fall of 1949 Dr. Hohlfeld was appointed associate professor of linguistics in the Kennedy School, teaching languages to missionaries in training. Dr. Hohlfeld and his wife, the former Emma Schlegel, a co-worker in the Lansdale church, whom he had married in 1946 and who would join him in his world literacy teaching travels, thereupon made their home in Hartford, Conn. In 1957 Dr. Hohlfeld was appointed professor of linguistics in the Kennedy School, a post which he held until the end of his life. He also served as acting dean of the school during 1952-1953 and as academic dean of the Hartford Seminary Foundation from 1963 to 1966.

In January of 1950 the Hohlfelds joined Frank Laubach, Robert Laubach, and several others on a four-month tour of Africa, consulting with missionaries, preparing reading primers in local languages, and generally promoting literacy programs in the countries they visited. After Dr. Laubach and his son left for Mozambique, the Hohlfelds revisited stations which Dr. Laubach had visited on an earlier tour to observe the progress there and to rekindle enthusiasm, which often slowed down once the motivating spirit of Dr. Laubach's presence was removed. Then in 1954 and 1955 the Hohlfelds made two visits to Iran, one an extended stay of six months in Teheran, during which Dr. Hohlfeld helped to prepare second-stage literature for villagers to give them material on health care, infant care, farming, etc. He wrote a teaching manual, *Teaching Adults To Read*, translated into Farsi (Persian) by Mohammed Ali Khorouzan, and co-authored a book, *Writing Simply In Farsi*, with Shamsi Mossaheb, published in English and Farsi. There followed assignments for the Laubach Committee in Central America, and in 1958 a visit to Mysore, India, as a visiting senior linguist under the auspices of the Rockefeller Foundation. He held summer lectureships in various church-sponsored retreats and gave courses in linguistics and literacy education, preparing missionaries for their assignments in various parts of the world. In 1971, after a tour of the churches and missions in North and South Dakota sponsored by the Stewardship Council of the United Church of Christ, he became concerned about the education and welfare of the American Indians.

Throughout this time Dr. Hohlfeld wrote frequent articles and reports for the *Schwenkfeldian* and spoke at numerous Schwenkfelder conventions. He preached the funeral sermons for both Rev. Heebner and Rev. Hoffman. In 1964 he received the Distinguished Alumni Award of Temple University and in 1970 a distinguished service award from the Schwenkfelder Mission Board. Rev. Hohlfeld died in Hartford, Conn., on March 7, 1973, and was buried March 10 in a lot reserved for Schwenkfelder ministers in The Garden of Memories at the Central Schwenkfelder Church. Mrs. Hohlfeld continued to reside in Hartford, where she was employed with the Connecticut Conference of the United Church of Christ, until 1979, when she returned to Trappe, Pa., and took a position in the Collegeville office of the Pennsylvania Southeast Conference of the church.

Am I My Brother's Keeper?

While not strictly a "mission" project in the usual sense, the response of the Schwenkfelder congregations to the appeal for help from Silesian refugees expelled from their devastated homeland and transported to western Germany to fend for themselves in the already-disorganized economy there following the end of World War II proved a dramatic expression of Christian love and charity.

The 1934 Pilgrimage group received a warm welcome in Harpersdorf, the heart of the Schwenkfelder Silesian homeland. A good portion of the population of Harpersdorf and surrounding villages gathered in front of the local hotel; their band played, and their choir, under the direction of Kantor Knörrlich, sang, and village and church officials, led by Pastor Nierlich, exchanged formal greetings with the leaders of the tour group. While the band played appropriate music, the entire group joined in the procession to the Viehweg monument and in the ceremonies there. Names of Meschter, Anders, and Schultz confirmed the family relationships of the two groups—one descended from families who emigrated in the 1720s, and many of the others from families who stayed behind.

The last days of World War II ushered in a disastrous period of misery and suffering for the residents of the entire Harpersdorf area. During the cold days of January 1945 German refugees from the east sought temporary refuge in their flight from the advancing Russian armies, overwhelming town lodging facilities. By early February, as the battle line moved into the villages, the residents were ordered by the German army to evacuate, and they joined the trek westward. Russian Siberian regiments, a "drunken, howling, and plundering rabble," created scenes of unbelievable chaos, convincing the Harpersdorf refugees to seek to return home by a circuitous route. Harpersdorf had been right in the middle of the battle line. Homes and the church were destroyed, cattle driven off, and everything movable plundered. Insides of houses were left in the wildest disorder. Without matches, convex lenses and decayed willow-wood had to be used to start fires. Throughout the spring and summer the people struggled to bring some order out of chaos, to bring in the harvest, and to gather wood for the winter. With water supplies polluted, typhus ran rampant. Women and girls suffered severely at the hands of the debauched Russian soldiers occupying the village.

Then at the end of July Polish militia ordered the second evacuation of the village and the refugee trek began again. The Polish militia, however, lacked authority for this act, and when their guards drifted off, the people returned to their devastated villages for a second time. This time the work was organized according to the Russian pattern of forced labor and collectivized farming, with its trying inefficiencies. During the winter an increasing flow of Polish peasants moved into the area, confiscating houses, plundering any remaining belongings, and designating a list of men and women as hostages who would be hanged if harm came to any Pole. Imprisonment with or without reason became common. The Polinization of the area was carried on with great zeal. German road signs were replaced with Polish, German books were confiscated, letters in German refused delivery, and German teachers replaced by Polish teachers in the schools, where lessons in German were outlawed. German church services were repeatedly disrupted.

By July of 1946 the first order of expulsion was received and the Harpersdorf refugees moved to a concentration camp in Haynau, where they were loaded into freight cars of a transport train bearing them slowly westward out of the Russian zone. One large group of refugees, including the chorister, Siegfried Knörrlich, found themselves in the village of Gummersbach, in the English zone of occupation, without belongings, without housing, without means of earning a livelihood, and with only the most modest hope of assistance from the people there, who were already suffering the depression of the broken German economy.

In trying to maintain order in his Harpersdorf study, Mr. Knörrlich had come across an issue of the *Schwenkfeldian*, and on some premonition cut out the name and address of Mr. Wayne C. Meschter, then moderator of the Schwenkfelder church. In August of 1946, after arrival in Gummersbach, Mr. Knörrlich addressed a letter to Mr. Meschter describing their trials and their condition. Upon receipt of this letter Mr. Meschter investigated possibilities of communications, and found that postal authorities were accepting only packages of less than eleven pounds, with delivery uncertain. Some twenty-five well-organized relief organizations in the United States had joined to form a non-profit organization, CARE, Cooperative for American Remittances to Europe, Inc. The War Assets Administration turned over surplus food and the U.S. Department of Agriculture, the Department of State, and the Army worked out arrangements with the governments of Europe to protect and provide for delivery of food relief packages. With the food already in Europe, and much of it already made up into packages, 25,000,000 pounds of food were placed in the hands of war victims by Christmas of 1946. Regulations stipulated one 30 lb. package per person per week. The price in the United States was fixed at $10.00 per package.

Mr. Meschter immediately forwarded six packages and a letter to Mr. Knörrlich requesting more detailed information. Through the CARE office in New York he forwarded a telegraphic request for a list of fifty names. On January 13, 1947 one-hundred CARE packages were ordered, two for each of the fifty families listed. Then at Mr. Meschter's suggestion, Mr. Knörrlich agreed to supervise distribution of all packages among the refugees, supplying the most needy first. The list of fifty names and addresses was also circulated to the several churches so that clothing packages, now permitted at the rate of one package per address per week, could be forwarded.

By the beginning of 1947, encouraged by Mr. Knörrlich's acknowledging receipt of numbered packages, the relief work went into high gear. The moderator appointed a committee of Royal Dresher, Lansdale; Frederick Hevener, Pennsburg; Mrs. Wilbur Kriebel, Chester; and Curtis Weigner, of Lansdale, representing the several churches. Funds were received from many sources to support the work. A second hundred food packages were forwarded in February and fifty-six blanket packages in March, eliciting a most heart-warming letter from Mr. Knörrlich. Individual correspondence also lent support to the effort. On May 17, 1947 the Schwenkfelder General Conference formally confirmed the arrangements for forwarding and distributing relief packages. By summer the refugees were gathering together in meetings and gradually communicating with refugees relocated in other parts of Germany. CARE packages were forwarded to such otherwise isolated individuals where possible.

By 1948 some 2,000 CARE packages and another 1,000 parcel post packages had been forwarded. Many questions were raised. Who are we helping? Why are we helping them instead of millions of other people in need? What are the future prospects of those being helped? On August 10, 1948, when air travel became possible, Mr. Meschter, accompanied by his son Spencer, set out on a month-long visit to see for himself the situation among the refugees. By way of Frankfurt and Cologne, where they walked the streets shocked at the destruction and destitution around them, they made their way to Gummersbach, about forty miles from Cologne. Here they found that Mr. Knörrlich had arranged five group meetings of the refugees, in Gummersbach,

Bakum, Uepsen (Asendorf), Hildesheim (Göttingen), and Erndte-brück. The groups that congregated numbered from 85 to 154, permitting the visitors to meet with some 600 of the refugees. For two weeks they lived with these groups, ate with them, and talked with them individually, in small groups, and in large formal meetings. They heard over and over again recitals of their experiences of the last three years, and observed first-hand the desperate conditions under which they continued to live. The change of currency, a good harvest, and Marshall Plan aid had noticeably improved conditions, but housing remained primitive, many families living in converted chicken coops and other converted outbuildings. Over and over again the visitors were thanked for the CARE packages, without which many of the refugees could hardly have survived the first winter months of their exile. The most frequent question encountered was, "Will the Americans stay in Berlin?" Their greatest fear was renewed war with the Russians. Should the Russians press farther west, where would the refugees go next?

At each meeting, frequently attended by local church and town officials, formal expressions of thanks were tendered, "with the assurance that you and the Schwenkfelder Churches in Pennsylvania, through this large scale relief work, have established for yourselves in our hearts an abiding monument of veneration and Christian love of neighbor; and, in the name of all who cannot be present, I grasp your hand with the sincere prayer: May the mercy of God be daily new over you, your house, your family, and over the entire Schwenkfelder congregation which has found a new home in the new world and yet has not forgotten the misery of the old Silesian homeland. God grant it!"

The steady stream of CARE and individual packages continued into 1949, when pressures began to ease. "The Moderator's report to the General Conference of The Schwenkfelder Church, April 24, 1950, shows an aggregate of $28,914.08 contributed and disbursed for Silesian-German Relief, 1946-50. No accurate record was kept of the number of clothing packages shipped. The estimated number is approximately 1200-1500. The Relief-Work included in its scope also several friends of the *Corpus* editorial staff, and members of the Harpersdorf Von Lucke family."

Correspondence over this period, principally concentrated between Mr. Meschter and Mr. Knörrlich, included 530 German letters from Mr. Knörrlich, most of them translated by Mrs. Selina Schultz, and 790 comprising Mr. Meschter's replies, his correspondence with the CARE office in New York, and with pastors, members of the relief committee, and contributors among the Schwenkfelder congregations. Some 1,850 items of this correspondence have been preserved in the Schwenkfelder Library. Excerpts from the correspondence and from Mr. Meschter's report of his trip have been published by the Board of Publication as Vol. II, No. 2, of *Schwenckfeldiana*, under the title, "A Challenge: Am I My Brother's Keeper." The descriptions of suffering and despair, and the following expressions of heartfelt thanks, offer a moving testimony of "Man's Inhumanity to Man," and "The Dismantlement of Despair." In the words of Mr. Knörrlich, " . . . the entire Schwenkfelder relief-activity of the last three years has become an imperishable golden page in the annals of the Schwenkfelder Church in Pennsylvania—in the hearts of the Harpersdorf congregation the faithful Schwenkfelders have erected a second monument bearing the words of Christ: Inasmuch as ye have done it unto one of the least of these my brethren, ye have done it unto me."

In the spirit of a fitting memorial, in 1963 Mr. Siegfried Knörrlich prepared and had published in Germany, *Die Zufluchtskirche zu Harpersdorf in Schlesien,* a reminiscence of the Harpersdorf church and a short history of the experiences of its congregation during World War II. In 1979 this work was translated by Sherman L. Gerhard and published by the Society of Descendants of the Schwenkfeldian Exiles under the title *The Refuge Church in Harpersdorf.* In 1957 Mr. Knörrlich's son, Wolfgang, prepared and published his doctoral dissertation, "Caspar von Schwenckfeld and the Reformation in Silesia," submitted to the philosophy faculty of the University of Bonn

New Mission Interests

For many years Rev. Harvey K. Heebner had been the key generator of mission interest and support among the Schwenkfelder congregations. The Taiku mission was, of course, close to his heart. As an active Oberlin alumnus, he counted among his personal friends many workers in the mission field as well as many members of the staff of the American Board. As secretary of the Schwenkfelder Mission Board and editor of the *Schwenkfeldian*, he kept up a lively stream of communications between workers in the field and members of the several Schwenkfelder congregations. With his passing in April of 1963 much of the sense of intimacy which he engendered was inevitably lost, and mission initiatives devolved more and more upon the mission committees and boards of the individual churches. Mission activity assumed a more ecumenical and less Schwenkfelder denominational orientation.

With Rev. Heebner's passing, the time and energy of the Mission Board, under the leadership of Rev. Rothenberger as president, and Mr. Donald Hamme as recording secretary, almost immediately became absorbed in the administration of the mission at 30th and Cumberland Streets. Commitments for the support of the Philadelphia church soon doubled the Mission Board budget, continuing through the 1970s and early 1980s to account for roughly half of the board's total disbursements, while the total budget remained flat, fluctuating from $30,000 to $40,000 per year.

During this period the records of the treasurer of the Mission Board reflect contributions for the support of more than eighty-five different mission activities, many, however, reflecting special contributions taken in the churches and forwarded through the board, earmarked for specific projects. The principal home missions supported by the board were Perkiomen School, the migrant mission work sponsored by the Pennsylvania Council of Churches, and work among the Navaho Indians conducted by the Mennonite Church Mission Board.

Annual contributions were made to the Interdenominational Evangelical Theological Seminary of Puerto Rico, jointly supported by a number of U.S. denominations to prepare Spanish-speaking pastors for service in Central and South America and to provide Spanish language literature for their use. In the fall of 1965 Rev. Eric Braund visited the Seminary and came away "filled with enthusiasm and admiration for that strategic, Christian work." The fifty-five students (later 150-200) then enrolled came from Mexico, Cuba, Guatemala, Brazil, Dominican Republic, U.S., and Puerto Rico. Rev. Braund went on: "An ecumenical center for the crossroads of the West Indies! Here are students concerned with the problems of their people: freedom, hope, fulfillment amidst the contrasts of poverty for many, wealth for a few. They have a lively concern to bring the light of the Gospel to the deepest and darkest needs of their people and to do so in cooperation and concert with their brother ministers in Christ of other denominations. The greatness of this school lies uniquely in the fact that it is interdenominational as well as international—and the only graduate seminary in the Caribbean, Spanish speaking area." Dr. and Mrs. Claude Schultz, Jr. of the Palm Church visited the Seminary in early 1971, and caught the same spirit of enthusiasm.

When in 1957 the Congregational churches and the Evangelical and Reformed churches merged to form the United Church of Christ, mission work was consolidated under the United Church Board of World Ministries. Beginning in 1965 foreign mission contributions were channeled through the Southeast Pennsylvania Conference office of the United Church of Christ. The result was even longer channels of communication and the Schwenkfelder Mission Board continually struggled to keep itself and congregation members informed in a timely manner. The proliferation of projects and the relatively small contributions to each, usually providing less than 10 percent of a missionary's support, impeded development of close personal ties and made enthusiasm within the congregations difficult to sustain. While the missionaries supported made it a point to visit the several churches during their furloughs, these visits were, for the most part, too widely separated to maintain a continuity of interest. An effort was made to assign a missionary to each member of the board, with responsibility for maintaining correspondence. A one-week "School of Missions" was considered, when the churches were asked to devote one night to foreign and one night to home missions during the week of the fall conference each year. Special Missionary Sunday programs and dinners were arranged.

Throughout this period an annual contribution of $5,000 was channeled through the United Church board for the support of overseas missions. This was generally divided into four or five shares, forwarded to missionaries recommended by the United Church board. These included, at different times, Rev. Anna Dederer, Rev. Robert Simon, and Rev. and Mrs. Walter Snowa, Jr. in the islands of the South Pacific; Rev. Wills, Rev. Thomas Puroff, Mr. and Mrs. Mullholland, and Dr. Joyce Baker, in Honduras; Miss Louise Torrence, Mrs. Emery Rudolph, and Rev. and Mrs. John Parsons, in Rhodesia, South Africa; and Dr. Raj and Maybelle Arole, medical doctors who in 1974 opened an outpatient clinic in the rural area of Maharashtra State, in India, which was soon flooded with patients. Support for Mabel Reiff during her term of service in Japan was also forwarded through these channels.

Miss Anna Dederer had grown up and been educated in Germany, attending a school for missions and spending two years in nurses' training. She went out to Micronesia in 1934, serving on four different islands, learning four separate languages. The war cut off support from the German churches, and when the Japanese invaded the islands she and other missionaries were taken prisoner, surviving only on food smuggled in to them by faithful natives. After the war she found her way to Honolulu, where she was befriended by Dr.

Charles Hoskinson, minister of a Congregational church there. Here she was ordained as a Congregational minister, and returned to the islands where she served until retirement in 1970. Through visits to the Palm church, she made a number of close friends, who kept in touch with her during her service in the islands and her years of retirement.

Dr. Joyce Baker, also one of the missionaries better known to the Schwenkfelder congregations, works as a medical doctor in Pinalejo, Honduras. Her ministry is in a mobile clinical program bringing health care and preventive medicine to remote villages in Honduras. One of the handicaps of her ministry was the handling of water. Each night they had to fill buckets and basins with water for use in the clinic and house for the following day. In a letter dated September 1978, she wrote, "A major blessing was the installation of a water system including a two thousand gallon underground tank and two small elevated tanks which enable us to have water both night and day." The word "day" was underlined. Dr. Baker is also involved in training of others such as the midwives program and the training of village health workers. These health workers were called "guardians of health."

Of recent missionaries, perhaps the best known to Schwenkfelder congregations is Miss Joan Hunsberger. An immigrant descendant through her paternal grandmother, Ida Mae Kriebel Hunsberger, at the age of 13 she was baptized by Rev. Hohlfeld and became a member of the Lansdale church. A few years later she accepted Jesus Christ and found new life in Him through the ministry of Jack Wyrtzen of Word of Life. She was active in the Lansdale church as Sunday school teacher, leader of Junior Christian Endeavor, and a young people's officer. She attended Christian Endeavor retreats and camps, which greatly influenced her life. After concern for her father's health prompted the family to move to Florida, she continued her interest in Christian service, and in June of 1956 graduated from the Miami Bible Institute, today Miami Christian College. At a youth retreat in Boca Raton, Florida, she was challenged through a pastor who had visited Brazil with the need and ready response of the Brazilian people to the gospel. She felt the Lord was leading her to work there. Supporting herself through part-time work, she continued her education at Trinity Seminary and Bible College, the Evangelical Free Church school in Chicago. Here she came into contact with the Unevangelized Fields Mission, an interdenominational faith mission with over 500 missionaries throughout the world, whose headquarters are located in Bala-Cynwyd, Pennsylvania. Following graduation, she was accepted as a candidate and with the support of some faithful friends she was able to sail from New York harbor for Brazil on March 18, 1959.

After eight months of intensive Portuguese language study in Belem at the mouth of the Amazon River, she traveled to the city of Sao Luis, along the Atlantic coast, where she has lived ever since. Her first ministry was teaching Christian education and Bible-related subjects in the Northern Christian Evangelical Seminary. There she also organized the library, served as treasurer, took students to Christian work assignments, and helped to organize a new church in the suburb of Saint Anthony. She has been active in the national church organization with sixty-three churches across the north of Brazil, serving as treasurer of the administrative board, and in the women's work, serving several times as president of the organization. She has been director of the women's quarterly magazine called *Ebenezer.*

During the 1970s she was instrumental in organizing the Jet Cadets for young people aged 11 to 15. The name and original materials came from Success with Youth in Tempe, Arizona. These have been translated and adapted and new ideas have been added to the program. When the work was ten years old in 1982, fifty-five groups had been organized, reaching about 1200 young people in their teens. Miss Hunsberger prepared many of the materials and journeyed to the churches to teach the leadership courses and encourage the young people.

Besides the annual Mission Board contribution towards her support, individual churches and church organizations have also come to her assistance, making it possible for her to purchase a Volkswagen in 1968 and more recently, as the Volkswagen gave out, a new car. They helped her purchase her Sao Luis home in 1974 and a home and office in Belem, to serve as headquarters for the work there.

The establishment of the Jet Cadets goes well beyond the youth of the land of Brazil. Many of the pastors that presently serve the native churches in Brazil have come from the Jet Cadets where they found the Lord Jesus Christ and were convicted to serve Him with their lives. Besides frequent speaking visits to the Schwenkfelder churches, interest in Joan's work has been sustained by a visit with Joan in Brazil by Mrs. Ruth Weber and Gail Carlen, members of the Lansdale congregation, in October, 1975 and through a visit by Rev. Bond in 1976.

In an effort to bring into focus overall missionary activity within the Schwenkfelder denomination, the Mission Board in 1978 made a survey of giving for missions in the several churches, and the results were published in the *Schwenkfeldian* of April 1979. The results reported may be summarized as follows:

	To Conference Board	Other	Total
Norristown	$ 5,100	$ 3,250	$ 8,350
Lansdale	4,015	4,731	8,746
Palm	8,216	5,179	13,395
Central	16,229	42,060*	58,289
Total	$33,560	$55,220	$88,780

*Includes $7,000 subsidy for pastor's salary, paid directly to the Philadelphia church.

Of the Conference Mission Board budget, about one-half was directed to the Philadelphia church and $7,000 to other home missions, leaving $8,800 for foreign missions. This included $5,000 to the United Church Board of World Ministries, $1,250 to the Puerto Rico seminary, and $2,550 to Miss Hunsberger in Brazil. Thus home missions, including the Philadelphia church, accounted for about two-thirds of overall mission giving, with the remaining one-third devoted to foreign missions. While the level of giving increased, the general pattern set forth here continued into the early 1980s.

There seems no end to human need, and in the shrunken "one world" of the 1980s it seems more visible and more pressing, both at home and abroad. Throughout the world, hospitals, schools, and churches, many staffed by local workers trained and inspired by missionaries, seek to alleviate suffering and uplift spirits. The missionary tradition may also be seen at work in the mammoth health, education, and relief projects of governments and United Nations organizations, which often build upon field-work pioneered by Christian missionaries. Missionary support is firmly embedded in the Schwenkfelder tradition. The Schwenkfelder congregations continue to reach out in Christian fellowship to those less fortunate and to spread abroad the good news of the Gospel Message.

Chapter Seven

The First Schwenkfelder Church of Philadelphia

The First Schwenkfelder Church of Philadelphia and the Schwenkfelder Mission Board evolved from the same initiative by Mr. William Y. Meschter and Dr. James Meschter Anders. Both had been reared on Schwenkfelder farmsteads, Mr. Meschter on that of his father, Rev. Jacob Meschter at Palm, Pa., and Dr. Anders on the family farm at Fairview Village. First cousins, both had been raised to respect and revere their Schwenkfelder heritage.

In 1883 Mr. Meschter moved to Philadelphia to become bookkeeper, and later treasurer, director, and part owner of the American Preserve Co. Dr. Anders graduated from the University of Pennsylvania in 1877, having "read medicine" with his more distant cousin, Dr. George K. Meschter, well-known Worcester physician, and in the same year was awarded his Ph.D. by the university and a prize for his original dissertation on "The Transpiration of Plants." Shortly thereafter he embarked upon his long and distinguished career as medical practitioner, author, administrator, and for many years as professor of medicine and clinical medicine in the Graduate School of Medicine, University of Pennsylvania.

By the year 1894 both men, then aged 42 and 40, were well established in Philadelphia, and both were active members of the Oxford Presbyterian Church. They missed, however, their home churches, a church association with like-minded relatives and friends, and the spirit and traditions in which they had been steeped by their deeply religious parents. In one of Dr. Anders' favorite phrases, "The religion of my mother is good enough for me." They shared a desire for a Schwenkfelder place of worship in Philadelphia and laid the matter before Dr. O. S. Kriebel, who in turn presented it to General Conference with the result as we have seen, that the Schwenkfelder Mission Board was organized and chartered. A mission in Philadelphia became the first priority of this board.

This mission first took the form of a Sunday school. At the Mission Board organization meeting at Dr. Anders' home, 1603 Walnut St., on June 14, 1895, Dr. George K. Meschter was elected president, Elmer E. S. Johnson secretary, and Dr. Anders treasurer. The Board commissioned its treasurer a committee of one to procure a meeting place in Philadelphia for a mission school under the auspices of the board. By fall Dr. Anders had arranged rental at $5.00 per Sabbath of a hall on Huber St. (between 19th and 20th Streets) above Susquehanna Ave., and the Sunday school duly opened with Elmer K. Schultz as superintendent, Charles K. Meschter as assistant superintendent, Samuel H. Schultz as secretary and Mrs. Joseph B. Bechtel as organist. By the following spring, however, the hall had been found unsatisfactory and the school was temporarily closed. It reopened December 1, 1896 in Thomas Hall, 31st St. and Ridge Ave., this time with Elmer E. S. Johnson, a student at Princeton University, as superintendent. Here the school flourished, and monthly preaching services, conducted by Dr. O. S. Kriebel and other guest preachers, were soon inaugurated.

During the summer of 1896, building operations were being vigorously extended in the northwestern section of Philadelphia, westward from 20th St. and northward from York St. toward Lehigh Ave. In this attractive field the Mission Board decided to seek an appropriate location for the new church now envisioned. At the April 17, 1897 meeting of the board Dr. Anders moved that the purchase of a lot at the corner of 30th and Cumberland Sreets be investigated, and by the October meeting the purchase was authorized. It was the sense of the meeting that the required funds should be solicited from members of the entire denomination. At the Mission Board meeting January 21, 1898 Dr. Anders reported that $4,032 had been collected toward the $4,400 purchase price, and by the April meeting, that the lot had been purchased and paid for.

In May of 1898 the board appointed Elmer E. S. Johnson and Allen A. Seipt to make a canvas of those persons willing to support a church on the 30th and Cumberland lot. They secured signed pledges of support from seventeen individuals. The spring General Conference empowered the Mission Board to build a chapel on the site, to mortgage the property, and to organize a church. The board contracted with Mr. Burd P. Evans to erect the building at a cost of

$3,945. The new chapel was duly dedicated on the last Sunday in October 1898.

On November 19, 1898 the seventeen charter members formally organized The First Schwenkfeldian (sic) Church of Philadelphia, electing Dr. James M. Anders, moderator; Samuel A. Seipt, secretary; W. Y. Meschter, C. G. Schultz, and E. K. Schultz, deacons; George K. Heebner and Allen A. Seipt, Trustees; and Frank M. Underkuffler, treasurer. George K. Brecht, Esq., shortly had recorded a deed transferring the property from the Mission Board to the Philadelphia church trustees. At the building dedication Rev. William S. Anders, who presided, called upon Dr. Anders to report on the financial situation and to make a plea for contributions to discharge the $1,000 deficit, whereupon the deficit was duly subscribed by those present. The mission continued under the jurisdiction of the Mission Board until May 1899 when, having been organized and become self-supporting, the First Schwenkfeldian Church of Philadelphia was formally received as a member of the General Conference of the Schwenkfelder Church, marking the beginning of the expansion of the church beyond the boundaries of the original settlement communities. The new "Lower District" transformed the previous "Lower District" into the present "Middle District," now with its "Central Church."

During the early years various pastoral supplies, ordained and lay, from both Schwenkfelder and outside churches, conducted the preaching services. Rev. A. N. Stubblebine, of the Reformed Church, then a senior student in the Ursinus School of Theology, served from May 1899 to October 1900. From March 1901 to August 1902 Rev. H. A. Bomberger of the Reformed Church served as acting pastor. In September 1902 Elmer Johnson, having graduated from Hartford Theological Seminary, was installed as pastor and the next year Flora Heebner came to Philadelphia to work as home missionary. By this time the open fields originally surrounding the 30th and Cumberland lot had been largely built up and the church found itself firmly established in the midst of a thriving new community.

The Sunday school, which had initiated the "Mission," continued a principal source of strength, drawing in children of new families moving into the community and through them attracting their parents to the church. While the church edifice was under construction during the summer of 1898, Sunday school services were moved from Thomas Hall to a tent set up on the unused portion of the lot at 30th and Cumberland with Allen A. Seipt as superintendent. He was a graduate of West Chester State Normal School and was studying at the University of Pennsylvania, from which he graduated in 1900. During 1901 he devoted himself "voluntarily and exclusively" to the interests of the "Mission" in Philadelphia, and then entered the Graduate School of the University of Pennsylvania to earn a Master's degree. In 1906 he earned a Ph.D. with a dissertation entitled: "The First Printed Hymnbook of the Schwenkfelders and its Sources." In December of 1906 he received an offer of an instructorship in German at Ohio Wesleyan University, Delaware, Ohio, taking up his new duties with the winter term beginning in January 1907. He retained his interest in the publication of the *Schwenkfeldian* and returned to the Sunday school on holidays and during vacations. However, it was no longer possible for him to continue his active leadership role in the Sunday school. He later served briefly as assistant editor for Vol. II of the *Corpus*.

Rev. Johnson and Allen Seipt were responsible for one initiative destined to have long-term influence upon the entire Schwenkfelder denomination. A church historian by education, Dr. Johnson felt the need for a congregational periodical to chronicle events and bind the several congregations more closely together. In December of 1903 he brought out Volume I, Number 1 of the *Schwenkfeldian*, the masthead of which proclaimed, "Published every month in the interest of the First Schwenkfeldian [sic] Church, Thirtieth and Cumberland Streets." The editorial staff was listed as Rev. E. E. S. Johnson, editor; Allen A. Seipt, associate editor; C. M. Gilbert, Jr., business manager; and Alex. S. Day, circulation manager. "Subscriptions, 25 cents a year in advance. 35 cents a year by mail." Its second news paragraph duly noted: "All services in this church are conducted in the English Language." The third issue proclaimed a circulation of 1,000. By the July issue of 1904, with Rev. Johnson's departure for Germany, Dr. Samuel K. Brecht, then a member of the new Norristown congregation, took over as acting editor. By the September issue the masthead announcement was amended to include "in the interest of the Schwenkfelder Churches." From the beginning the paper had included news reported from the other districts, and the spring General Conference of 1905 adopted the paper as the official church publication. The July 1905 issue announced its publication under the auspices of the Board of Publication.

In June of 1904 Rev. Johnson left for Wolfenbüttel to assist Dr. Hartranft in editing the *Corpus* and Flora Heebner left for China. Once more the church was obliged to seek new pastoral leadership. In August Rev. Harvey K. Heebner, then a student at Union Theological Seminary in New York City, was appointed stated supply, but the following year he asked to be relieved to complete his studies. Rev. David W. Ebbert, D.D., of the Reformed Church, president of Ursinus College, served as acting pastor during the spring of 1906. In June of that year Rev. Heebner graduated from Union Theological Seminary and was called as pastor. After some hesitation, occasioned by an inner prompting that perhaps he should join his sister, Flora, in the Taiku Mission, he was prevailed upon to serve here at home, accepting the call to the Philadelphia church. He was formally installed Sunday evening, September 23, 1906, beginning a lifetime of service to his church, denomination, community, and the church at large, terminated only by his death fifty-seven years later on April 8, 1963.

The seventeen charter members proved a loyal and durable band. Dr. Anders continued as moderator of the church until his death in 1936, Samuel A. Seipt as secretary until his death in 1939, and George K. Heebner as trustee until his death, also in 1939. These three averaged forty years of service to the church. On Saturday, September 1, 1902 the young Wayne Meschter arrived in Philadelphia. On the following day his uncle, William Y. Meschter, brought him to 30th and Cumberland, where he immediately became a regular attender and shortly an active worker. In 1915 Dr. Samuel K. Brecht moved his residence from Norristown to Manoa and transferred his church membership to the Philadelphia church. The regular Sunday morning services drew these men together. Their collective efforts provided strong lay support for the activities of the local church and for the interests of the Schwenkfelder denomination.

On the day following Rev. Heebner's formal installation the September 24 annual Memorial Day services were held for the first time in the Philadelphia church. The proceedings were duly reported for the *Schwenkfeldian* by Rev. Heebner, thus initiating him as a literary contributor to the church paper. In January of 1907 Rev. Heebner was appointed an assistant editor along with Allen A. Seipt and Samuel A. Anders. Years later, when Dr. Brecht undertook editorship of the *Genealogical Record*, Rev. Heebner took the title of "Acting Editor." Although he performed the duties, it was not until 1935 that he was prevailed upon to print his own title as "Editor."

By the first year of Rev. Heebner's pastorate the Sunday shool reported an enrolment of 134 adults and 88 children, with an average attendance of 74 adults and 41 children. On Sunday, October 2, 1906 the Sunday school celebrated Rally Day and the eleventh anniversary of the school, with record attendance of 160. By comparison the church reported a membership of 76 and an average attendance of 60, once again evidencing the strong supporting role of the Sunday school.

Sunday worship services were regularly scheduled for 10:45 a.m. and 7:45 p.m., Sunday school at 2:30, and prayer meetings Wednesday evenings. During summer months the Sunday school services were moved up to 10:00 a.m., while the evening services, weather permitting, were held on the church lawn, where the gospel was "proclaimed in sermon and song," open to the notice of neighbors and passers-by. Communion services were held the first Sundays of January, April, July, and October. The Ladies' Aid Society met the last Monday evening of each month and conducted socials, rummage sales, block parties and similar affairs to raise money to supply food baskets to the needy, to pay off the balance due on the primary department piano, and for many other small but useful services. A church library was started. On January 9, 1904 the young people met at the home of Rev. Johnson to organize the Young People's Society of Christian Endeavor, with James E. Hoffman as president. The Home Department, organized by Flora Heebner, had a membership of 30 when she left and the responsibilities of superintendent were assumed by Miss Carlotta Schultz.

On September 12, 1907 Samuel A. Anders, professor of German at Temple College and an associate editor of the *Schwenkfeldian*, was installed as superintendent of the Sunday school. Professor Anders served as Sunday school superintendent until 1915, when Mr. Wayne C. Meschter began his lifetime tenure of forty-eight years. On September 17, 1908 the men's "Brotherhood of Andrew and Phillip" began meeting at 10:00 a.m. on Sunday mornings before church, for prayer and an inspirational message. They also organized Sunday morning prayer breakfasts, attracting inspirational speakers from around the city, and participated with other like-minded church groups in city-wide activities.

As reported in the *Schwenkfeldian*, the year 1910 seems to have been an active one, ushered in by a blizzard the Sunday morning before New Year's Day which prevented all but seven hearty souls—some of them living almost next door—from getting to the church. By February, "The Sunday School has had an increase in interest and attendance since the blizzard. On Sunday, January 23rd the highest attendance in the school's history was recorded, 207. All shoulders to the wheel!" Miss Louise Livesey organized a Junior Christian Endeavor Society for young people between the ages of 7 and 16 years. "The pastor has a 'phone installed in his residence. The call number is Diamond 2223D."

In April the men of the church formed an "Ushers' League, to aid the pastor and the church, to increase the sociability of the men, to welcome strangers and to make the congregation comfortable in the house of prayer." "An exceptionally good entertainment was given by the primary scholars on Tuesday evening, April 19, under the direction of Mrs. Alex Day and her assistants, Carlotta Schultz and Mrs. Nellie Brown. . . . The receipts were over twenty dollars, to be used for improvements in the primary department." In June the annual Sunday school picnic was held at Strawberry Mansion, nearby in Fairmount Park, and "everyone had a good time. The rain and hail storm sent the whole party scamping for shelter under the music pavilion just after supper was hastily finished." "Members of our congregation welcomed home very heartily Mr. and Mrs. Allen A. Seipt, who worshiped with us July 31, after an absence of one year in Germany, where, with Rev. and Mrs. Elmer E. Johnson they have been assisting Dr. Chester D. Hartranft in the publication of the works of Schwenckfeld. They are enthusiastic about the fatherland." In September Dr. Seipt began his work as instructor of German in the University of Kansas at Lawrence.

In June, "Our Sunday School has organized a baseball team that is now numbered with the North West Church Base Ball League. There are eight teams and the schedule of games extends into September. The boys are playing well and should be encouraged, for it is theirs to show that athletics can be played clean and fair. The moral rules for the games are stringent. Methodists, Baptists, Reformed, and Presbyterian are the other denominations represented. One game won out of four is the record for our team thus far. As the team gains practice we may expect more victories."

"The Harvest Home services held in the church on October 9th, proved to be a source of joy and thanksgiving. Members and friends of the church brought fruits, vegetables, flour, flowers, etc., which were banked into a pyramid before the pulpit. Field corn and forest leaves decorated the walls, making the church auditorium appear very beautiful. The next day, under supervision of the Ladies Aid Society, the generous supply of donations was divided into portions and distributed amongst the needy."

"November 20th was Missionary Sunday. Miss Flora Heebner, home on furlough, addressed large audiences at the morning and evening services. A feature of the morning service was her presentation of a silk banner from the native church in Shansi, upon which was written in Chinese characters a salutation to us the "Old" church in return for the communion service sent them three years ago."

Early in 1911: "New Gas lamps of greater power have replaced the former ones in use in the church and annex. The improvement is marked. Thanks are due to Mr. William Mevins and Mr. Clark, who donated the labor." A Boy Scout Club was organized under the leadership of Mr. William Anders, Jr., with Dr. Andrew Anders giving a course on first aid to the injured. "The men of the church registered their earnest protests against the application for a saloon at the corner of Stanley and Cumberland Sts, only a half square away from our church." In addition to the primary and junior picnic at Strawberry Mansion, the teachers, officers and senior departments of the Sunday School initiated their annual picnics at Belmont Mansion, the regular feature thereafter being a baseball game between the married men and the single men, with Rev. Heebner in the unenviable position of umpire.

During the summer of 1912 Sunday shool superintendent Samuel A. Anders and *Schwenkfeldian* editor Professor Samuel K. Brecht toured western Europe, Professor Anders to visit European universities and Professor Brecht to make a special study of places renowned in Schwenkfelder history. Dr. Brecht visited the *Corpus* staff in Wolfenbüttel and in company with Dr. Johnson toured the Schwenkfelder homelands around Harpersdorf, visiting the old Schwenckfeld Schloss in Ossig, whose then resident, Major von Lücke, sent his carriage to meet the travelers as they arrived by train at Lüben, two miles away.

In the early summer of 1914 Rev. Heebner was granted a 2-1/2-month leave of absence for an extended trip to the Holy Land. He sailed April 25 on the North German-Lloyd steamer "Berlin" bound for the Azores, Gibraltar, Algiers, and Naples, with a visit to Pompeii. "Vesuvius is smoking, but otherwise behaving himself very well." Then on to Egypt and Palestine, circling the walls of Jerusalem on a donkey and spending a week visiting the sacred places, assisted by Mr. J. P. Spafford, president of the American Colony, as a guide. There being no railroad north out of Jerusalem, a hard three-day carriage ride took him to Galilee, "where the Savior longed so much to be," and then on by rail to Damascus and Beirut. From Damascus he wrote, "If the next few days continue auspicious, we can report a very successful nineteen days' visit to the Holy Land. We worked pretty hard for this hot weather, and last night we unanimously decided to express our thanks to the Almighty for the part of the trip safely and happily accomplished." He then traveled by way of Constantinople and Athens to Rome, where he wrote, "I never worked harder in the hay field than this week here among the historic and present day sights of Rome." Then on to Florence, Venice, Switzerland, a visit with the *Corpus* staff in Wolfenbüttel and back home to a friendly welcome service at 30th and Cumberland.

Upon his return he lectured on numerous occasions, showing about 100 slides of Jerusalem, which he had purchased while there. Jerusalem had suffered destruction on numerous occasions down through the centuries. Rubble had raised the city some thirty feet above the level of the gospel city, filling in nearby valleys in some places to a depth of sixty feet. During Rev. Heebner's visit the country was a province of the decaying Turkish Empire. The atmosphere of the place was, however, still conducive to imagining life as lived at the time of Christ and ever after Rev. Heebner's New Testament sermons had an authentic ring as he drew upon his recollections of the countryside and the people there. He was doubly fortunate to arrive home just before the outbreak of World War I, and to have visited the Holy Land before the dramatic disruptions of two world wars and the establishment of the State of Israel.

In December of 1914 the *Schwenkfeldian* reporter noted, "Electric lighting has been installed in the church by Mr. William Mevins assisted by Hudson McMurtrie and Mr. Frank Clark. The improvement is much appreciated and the auditorium looks very inviting."

For nine weeks during January and February of 1915 the Billy Sunday evangelistic campaign visited Philadelphia, dramatically strengthening the religious life of the city. A committee from the church cooperated in arrangements for the campaign. Sunday evening services were dispensed with so that members could attend the revival meetings in the great tabernacle at Nineteenth and Vine Streets, where some two million people participated in the services. An estimated 150,000 people publicly determined to lead a better life and 40,000 took their stand by "hitting the trail" in the tabernacle. The church received fifty-five decision cards through the tabernacle post office, from which twenty-five new members were enrolled. The men's and women's adult Bible classes doubled their attendance. During the year the church enrolled sixty-two new members, largely reflecting the stimulus of the campaign, which Rev. Heebner found to be the principal topic of conversation in most of the homes he visited during the year.

January 1916 saw the initiation of the "Leaflet," a combination newsletter and worship program, which Rev. Heebner issued for distribution each Sunday. The Men's Brotherhood underwrote the cost of the first issues. During the fall, Sunday school services were interrupted by concern over the infantile paralysis epidemic then rampant throughout the city. Those families who could arrange it removed their children to the nearby countryside.

The year 1917 marked the 400th anniversary of the Reformation, "when the human soul was emancipated from the bondage of medieval oppression." April was celebrated as Reformation month, during which Rev. Heebner keyed his sermons to Luther and Schwenckfeld. Then during Holy Week, in early April, after a moving message from President Wilson, Congress passed a declaration of war against the German Empire, which the president signed, ironically, on the afternoon of Good Friday. Despite the obvious rupture of emotional ties with the fatherland, the Schwenkfelder congregation, along with the entire city, was swept along into the preparations for participation in the war. The church participated in patriotic rallies and in Liberty Bond drives. By the summer a number of members were writing the pastor from training camps and a few from France. Delegations of sailors and soldiers from the Navy Yard were entertained at Sunday services and in individual homes. Letters written by the local hosts to parents of boys so entertained elicited grateful replies from their families anxious for information as to their sons' welfare.

In all, thirty-seven members entered the armed forces. The name of Walter Garden, an early enlistee from the Sunday school, was the first to appear on General Pershing's injury list, but he was later able to return to his unit. A memorial service was held in September 1918 for John Meyers, an early Sunday school volunteer, killed in action "somewhere in France." Two of the number were seriously wounded.

Church Treasurer Dr. Andrew Anders enlisted in the Medical Corps and served with the 29th Division, which saw action in France. Rev. Heebner enlisted, initially for a three-month term, as a chaplain in the YMCA. On May 6, 1918 he left for Camp Stuart, Newport News, Virginia, where he served as secretary of the Margaret Wilson YMCA Hut. Camp Stuart was an embarkation camp through which units passed on their way to France. Rev. Heebner experienced many emotional moments working with service men there. His term was extended several times, until he spent nine months at Camp Stuart and another month as representative of the YMCA on a fund-raising tour for war-relief agencies through Culpepper Co. in Virginia. Local pastors and friends supplied the pulpit during Rev. Heebner's absence; church and Sunday school officers and the brotherhood assisted in conducting services. In October services were canceled in compliance with an order from the Director of Health because of the influenza epidemic sweeping the city.

On Tuesday evening, March 11, 1919 the Ladies' Aid organized a reception to give Rev. Heebner a rousing "welcome home." Moderator Dr. Anders, on behalf of the congregation, "pledged Rev. Heebner the loyal and undivided support of the congregation in welcoming him back to the pulpit. . . . By entering the U.S. Service he stated that Rev. Heebner had carried the activities of the church to Camp Stuart and thus gave the congregation a wider field of labor." Mr. Albert Harvison, on behalf of the deacons, thanked the entire congregation for their helpful support during the pastor's absence. "In response Rev. Heebner spoke of some of the experiences in camp and the impressions received from service in the army; of the strain under which all Y secretaries worked; and of the appreciation of the services rendered, by the men in khaki." In his annual report Rev. Heebner observed, "The American Army is demobilizing because they have won their objective—the defeat of autocracy and oppression. The army of the Kingdom of God has not as yet won its objective, the evangelization of the world, and therefore, let every member of the church work faithfully in 1919 and on through the years, whether at the front or far behind the lines, with the untiring devotion that springs from the thought that there is no discharge in the war against ignorance, intolerance, and sin, and that we are under the command of the Captain of our Salvation who has never lost a battle."

The safe return of the *Corpus* staff in April 1919, together with their editorial materials, concluded the long period of intense preoccupation with the war, and church life again resumed a more normal course.

By the 1920s the once new houses in the neighborhood increasingly showed signs of age and the original settlers began to move farther out in the city or into the suburbs. More and more the active workers commuted longer distances to attend church services and activities. An influx of Jewish families gradually changed the makeup of the neighborhood immediately surrounding the church. A Hebrew synagogue flourished less than a block away from the church on Cumberland St. In January 1924 Rev. Heebner noted: "Evidently there is a large field right here to be cultivated and our commendation goes to the workers who stand so nobly by their tasks in a situation where the gentile is in the minority." He cheerfully reported: "Christmas morning services were held at 6 o'clock, the pastor speaking upon the "Joy of the Shepherds." The C. E. were out caroling around the neighborhood after midnight. This brought the Message in song to our Hebrew population."

Nevertheless, during the decade following the war, all activities of the church seemed to flourish. Church membership fluctuated narrowly around 450 members. Sunday school enrollment reached a peak of 697 in 1924 while record average attendance for the year 1923 reached 204. Both slowly but steadily declined thereafter.

Early Sunday school scholars grew to middle age and furnished new leadership support. Mr. Albert Harvison served many years as assistant Sunday school superintendent, as advisor to the senior C. E., and as a leader in the Men's Brotherhood and Wednesday evening prayer meetings. His wife was assistant superintendent of the Sunday school primary department and advisor to the junior and intermediate C. E. societies. Harry Paynter, perennial catcher on church baseball teams, served as Sunday school pianist and active worker in C. E. and young people's activities. Bob Tweedie, Albert Chaplin, Lillian Wheatly, and many others worked joyfully and faithfully. In June of 1923 the church purchased the property at 2509 N. 30th St., on the third floor of which Rev. Heebner had lived from the time of his arrival as pastor. The ground floor front was converted into a Sunday school room and the kitchen remodeled to provide facilities for church dinners, etc. It shortly became a rallying place for church and Sunday school workers, those commuting from a distance frequently spending the day at the Church, eating picnic meals in the church house or in nearby Fairmount Park.

One of the most active groups was the Schwenkfelder Cadet Corp, under the energetic leadership of Captain William Day. They met regularly on Thursday evenings and conducted fund-raising concerts, entertainments, block parties, etc., to finance the purchase of equipment and their ten-day to two-week encampment on the beach near Corson's inlet at the end of Ocean City, N.J. Their first camp was in 1918 and their outings continued through most of the 1920s, becoming a regular summer feature. Rev. Heebner spent his vacations on visits to Dr. Anders' summer home in Blue Hill Falls, Maine, evangelistic services at Ocean Grove, and a visit to the cadet camp. In 1920 the *Schwenkfeldian* reported, "The Cadets spent the week before Labor Day upon the beach near Corsons' Inlet, Ocean City. They enjoyed favorable weather and the only enemies that penetrated the guards were mosquitoes. The sea last Spring wrecked the tip of the town near their camp and they made good use of the kindling wood, furniture, etc. which was donated to them." On Sunday, September 4, 1921, "Camp Heebner" entertained fifty parents and guests at services conducted by Cadet Chaplain James Gardner. The next year the *Schwenkfeldian* reported, "Here on the level floor of sand near the sounding sea they pitched their tents and set up their program of activities. Their daily routine followed very closely that of a day in one of the military camps, beginning with reveille and ending with taps. Many of the parents and friends of the Cadets went to camp at Ocean City on Sunday, September 3. All assembled in one of the tents and religious services were held, at which Mr. Albert A. Harvison, whose son is one of the Cadets, preached. Since they have returned we notice that the tan is disappearing, but the smile is remaining."

Junior, intermediate and senior Christian Endeavor societies were especially active, not only within the church but in Schuylkill Branch, combining the activities of some forty neighborhood church societies, and in the city-wide Philadelphia Christian Endeavor Union. In 1922 Joel Forsythe, having served as president of the Schwenkfelder Society, was elected president of Schuylkill Branch C. E. Bob Tweedie served as president of Schuylkill Branch in 1929 and of the Philadelphia Union in 1933. The Junior C. E. was a frequent winner of attendance banners at Schuylkill Branch rallies.

Under Rev. Heebner's dedicated leadership the church, besides its concentrated support of the Taiku mission, reached out into the community and city, participating generously in cooperative activities. In his annual report to the Philadelphia District Conference in January of 1924, Rev. Heebner gave some idea of the breadth of this outreach.

> It is our aim to bring to our people speakers and causes that will constantly enlarge our vision of service and make us feel that we live not unto ourselves but are members of the larger Church of Christ around the world. We certainly commend our people upon the attention and courteous treatment given to visiting speakers. The Philadelphia Federation of Churches has been represented by the secretary, Rev. Elim Palmquist and by Mrs. Jennie Griffith. . . . Several attended the Congregational Assembly of Young People in the Perkiomen School, August 6-13, and we would recommend that many more attend this friendship making and inspirational meeting this year. . . . Here are added names and causes represented in our pulpit last year: DeMar, of the Philadelphia Record; Chief Manitowang, of a Western Indian Tribe, Evangelist; Bert Rudolph, Rev. Kitto, and the state secretary of C. E.; Rev. Levi S. Hoffman, of the Middle District; Prof. Frey, of Girard College; Miss Grace Mayette, of the Y.W.C.A.; Rev. William Somers, Supply; Mr. Ramsden and other mission workers; Mr. John Emlen and Mr. Manley, of the Armstrong Association, a colored organization; Rev. Paddock, of

the Rocky Mountain Institute of Idaho; Rev. Faulkner, of the Anti-saloon League; Mr. Brewer Eddy, of the American Board of Commissioners for Foreign Missions; Rev. Percy Shelley, of the Lord's Day Alliance; and others.

On the evening of Saturday, April 28, 1925 forty-five teachers and officers of the Sunday school were guests of Superintendent and Mrs. Wayne C. Meschter in a tenth-floor dining room of the Manufacturers Club at Broad and Walnut Streets, Philadelphia, in what proved to be the first of more than twenty annual teachers' and officers' dinners. Given to recognize the loyal service of those invited, the events proved to be high spots in the Sunday school year. Guest speakers over the years included Dr. James M. Anders, Dr. W. D. Reel, secretary of the Philadelphia Sunday School Association, Rev. H. H. Kinkler, chaplain of the Eastern State Penitentiary, Rev. Hoffman, Rev. Lester Kriebel, Mr. Oscar Schultz, superintendent of the Palm Sunday school, Rev. Elliott D. Parkhill, of the American Sunday School Union, Dr. Conrad Hauser of the Reformed Church board, Rev. Eric T. Braund, later pastor at the Central church, and most unforgettable, Dr. Forest Dager, pastor, professor, and co-founder of Temple College. Unpretentious in stature and grooming, Dr. Dager on two occasions held his audience spellbound with carefully blended humor and serious moral anecdotes. Sid Coleman regularly tickled the ivories and led group singing. Carlotta Schultz Hoffman, Helen Schultz Cook, and Raymond Seeburger furnished special music. On one occasion Prof. Bruno Steyer, teacher of piano and violin at Temple College, played violin solos, accompanied by Sunday school member Aileen Ibart. And then there was Edward Hohlfeld, playing his solo harmonica and regularly condescending to render "Nola" as an encore. Eddie won several city-wide harmonica playing contests, and played with the Philadelphia harmonica band at the White House in Washington. The full-course dinner usually featuring chicken à la king, a Manufacturers Club specialty, left all in a mellow mood to enjoy the entertainment and message of the evening.

A high event of the year 1927 was a testimonial dinner tendered Dr. James M. Anders in honor of his fiftieth anniversary in the practice of medicine. Sponsored by a committee of leading doctors in the city and supported by an honorary advisory committee of almost 200 leaders in the medical profession, the guest list of some 500 assembled in the grand ballroom of the Bellevue Stratford Hotel on Tuesday evening, November 29, read like a "Who's Who in Philadelphia." Provost Josiah H. Penniman of the University of

Pennsylvania served as toastmaster. Dr. George L. Omwake, president of Ursinus College, spoke of Dr. Anders' commitment to liberal education. Dr. Judson Daland related Dr. Anders' influence as professor of medicine, first in the Medico-Chirological College, and after the merger, of which Dr. Anders was one of the prime movers, at the Graduate School of Medicine of the University of Pennsylvania, and as author of the medical textbook, *The Theory and Practice of Medicine.* This textbook, the most widely used of its time, was first published in 1898, and then over the next twenty years in fourteen revised editions, each reflecting painstaking efforts to keep the text abreast of medical progress. Over 50,000 copies were sold. Dr. David Reisman spoke on "Dr. Anders in Public Health Work and Medical Organization" in the City of Philadelphia. Outstanding surgeon, Dr. John B. Deaver, unveiled a bust of Dr. Anders. Dr. Anders responded in his usual gracious manner: "This occasion marks the brightest moment of my life. As I look about me, I could desire no better fate than to have been awarded this exceptional honor. The respect and reverence you have shown to my years, I deeply appreciate." Seventeen Schwenkfelder co-workers from the several churches joined in the testimonial dinner.

On Sunday, November 18, 1928 the church celebrated the thirtieth anniversary of the November 19, 1898 organization meeting at which the Philadelphia church was formed. Twelve of the seventeen original charter members were still living. Dr. Anders prepared a history of the early church which, however, Rev. Heebner read, as Dr. Anders refrained from delivering it because of the death of a brother. Early ministers Rev. Albert Stubblebine, Rev. Henry A. Bomberger, and Dr. Johnson reminisced, while Dr. O. S. Kriebel gave the message of the morning. During the Sunday school hour the Norristown church choir sang, and Rev. Gottschall gave the message. In the early evening Mr. Harvison presided at a C. E. reunion which brought out many old members. Rev. Hoffman and Rev. Lester Kriebel spoke at the evening service. The following Monday evening the choirs of the Lansdale, Worcester, Towamencin, and Palm churches presented a musical program.

During the decade of the 1930s, with country and city in the grip of the great depression, the church struggled also with a changing, and certainly less supportive, community. The almost entirely Jewish neighborhood began to experience an influx of black families, who by mid-century clearly dominated the community. Social services assumed increasing prominence in the church program.

Distribution of food baskets to needy families at Thanksgiving and Christmas, long the practice of the C. E. societies, the Ladies' Aid, and other church organizations, was now greatly expanded. At Harvest Home services in the fall, groceries and canned goods were collected and delivered to the Keeler Home for disadvantaged children. Rev. Heebner noted, "There are many cases of poverty and dire need that challenge the attention and neighborliness of our people. In five families upon which the pastor called in succession, partial or no employment was reported." The young people brought needy children into the church house, entertained them in the afternoon, and then fed them a substantial supper before sending them off to their homes.

On several occasions the church heard Harry Heebner, manager of the Shelter for homeless men. Early in 1930 the "Lloyd Committee" of concerned citizens raised some $9,000,000, and administered another $2,500,000 contributed for "relief" by the State legislature. As one of their projects they operated a shelter in one of the old Baldwin Locomotive buildings, idle since the war. Facing on Hamilton St., the building ran the full block between 18th and 19th streets, enclosing some 320,000 square feet. Made marginally habitable by volunteer workers, it housed and fed thousands of men completely down and out. Church organizations throughout the city, including the Schwenkfelder church, directed clothing, supplies, and volunteer help to the shelter. One of their projects involved canning available donations of fruits and vegetables for distribution during the winter months. Harry Paynter and Albert Chaplin of the American Preserve Co. were drafted to bring some order into this operation, which somewhat daunted willing housewives, each with her own home canning recipes. Some 10,000 jars were processed, all by volunteer help, for distribution during the winter. Perhaps as important as the product turned out was the sense of "doing something" instilled in the workers to combat the rampant discouragement of the times.

The year 1932 also saw the inauguration of a baby clinic in the church annex. Conducted by the Baby Welfare Association of Philadelphia, a neighborhood physician and three trained nurses, assisted by members of the Ladies' Aid, staffed the clinic each Tuesday morning from 11:00 a.m. to 1:00 p.m. Initially some thirty-five babies were brought by their mothers, who received advice on hygiene, formula feeding, inoculation, health, and corrective treatment by a hospital or family physician. This service became increasingly valuable to the community as the years passed.

An inevitable burden of advancing years is the passing of friends and co-workers, and with his wide circle of personal contacts, Rev.

Heebner was to experience his full share of such partings. Whatever the emotional cost to him, however, his presence and confident faith in the loving care of our Heavenly Father brought comfort to the bereaved families, whatever their station in life, whether Protestant, Catholic, or Jewish. His funeral sermons, born of intimate lifetime acquaintance, struck just the right notes of faith, comfort, and eulogy.

On Saturday, February 20, 1932 he journeyed to the Palm Schwenkfelder Church to preach the funeral sermon for Dr. O. S. Kriebel, that fountainhead of inspiration to all Schwenkfelders, Rev. Heebner notably included.

Four years later an even closer personal association was broken with the passing of Dr. J. M. Anders, August 29, 1936 at his beloved "Walkonda," Blue Hill Falls, Maine. The long association of Rev. Heebner and Dr. Anders had been a source of mutual inspiration and respect. Each summer Rev. Heebner had spent at least a week, sometimes two, as the guest of Dr. Anders at "Walkonda," and always he returned refreshed and recharged, both physically and spiritually. Considering the increasing difficulties under which Rev. Heebner labored and the often distressing suffering he witnessed around him, who can estimate the therapeutic benefits of these uplifting interludes. Speaking at the memorial service held in the Philadelphia church, with Mrs. Anders and many of Dr. Anders' medical associates present in the overflow audience, Rev. Heebner recalled that two years before Dr. Anders had told him, "I am now 80 years of age, and if there is still work for me to do, as I feel there is, I must make every moment count. . . . I must be about my Father's business." Rev. Heebner then appropriately quoted: "To serve this present age, my calling to fulfill, / O may it all my powers engage to do my Master's will."

At the recommendation of the Board of Publication Rev. Heebner prepared a special May 1937 supplement to the *Schwenkfeldian* as a memorial to Dr. Anders. He was a founder of the Philadelphia church and until his death its only moderator. From 1910 on he was a trustee of Perkiomen School and president of the board at the time of his death. In 1926 after the death of then moderator of the Schwenkfelder General Conference, John H. Schultz, when efforts to select a new moderator were not meeting with success, and when the situation was related to Dr. Anders, he soon replied, "If agreeable, I shall be glad to accept that office for a few years in honor of my worthy father, who, I believe, served in a similar capacity for more than thirty years. I think it would be a fitting tribute to his memory for me to follow in his footsteps." Then past 70 years of age, he took on this new responsibility, which office he filled acceptably until 1932, when he resigned, saying it was now time for a younger man to succeed him!

Dr. Anders was the recipient of many honorary degrees, including that of Doctor of Science from his alma mater, the University of Pennsylvania. He was thrice honored by Ursinus College. He served there as trustee for over forty years, beginning in 1894. He followed keenly the work of the brilliant biologist, Professor P. Calvin Mensch, and was instrumental in instituting modern courses in science and in planning a group of pre-medical studies. Years later the pre-medical students formed themselves into the James M. Anders Pre-Medical Society. In 1890 Ursinus conferred the degree of Doctor of Philosophy, six years later the honorary degree of Doctor of Laws, and again in 1927, the degree of Doctor of Science. He was the only alumnus to be so repeatedly honored.

December 6, 1936 was designated recognition Sunday, celebrating "Thirty Years at Thirtieth and Cumberland" by the pastor, Rev. Heebner. The roster of those participating reflects the active laymen who maintained the momentum of church activities during this difficult period. At the Sunday morning service the choir, with Miss Carlotta Hoffman at the organ, sang "Send Out Thy Light," and brief greetings were given by Wayne C. Meschter, who presided, for the denomination; Samuel A. Seipt, for church progress; Samuel K. Brecht, for the *Schwenkfeldian*; Mrs. Ellen Schultz, for the Ladies' Aid Society; Mrs. Carlotta Hoffman, for the choir; and Miss Flora K. Heebner, home on furlough, for missions. The recognition service in the Sunday school was continued after the church service with Robert J. Tweedie, Jr., associate Sunday school superintendent, speaking for the young people; Lillian Wheatly, for the prayer meetings; Sidney Coleman, for social life; Mrs. Dobelbower, for the cradle roll; Joel Forsyth, for Christian Endeavor; J. Maurice Hohlfeld, on spiritual advisor; Mrs. Sara Jamieson, on the home department; and Albert Harvison, on the pastor. Characteristically the pastor responded, "You have spoken about a person who I am not, but as an ideal high above myself to which I fain would attain. What is left for me to do now is to try to live up to the expectations and to live down the exaggerations. How small after all is the part of the under-shepherd in view of Christ the Good Shepherd, whose we are and whom we serve."

In November 1938 the church celebrated its fortieth anniversary with all-day services. During the morning service Rev. Albert

Stubblebein and Rev. Elmer Johnson reminisced about the early days of the church. In the afternoon Bob Tweedie conducted the Sunday school services. A Christian Endeavor rally in the early evening brought out a number of old timers, and at the evening service Rev. Lester Kriebel and Rev. Hoffman contributed messages appropriate for the occasion. Between the morning and afternoon services, a dinner was served in the church house for the church officers and their families, the out-of-town guests, visiting clergymen, and six of the eight living charter members, to dedicate the new church hall. The property at 2511 North 30th Street, next to the church house, had been vacant for some time. Mr. Meschter purchased the property and arranged for structural improvements to combine the first floors of the two properties into an enlarged Sunday school room, to improve the kitchen facilities, and to combine the third floors of the two properties into expanded study, living, and sleeping quarters for the pastor.

In August 1938 Mr. Samuel Seipt passed away; in April 1939, Dr. Brecht; and in September, George K. Heebner. With Mr. Meschter seriously incapacitated at the time, lay leadership for church and Sunday school activities became a serious concern. Attention fixed upon two among the younger members. The obvious choice as a successor to Mr. Meschter as Sunday school superintendent was Mr. Robert Tweedie, associate superintendent of the Sunday school, a capable speaker, actively engaged in Sunday school and Christian Endeavor activities, and experienced in Schuylkill Branch and Philadelphia C. E. Union administration. Mr. Tweedie, however, employed in the real estate department of Atlantic Refining Co., was shortly required to remove his residence to Pittsburgh.

A second promising young person was J. Maurice Hohlfeld, active in young peoples' activities, particularly in Christmas and Easter dramatic presentations, which became quite ambitious productions against backdrops of biblical scenes chalked by artist Robert Jamieson, and which drew capacity audiences, sometimes requiring repeat performances. Maurice graduated from Northeast High School in 1927, and became an apprentice tool-maker, at which trade he worked for some ten years. During Christian Endeavor conferences at Beaver College, Jenkintown, Maurice took definite "forward steps" in consecration and commitment to full-time Christian service. He came to realize "What the world needs is not better tools, but better men." Employed during the day, he attended afternoon and evening classes at Temple University. He completed the college course and went on to graduate from the School of Theology in June of 1940.

Having assisted during his final school years in the pulpit of the Lansdale Schwenkfelder Church, upon graduation he was ordained as a Schwenkfelder minister and installed as pastor there. He later entered upon a distinguished career as linguist, professor, and missionary.

Mr. Meschter's health was fortunately restored, and he and Rev. Heebner, together with a dwindling corps of loyal workers, continued the principal pillars of the Philadelphia church over the next twenty years.

During the 1940s another protégé was inspired by Rev. Heebner to pursue the Christian ministry. Rev. Carl Davis Bader graduated from Northeast High School in 1943 and then from Temple University and Temple School of Theology. He undertook graduate studies at Princeton Theological Seminary and then earned a Master of Science in Education degree from the University of Pennsylvania, where he majored in counseling. He was ordained June 2, 1949 at the First Congregational Church of Germantown, with Rev. Heebner giving the invocation and Rev. Dr. J. S. Ladd Thomas, dean of the Temple School of Theology, preaching the sermon. Carl went on to an active career as pastor, school counsellor, and social worker for the City of Philadelphia. He composed several hundred poems and hymns, among which was "Water of Joy," written in 1975, with the dedication, "Written by his "Timothy" to honor the life and ministry of Rev. Harvey K. Heebner."

On January 25, 1963, at his home in Glenside, Mr. Meschter passed away. He had served as moderator of the Schwenkfelder General Conference from 1932 to 1957; Sunday school superintendent and moderator of the Philadelphia church; president of the Board of Publication and of Schwenkfelder Library; trustee of Perkiomen School; first president of the Commercial Alumni of Temple University, active in Temple alumni affairs and recipient of the honorary degree of Doctor of Laws for his services to the college; president of the Abington Township School Board; and in many church, business, and community activities. His presence, encouragement, and support would be widely missed, but nowhere more than at 30th and Cumberland and by its pastor, Rev. Heebner, friend and co-worker for almost sixty years.

Preaching the funeral sermon at the Palm Schwenkfelder Church, Rev. Heebner reminisced with moving eloquence. Using as text Romans 12:11, "Not slothful in business, fervent in spirit, serving the Lord," he went on, "In the passing of Wayne C. Meschter from our midst . . . we all have lost the inspiration of a loving and faithful friend and co-worker." He reviewed Mr. Meschter's many activities from intimate lifetime acquaintance, not forgetting the Sunday school outings in the park, with their married men vs. single men baseball games. "Entering heartily in this sport, he hit a home run in the area of the Museum. The ball has not been found and his mechanic at the factory said it now might be a satellite among the stars. . . . A man's character and worth are largely measured by the little acts of fellowship and kindly human interest, the best part of life itself." In concluding, Rev. Heebner quoted Longfellow's "The Psalm of Life," ending with the familiar words:

> Let us, then, be up and doing,
> With a heart for any fate;
> Still achieving, still pursuing,
> Learn to labor and to wait.

The funeral sermon for his friend and co-worker preached, the vitality of life seemed to drain from the surviving pastor. Many have remarked that from that time on Rev. Heebner entered a steady decline. It was not long before he was hospitalized in Women's Medical College Hospital, where on April 8, less than three months after Mr. Meschter's death, he too passed to his eternal reward, aged 86.

Dr. J. Maurice Hohlfeld, at this time professor and academic dean at the Hartford Seminary Foundation, preached the funeral sermon at the Central Schwenkfelder Church. He recalled that twenty-five years before, faced with his first funeral sermon, he had sought out Rev. Heebner in his "upper room" at 2509 North 30th St. to ask, "What should one say at a time such as this?" "Tell them of the great KNOWS of the Bible—I KNOW that my Redeemer liveth—We KNOW that all things work together for good—I KNOW in whom I have believed." Maurice continued, "This is his sermon outline. He gave it to me twenty-five years ago. I give it to you on this Holy Thursday, 1963. . . . Holy Thursday is going to be just a little bit holier for our fellowship of believers as the years go by. Many will partake of the cup and the bread tonight in remembrance that God so loved the world that he became enfleshed in the person of Jesus Christ and it was He who reconciled the world unto himself. But He also gave us the ministry of reconciliation and the spirit of the Almighty became enfleshed in our own departed friend, colleague, pastor, and brother in Christ." He recalled that of the seven churches in Revelation, that at Philadelphia was the church with the worldwide mission, the church of the open door. Spoken from intimate acquaintance, it was a sermon preached from the heart, worthy of Rev. Heebner himself.

Rev. Heebner was the personification of Christian discipleship. Truly he could "walk with kings, nor lose the common touch." He was sensitive to human need, physical and spiritual, of which he witnessed certainly more than his share, yet perennially optimistic and cheerful. He was unassuming and humble, yet where service to his God or fellow man required it, he harbored a will of steel. His sermons were simple and direct expositions of biblical truths yet embellished by broad intellectual interests and wide personal experiences. He tasted life to the full and preached from the heart, giving a little of himself in each sermon. He was so deeply immersed in church affairs that without notice he could capture the spirit of the moment in any meeting and give it expression in brief and pointed phrase.

Never hospitalized until his last days, Rev. Heebner maintained his robust health by sober living, sensible eating, and a vigorous walking gait, which served as his principal means of city transportation. He never owned a car, nor learned to drive, but thought nothing of walking into center city, or on occasion to the family farm in Worcester, to which he regularly retreated for physical and spiritual refreshment. A lifelong bachelor, his only residence was the parsonage at 2509 North 30th Street. His third-floor front study served as church, *Schwenkfeldian* and Mission Board office. Its bay window offered unobstructed vision up and down 30th Street and over the intersection with Cumberland St. Little that went on there escaped his observation.

The attractive parish to which he had been called in 1906 had changed into a Jewish enclave and then into a predominantly black neighborhood, totally unrecognizable to a returning visitor from the early days. Yet through it all, Rev. Heebner went his way unperturbed. All who sought counsel, advice, or comfort were received in his study and sent on their way encouraged and heartened. Whatever the need, Rev. Heebner visited the neighborhood homes, preaching by example the gospel message. All were his flock. He walked among them as friend and pastor. Yet with it all he led the Philadelphia church to a distinguished place among the conference of Schwenkfelder churches, providing over the years its full share of leadership in denominational activities, educational and missionary endeavors, and service within the church at large.

The Philadelphia church would now enter a new era.

Once Again a Mission Church

As reported in the 1960 census, the area surrounding the First
Schwenkfelder Church of Philadelphia contained a total population of
16,796, of which 1,818 were white, 14,946 black, and 32 of other
races. The median school years completed was 8.9, the median family
income $4,666, and the median value of housing units—almost all
over 50 years old— was $7,000. Rev. Heebner had served to preserve
the interest and support of a dwindling core of long-time church
members, many of whom traveled some distance to attend services.
At the same time, his conscientious ministry to any family in need in
the community assured the black community's acceptance of him as a
Christian pastor. His passing threatened both pillars of support.

A core of loyal church members under the leadership of Mr. and
Mrs. William Ayre and Mr. and Mrs. Charles Tomlinson was
determined to carry on. They sought the assistance of the General
Conference Mission Board, which had initially sponsored the
Philadelphia church. The board accepted jurisdiction and the spring
General Conference of 1965 approved a program whereby a new
Church Council assumed administrative responsibility for a two-year
interim period, during which the Mission Board underwrote the local
budget. It was estimated some $8,000 to $10,000 per year would be
required, meaning the mission assessments of the denominational
churches would have to be increased by the equivalent of about $3.00
per member. It was agreed the church property would be neither
encumbered nor sold. If no viable program evolved, it would revert to
the Mission Board at the end of the two-year trial period. As finally
operative, the council was composed of Mr. and Mrs. Ayre, Mr. and
Mrs. Tomlinson, and Miss Beatrice Emmons (shortly replaced by
Mrs. James Hoffman), representing the local church, and Mrs.
Melvin Ruth of Lansdale, Mr. Paul Bieler of Palm, Rev. David
Crowle of Norristown, and Mr. Donald Hamme of Central, representing the Mission Board.

The committee struggled mightily with problems simply
beyond their comprehension and certainly not amenable to traditional solutions. The Sunday school had long attracted neighborhood
children, and such programs as the day care center and clinic operated
in the church house were well supported, but few neighborhood
adults attended church worship services or cared to participate in
church affairs. They simply did not relate to the worship programs
which the white core sought to preserve.

A series of Schwenkfelder and neighborhood pastors filled the pulpit and lay workers assisted where possible. During the fall of 1963 Mr. Ernest Moritz, of a Presbyterian congregation, was licensed by General Conference, and on Sunday, November 10 installed as minister. Married and father of five children, Mr. Moritz had left a thriving dairy business to pursue further education and a career in the ministry. At this time he was a second-year student at the Conwell School of Theology at Temple University; he had served three years as lay minister with the Neshaminy-Warwick Presbyterian Church in Hartsville, Pa. He served the congregation well, involving himself in community affairs, with the result that the church emerged unscathed from the city-wide riots that wracked the surrounding area and ravaged nearby Simon Gratz High School. Pursuant to a directive of the mayor, no services were held on Sunday, August 30, 1964 while efforts were under way to restore calm. Then in June of 1965 Mr. Moritz received his B.D. degree from the Conwell School, and shortly thereafter was called to the Doylestown Presbyterian Church. He did not, however, forget his friends in the 30th and Cumberland community; for a number of years the Doylestown church forwarded significant financial support to the Philadelphia church, used principally for structural renovations better to fit the church house to serve as a community center.

Through the good offices of Rev. Paul T. Slinghoff, Conference Minister of the Pennsylvania Southeast Conference, United Church of Christ, the committee was put in touch with Mr. James Serdy, a native of Phoenixville, a graduate of Ursinus College, where he majored in political science, and a recent graduate of Andover Newton Theological Seminary. Mr. Serdy was trained in social work, had pursued clinical training at the Danvers (N.Y.) State Hospital, and had served a 1963-1964 intern year in Bangalore, South India. He was ordained in his home church in Phoenixville October 3 and installed as the Philadelphia pastor November 28, 1965.

Prompted by his training and natural inclination, Rev. Serdy lost no time in involving himself intimately in community activities. Using the facilities of the Sunday school annex and the church house, he promoted the Well Baby Clinic, a tutorial program, the day care center, and a hot lunch program, serving the elementary school children who returned at lunchtime to empty homes because both parents were working. He undertook to establish a branch of O.I.C.—Dr. Leon Sullivan's Opportunities Industrial Center—and initiated negotiations for a federally funded "Get Set" program, seeking to give small children a better start in school. He was well received in the community and by early 1967 delivered an enthusiastic report to the Mission Board. "We face an unidentified ministry in an unicentified community. There are no accepted procedures, no standing committees. Everyone is feeling their way." Rev. Serdy reported he started with three strikes against him: he was single, he was white, and he was young, but gradually he gained acceptance.

Numerous attempts were made to involve supporting staff. In the summer of 1967 Mr. Fred Lee, a Taiwanese student in the master's program of journalism and public relations at Boston University, was hired to improve the church organization. He increased the church's presence in the community by mimeographing monthly the *Schwenkfelder Post*. He organized two committees, one supporting Rev. Serdy in his community activities and one to build up the church program. The United Church of Christ assigned a free-lance person, Mr. Ken Ross, to assist. The Voluntary Service Center in Pottstown supplied Miss Irma McCreedy, a social worker. But community needs simply seemed to overwhelm all efforts. The blacks complained that neither the music nor the sermons reached them— are we both talking about the same God? Church attendance many Sunday mornings of fewer than a dozen adults was a discouraging measure of success for the evangelistic program. Then when the Vietnam and civil rights protests aroused the black community, Bill Ayre took exception to injection of these issues into the sermons. Rev. Serdy also took to circulating literature, the inspiration for which was not clear, and this so disturbed Mr. Tomlinson that after several reconsiderations he finally resigned as treasurer.

When Bill Ayre died February 19, 1968 Mr. Michael Beauford, a student at Cheney State College and active in the Strawberry Mansion Co-op, was elected moderator; he soon clashed with Rev. Serdy. Mr. Beauford claimed Rev. Serdy was dictatorial, did not communicate with the congregation, did not delegate, and would not allow anyone else to get things done. "Rev. Serdy wants a society, not a church." In March of 1968 Rev. Serdy took a leave of absence to join a student group visiting South America. While he was away arrangements were made for Rev. Lorenzo Handy, a black Episcopal deacon, to be licensed as associate pastor to work part-time to strengthen the church effort. Mr. Barry Wally was also licensed and installed December 8, 1968, but he survived for only a few weeks and early in 1969 the Philadelphia congregation asked for the resignation of Rev. Serdy.

The one enterprise which seemed to unite church and community in a joint effort was the Strawberry Mansion Co-op. A group of people interested in cooperative purchases of food, etc., were granted permission to use the basement of the church house as a distribution point. Then a committee was formed formally to organize a co-op. When a store property directly across 30th St. from the church became available, this committee, the Church Council and the Mission Board entered into intense discussions as to financing. A plan was finally worked out whereby the co-op raised about $1,000 through sale of stock, the Philadelphia church advanced $2,000, and the Mission Board granted an interest-free loan of $6,000. In presenting the project to the Mission Board Mr. Robert Stroehman, a UCC-supported pastor in the urban area, explained the black philosophy. "They feel the organizations that regulate their lives should be their own—the banks, stores, schools, churches etc." The co-op led a precarious existence for several years, but unfortunately no longer survives.

On February 28, 1971 Mrs. June Abrams was installed as pastor, only to leave again by the end of June. During these periods of uncertainty, the church work was carried on by the moderator, Mr. Don Chestnut, and most effectively by The Rev. Dr. Havis Davis, made available on an interim basis by the American Sunday School Union. Here finally was a distinguished black preacher, able to communicate with the black congregation in their own idiom. Attendance picked up to some fifty per Sunday.

This time the local congregation set up their own search committee. To assist them in securing a better qualified person, the Central Church Mission Board, through the influence of Betty Jean Rothenberger, pledged $5,000 specifically to supplement the salary the Philadelphia church was able to pay. After a careful search, the congregation called Rev. T. Arnold Brooker, a native of south Philadelphia, ordained as an African Methodist Episcopal minister and uniquely qualified for the 30th and Cumberland assignment. His father, also a minister and semi-retired at the time, assisted in the initiation of more impressive church worship services, this time attuned to the temper of the community. His brother shortly assisted also, serving as moderator of the church. His sister, an accomplished musician, developed an outstanding musical program. Her several choirs added immensely to the spirit of the worship services. They also came to be featured participants in numerous denominational activities, offering stirring musical selections and joining in Schwenkfelder United Choir presentations.

After serving on an informal basis for about a year, Rev. Brooker was formally installed as pastor on October 21, 1973 and almost immediately a new spirit seemed to infuse the congregation.

New members were taken into the church and the Sunday school, and community activities, centered in the church house, were reactivated. By this time the church and church house were seventy years old and badly in need of deferred maintenance. The stained glass windows on Cumberland Street threatened to fall out and had to be reinforced. The perennially faltering heater had to be replaced. With the assistance of some fourteen workers subsidized by the Anti-Poverty program, a clean-up, paint-up, fix-up campaign was undertaken and the properties gradually returned to more respectable order. The remodeled church house became the center for a thrift shop. Through the months of July and August a day camp was organized. By 1975 Rev. Brooker reported 125 on the church membership rolls, with from 65 to 90 regularly in attendance at Sunday worship services. The weekly offerings averaged from $60 to $70, enabling the church to raise a good part of its budgeted $6,000 annual commitment. This together with $16,000 from the Mission Board and $4,800 from the Central church, along with help from numerous other sources, kept the church financially afloat.

The church was located close to the turfs of four different gangs and any non-gang member was suspect all around. Nevertheless, Rev. Brooker undertook to meet each young person on a personal basis, often working between the police, the gangs, and the young people of the community. He sought to gather them together into a fellowship and a personal relationship with Jesus Christ. He undertook to establish a drug rehabilitation program. The ministers of the area coordinated a prayer chain initiated because of the many killings taking place. They rotated riding with patrol policemen over weekends, seeking to reduce tension between police and residents. Arrangements were made for bus trips to take elderly residents shopping, each group accompanied by two men to guard against purse snatching and ladies being knocked down.

In the July 1978 issue of the *Schwenkfeldian*, Mrs. Annie Hyman described Rev. Brooker's ministry as follows:

> Five years ago, the members of First Schwenkfelder Church, Philadelphia, were fasting and praying to hold on as a church and that God would see the need to send us a pastor who would build and nourish the spiritual side of our church and also serve our community with its overwhelming problems. Not only did God send us a pastor, He sent us a whole family of Christians who have worked to build and develop First Schwenkfelder Church.
>
> Yes, we still have problems, because the congregation we have built are people who exist, for the most part, on a fixed income . . . we

leave this problem to our Lord Jesus Christ. We continue to grow in spirit and grace under Rev. Brooker. The other part of his ministry goes on and on. No one hesitates to call on Rev. Brooker 24 hours a day. His crises-filled day goes something like this: responds to gangs who feel they need him; drug addicts in need of a fix or on a bad trip or trying to go cold turkey; prisoners in jail, in court, being arrested—again; the street-walkers; the parent who feels she wants to kill her child.

We ask God to give Rev. Brooker the strength to hold on for the First Schwenkfelder Church's mission has to continue. We need our brothers and sisters of our sister churches just as we always have. First Schwenkfelder, being a mission church doing a missionary work in this inner-city community, needs your continued financial support along with your prayers. . . . We are thankful and appreciative for your help.

Gradually the results of Rev. Brooker's long hours and untiring efforts began to show in the church congregation. By 1978 a membership of 167 was reported and encouraged by the music of the excellent choir, church attendance steadily increased. Rev. Brooker became interested in Schwenkfelder denominational affairs, joined the Schwenkfelder ministerium, a monthly meeting of the pastors of the five churches, and led members of his congregation in participation in denominational activities. He has represented the denomination on the Social Ministries Committee of the Pennsylvania Council of Churches, and has served effectively on the subcommittee which initiated and carries on "Project 60" to work with persons over 55 years of age preparing for their release after serving prison terms. Over his eleven-year pastorate he has firmly established the Philadelphia Schwenkfelder Church as an integral part of the community, preaching the gospel and seeking to alleviate the extreme hardship under which many families in the community live. The Philadelphia Schwenkfelder Church is the most visible, the most timely, and quite possibly the most worthwhile, of the more recent missionary activities of the Schwenkfelder congregations.

Chapter Eight

The Norristown Schwenkfelder Church

From its initiation, and while the Philadelphia mission was being launched, the Schwenkfelder Mission Board had considered the Lansdale and Norristown areas as possibly ripe for local church and Sunday school organizations. A special committee of the board, "with authority to increase its membership by adding brethren in Lansdale," after a number of meetings finally reported its conclusion that a mission undertaking there should be deferred. Norristown, however, proved an immediately more fruitful field.

In 1900 the Borough of Norristown reported a population of some 22,000 people, drawn there by the mills and factories of Bridgeport, its sister town across the Schuylkill River, the Swedeland furnaces of the Alan Wood Steel Co., the nearby State Hospital for the mentally ill, and the rapidly growing bureaucracy associated with Norristown as the county seat of burgeoning Montgomery County.

In its second issue, January 1904, the *Schwenkfeldian* reported, "There are about thirty Schwenkfelder families in Norristown and Bridgeport." These families, too, felt the need for a local center of worship and spiritual training, and indeed seemed almost poised to undertake, on their own initiative, organization of a local Schwenkfelder church. On January 18, 1904 President John H. Schultz convened an afternoon meeting of the Schwenkfelder Mission Board at the Norristown home of Isaac Yeakle, to acquiesce in the commissioning of Flora Heebner to China and to consider establishment of a mission church and Sunday school in Norristown. That evening about twenty-five interested persons congregated at the home of John E. Brecht. Under the leadership of John Schultz and

245

Dr. Johnson they formed a local committee on arrangements consisting of George K. Brecht, Samuel K. Brecht, J. Leidy Anders, Mrs. Charles Kriebel, and Mae S. Longacre. At the suggestion of Dr. Johnson, ten of those present signed a resolution, "Resolved, that we, the undersigned persons, hereby agree to encourage cordially and support actively religious services under the auspices of the Schwenkfeldian denomination in Norristown, Pennsylvania, with the purpose of ultimately effecting a permanent organization." The Mission Board appointed its secretary, Dr. Johnson, a committee on supply, "to see that ministers be at the service of the Schwenkfelders of Norristown." Dr. O. S. Kriebel suggested that the Mission Board ask the Philadelphia church to have Dr. Johnson supply the pulpit as often as possible, and that church services be held every two weeks and Sunday school every week.

At the call of the local committee a second meeting was held January 25, at the home of Mrs. Charles Kriebel, John Brecht having been taken ill. The list of signers had been expanded to twenty-nine; the local committee was formalized with George K. Brecht as chairman, Mae S. Longacre as secretary, and Wilson K. Heebner as treasurer. In eloquent testimony to the energy and dedication of those present, less than one month later, on February 7, Dr. Johnson conducted the first worship service, held at the home of Mrs. Kriebel, 930 W. Marshall St., with forty-five in attendance.

Meanwhile, at a February 15 meeting at the home of Mrs. Kriebel, a Sunday school was organized with Samuel K. Brecht as superintendent, Mae S. Longacre as assistant, and Laura Anders as organist, with the first session scheduled for Sunday, February 21. Two other locations proving unavailable, arrangements were made with the Norristown School Board to use the Chain Street School building for Sunday school services every Sunday at 2:00 p.m. and church services every other Sunday at 3:00 o'clock. The Mission Board was to be paid $5.00 per month for supplying the minister and a janitor the same fee for maintaining the meetingroom. Wilson Heebner was authorized to purchase an organ for $27.50, but Samuel K. Anders presented the organ as a gift. Leidy Anders was charged with responsibility for publishing notice of weekly services in the Norristown papers.

The Brecht family was among the most active supporters of the early Norristown church. John E. Brecht had been a farmer in nearby Worcester Township and an organizer and lifelong director of the Farmers' Creamery at Center Point. He was a director of the People's National Bank of Norristown (now absorbed by American Bank and

Trust Co. of Pa.) and of the Girard Ave. Farmers' Market Co. of Philadelphia. The latter organization operated a farmers' market at 19th and Ridge Ave., where many Philadelphia Schwenkfelders regularly shopped and gossiped. He had married Sarah Kriebel, a descendant of immigrant Melchior Kriebel. When he retired from farming he took up residence at 926 W. Marshall St., Norristown, where he died only a month after the first meeting at his home. His widow continued to live there until her death in 1933. She drew her children into the line of Schwenkfeldian descendants and seems to have been a source of spiritual inspiration to them. Her son, Samuel K. Brecht, affectionately dedicated the 1923 *Genealogical Record* to his mother, "through whom he is honored as a descendant of one of the most noble groups of religious exiles who sought Pennsylvania as a refuge.'

George K. Brecht, 37 years of age at the time, and well launched on a distinguished life-long legal career at the Montgomery County Bar, was elected chairman of the organizing committee. He served the Norristown church as moderator for fifty years, and the General Conference as treasurer for almost as long. Samuel K. Brecht served as Sunday school superintendent until October 1906, when he moved his residence to Lansdowne, Pa. He subsequently transferred his membership to the Philadelphia church, where he served the local church and the denomination with distinction in many capacities.

J. Leidy Anders, a descendant of immigrant Anna Reinwald Anders, was a teller with the First National Bank of Norristown and later a vice-president of the Montgomery Trust Co., into which the former merged (now Continental Bank). He was a member of the original committee on arrangements and later served the church as secretary, deacon, and trustee. For many years he served the Conference Board of Publication as treasurer and as business manager of the *Schwenkfeldian*. In 1905 he married Mae Longacre, a descendant of immigrant Christopher Schultz. Mae Longacre was the original secretary of the church, and served as superintendent of the primary department of the Sunday school, deacon, and representative on the Pennsylvania Council of Churches.

Wilson K. Heebner, a descendant of immigrant David Heebner, and his wife, Susan Helen (Kriebel), a descendant of immigrant Melchior Kriebel, were both charter members of the church Mr. Heebner, a machinist and foreman at Wildman Manufacturing Co. in Norristown, served the church as treasurer for fifty years, while his wife was treasurer of the Ladies' Aid Society for forty-three years. Minutes of the organization meeting note that he was initially assigned to shovel coal into the basement heater to keep the meetingroom warm on Sundays.

While not a charter member, John H. Schultz shortly became a member. As President of the Mission Board he played a significant role in the development of the church and Sunday school. He was born May 10, 1855 on the family farm at Clayton, near the Schwenkfelder Washington Meeting House, and educated in the local schools and Kutztown State Normal School. After stints at teaching and two years "pioneering" in Florida, he settled on a farm in East Norriton Township, which he operated for thirty years. In 1905 he organized the Reading Bone Fertilizer Co., which he served as director and president until his death. He was also a director of the Penn Trust Co., later Norristown Penn Trust Co. (now also Continental Bank). In 1911 he moved to Norristown, where for many years he taught an adult Bible class in the Sunday school. He served as moderator of General Conference from 1918 to 1926, as president of the Mission Board, as a member of the Board of Publication—where he was treasurer of its various funds—and for twenty years as a trustee of Perkiomen School. In 1880 he married Ellen Meschter Anders. The couple had eight children, all at one time members of the Norristown church, including Irma Schultz and Christine Shearer, later active in the Middle District, and Claude Schultz, long-time moderator of the Palm church. John died November 26, 1926.

Regular services were maintained at the Chain Street School until June 1905, except when a scarlet fever epidemic among the school's students made the facility unavailable from January 22 to March 1, 1905. The pulpit was supplied principally by Rev. Dr. George K. Meschter, Worcester physician and senior minister of the Middle District as well as regular pastor of the Norristown Church from 1905 until 1908, when ill health forced his retirement. Supply pastors during 1904 included Rev. O. S. Kriebel from Palm, Dr. Johnson, Rev. Harvey Heebner, Rev. Frank Gabul, pastor of the Germantown Mennonite Church, Professor Charles K. Meschter, and Rev. Mahlon Custer. At the first regular annual congregational business meeting, January 30, 1905, the Sunday school reported an enrolment of 51 and average attendance of 38. Twenty-five church services had been held, with an average attendance of 57; the largest attendance, at Rev. Johnson's farewell service, was 90.

The Chain Street School building was not really conducive to a religious atmosphere. Following the scarlet fever epidemic attendance declined seriously as parents were reluctant to expose their children to possible contagion. This interruption seems to have been the catalyst activating the already latent desire for a suitable house of worship. The Mission Board was consulted. It strongly recommended acquisition of a site and construction of a new church building, noting that all other Schwenkfelder churches had been erected by the respective congregations.

Just at this time, however, the Grace Lutheran Church was planning its impressive new edifice on Haws Ave., and their church building at George and Marshall Streets came on the market. Although originally constructed in 1886, a careful inspection showed the property to be in excellent condition, with $200 worth of new carpet and a $1,500 pipe organ just installed. At the offered sale price of $9,700, the Mission Board and the Norristown church officers decided it would prove substantially less expensive than construction of a new church building. After a series of meetings a decision was made to purchase the property, and it did indeed prove quite satisfactory. A purchase agreement was executed, providing for joint use of the church until the new Grace church was completed in August of 1906.

At 2:00 o'clock, Sunday afternoon, June 11, 1905, the first service in the new church was held, with the Mission Board occupying a front pew and the auditorium "filled by brethren from all the districts, and friends from neighboring churches. . . . The sweet tones of the new pipe organ were much enjoyed, and the excellent vocal music was very greatly appreciated."

Shortly thereafter the Mission Board held a special meeting at which "a resolution was unanimously adopted that an effort be made to raise the entire church debt within a year," a goal almost, but not quite, achieved. At the spring General Conference, Rev. George K. Meschter, secretary of the Mission Board, reported that the debt had been apportioned and $8,129.75 collected to date, as follows:

	Debt Apportioned	Collected to date
Philadelphia	$ 700	$ 350
Norristown	1,500	1,330
Upper District	3,000	3,000
Middle District	4,500	3,449
Total	$9,700	$8,129

Adding settlement costs and interest, a debt of just over $1,700 remained. Although steadily reduced, the Mission Board carried also the operating expenses and the minister's salary, and it was not until 1913 that the debt to the People's National Bank was finally discharged in full.

The first congregational meeting in the new church building was held October 19, 1905. By year end membership was reported as thirty-three. "Of the new members admitted, only two are children of Schwenkfelders." The next month separate church and Sunday school organizations were established, both operating under the general supervision of the Mission Board. At Christmas time the church joined in the support of foreign missions by forwarding a gift to Miss Heebner. The next year weekly prayer meetings were begun and monthly collection envelopes adopted, replacing the previous arrangements for meeting all expenses through subscriptions. A Ladies' Aid Society and Christian Endeavor societies were organized. From the beginning, the Norristown congregation was active in denominational and interdenominational Sunday school associations, hosting several Sunday school conventions.

In a January 7, 1908 letter addressed to the Mission Board, Rev. George K. Meschter resigned his pastorate at Norristown, "on the advice of my physicians, who advise me to give up all work." He preached his last sermon the following Sunday and retired to Florida, where the more temperate climate prolonged his life another two years. Arising early as usual on the morning of June 4, 1910 he went into his yard to trim some small trees on the lawn. Not feeling well, he went into his library about 6:15 a.m., lay down on the sofa, and a half hour later was dead of a cerebral hemorrhage. Quoted Rev. Heebner in his funeral address: "Dead he lay among his books! The peace of God was in his looks." He was laid to rest in the cemetery of the Worcester Schwenkfelder Church.

Upon the resignation of Dr. Meschter, the Mission Board had turned to Robert Jacob Gottschall to serve as lay minister. Mr. Gottschall had supplied the pulpit at Norristown on a number of occasions during the previous three years, had conducted a singing school in the Farmers' Hall at Worcester, and was well known and well liked by the members of the congregation. He had been born in 1883 in Adamstown, Pa., the third of seven children of Andrew M. and Emma B. Gottschall. Educated locally, he received a provisional certificate and taught in the schools of Lancaster County. He attended Millersville State Normal School, where he earned his permanent teaching certificate. He then enrolled in Perkiomen School, where he taught in the lower grades and did substitute teaching and preaching in Clayton and East Greenville to help pay expenses. While the only

Schwenkfelder minister of his day not of Schwenkfelder descent, he absorbed the spirit of Dr. Kriebel at Perkiomen. On the Schultz farm at Clayton he met his future wife, Sue Deysher Schultz, descendant of immigrant Christopher Schultz. In 1908 he enrolled in the University of Pennsylvania, and in 1912 earned his B.A. degree and a Phi Beta Kappa key, which he proudly wore on a watch chain across the front of his vest for the rest of his life. Wishing better to prepare himself for his life work, he resigned from his pastorate and entered Union Theological Seminary in New York City. Here he graduated in 1915, having specialized in church history and religious education. He also took courses in sociology at Columbia University, receiving his A M. degree the same year.

When Mr. Gottschall left for New York the Mission Board approved Rev. J. A. Swingle as pastor effective November 1, 1912. Rev. Swingle, the husband of Ida Meschter of Palm, was installed Sunday evening, November 3, with appropriate ceremonies, in which representatives of the Mission Board and the other Schwenkfelder churches participated. In 1914, however, he resigned to accept a position with the American Sunday School Association to organize new Sunday schools, and removed to Harrisburg, Pa.

On its tenth anniversary in February 1914 the church reported membership of seventy and the Sunday School 143, with the original principal officers still in service. Upon the recommendation of Rev. Levi S. Hoffman, Rev. G. E. Wolfe served a brief term as pastor, July to September 1914. Rev. Harry Spinks of Philadelphia supplied the pulpit during October and November, and then Mr. Charles Deininger, a student at Ursinus College, Professor Montford Melchior of Girard College, and Rev. Hoffman of the Middle District, each served short supply stints.

While in New York City Mr. Gottschall served as religious director of the 44th St. Boys' Lodging House for three years and chorister of Hope Chapel on East 4th St. for two years, as well as pastor-in-charge there during April and May 1914. During the winter of 1913-1914 he had charge of boys' work in the Church of Sea and Land, preaching there a number of times, as well as in other New York City pulpits. During the summers of 1913 and 1914 he was employed by the Chautauqua Association of Swarthmore, Pa., as advertising manager, requiring him to travel extensively through the middle Atlantic and southern states. He became a member of the Religious Education Association, the American Sociological Society, and the American Historical Association. In these pursuits he formed habits of a lifetime, during which he was especially active in Sunday

School Association and local and state-wide church-related activities.

Mr. Gottschall maintained his contact with the Norristown congregation. On March 21, 1915, he journeyed to Norristown to conduct all the worship services that day. A formal call was issued by the Mission Board, and at its meeting in the Norristown church on Wednesday, April 21, Rev. Heebner, secretary of the Schwenkfelder Mission Board, read a letter from Mr. Gottschall "in which he accepts the call to become the stated Pastor of the Norristown Mission on or about June 1, 1915. The Board expressed their gratification upon the spirit and substance of the letter and entertained high hopes for the continued growth of the work in Norristown under his pastorate."

On Thursday, June 24, at the home of Mr. and Mrs. Morris Schultz in Clayton, Pa., Rev. Gottschall was married to Sue Deysher Schultz. The bride had graduated from Perkiomen School and Oberlin College and was teaching at Perkiomen. Mr. Gottschall was appointed head of the history department at Perkiomen and the couple took up residence in Pennsburg while the new pastor commuted to Norristown to take charge of the activities there.

Completing an eventful two months, on July 11, before a large congregation in the Norristown church, Rev. Gottschall was formally ordained to the Christian ministry. Moderator George K. Brecht presided, Rev. Heebner preached the ordination sermon, Rev. O. S. Kriebel delivered the charge to the people, and Rev. Hoffman delivered the charge to the minister.

Perhaps the word *energetic* best described the young pastor, and the small congregation was challenged and inspired by his initiative and enthusiasm. He loved singing and regularly blended his fine tenor voice in the Norristown and the united Schwenkfelder choirs. He had a ready flow of language and an easy delivery, fluent in both English and German. He was a frequent visitor in homes and hospitals, always with a fresh flower in his buttonhole, and people responded naturally to his pleasant, friendly personality. His wife, more gentle and softspoken, complemented his personality. Her equally enthusiastic participation in church and Sunday school activities endeared her also to the members of the congregation. Their enthusiasm was contagious, permeating the church, Sunday school, and young people's activities, spawning numerous special classes, clubs, and societies within the church congregation, prompting anniversary celebrations, inspiring special projects, and spreading to community, county, and state organization activities.

With the objective of "Winning Norristown and vicinity for Christ," for six weeks from February 20 to April 2, 1916, a Tabernacle

Evangelistic Campaign led by Dr. W. E. Biederwolf and his evangelistic party filled the great tabernacle tent on Markley St., lifting the moral social life of Norristown "several steps higher." "The faces of worshipers are lit up with a new joy. Thousands more are willing to do personal work. . . . The Norristown Schwenkfelder Church has been warmed into a new life and great results are confidently expected. The field is white unto the harvest. Our prayer is that workers may not be lacking nor languishing to garner in the precious grain."

At a congregational meeting on Friday evening, February 2, 1917, after thirteen years of steady, faithful work, the Norristown Mission Church decided to be from thenceforth a self-supporting church, and petitioned the Schwenkfelder Mission Board for its independence. The original band of 29 had grown to a church membership of 97, and a Sunday school enrolment of 169, with an average attendance of 78. On the first Sunday in June 1917 the church celebrated its independence. Rev. Gottschall, Moderator George K. Brecht, Edwin K. Schultz, moderator of General Conference, and John H Schultz, chairman of the Mission Board, participated in special services observing the occasion. Rev. Levi S. Hoffman, Rev. Harvey K. Heebner, and Dr. O. S. Kriebel brought greetings from the sister churches.

Since the officers of the church were not charged with responsibility for program, a church council was formed in January of 1919 under the leadership of Earl T. Moore, assistant superintendent and treasurer of the Sunday school. Employed for many years by the Reading Railroad, he later became president of the Central Railroad of New Jersey. The council had a two-fold purpose: to devise ways and means of holding members and gaining new ones and to initiate new activities to involve more church members as well as members of the community. Composed of representatives from each of the various organizations within the church, the council adopted the following agenda:

1. Preparation of a church calendar
2. Promoting an active men's organization
3. Compiling and maintaining a complete mailing list
4. Developing interest in the *Schwenkfeldian*
5. Reducing tardiness on the part of teachers and scholars
6. Defining work assignments of various committees
7. Establishing more open lines of communication

These items appeared regularly on a monthly agenda sent to all members of the council until sufficient progress was reported to warrant elimination from the agenda. The church officers also were prompted to adopt their own goals, to place a minister on the field, and to double the church membership.

By the end of 1921 church membership had reached 148 and enrolment in the Sunday school 248. John H. Schultz's Sunday school class had installed new electric lights in the sanctuary; the Ladies' Aid Society had recarpeted the main auditorium; the church had issued a 1921 directory; and the congregation had joined in the newly organized Norristown Council of Churches.

On April 14, 1923 the congregation unanimously accepted the offer of Rev. Gottschall to become resident pastor at a salary of $2,000 per year and a parsonage. The church thereupon purchased the dwelling at 1021 W. Marshall Street as a parsonage for Rev. and Mrs. Gottschall and their seven-year-old son, Robert M., thereby happily bringing to an end eight years of commuting by the pastor between his home in Pennsburg and the Norristown community. In this parsonage communicants, neighbors, and visitors from near and far received a warm and friendly welcome. Along with the church, it became a meeting place for committees and other small groups. The writer recalls with a certain nostalgia his first date with his wife-to-be at a dinner at the Gottschalls preceding Barbara Hertwig's November 19, 1939 report to the evening church service on her experiences at the World Conference for Christian Youth in Amsterdam, Holland. It was an exemplary Christian home, setting a fine example for all to witness.

As the church and Sunday school grew, various organized groups were formed to accommodate different age levels and study and service interests. Wednesday evening prayer meetings continued as a regular feature. Junior, intermediate, senior and adult C. E. societies were active. A Ladies' Aid Society, Men's Club, Ushers' League, Women's Missionary Society, an Atta Girls Club and a junior Boys' Club flourished. The pastor's adult Bible class, organized in 1917 with eight members, steadily grew and actively participated in the Pennsylvania State Federation of Adult Organized Bible Classes. George K. Brecht taught the "Friendly Bible Class."

The following excerpts from reports in the *Schwenkfeldian* during 1927 will suggest the breadth of activity and interest:

January—"The Norristown Community Training School for Christian Workers opened on Thursday evening, December 2 (1926). To date 150 teachers and officers have enrolled for serious study in six courses. From our school the following enrolled, . . . [ten names follow]. . . . Our pastor . . . teaches the course on church school administration and is vice-president of the board of trustees and publicity manager for the campaign."

February—"Under the auspices of the Council of Churches, a series of Community Gospel Services were held in Norristown, Bridgeport and Jeffersonville from January 10 to 23. . . . The choir of the church met for organization on Friday, January 28. The Director, Rev. R.J. Gottschall, was elected President."

March—"Our church was very active in the celebration of C. E. Week. . . . Mr. J. Leidy Anders, trustee of our church, recently was elected Vice-President of the Montgomery Trust Company, Treasurer of the Kiwanis Club and Treasurer of the Associated Charities. Mrs. Anders continues her office as Secretary of the Executive Committee of the Probation Society and Treasurer of the Garden Club. Mr. Anders was also elected a Director of the Norristown Y.M.C.A."

April—"The first Mother and Daughter Banquet was held on Saturday evening, March 5, in the Cold Point Grange Hall. Members of the Men's Club prepared and served the meal. . . . Our Pastor, as General Chairman of a County Committee, arranged for an Educational Dinner Conference on Law Observance. . . . From lower Montgomery County 150 persons were present to hear an inspiring address by Judge Harold G. Knight."

May—"As President of the Montgomery County Sabbath School Association, our pastor entertained the District Presidents of the County at a dinner in the Valley Forge Hotel, on Saturday, April 9."

June—"Our church was honored during May with the following appointments: J. Herbert Weber, President of the Montgomery County C. E. Union; Rev. R. J. Gottschall, Intermediate Superintendent of the Montgomery County C. E. Union; Mildred Schultz, Secretary of the Intermediate C. E. Union of Montgomery County; Rev. Robert J. Gottschall, President of the Norristown Council of Churches and President of the Montgomery County Sabbath School Association; J. Herbert Weber, President of the Norristown Branch of the Montgomery County C. E. Union. . . . "

August—"Miss Marion Weber and J. Herbert Weber, who were delegates to the Cleveland C. E. Convention, presented full and interesting reports to our Sunday School on July 17, 24, and 31."

October—"During the week of September 25, twelve Protestant churches of Norristown and Bridgeport made a religious survey of the two boroughs. Ten workers of our church signed up for one hundred hours of work."

November—"During the week of October 9-16, workers in our

church were engaged in a Visitation Evangelism Campaign. Two by two they visited in the homes of prospects secured during Survey Week, conducted two weeks previous to the above date, and urged decisions for Christ and for the Church. As a result to date twenty-five persons—all adults—have been received into membership of our church."

December—"The Second Annual School of Missions was held on successive Wednesday evenings from October 26 to November 16th. Four lectures were given:. . . . "China and Japan" (illustrated) by Rev. H. K. Heebner; November 2, "The Women of Japan," by Mrs. George K. Brecht; November 9, "The Men of Nippon" (illustrated), by Rev. Robert J. Gottschall; November 16, a review of Margaret Burton's book, *New Paths for Old Purposes,* by Mrs. George K. Brecht, Mrs. J. Leidy Anders, Mrs. R. J. Gottschall and Mrs. E. G. Kriebel."

While a host of workers participated, the imprint of the pastor's personality and training was clearly stamped on the program of activities. He was a member of the Kiwanis Club, chaplain of the Fire Department, a member of the School Board for over twenty years, and president of the Tuberculosis Society. Mrs. George K. Brecht also served as a member and two terms as president of the Norristown School Board. The pastor and numerous Sunday school organizations regularly conducted services and assisted in other ways at the Montgomery County prison and at the nearby State Hospital for the mentally ill. His interest in Sunday school activities led him to play a leading role in the annual Schwenkfelder Sunday school conventions, on the board of the Pennsylvania Sunday School Association, and later on the International Council of Religious Education. Enjoying a healthy appetite, he reveled in church and Sunday school dinner affairs, frequently performed as toastmaster and could always be found at the center of any dinner table conversation. During one Sunday school convention banquet, Rev. Gottschall was especially loquacious throughout dinner and following dessert, whereupon Andy Berky, seated at the same table, leaned back in his chair, fixed his gaze upon the pastor, and in a slow Pennsylvania German drawl, goodnaturedly challenged him, "Why don't you turn off your motor and glide for a while?" Rev. Gottschall never seemed to turn off his motor, and church and Sunday school activities proliferated and prospered under his leadership.

The church auditorium proved reasonably adequate for church services, but by the mid-1920s the Sunday school and young people's organizations had completely outgrown their relatively limited facilities and overcrowded conditions severely hampered their activities. In 1925 the church council adopted the project of providing additional space. A building fund was created, to which members were urged to contribute. By 1928 the trustees were directed to ask General Conference (in whose name, at that time, the church property was held) for permission to create a loan. Conference Secretary Samuel K. Brecht duly notified the Norristown congregation that Conference had

> RESOLVED: that Conference approve of the proposition of the Norristown Church to build an addition to the present edifice in accordance with plans and specifications adopted by said church.

A contract in the amount of $9,500 was given to Harry M. Alderfer for the erection of an addition on the rear of the existing structure to contain Sunday school rooms on two floors and a large meeting room in the basement, equipped with a kitchen to accommodate church suppers and similar affairs.

Meanwhile, however, the church building itself was showing signs of age. Individual contributions were applied to its refurbishing. During the summer of 1929 the carpet was taken up, cleaned, and relaid; the organ cleaned, repaired and tuned; new electric lights installed in the sanctuary; the outside woodwork painted; and a new vapor heating system installed. The church auditorium was rededicated with appropriate ceremonies Sunday evening, November 3, with Rev. E. E. S. Johnson, one of the first pastors of the congregation, preaching the sermon.

Mr. Alderfer's work was also completed during 1929, but furnishing and equipping the addition required additional time since the majority of the work was undertaken by various organizations of the church and Sunday school; much of the labor was performed by church and Sunday school workers. The addition was dedicated Sunday morning, June 30, 1930 with Rev. Gottschall in charge of the ceremonies and Dr. George W. Wellburn, of Swarthmore, Pa., superintendent of Christian education for the Pennsylvania State Sabbath School Association, delivering the message on "The Objectives of Christian Education."

In May 1929 the church requested permission of General Conference to incorporate and to hold real estate in its own name. Approval received, Judge Knight of the Common Pleas Court of Montgomery County granted the church a charter on May 15, 1930. A By-Laws Committee was appointed consisting of Rev. Gottschall, Daniel M. Anders, Mrs. J. Leidy Anders, J. Herbert Weber, and

George K. Brecht; by-laws were approved by the congregation January 21, 1931. In 1932 General Conference turned over to the new corporation deeds to the church building and to the parsonage. It was now a fully independent church, affiliated with the Schwenkfelder General Conference. Three years later the church council was reorganized to conform with the provisions of the new by-laws. Rev. Gottschall was elected the first president and Elizabeth Weber the first secretary.

The great depression called forth special efforts by the Norristown congregation to help needy families within the congregation and to extend the outreach of the church to such families in the surrounding neighborhood. The deacons established a deacons relief fund quietly to assist the pastor in meeting needs he encountered in his visitation ministry. Food, milk, coal, and some money were distributed to those most in need. The parents of non-member families were encouraged to send their children to Sunday school and invited to attend church worship services, and some of these were added to the church rolls. Special efforts were made to deepen the spiritual life of the people in the home, and in the work and worship of the church.

The thirtieth anniversary of the Norristown church in 1934 coincided with the denomination-wide Bicentennial Celebration. Observing the local anniversary on Sunday, February 4, Rev. Harvey K. Heebner of the Philadelphia church preached while Rev. Gottschall occupied the pulpit in Philadelphia. The evening service was a joint celebration with the Christian Endeavor, and the last of a series of youth conferences. Rev. Freeman H. Swartz, pastor of the Eden Mennonite Church of Schwenksville, brought the message. Five members of the congregation joined the bicentennial Pilgrimage to Silesia. A number participated in the historical drama, "Faith of our Fathers," presented in Salford Grove, with Rev. Gottschall giving an impressive portrayal of Pastor Neander, the local Harpersdorf pastor just before the Schwenkfelders fled the area.

By the end of 1936 church membership had reached 396, Sunday school enrolment 632, including the home department, and Sunday school average attendance 240. $7,500 of the debt incurred to build the church school addition remained outstanding and this debt was standing in the way of projects to accommodate other pressing needs. Since this was the only debt owing by any of the churches at that time, the entire Schwenkfelder community—with the approval of General Conference—was circularized in an appeal to clear the debt that year, the twentieth anniversary of the church's independence from the Mission Board. By September 1, 1937 the campaign committee reported contributions and pledges totaling $4,000 and the local congregation launched a renewed effort during the fall. With $3,000 remaining, however, during the year 1938, in anticipation of the 35th anniversary of the church in 1939, the church adopted the slogan, "We won't owe a dime after '39," and initiated a campaign to clear the balance, this time eliciting a better response. By the end of 1939 the funds had been raised. Mr. and Mrs. George K. Brecht hosted a celebration dinner at the Y.M.C.A. for all the church officers and their wives. The church was finally free of debt.

The year 1940 brought the National Selective Service Act. As Rev. Gottschall wrote, "The churches face a challenge and opportunity in their ministry to "our boys" who may be drafted. . . . The denomination has not taken a definite stand on "Conscientious Objectors," but will help in every way possible to defend those who register as such. It will also serve those who are inducted into service." An "Honor Roll" of those serving in the armed forces was placed in the rear of the church and updated and rededicated each year throughout the war.

Following the war the moderator, Mr. George K. Brecht, appointed Albert B. Meyer, Wilbur C. Kriebel, and Robert J. Gottschall a committee on Aid to Returning Service Personnel. On May 25, 1946 the committee joined with the Ladies' Aid and members of the Semper Fidelis Club to sponsor a dinner for returned service men and their guests. Following the dinner the senior choir sponsored a musical program and the Willing Workers' Class a reception attended by 150 persons. The church, and many individual members, took an active part in providing food, clothing, and other necessities to the Harpersdorf and European refugees as part of the General Conference relief project. More than 100 cartons of clothing and over $2,300 were contributed. Additional clothing was sent to New Windsor, Maryland, to Church World Service.

In September 1947 a retirement fund for the pastor was authorized and the funds placed in the Norristown Federal Savings and Loan Association. For a number of years the young men's Bible class sponsored an oyster supper to raise money for this project, a regular guest being Judge Holland of Montgomery County Orphans Court. No oyster supper was ever complete until Mr. A. K. Rothenberger arrived, usually after 8:00 p.m. His order was always the same—a large oyster stew and a double portion of fried oysters. This serving signaled the end of the supper. While the young men of the church were frying oysters in the kitchen, the Brecht Sunday school class held a bazaar and cake sale on the first floor in the Sunday school building. Working together these two groups raised a substantial sum for the minister's retirement fund.

In May of 1949 Rev. Gottschall became critically ill and was hospitalized when peritonitis set in following a ruptured appendix. Only his hearty constitution saw him through a week-long crisis. Rev. Maurice Hohlfeld, living in nearby Trappe, supplied the pulpit. During the summer, while the pastor was convalescing, the church officers engaged the services of Mr. Harlan Durfee, a resident of Glenside, Pa., a member of Carmel Presbyterian Church and a junior student for the ministry at Princeton Theological Seminary, to serve as assistant to the minister. Mr. Durfee had been teacher of the young men's Bible class since his undergraduate days at Ursinus College. He was president of the Pennsylvania State Youth Temperance Council and was in charge of the Council Camp at Newton Hamilton, Pa. Beginning November 1, Mr. Durfee was employed as director of youth activities, working Saturdays and Sundays, and teaching the young men's Bible class in the church school. Following his graduation from seminary, Mr. Durfee was ordained to the Christian ministry at the Carmel Presbyterian Church near Glenside on June 27, 1951. That fall he was called to become pastor of the Mt. Joy, Pa., Presbyterian church, where he assumed also responsibility for Donegal Church, an historic church similar to Salford.

Following the lead of their energetic pastor, lay leaders and workers in the Norristown church participated actively in a wide variety of community, county, and state association programs. Workers attending these functions returned to report, serving to uplift the spiritual and social life of the Norristown congregation. The Montgomery County Sunday School Association conducted annual conventions featuring courses in Bible study, methods of teaching, music, social activities, and a closing inspirational message. Along with leaders from various denominations, Norristown teachers presented courses as outlined by the International Christian Education Board at the Norristown Community Training School for Christian Workers. Elizabeth K. Weber served as dean of this school for its last five years, after which the Norristown Council of Churches took over responsibility for the school. Each year two young people active in the local church were selected to go to Camp Kanesatake, a summer retreat at Spruce Creek sponsored by the Pennsylvania State Sabbath School Association. Many workers, particularly young people, assisted faithfully in the community Daily Vacation Bible School sponsored by the churches of the west end of Norristown and usually held in the Calvary Baptist or the Central Presbyterian churches, which had larger facilities to accommodate the activities of the school.

In the early 1940s the men's fellowship class (older men) started a Saturday afternoon outing where they pitched horseshoes and enjoyed a meal of steamed clams, corn on the cob, etc. The first host was Bert Clemens at his home on Gravel Pike in Delphi. For this event Bert made a clam steamer, which has been used every year since. About 1949 the fellowship class invited the young men's Bible class and their wives to join them for this event. The two groups, which included all the men of the church, later became known as the Norschmen. For about five years in the early 1950s Robert and Margaret Scheid hosted the clam bake at their spacious place on Berks Road. Hot dogs and hamburgers were added to the menu, and the entire families of the men were included. About 1955 the event was moved to the home of Victor and Thelma Glenn at 1939 W. Marshall St., where it continued for over twenty-five years. The men of the church continue to organize the outing, which is held the first Saturday after Labor Day and is supported by "passing the hat."

In 1951 a church directory was prepared, a ready reference helping to draw new members into the activities of the church.

The year 1954 marked the golden anniversary of the founding of the church. The thriving congregation had grown to a membership of 629, the Sunday school to an enrollment of 571, including the home department, with an average attendance of 172. The church budget reached $12,500. A committee of Thelma Glenn, Ethel Beideman, Mildred A. Kriebel, and Helen Felton scheduled monthly activities throughout the year to honor all the various active church groups. These included the family, church school, Boy and Girl Scouts, Philathea Class, Ladies' Aid Society, missionary groups, athletic groups, Semper Fidelis, the choirs, Atta Girls and the Brecht Sunday school class, the men's club and Christian Endeavor. The Ladies' Aid Society was especially feted for its continuous role in supplying financial support, courage, and fellowship for the many projects envisioned. The members had placed in the church a pulpit Bible, communion linen, a clock for the sanctuary, hymnals, a piano, and the baptismal font, beside supporting virtually every project undertaken on behalf of the church. How busy these church women must have been! The services of Mrs. Frank H. Anders, Mrs. Wayne N. Alderfer, and Mrs. William H. Michener, the first three presidents of the society, were particularly noted. The society had raised $6,523 for the use of the church, including $1,500 for the parsonage fund.

They had supported missions, including Flora K. Heebner, Harpersdorf refugees, and the Hindman School in Kentucky.

After fifty years of faithful service as treasurer of the church, Wilson K. Heebner resigned and Mildred A. Kriebel was elected in his place. The moderator, George K. Brecht, was feted by the Ladies' Aid Society at a surprise 87th birthday party. He had served as treasurer of the Montgomery County Bar Association for more than a quarter century and as secretary of the Montgomery County Historical Society for twenty-four years. His wife, Rebecca Wood Brecht, had died in 1949.

Over the fifty years, besides Schwenkfelder Missionaries Flora Heebner and Mabel Reiff, the church had supported Dr. Frank C. Laubach in various parts of the world, the Christian Literacy work in which Rev. Hohlfeld followed Dr. Laubach, missionaries in India, Africa, Micronesia, and leper work.

Free of debt, in January 1955, the pastor announced plans for developing a church missionary group, a committee for supervising a three-year plan for the "Share our Surplus" crusade, and a committee on evangelism and membership. The group voted donations of money to the Pennsylvania Council of Churches, Pennsylvania Temperance League, State Lord's Day Alliance, Philadelphia Council of Churches, Greater Norristown Council of Churches, American Leprosy Missions, American Mission to the Greeks, the Near East Foundation, American Friends Service Committee, Church World Service, American Bible Society, World Literacy Inc., Hindman School, and to work among lepers in Africa.

Religious instruction of the young was based, during the early years of the twentieth century, on the catechism prepared by Reverend Christopher Schultz, first printed in 1763 and revised in 1784 and 1855. Then during the 1920s Rev. Levi Hoffman was appointed to write a new catechism which was printed by the Board of Publication. To many teachers and young people, however, the language of this catechism appeared too stilted and academic, and a simplified version was deemed necessary. Rev. Gottschall was appointed to prepare the revision, and in 1955 the Board of Publication published his *Handbook for Instruction of Catechumens in the Schwenkfelder Church*. Included in this volume was a section on the most distinctive beliefs and doctrines of Caspar Schwenckfeld von Ossig and a brief history of the Schwenkfelders from 1561 to 1954, prepared with the assistance of Mrs. Selina G. Schultz. Notwithstanding some reservations by Rev. Hoffman, the new catechism was generally accepted and remains the one in use down to the present.

On June 10, 1955, the Schwenkfelder United Choirs and the Junior Choir of the Norristown church presented a special music festival in the Stewart Junior High School auditorium. After the rendition of several selections, there began the special surprise program—"This is Your Life,"— for Rev. and Mrs. Gottschall in celebration of the fortieth anniversary of Rev. Gottschall's ordination into the Christian ministry and the couple's fortieth wedding anniversary. As a climax to the evening, church members and friends presented the Gotschalls with a new 1955 Chevrolet car. Of course, Mrs. Gottschall was to be the driver, for Rev. Gottschall, as Rev. Heebner, never learned to drive a car. It was commonly remarked that Rev. Gottschall was always so busy waving to his many friends that he could never have kept his hands on the wheel long enough to drive a car! A reception in the dining room of the church followed the choir presentation. A special booklet written for the occasion by Robert M. Gottschall, Rev. Gottschall's son, was one of various features announced during the evening. Relatives and friends from near and far attended this memorable occasion. In his response Rev. Gottschall expressed the need for more evangelistic effort and the witnessing and disciplining of our lives to give spiritual strength so that God might work through us to bring about His Kingdom on earth.

In 1957 Mr. Milton P. Ryder of Brockton, Mass., a student at Eastern Baptist College, was selected to be assistant to the pastor, with responsibility for youth work. His dynamic personality and enthusiasm attracted the young people, who readily responded to his leadership. He coordinated the activities of the church school and Christian Endeavor. Bible study became a part of every Sunday school hour. How to use the Bible, where to find a reference and how to find help for one's self were among the topics which Mr. Ryder used. He led them in a study of action verbs in the New Testament, reminding them that Christianity was an active religion to be lived.

Four Christian Endeavor Societies functioned independently, although in cooperation with other church activities. They took an active part in the Norristown Branch and Montgomery County C. E. activities. During the summer months outdoor worship services were held, spelling bees enjoyed, and special speakers from Eastern Baptist College brought in. One group was challenged to "FLEE the lusts of this world, FOLLOW Christ always, and FIGHT the good fight of FAITH." Mr. Ryder took the young people to the Montgomery County Labor Day weekend retreats at Camp Council, near Phoenixville, where along with a lot of fun and frivolity they enjoyed the spiritual benefits of the camp. The decision services, outdoor candlelight communion services, Bible conferences, and C. E. workshop periods made lasting impressions upon the developing young people, increasing their awareness of the presence of Christ.

Since transportation was a problem, Mr. Ryder bought an old hearse and equipped it with benches. This vehicle was a highlight in the parade of the International C. E. Convention in Philadelphia in 1959. That same summer a number of Christian Endeavorers bade Milton farewell at his wedding in Rhode Island.

Having experienced the positive influence exerted by young men such as Harlan Durfee and Milton Ryder, the church arranged to have college students work with the congregation, giving them the title of director of youth activities. Over the years those serving the church as youth directors included John Bammesberger, Jack Wallace, Paul Marmon, Douglas Cook and George McCurdy. Some time later church council engaged seminary students as intern pastors to assist the church with its program and to give training and experience to these persons. Seminary student Penelope Rahm worked with the church during the school years 1979 to 1981, and John Goodwin during the years 1981 to 1983.

In January of 1962, George K. Brecht retired as moderator, although continuing as moderator emeritus, while younger leadership was elected to the church board. C. Harold Beideman was elected moderator and Robert Scheid, vice-moderator.

By 1962 Rev. Gottschall was 79 and the incessant activity over the years began to take its toll. He reluctantly began to accept the prospect of retirement. A pulpit committee was appointed. The next spring Rev. Gottschall fixed the date of May 1, 1963 for retirement after fifty-three years as pastor of the Norristown church. He was immediately elected pastor emeritus, to continue residence in the parsonage, and to maintain for another five years his extensive program of regular visitations in Norristown's hospitals and to work in organizations of the community.

The pulpit committee selected the Rev. Ronald Wayne Lockhart, who was installed as pastor Sunday, May 5, 1963. A native of Van Buren, Arkansas, he had earned a B.S. degree in chemical engineering from the University of Tulsa, Oklahoma, and taken a position as process engineer with the Carter Oil Co. He left this job to seek a B.D. degree at Crozer Theological Seminary in Chester, Pa., following which he began graduate work at the University of Pennsylvania. Dr. Maurice Hohlfeld preached the installation sermon, Rev. Gottschall gave the charge to the new pastor, and Dr.

Kenneth L. Smith of Crozer Seminary delivered the charge to the congregation. Ministers of the other Schwenkfelder churches also participated.

After over fifty years under the energetic leadership of Rev. Gottschall, it is hardly surprising that the new leadership experienced a difficult transition period, and indeed Rev. Lockhart's two-year pastorate proved less than a happy experience for both the pastor and the congregation. The younger leadership set out ambitiously enough to promote more participation in the work of the church, to increase attendance, and to encourage personal spiritual growth. Many adult members were called upon to serve on various committees or to keep in touch with absentee families. Church school members were urged to invite their friends.

The new pastor suggested a complete change in the adult department of the church school. The International lessons were replaced by elective courses, selected by the adults. This new plan created some confusion. The regular teachers felt inadequate to teach a mixed age and sex group, dealing furthermore with questions and issues of which they often had little or no knowledge. Although it was a challenging plan, perhaps in harmony with the disturbed conditions of the 1960s, many of the adults felt uncomfortable in discussion groups and it was difficult to find qualified new teachers. Attendance gradually declined, seemingly defeating the ambitious goals which the new leadership had set for itself. The multiplicity of "Indians" and the paucity of "Chiefs" plagued the church for some years.

In 1963 the church purchased the house at 620 George St., across Blackberry Alley from the church. The men of the church substantially renovated the interior and the ladies redecorated it to serve the young people's departments of the Sunday school, as well as a variety of educational purposes. The building was dedicated October 13, 1963, at which time a plaque was unveiled identifying it as the "Gottschall Annex" in honor of Rev. and Mrs. Gottschall. Since 1966 the Gottschall Annex has been used by the West End Pre-School, a community effort of the west end churches to provide enrichment for four-year-olds, particularly of middle and lower income families, and to prepare them for a happy adjustment when entering kindergarten the following September. A church office, essential to the effective operation of the church, was placed to the rear of the church on the first floor of the church school building. A legacy under the will of Wayne C. Meschter provided funds for this project. A gift provided by Mrs. Duncan Forsyth in memory of her husband was used to supply the furnishings.

At the annual congregational meeting January 27, 1965 the church voted to have associate membership with the United Church of Christ. Of the ninety-nine members voting, 78.7 percent of the ballots were in favor of the affiliation. It was anticipated that wider access to educational and evangelistic resources and fellowship with the larger Christian group would be mutually beneficial to the local church and to the Church of Jesus Christ. The move did not in any way affect the church's relationship with the Schwenkfelder Conference.

On May 30, 1965 Rev. Lockhart resigned to pursue further seminary education with a view to ordination in the Episcopal church. In a friendly, but candid, article in the July *Schwenkfeldian* he set forth his reasons for resigning. They are cited here in some detail as they throw light on the general structure of the Schwenkfelder church, and because they raise issues which may well be pondered with profit. He commended the Norristown church for the freedom of expression granted him in the pulpit, for upholding his absolute right to speak as hopefully he was inspired by God, for their openness and involvement in the community as a whole, and for their participation in ecumenical activities. He felt, however, that he would better develop personally in a more structured church organization. He cited deliberations of General Conference, whose decisions ultimately arrived at are as quickly made subject to ratification by the local churches. Furthermore, he felt in the Schwenkfelder church the priesthood of the laity was elevated above the priesthood of the clergy, and went on:

> In all kindness, I must state that the ministry of the Schwenkfelder Church as a denomination is almost nil. Furthermore, Conferences have become "ritualistic" as opposed to decision making sessions which affect the ministry of the local church. General Conference must be devoted to grappling with issues that confront 20th century society and the role of the denomination in attempting to solve these problems. . . . We are Christians first and Schwenkfelders, Methodists, Episcopalians, etc., second. The God revealed to us in Christ cannot be ignored for the sake of hereditary culture, or denominational affiliations. The cause of Christ must receive our primary loyalty.

The pulpit committee now recommended Rev. David R. Crowle. He conducted the services on Sunday, August 1, 1965 and was called as pastor at a congregational meeting immediately following. Rev. Crowle, a native of Williamsport, Pa., and a graduate of Elon College in North Carolina, had earned a B.D. degree from the

Oberlin Graduate School of Theology. Since 1960 he had served as pastor of the Park Congregational Church, U.C.C., in East Falls, Philadelphia. Denominationally he had served as chairman of the Philadelphia Association Committee on Ministries to Institutions (Hospitals and Prisons) and as chairman of the Social Action Committee. "Mr. Crowle is an industrious minister of the gospel who exhibits a great deal of initiative as he confronts and attempts to solve church and community problems."

The church was completely renovated in 1965-1966 and dedicated October 2, 1966. The beautiful symbols in the plate glass windows at the rear of the sanctuary were designed and interpreted by Rev. Crowle. They symbolize the progressive witness of the church to God and to the nature of man's commitment to Him. Since some of the existing memorials were to be altered by the renovations, Paul E. Haines photographed them and placed the pictures in a memorial book arranged by Nancy M. Breuninger. The names of the contributors of monetary gifts were also listed therein. Marian Ragan and Elaine Smith have kept this book up to date. It is kept on display in the desk case in the narthex.

In 1966, faced with declining health, Rev. and Mrs. Gottschall gave up the parsonage and moved to the home of their only son in Chadds Ford, Pa. Since the younger pastors preferred to own their own homes, the parsonage was sold in December of that year. After a year of incapacitating illness, Rev. Gottschall passed away on July 19, 1968, aged 85. Mrs. Gottschall moved near her son, at this time living in Tempe, Arizona, where she died February 15, 1974. Rev. David Crowle conducted her funeral service in the Norristown church, following which she was buried beside her husband in the Schultz family plot at the Bethesda church cemetery, Clayton, Pa.

The Norristown congregation decided to establish a memorial for Rev. and Mrs. Gottschall. At a special service Sunday morning, June 1, 1975 Miss Nadine Cameron spoke of the couple, "both of whom were for many years dedicated to the love of Christ and to the Congregation of the Norristown Schwenkfelder Church. Not only our church, but the entire community felt the influence of these dear people. Theirs was a ministry of true LOVE. Many people remember the words of comfort and cheer which Mr. Gottschall spread on his regular visits to the hospitals. Many, many, children felt the loving influence of Mrs. Gottschall as she guided their lives in the church school and in junior Christian Endeavor, so we would like to share in a memorial to these fine people." She then introduced Mrs. Katherine Jacobs, who presented a check for $1,375 to the Rev. Fred I. Lesten of the American Bible Society for its work in translating the scriptures into various languages. The gift was presented as a memorial to Rev. and Mrs. Gottschall, who took a deep interest in the work of this society.

Over the years the Norristown congregation assumed its full share of leadership roles in the General Conference. Wilbur C. Kriebel and his wife Mildred were active in many of the Norristown activities, Wilbur serving as recording secretary from 1937 to 1945, adult church school superintendent, and teacher of the men's Bible class. In 1938 he succeeded Dr. Samuel K. Brecht as secretary of General Conference. He was proprietor of a print shop in Chester, Pa., where he later resided, was tour promotional director for Chester County, and served as head of the Chester County Bicentennial Committee for their 1976 celebration.

J. Herbert Weber, a native of Norristown and graduate of Temple University, served as secretary and assistant to George K. Brecht in his law office, and during Mr. Brecht's later years performed many duties usually assumed by a law clerk. He became involved in building and loan activities. For more than twenty-five years he served as court clerk in the Montgomery County courts. In 1928 he was elected president of both the Norristown Branch of C. E. and the Montgomery County C. E. Union. He then served two years as secretary of Southeast Pennsylvania District, and in 1932 was elected treasurer of the Pennsylvania C. E. Union. He served as teacher and long-time financial secretary of the Sunday school, as well as treasurer of the Conference Mission Board, and in 1942 succeeded George K. Brecht as treasurer of General Conference. In 1953 he was elected vice-moderator, and in 1958 succeeded Wayne C. Meschter as moderator of General Conference, in which capacity he served until 1971, when he turned the gavel over to fellow Norristonian, Vincent W. Nyce. In 1932 he married Elizabeth Krauskopf, a Lutheran, active in the North Penn Branch of Christian Endeavor, in which activity the couple met. Elizabeth graduated from the Philadelphia Normal School and Temple University and taught for a number of years in Philadelphia, and then in Norristown, where she also served as an elementary school principal. She devoted herself to Christian education, both in the Norristown church and in the community, and was several times recognized for her service to young people, both in teaching and in girl scouting.

Vincent W. Nyce gained entry into the Schwenkfelder "Vereinschaft" through his marriage to Mildred Beyer Schultz, a descendant of immigrant George Schultz. Educated at Schwenksville High,

Drexel, and R.C.A. Institutes, he served a four-year term in the infantry during World War II and, after sixteen years in the reserves, retired with the rank of Lieutenant Colonel in 1962. During most of his working life he was employed at the Norristown State Hospital, retiring as business manager in 1973. He served the Norristown church as deacon, church school treasurer, church school teacher, chairman of the Boy Scout Troop Committee, and moderator of the church. He was a trustee and treasurer of Perkiomen School and succeeded J. Herbert Weber as moderator of General Conference from 1971 to 1977. Mr. Nyce was an original incorporator and director of Advanced Living, Inc., the sponsoring body for Schwenckfeld Manor. He served as chairman of the building committee, the first administrator, and, after completion of Schwenckfeld Manor East in 1979, as administrative consultant.

Concern for persons released from the State Hospital resulted in a luncheon program and an "After Care" social hour. A number of church women prepared the weekly meals. An effective ecumenical project, "Key 73," sponsored locally by the west end churches, but observed by churches nation-wide, found church members participating in the twenty-four-hour prayer vigil centered in the Haws Avenue United Methodist Church.

In October of 1974 Rev. Crowle, after serving the congregation for nine years, resigned to pursue secular work. Dr. Frank E. Sharp, a retired Baptist minister, served as interim pastor while the pulpit committee searched for a candidate to fill the vacancy. During the Christmas season Dr. Sharp initiated a Christmas Eve family candlelight service, which was very well attended and became a tradition in the church calendar. Three young people, Susan Ragan, Donna Miles, and Lynn Munshower, directed the program.

Upon the recommendation of the pulpit committee, a special congregational meeting called as pastor Rev. Herbert H. Dewees, who was installed Sunday evening, November 2, 1975. Rev. Dewees was born and educated in the Norristown area, at Temple University, at the Russel H. Conwell School of Theology, and did graduate work at the University of Pennsylvania. He came to the Norristown church from a six-year term as minister of the Hegins Valley charge of the United Church of Christ. A former president of the Norristown Council of Churches and its hospital chaplain, he had served as a member of the board of managers of the Bethany Children's Home, Womelsdorf, Pa., as industrial chaplain for the Alan Wood Steel Co., and as assistant minister at the Haws Ave. Methodist Church in Norristown. The following May church groups organized a musical and reception at which friends old and new helped him celebrate his twenty-fifth year in the ministry. The couple easily came to feel at home, as Rev. Dewees was a lifelong resident of the area, and Mrs. Dewees, a descendant of Schwenkfelder immigrant David Heebner, had been a member of the Norristown church before her marriage.

In the summer of 1976 the Schwenkfelders observed the American Bicentennial with a new presentation of the pageant "Faith of our Fathers," originally presented in 1934. Mildred and Vincent Nyce, Clarence Baker, and J. Herbert Weber assumed leading roles, while Thelma Glenn assisted with costumes.

The month of February 1979 marked the 75th anniversary of the beginning of the church and Sunday school. Verda Anders Cameron, a member of an adult class, was honored as the only living member of the original Sunday school class. Verda Anders Cameron, Russell Brecht Weber and J. Herbert Weber, all of whom joined the church in 1916, were recognized as the living members with the longest terms of membership. Rev. Jack Rothenberger of the Central Schwenkfelder Church, preached the anniversary sermon in May 1979, challenging the congregation to look forward to the future of the church. This service was followed by a congregational luncheon. A 75th-anniversary bulletin presented an historical statement of many years of worship and service. Nadine Cameron and Susan Ragan arranged an interesting display of articles and artifacts collected by various members, a display which created much fun and laughter.

After the formation of the church council in 1964 the Sunday school once more became a part of the church organization, with the Board of Christian Education directing its activities. Classes on the life, work and teachings of Schwenckfeld were presented regularly for teachers, leaders, and members of the congregation. High school graduates were presented with the book, *The Iron Collar,* by Fedor Sommer, translated by Andrew S. Berky. College graduates received *Caspar Schwenckfeld von Ossig,* the biography by Selina Gerhard Schultz. Presentation of these books continues as an annual tradition.

There was renewed interest in providing scriptures for new Christians in other parts of the world. Some were sent to the Maxakali Indians in Brazil, Naraki tribe of New Guinea, and the Kekchi tribe of Guatemala. In 1981 efforts were directed to "Bibles for India," where the indigenous churches need thousands of copies in sixteen languages and 150 dialects. Through the efforts of the Home Bible League and the Wycliffe translators this great work is being accomplished.

Rev. Dewees came to the Schwenkfelder pastorate as a mature pastor and experienced administrator. His eight-year pastorate from 1975 to the end of 1983, when he planned to retire, was a rewarding one, and the church generally prospered. His ministry was Christ-centered: "If we really seek the will of Christ for our lives and for this church, then the Holy Spirit, like a mighty rushing wind, will sweep through our church, and truly we will all be changed."

At the time of his arrival there were two active but separate groups dividing the women of the church. There was the Brecht Bible class with many dedicated women who held on to the memory of a wonderful teacher and leader of the church, Rebecca W. Brecht, wife of long-time moderator George Brecht. But there were as many women of the church who did not have that personal relationship and who did not feel a part of that group. There was also a Semper Fidelis Club comprised of another generation of wonderful, faithful ladies, but who were not attracting the younger women and who found they were not able to function as a working group. At the gentle but firm urging of the new pastor the separate groups were merged into a new Women's Fellowship, and the pastor announced that all women members of the church were at the same time automatically members of the Women's Fellowship group. The result was a greatly strengthened role for the women in the life of the church. They plan monthly programs of general interest and are called upon to serve receptions, dinners, housecleaning projects, and money-raising events in the form of Christmas bazaars, strawberry festivals, rummage sales, etc. With the funds so raised, monetary gifts have been made to the church, for Bibles for India, for support of an Indian child and a Haitian child, for the stuffing of stockings for patients at the Norristown State Hospital, for groceries for needy families at Christmas, for the migrant ministry, and for any need that can be met. As long as there are Lydias, Dorcases, Ruths, Esthers, Marthas, and Marys exemplified in the lives of church women everywhere, the church will live on. This is our heart's desire.

A second strong group in the church has been the Missionary Committee, which, with a truly ecumenical outreach, has supported such agencies as the Faith Mountain Mission in Kentucky, Norristown's Interfaith Mission, the Migrant Ministry, Joan Hunsberger in Brazil, and many independent missions in addition to the projects of the Schwenkfelder Board of Missions.

As Rev. Dewees contemplated his retirement he expressed his appreciation for the love, cooperation, and support from the congregation which had made his ministry a joy. He saw a fine choir of great loyalty, a finely organized church school staff, and usually an intern pastor from Eastern Baptist Seminary.

Asked about the future, he responded, "Wouldn't it be wonderful to peer into the future and to know how to plan and work with the best results? But, if that were possible, where would the challenge be? What about our faith? No, I think it was God's will that the future be hidden from our eyes so that we simply must practice the faith that we profess, and trust and obey. I cannot believe that a church with so rich a heritage can come to naught in God's plans. I do not think that God is finished with the Norristown church. What the future holds is an intriguing speculation, but it is all in God's hands."

Chapter Nine

The Lansdale Schwenkfelder Church

Among those who sought to establish homes in the new land, about 1729 there came from Wales one Jenkin Jenkins, whose family became the principal pioneers in the establishment of a community in eastern Montgomery County which later took the name of Lansdale. His son John Jenkins inherited from his father 150 acres, upon which he built a farmhouse, still standing on the north side of Jenkins Avenue between Chestnut and Line Streets, presently owned by the Borough and diligently cared for by the Lansdale Historical Society. John Jenkins' grandson, also named John, was president of the road company that built the Springhouse to Sumneytown Turnpike, and his son John S. Jenkins in 1856 opened the first General Merchandise Store and in 1860 became the first postmaster. In 1864 the first bank was formed; John S. Jenkins' son became its first president. In 1856 the community took the name of "Lansdale" from Philip Lansdale Fox, who was the chief surveyor for the North Pennsylvania Railroad. On August 24, 1872 the Borough of Lansdale was incorporated.

By the early 1900s the town had become something of a transportation hub and a center for a wide variety of manufacturing activities. Even then the Bethlehem branch of the Reading Railroad offered commuter service to Philadelphia. There was express trolley service to Allentown and to Sixty-ninth St. The Lehigh Valley Transit Company trolley offered conveyance to Chestnut Hill for 25 cents, from which point for a nickel fare the rider could connect with almost any trolley line in Philadelphia, although it took time. This trolley came into town along Railroad Avenue, stopped at the Trolley Station, then almost immediately made a left turn on to West Main

Street, passing by the corner of Main Street and Towamencin Ave., later to become the site of the Lansdale Schwenkfelder Church. Schwenkfelder Irwin S. Kriebel, later a charter member of the church, became a lineman and then a motorman on this line, a position which he held until 1914 when an unfortunate accident in the trolley barn in Souderton made it impossible for him to continue working.

Perhaps at this time the most notable industrial concern located here was Heebner and Sons, makers of agricultural machinery. This business was originated by David S. Heebner, a lifelong active member of the Worcester Schwenkfelder congregation, who gained a local reputation as a maker of clocks on his Worcester Township farm. Neighbors and friends prevailed upon him to direct his attention to invention and development of labor-saving agricultural implements and machinery, which they so desperately needed. In 1840 he made his first machine, devoting six weeks to the task; gradually his machinery business developed. In 1852 he retired from farming, sold most of the farm, and moved his agricultural machinery works to an eleven-acre corner tract which he retained. In 1862 he took his two sons, Isaac and Josiah, into partnership. In 1868 Isaac withdrew to set up a machine repair shop at Main and Broad Streets in Lansdale. Two years later the youngest son, William D., also left his father to join Isaac in Lansdale. Then in 1872, attracted by the availability of railroad siding facilities, David joined the move to Lansdale, leaving only Josiah in Worcester. By 1873 the Lansdale enterprise became Heebner and Sons, and was set up in a large new building adjoining the Broad and Main St. property. The company manufactured horse-powers, grain threshers to take the place of the flail, and ensilage cutters for greater economy in feeding of stock. They not only developed agricultural machinery but invented diverse tools facilitating the manufacturing process. Their machines were demonstrated and carried high honors at the 1876 Centennial Fair in Philadelphia and at the Chicago World's Fair in 1893. Before World War I Germany and Russia were large buyers; disassembled machines were packed by muleback through the mountain passes of Mexico and by camel into remote Asian provinces. In 1887 son William D. Heebner bought out the other partners and became sole proprietor, continuing until his retirement in 1925. He died in 1933.

For twenty years following its inception in 1895 the Schwenkfelder Mission Board investigated and studied the feasibility of establishing a mission in this thriving community, which was drawing numerous Schwenkfelders from the surrounding countryside, but plans were never pushed to consummation. In 1910, when Rev. Levi S. Hoffman was ordained and installed as minister in the Middle District, no manse was available for him and his new wife. Theretofore the Schwenkfelder ministry in the Middle District had been an avocation and the ministers continued their regular activities, usually farming. Farmsteads regularly passed from father to sons, and only infrequently came on the market. The new minister boarded for two years with parishioner George Kriebel, but upon the marriage of his host's son, these quarters became unavailable to him. Unable to locate suitable quarters nearer the churches which he served, Rev. Hoffman in 1912 purchased a home at 739 West Main Street in Lansdale, where he was to live for the next forty-four years. From the first a member of the Schwenkfelder Mission Board, he shortly became the moving spirit in the establishment of a Schwenkfelder mission in Lansdale.

At this time Schwenkfelders living in Lansdale attended church and Sunday school services in the Towamencin Meeting House only with considerable difficulty. For some time they took the trolley to the Upper Gwynedd School House, from which point they were conveyed to the meeting house in Mr. William K. Heebner's large wagon. Then the trolley route was changed and the ministers and deacons arranged to hire a coach for the round trip from Lansdale. But this coach ran only for regular worship services. On special occasions it could not handle all who wished to attend and it made no provision for young people attending Sunday school, Christian Endeavor, or other activities. In any event, worship services alternated with Worcester and in the summer with Salford, reducing attendance opportunity to every other Sunday, or only once a month. It was no wonder Lansdale Schwenkfelders drifted to other local churches and that their children were enroled in local Sunday schools.

Young Pastor Hoffman had studied Schwenkfelder history and was acutely aware that after 1740 those Schwenkfelder descendants who had remained in Europe, in the absence of an organized Schwenkfelder church, had gradually been absorbed into other churches, and that the Schwenkfelder community had disappeared. As he called upon Lansdale Schwenkfelders he was chagrined to observe the same tendency at work there. Lansdale's most prominent Schwenkfelder, the Hon. William D. Heebner, proprietor of the agricultural machinery company, two-term representative in Harrisburg and a state senator, was a member and chorister of the Lansdale Methodist Church. His brother, Isaac, who built the Tremont House, was also a member there. The Anders Shirt Factory had been started by Schwenkfelders, who by that time were members of Trinity Lutheran Church. Mrs. Daniel Zweier, owner of the Eitherton Hotel, was an active member of the Reformed church. These were prominent Lansdale people, potential supporters of a Schwenkfelder church there, but actively working in other churches.

As a member of the Mission Board, Rev. Hoffman was also keenly aware of the progress of the Philadelphia and Norristown missions and felt badly about the time wasted in delaying the establishment of a mission in Lansdale. The statistical report to General Conference for 1915 listed a total denominational membership of 1,042, of which Philadelphia accounted for 242 and Norristown 70, while out of a total Sunday school enrolment of 1,612, Philadelphia accounted for 430 and Norristown 156. Thus the two mission churches comprised roughly one third of total denominational membership. It was noted further that over seventy people of Schwenkfelder descent lived in Lansdale, more than in the entire Philadelphia membership. Rev. Hoffman laid his concerns before his old pastor, Rev. O. S. Kriebel, who characteristically offered encouragement, and with little difficulty he assured himself of the support of Conference Moderator E. K. Schultz and Mission Board Secretary Rev. Harvey K. Heebner.

Not to be further put off, on Tuesday evening, February 22, 1916, Rev. Hoffman called a meeting in his home at which he frankly discussed the situation with three young men, Harry Ruby, Henry Godshall, and William Cassel. They considered not only the possibility of establishing a Sunday school, but made a survey to estimate what could be expected in the way of membership. They were surprised to discover at least seventy persons were potential members, and that in addition there was strong sentiment for making a Sunday school accessible to the youth outside the Schwenkfelder faith and tradition who lived in the west end of town, not then served by a local church.

A week later, on March 2, 1916 a larger group met in the pastor's home. At this time Rev. Hoffman expressed his views and purpose in greater detail. He then called for a vote and only one spoke out against the new venture. When that one realized he was in the minority, he, too, agreed that he would not oppose the movement. A Sunday school organization was formed, and officers elected by acclamation as follows: President, Irwin S. Kratz; Vice-President, William Moyer; Superintendent, William Cassel; Assistant Superintendent, Harry Ruby; Secretary, Mrs. Raymond Dresher; Chorister, Henry Godshall; Managers, Raymond Dresher, Elmer Hunsberger, and E. Stott.

Two locations were considered for a meeting place—Moyer's Hall on West Main Street adjacent to the railroad crossing, and Music Hall located on North Broad Street. At a meeting again held in the home of Rev. Hoffman, it was unanimously decided to rent the second floor of Music Hall, which was available for $100 per year with heat, light and janitorial services provided. At a second meeting at the home of Mr. and Mrs. Raymond S. Dresher it was decided to hold the first Sunday school session in the form of a Rally Day service, on March 26, 1916 at 2:00 p.m. in Music Hall.

Seventy-two persons attended this first session. The superintendent, Mr. William Cassel, presided and Rev. Hoffman spoke on "The Birth and Growth of the Christian Church as Recorded in the Acts of the Apostles," making practical application of the teachings of the Holy Scriptures by encouraging the founding of a Lansdale Schwenkfelder Church. Mr. A. K. Dresher, superintendent of the Towamencin Sunday school, and his assistant also addressed the gathering. The Philadelphia church was represented by Mr. William Anders. Interestingly, Mrs. Joseph Schultz and Mr. Reuben Kriebel, both members of the first Sunday school which the Schwenkfelders started in the Middle District in 1861, were present at this initial session in Lansdale.

While without a formal church organization, the first worship service was held in the rented hall on June 25, 1916. At this service there were 121 present and the offering amounted to $4.54, an average contribution of slightly under four cents per person.

The enterprise launched, pressure for a proper house of worship soon became irresistible. The Mission Board recommended to the spring General Conference of 1916 that a mission be established. Encouraged by Conference, the Mission Board as its agent shortly thereafter purchased a lot on the corner of Main Street and Towamencin Ave. An opportunity to purchase the abandoned Methodist church building on Walnut Street was rejected, as it was located on a back street. There was strong feeling the church should be visibly located on Main Street.

This site, once a part of Hatfield Township, had been acquired in 1881 by the Lansdale Creamery Association. The Association came into default on $3,123.33 in debts and taxes, and Towamencin Schwenkfelder Andrew B. Kriebel bought the property at sheriff's sale for $100. In 1916 he sold the property to H. L. S. Ruth for $3,450. Mr. Ruth, president of the local Citizens National Bank, lived opposite the property on the corner of Main Street and Towamencin Avenue. That same year, and for the same price, the Schwenkfelder Mission Board acquired the property from Mr. Ruth for a $450 down payment and a $3,000 note bearing interest at a rate of 4 1/2 percent.

In recommending the purchase of this site, the Mission Board noted that:

1. It is located on Main Street where people always go to and fro; where the church will be accessible and where it will be advertised.
2. The site is west of the railroad in a part of the town that is building up rapidly, and away from the amply churched section south of the railroad, commanded by the Methodist and Baptist churches. Moreover, two-thirds of our Schwenkfelder families live in this section and will continue to reside here if the present inflow from the country is any indication.
3. The site offers practically the only desirable corner lot in Lansdale. Several lots for sale in the outskirts and in the middle of blocks, although offered at cheaper figures, for many reasons did not seem to be desirable.
4. Considering the favorable location in a section where property values are rising rapidly, and also the terms of purchase, the price of $3,450.00 seems reasonable. The two houses on the property can be utilized in the construction of the future church. . . .
5. The members of the Lansdale Mission and the clergy and representative business men of the town favor the location. . . .

As usual, the ownership of property carried with it citizen obligations. The Sunday school minute book, under date of January 4, 1917, notes:

A bill for seventy five cents was handed in by Reverend Hoffman for shoveling snow from the pavement around the church lot . . . it was moved and seconded that the Sunday School pay the bill since Rev. Hoffman promised after this he would shovel the snow himself and not have any more bills presented.

A building committee comprised of Reverend Hoffman, Reuben Kriebel, Aaron Snyder, Homer Kriebel and Raymond Dresher was appointed at a February 1917 congregational meeting. A decision to proceed with the erection of a suitable church building was ratified at a special session of General Conference convened for this purpose on April 2, 1917, the very day on which President Woodrow Wilson convened Congress to declare war on Germany. Conference also voted that the "Mission Board would give $10,000 for the church and Lansdale would make up the rest." This was comparable to the support pledged by the Mission Board for the Philadelphia and Norristown missions.

There was some apprehension about proceeding in the face of impending involvement in war. Rev. Hoffman later related that while he and Mr. John H. Schultz of the Norristown congregation were out soliciting contributions for the building, they met a man on the road going home with a load of lumber to build a pigsty. He told them this was no time during the war to build churches. Mr. Schultz used to laugh and say, "It is all right during war time to build pigsties, but not to build churches."

The old buildings on the site were demolished by volunteer workers and the lumber and bricks used in the erection of the new edifice. The church was not built by contract. The workmen were reputable mechanics who were paid the regular daily wages. Construction began in the summer of 1917 and was substantially completed by yearend. The dedication, however, had to be postponed until May 5, 1918, since shipment of the pews, purchased from a German firm in the mid-west, was delayed because of wartime conditions.

On the Sunday of dedication, all the other Schwenkfelder churches suspended services and large delegations attended the exercises. Its seating capacity of 330 was the largest of any Lansdale church auditorium at the time, but it could not accommodate the large congregation assembled, especially during the afternoon and evening exercises. All the Schwenkfelder ministers participated, as did the choirs of all the churches. All the districts had a share in the enterprise. Not only did they raise their allotted share of the Mission Board pledge of $10,000, but at the evening service, presided over by Dr. O S. Kriebel, individuals and church organizations pledged the $2,500 balance of cost, permitting the church to begin service free of debt. Editorialized the *Schwenkfeldian*, "The Lansdale brethren are to be warmly congratulated for their enterprise and enthusiasm, and the dedication of the new church building is a tribute to the Pastor, Rev. L. S. Hoffman, and the earnest work in which he has been engaged since residing in Lansdale."

On Saturday evening, May 5, 1918 the congregation formally organized, with sixty-three charter members affixing their names at the place provided in the pulpit Bible. The following officers were elected: Moderator, Homer Kriebel; Secretary, Wilson C. Moyer; Treasurer, Raymond Dresher; Registrar, John Kile; Deacons, George Hare, Charles Rittenhouse, Isaac Snyder; Trustees, Levi Kratz, Joseph Snyder; Chorister, A. K. Dresher; Assistant Chorister, Aaron Snyder; Pianist, Viola Kratz; Assistant Pianist, Edna Cassel.

As a consequence of Rev. Hoffman's commitments as pastor of

the Middle District churches, worship services were scheduled for Sunday evenings. Sunday school exercises alternated with those of Towamencin Sunday school—on Sundays when there was Sunday school at Towamencin, Lansdale exercises were in the afternoon; when there was no Sunday school at Towamencin, Lansdale exercises were in the morning.

In due time other organizations of the church were developed and the work progressed with all the enthusiasm of pioneers who have discovered new worlds and conquered them. The Lansdale Schwenkfelder Church was dutifully accepted into the town's Christian church fellowship and accepted the invitation to become a member of the Community Union of the Lansdale Churches.

Sunday school business meeting minutes of December 4, 1918, record:

> A suggestion by William Anders that the church receive all collections and pay all bills was turned down by Reverend Hoffman on the ground that the Sunday School was organized before the church and that it did not seem right that the church should dictate to the Sunday School since it was the first to exist and really was the organization that had done the most work. After which, Reverend Hoffman suggested the officers of the Sunday School and the Church have a meeting and agree on how to pay bills in unison, stressing that our finances should be straightened out by the first of the year so as to make a report to the General Conference.

And of a meeting December 3, 1919:

> Mr. Anders (Superintendent) next reported he had not as yet secured a charter for a front line Sunday School and could not conscientiously do so unless the Sunday School met the requirements of a front line school— that is, to have regular temperance and mission talks once a month.

And of a January, 1920 meeting:

> Temperance report for beginning of January—In as much as prohibition was put into effect January 16, 1920, a funeral service on "John Barleycorn" was conducted by Messrs. Ralph Snyder, Jacob Fretz (representing the Mennonite Community) and Reverend L. S. Hoffman.

The first organization formed within the church was a group of ladies, with the intention that three or four of them would hold social gatherings from time to time at each other's houses. However, at their first meeting they were agreeably surprised by having an attendance of forty ladies. It was then and there decided to call the society "Let Us Be Acquainted," a name that later, at the suggestion of Mrs.

Hoffman, was changed to "Willing Helpers," which name it retains to this day. Officers elected at the first meeting, May 13, 1918, were: President, Mrs. Edna Ruby; Vice-president, Miss Nora Cassel; Secretary, Miss Elizabeth A. Snyder; Treasurer, Mrs. Anna B. Lloyd. This organization rendered valuable services in various endeavors over the years. The first secretary of the Sunday school, Mrs. Raymond Dresher, was one of the guiding lights in the formation of the Willing Helpers, serving as its president for a number of years.

The first issue of "The Friendly Messenger," a church bulletin, was published on January 1, 1922. For many years the front page pictured the church building with the caption below the picture reading "The Place We Love." There was indeed a fine spirit, and talented and willing workers pursued any number of worthy enterprises. In at least some measure they made up for the dilution of the pastor's efforts, which necessarily resulted from his duties in the Middle District churches where on alternate Sundays he conducted services at Worcester and Towamencin. At Lansdale Rev. Hoffman regularly taught teacher training and leadership training classes, in both the church and the community. He somehow found time, however, to serve as a member of the Lansdale Board of Trade, encouraging the location of new industries there, and as a member of the committee organizing a new library in the town. He was a charter member of Rotary International. He was drafted to serve on the Lansdale School Board, serving eight years as vice-president and sixteen years as president, during a period of rapid development of the public school system in the town. High school baccalaureate services were frequently held in the church sanctuary.

Some ten years after the erection of the church building, it was made complete by the installation of a pipe organ, dedicated on July 5, 1926. Ruth Bothers (later Heckler) was selected as the first organist and Mr. Abram Dresher was elected chorister. Also in that year, the first Daily Vacation School was organized, and this became a regular feature of the church summer program. A few years later the first Union Good Friday service was held in the church, and the congregation has participated in these community exercises down to the present day.

By 1937 the leaders of the congregation felt the need for more regular worship services and, after consulting with Rev. Hoffman, brought the matter before the congregation. A suggestion to invite a visiting pastor to conduct a morning service the second Sunday of each month and to assist Rev. Hoffman with the evening service the same day was implemented. A committee visited Mr. J. Maurice

Hohlfeld, reared in the Philadelphia Church and about to enter the Temple University School of Theology, and arrangements were made for Maurice to serve as student pastor, with other Schwenkfelder ministers conducting communion services and assisting as required.

No sooner had this arrangement been put into effect than Rev. Hoffman, in the early fall of 1937, was temporarily, but seriously, incapacitated. While standing on the inside drive of Walton's Garage, he was struck by an automobile, suffering a compound fracture of his left leg and an incomplete fracture of his right leg. Thereafter the burden of preaching fell largely upon the student minister.

Beginning Sunday, February 6, 1938 morning and evening worship services were conducted every Sunday. During the summer months Mr. Hohlfeld and Dr. Alfred Sayres, pastor of St. John's Reformed Church in Lansdale, alternated in bringing the message to united evening services held on the lawn of the St. John's church, with the respective churches furnishing the music, ushering, supplying flowers, etc. A friendly spirit of cooperation developed between the two groups.

The Schwenkfelder General Conference granted Maurice licensure on October 15, 1938. In the spring of 1940 he graduated from the Temple School of Theology with a B.S.T. degree, and on June 23 he was ordained and installed as pastor in the Lansdale church. As usual large delegations from the other churches, particularly the Philadelphia church, attended and all of the Schwenkfelder ministers participated. The Lansdale Ministerium was represented by Rev. Olin Krehbiel, who noted that the Lansdale ministers already felt at home with brother Hohlfeld through his two years of service as acting pastor of the local church.

At the April 1938 meeting of the Schwenkfelder Mission Board, a petition was presented requesting that the status of the local group be raised to that of an independent church within the Schwenkfelder Conference. The spring General Conference meeting in Worcester unanimously granted the request. In the fall of that year the congregation was incorporated under the laws of the Commonwealth of Pennsylvania.

The Lansdale Sunday School entered a team in the Baseball Sunday School League of the area. One of the classes became known as the baseball class of "22 Good Batters." Eligibility to play required attendance at Sunday school classes at least twice a month. A Scout Troop was chartered soon after the church became independent and Victor Schultz was chosen as the first Scoutmaster. Also about this time a newly formed Fellowship League, a combination of all the men's classes, was contributed to the life of the church. On June 12, 1940 a program and dinner were held at the church to honor Mr. and Mrs. Raymond Dresher and Mr. Irwin Kratz for twenty-four years of continuous faithful service to the church and Sunday school since its founding. Mr. William Cassel, the first Sunday school superintendent, returned to speak of the organizational problems, which brought back many happy recollections.

The life of the church was greatly enriched by the musical ministry of Paul Bartholomew, the talented church organist. He arranged presentation of anthems and oratorios, and together with Rev. Hohlfeld planned special evening services featuring the great hymns of the church. The rich lore of the Christian heritage was recalled as Maurice described the lives of the authors of the hymns and the background of spiritual experience against which the hymns had been composed. Christian Endeavor young people frequently participated in these programs by reading the scriptures, reporting their spiritual experiences while attending Christian Endeavor retreats or conventions, and by presenting dramas at Christmas and Easter.

Mindful of his own experience as a young person, Maurice encouraged members of the Christian Endeavor to participate in Montgomery County C.E. activities, and to attend Labor Day weekend retreats, County hymn sings and other special events. They also took part in the Lansdale Community Youth Alliance (CYA), joining with other denominations in programs to offer assistance to newcomers in the community, to help in their orientation, and to introduce them to a new church home of their choice. The young people conducted devotional services and distributed copies of the "Upper Room" to patients in the hospitals of the community.

The year 1943 marked the twenty-fifth anniversary of the founding of the church. There was some hesitation as to planning a celebration, since almost one-tenth of the church's 250 members were in the service. But with Rev. Hohlfeld's counsel, "When the world is at its worst, the church must be at its best," a committee was appointed to prepare suitable exercises. The fact did not escape notice that the Lansdale church had been launched on the eve of one great war, and was celebrating this anniversary in the midst of another. The celebration covered three days, beginning Friday evening, May 21, with a community service addressed by Dr. Alfred N. Sayres of St. John's Reformed Church of Lansdale. Saturday rehearsed the work of the Sunday school, winding up in the evening with a banquet at which Mr. Wayne C. Meschter, Moderator of General Conference, brought greetings, and Rev. Mr. William Cassel, the first superintendent of the Sunday school and at this time pastor of the Grace Evangelical-Congregational Church of Kutztown, spoke. He compared the periods of struggle in the olden days with those of the 1940s, reminding the people that "Hitherto the Lord has helped us." On Sunday Rev. Hoffman reminisced as he spoke about "Visions Enacted," citing St. Paul who was not disobedient to the heavenly vision. Flora Heebner presented the worldwide appeal of the church and Rev. Heebner, secretary of the Mission Board, spoke on the "Romance of Missions."

While serving the Lansdale church, Rev. Hohlfeld commuted to Princeton, N.J., to earn his M.S.T. degree from Princeton Theological Seminary in 1942. As an undergraduate at Temple University studying Hebrew and Greek he had become interested in the study of languages, and before graduating from the school of theology, had received a scholarship for the study of German at the University of Munich. During the summer of 1939 the Lansdale church granted him a ten-week leave of absence to take advantage of this scholarship and to visit the Schwenkfelder homelands in Silesia. Nearing the end of his stay, while planning to extend his stay an additional two weeks, he was suddenly alerted to leave the country as war broke out at the end of August. He joined the rush of Americans clambering to get out of Germany. His parents and the Lansdale congregation had a few weeks of great concern for his safety. On his first attempt to cross the border he was turned back by Dutch customs, since he had no steamship ticket to leave from that country. With the help of the American Consuls in Munich and Cologne, however, he was able to get into Holland and then to Belgium. With two other Americans, who loaned him passage money, he was able to secure last-minute, spot-cash passage for three on the "Westernland," and in due course arrived in Hoboken, N.J.

A large number of the young people of the church joined the various armed services during World War II. Members of the church were faithful in communicating with them and sending packages of food and other items. Rev. Hohlfeld frequently sent messages about activities in the church to keep in touch and to let them know they were in the thoughts and prayers of those back home.

As of May 1, 1946 Rev. Hohlfeld presented his resignation as pastor of the Lansdale church to devote full time to what became a distinguished third career as linguist, teacher, and world missionary. He continued, however, as a member of the church for the rest of his life.

On August 7, 1946 a student for the ministry, Mr. Lester

Kister, began his service to the congregation. Mr. Kister received his Bachelor of Arts degree from Gordon College, Boston, Massachusetts, and his Bachelor of Divinity degree from Crozer Theological Seminary, Chester, Pennsylvania. Rev. Kister shortly concluded that he should pursue his life work outside of the ministry. He served only until January 12, 1949.

On July 8, 1946 it was decided by church council to purchase a parsonage on Delaware Avenue, Lansdale, for the sum of $9,750. A down payment of $500 was made, with the balance due in thirty days. A donor who wished to remain anonymous gave the church $7,500, interest free, to consummate the transaction.

On June 19, 1949 Rev. Edgar T. Chandler was accepted to fill the pulpit at Lansdale. He formerly was the pastor at New Britain Baptist Church, Pennsylvania. Reverend Chandler was a native of Benton, Kentucky, and a graduate of Georgetown College, Kentucky, class of 1939. He received his Bachelor of Divinity degree from Crozer Seminary in 1942 and also attended Lutheran Seminary. There soon was a mutual disenchantment between the congregation and Rev. Chandler and his services were discontinued on January 17, 1954.

Mr. Jack R. Rothenberger, an immigrant descendant, member of the Palm Schwenkfelder Church, and at that time a student for the ministry at Hartford Theological Seminary, commuted from Hartford to serve as acting pastor. When school began in the fall, however, he left to concentrate on the completion of his work at Hartford and supply pastors had to fill the void in the pulpit and service the needs of the congregation to the extent possible.

For the next two years Rev. Arthur F. Wagner served as pastor while continuing as a popular teacher and head of the history department at Springfield High School, Montgomery County, Pennsylvania. Rev. Wagner was an ordained Baptist minister who had given up the full-time church ministry to teach in the public schools. He had graduated from Colgate University in 1926 with a Bachelor of Arts degree, received his Master of Arts degree from the same institution in 1927, and in 1929 had earned a Bachelor of Divinity degree from Yale Divinity School. With his dynamic personality and sincerity of purpose, Rev. Wagner proved a fortuitous choice, furnishing a much-needed stabilizing influence in the congregation. Devoted to his tasks, his talents and personality seemed ideally suited to the needs of the congregation at that time. Unfortunately, early in 1956 ill health forced Rev. Wagner to give up his post. His departure was a further disappointment to the congregation seeking stable pastoral leadership.

Rev. Lester K. Kriebel and Rev. Jack Rothenberger, co-pastors of the Palm Schwenkfelder Church, offered their services and alternated each week in the pulpit. After completing his study at Hartford Seminary, Rev. Rothenberger was ordained on June 26, 1955 and installed as associate pastor of the Palm church. He was also to serve on the staff of Perkiomen School, counseling students, teaching courses in mathematics and Bible, and coaching basketball and track. Jack accepted a call from the Lansdale congregation and began his full-time pastorate there July 1, 1956. He brought to the congregation a renewed consciousness of the teachings of Caspar Schwenckfeld as they pertained to everyday life, and his sincerity and devotion were felt throughout the congregation.

Rev. Rothenberger placed new emphasis on the work of the Sunday shool. From the beginning the facilities for Sunday shool and young people's work had been quite inadequate. Under Jack's leadership a movement for a new Christian education building got under way in 1959. A building committee was appointed composed of: Mr. Arthur N. Anders, Jr., Chairman; Mr. Carl Quade, Treasurer; Mrs. Joseph (Hilda) Mininger, Equipment Chairman; Mr. Willard Bergey, Moderator; Mr. G. Donald Reichley, Mr. Nevin Kelly, Jr., Dr. Paul T. Bergey, Mr. Wellington Schlosser, Mr. Samuel Freed, Mr. Paul Rosenberger, Mr. Allen Eshbach, Rev. Jack Rothenberger. They selected Mr. Harold Wilson as the architect and Mr. G.L. Janke as the general contractor. The building was erected at a cost of $105,000 with equipment and furnishings donated by businesses in the community, individuals of the church family, and in memory of family and loved ones. With the new building came the use of the United Church of Christ curriculum in the Sunday school and a general expansion of activities.

Reverend Rothenberger felt that he could best serve the Schwenkfelder denomination in an administrative capacity at Perkiomen School and it once again became necessary for the Lansdale congregation to seek a new pastor. Rev. William E. Cameron, Jr. was selected and he began his duties April 24, 1963.

Rev. Cameron had received his Bachelor of Arts degree from Lafayette College and graduated from Chicago Theological Seminary. He had been student minister at the Asbury Methodist Church in Allentown and at the Woodlawn Methodist Church in Chicago while a seminary student there. A seminarian of the 1960s, Rev. Cameron's emphasis was on social issues. He had very strong feelings supporting desegregation, which he shared with the congregation. His convictions led him to personal involvement in the social problems of the day. After two years of service to the Lansdale congregation, he resigned to become associate director of the Delaware Valley Fair Housing Council in Philadelphia.

Rev. Rothenberger was again drafted into service and divided his time between Perkiomen School and the Lansdale church. After a year of this arrangement, however, Rev. Rothenberger decided to remain at Perkiomen in his administrative capacity and also to serve as chaplain and coordinator of religious affairs. The Lansdale Committee on the Ministry was once again activated to seek a new pastor.

Rev. Larry O. Bechtol, pastor of a Congregational church in the Frankford section of Philadelphia, expressed interest in the Schwenkfelder denomination and beliefs, accepted a proffered call, and began ministering to the Lansdale congregation May 29, 1966. Rev. Bechtol was a native of Dayton, Ohio, and received his Bachelor of Arts degree from Asbury College, Kentucky, and his Bachelor of Divinity degree from Union Theological Seminary in Dayton, Ohio. During his pastorate the "Young Minded" were organized to provide a means for couples of the church to develop closer relationships, an effort from which the church family derived significant benefit. Rev. Bechtol served the congregation for two years. The urge to return to his native Ohio became too great to resist when he was offered a pastorate there.

On April 20, 1969 Reverend Andrew H. Johanson, Jr. became pastor. After having served the First Congregational Church in Rushville, N.Y., Rev. Johanson graduated from Davis-Elkins College in West Virginia and received his Bachelor of Divinity degree from Crozer Theological Seminary, Chester, Pa. He had been a student pastor in Ridley Park, Pennsylvania, and served a one-year internship in the ministry of the national parks. Rev. Johanson served the church for two years and became very interested in pastor-counselor relationships. This interest became so dominant that he decided to pursue the counseling area full time. He left the ministry to do graduate work in counseling and psychiatry.

Rev. Hoffman had served the church for twenty years; Rev. Hohlfeld for nine years. Over the next twenty-five years new pastors had been installed ten times, serving an average term of less than three years. In 1937 the church reported a membership of 189 and a Sunday school enrolment of 222, with an average attendance of 145. The peak of church membership was reached in 1968 with a membership of 363 and a Sunday school enrolment of 210. But the frequent change of pastors and the changing times took their toll. By 1971 church membership had declined to 279, with an average attendance of only 100. Sunday school enrolment had fallen to 100, with average attendance down to around 60. A core of faithful workers nevertheless kept church and Sunday school alive.

The Willing Helpers carried on their program of activities. They prepared food for wedding receptions and other special affairs. They conducted auctions, rummage sales, bake sales and similar activities to raise money for church and Sunday school needs, and for home and foreign missions. They made quilts, sold Christmas and Easter candies, stuffed teddy bears, and were long noted for their delicious cherry pies. The entire congregation was drawn together in providing "Meats for the Needy" within the community. "Second Mile" offerings were taken at communion services and given to the Visiting Nurses' Association to purchase meat for those they found to be in need. To add to these funds each year a "Peach Festival" was held serving soups, hot dogs, barbeques, and fresh peaches with ice cream. These festivals were enjoyed by the guests as well as by the members who put forth such great effort.

The church entered upon a more stable era in the spring of 1971, when a call was extended to the Reverend Arlan M. Bond and he was duly installed on June 20. Rev. Bond graduated from Eastern Baptist College in St. Davids and from the Evangelical Congregational School of Theology in Myerstown, Pa. Sharing in the ministry to the Lansdale church have been his wife, Janet, and two sons, Randy and Steven, then age 14 and 11 respectively. Rev. Bond provided a leadership the church seemed to need. Prior to entering the ministry in 1971 he had been employed in industry, serving as a foundry engineer, and he felt a special rapport with the life of the average person in the pew. His strong commitment to the traditional family lifestyle, his conservative views of the scriptures, and a freely-expressed sense of humor gradually earned him the respect of the congregation. His love and common friendliness created an atmosphere of peace and harmony that the church had long desired.

He shortly reestablished Wednesday evening Bible study and prayer meeting sessions, with invited guests participating during the lenten season. In the fall of the year he introduced into the Sunday school the curriculum of the Gospel Light Publications. He considered these Christ- and Bible-centered lessons more appropriate than the United Church of Christ curriculum, more oriented toward social action themes. The new year of 1972 was begun with a New Year's Eve watchnight service, which observance was repeated annually over the next five years.

Because of a decline in Sunday school attendance in past years, classes had been eliminated for the summer months. Reverend Bond felt that this contributed to a continued decline and therefore reestablished summer Sunday school sessions beginning with the summer of 1972; the downward trend in attendance was reversed. In the fall of 1972 new *Great Hymns of Faith* hymnals for the church sanctuary and fellowship hall were purchased by members of the congregation as memorials to honor a loved one. The new hymnals contained many of the old-time favorites, which were sung with great enthusiasm.

The pastor devoted persistent effort to promoting the unity of the church and especially to strengthening of the families within the church. Under his guidance in the summer of 1973 an annual weekend retreat was established, where families spent the weekend on the Salford Meeting House grounds in tents and trailers, participating in activities consisting of fun, fellowship, and worship of God. In the fall of that same year Revised Standard Version Bibles for the pews were presented in memory of Jonas Y. Bergey, the father of Willard Bergey, who served as moderator of the Lansdale congregation for ten years, 1960 to 1969. The next year the organ was extensively rebuilt and expanded, and on November 24 the new Fritzsche pipe organ was dedicated to the glory of God before a capacity audience present to share in the occasion. In the fall of 1975 the active members of the church were organized into teams, each undertaking to visit three or four inactive families to encourage their participation in the worship services and other activities of the church.

During Rev. Bond's ministry two young men of the church family felt the call to enter the Christian ministry. In 1976 Darryl Lang, a son of Mr. and Mrs. Bernard Lang, having obtained a college degree, began his seminary training in the Hatfield Biblical School of Theology, in Hatfield, Pa. Upon graduation in 1980 Mr. Lang was called to Grace Mennonite Church in Lansdale. A year later he established The Open Bible Church, an independent church located on Jenkins Ave. in Lansdale. In 1979 Randy Bond, son of the pastor and his wife, also undertook a career in the ministry. He graduated from Eastern College, St. Davids, Pennsylvania, and began his seminary training at Eastern Baptist Seminary in Philadelphia. Upon graduation he was called to Zion United Church of Christ, Windsor Castle, near Hamburg, Pa. The congregation there responded quickly to his leadership with increased membership and attendance, testimony to the effectiveness of his upbringing and training, and satisfying to all in the Schwenkfelder congregation who had contributed scholarship aid for his education.

For a number of years the church has extended partial support, as have the Schwenkfelder Mission Board and other Schwenkfelder churches, to Miss Joan Hunsberger, a member of the Lansdale congregation serving as a missionary in Brazil under the auspices of the Unevangelized Fields Missions. In January 1977 a young couple, Bill and Bonnie Rush, entered the mission field. They were not from the church but during the year began to receive partial support from the church. They are presently serving in Indonesia with the Regions Beyond mission board.

To encourage outreach an evangelism training session was held for ten weeks in 1978. This was led by an outside consultant, Reverend David Brewer, who introduced the church to the Kennedy program of evangelism known as "Evangelism Explosion," an outreach program featuring visitation of homes in the neighboring community to present the gospel message. In the same year a Thanksgiving Eve service was initiated, devoted to fine gospel singing of visiting quartets, hymn singing and testimonials of thanksgiving for what God has done in individual lives. It was well received and continues a part of the church calendar.

An increase in the senior church choir required the purchase of new chairs for the choir loft and the original chairs were refinished to match. These were dedicated on June 3, 1979 along with a beautiful polished brass communion service set, in loving memory of Mr. LeRoy B. Rittenhouse, a charter member of the church.

Reverend and Mrs. Bond were guests of honor at a surprise celebration of their twenty-fifth wedding anniversary attended by over 200 guests on October 7, 1979. They were honored with "This Is Your Life," during which time they were introduced to members of their family, members of their wedding party, and many friends of their past. Among the gifts received was a monetary one to be used toward a trip to the Holy Land they had planned for the spring of the following year. The two weeks in Israel stirred them to new insights into the scriptures, giving them a feel for the land and great excitement, having "walked where Jesus walked."

Two exciting and meaningful programs were introduced to the Lansdale church during the year of 1980. The first was "Marriage Encounter Weekends." On these weekends the interested couples of the church experienced a forty-four-hour crash course on communications intended to help a good marriage become even better. These weekends, held in neighboring motels, increased the love between couples and improved the unity of the Spirit throughout the church.

During the year seventeen couples went on such weekends, most returning with great enthusiasm to improve their marriages. In a day when many marriages were in disarray, such a program offered many great benefits.

The enthusiasm aroused by the many couples of the church who had been "encountered" set the pace for a program that involved the entire church, the "Lay Witness Weekend." On this weekend laity came from other churches sharing a testimony of what God through Christ was doing in their lives. This gave confidence to the fellowship to allow them openly to express themselves concerning their own faith. The result was a weekend that has never been forgotten by the participating members.

During this exciting year the church sanctuary was redecorated with new paint, new curtains behind the cross, new paramounts, new carpeting, etc., the beauty of the sanctuary adding to the luster of the worship taking place there. The funds used for this redecorating, for the most part, came from a memorial fund for Rick Moyer, the 18-year-old son of Mr. and Mrs. Gerald Moyer, who was tragically killed in an automobile accident on January 28, 1980. The entire congregation rallied in a loving relationship to the support of this church family in their time of crisis.

Elective courses that had been launched in the adult Sunday school classes in the fall of 1980 continued with enthusiasm. These included a popular film series for the family entitled "Focus on the Family." In the spring of 1981 the Lansdale church entered a team into the local softball league. While the winnings were hard to come by, the games did serve to increase the fellowship among fellow believers.

Another experience of the church which will long be remembered was the observance of a Passover meal on March 22, 1981. This was led by the Reverend Mitchel Treistman from the American Board of Missions to the Jews. The ladies of the church prepared the unfamiliar dishes that were a part of the observance, doing a fine job. The evening was very informative concerning the Jewish Passover meal. As Rev. Bond wrote afterwards, "What added to the observance was to become aware of Christ's symbolic presence within that observance in a number of striking parallels. For instance, the unleavened bread, or matzoh, which is used in the meal is termed a "Unity." It is in three sections, reminiscent of the trinity. The middle matzoh is broken; so also our Lord was broken. When the matzoh is baked it is pierced and striped, a beautiful symbol of our Messiah, who was pierced and striped for the sins of the world."

The church fellowship at Main and Towamencin Avenues in Lansdale prospers, as traditional and new activities contribute to the strength of the church. In January of 1983 the church reported a membership of 326, a Sunday school enrolment of 161, and an average Sunday school attendance of 106. During his continuing pastorate of now more than twelve years' duration, pastor and congregation have grown in Christian fellowship, striving together, in all that is said and done, that God the Father, God the Son, and God the Holy Spirit may be glorified.

Chapter Ten

Perkiomen School

Education among the early Pennsylvania Schwenkfelders

The erudition of individual Schwenkfelder immigrants to America has been widely remarked. Most of them signed their own names to the Pledge of Allegiance upon arrival, itself remarkable for the time when many new arrivals had simply to make their mark. Books and manuscripts were prominent among the meager possessions they were able to bring with them on their long journey. Once in this country they conducted an extensive correspondence with friends and relatives left behind in Europe, as well as with fellow immigrants in sparsely settled parts of Pennsylvania. Much of this correspondence was of the nature of information and instruction, not infrequently written in Latin. Among extant correspondence is that between Balthasar Hoffmann and Christopher Schultz in which the former gives the latter instruction in the comparative study of Greek, Latin, German, and Hebrew.

The education of these early Schwenkfelder immigrants must necessarily have been obtained from private study and tutoring. Their political situation in Europe precluded formal church or school organization. Not a single record survives of a Schwenkfelder immigrant ever having attended any institution of higher learning in the old country. During the first thirty years in this country elementary education continued in the homes, no doubt aided by the religious leaders, George Weiss, Balthasar Hoffmann, and Christopher Kriebel as they traveled widely on horseback to attend to their pastoral duties, to conduct the equivalents of later Sunday schools, and to see to the catechetical instruction of the young.

By the end of the 1750s, however, there is evidence the Schwenkfelders were becoming increasingly alive to the importance of public secular education in a new country then feeling its way to independence politically, educationally, and religiously. They wanted to raise their children literate not only in their native German language but in English, the language in which business and government were conducted. The heads of families met on March 1, 1764 at the home of Caspar Kriebel in Towamencin Township, to consider more formal arrangements for the support of education. By summer they had raised a fund of 840 pounds principally in the form of sixteen-year loans by thirty subscribers. Melchior Schultz, Christopher Schultz, Christopher Yeakel, George Kriebel, and Caspar Kriebel were elected trustees to hold and invest this fund at 5 percent interest and to apply the income toward school expenses. They adopted a preamble strongly emphasizing religious and moral elements in education and a set of ten "fundamental principles" governing the management of the trust fund and the administration of the "school system." Two provisions are of special relevance to our subsequent narrative. While controlled by Schwenkfelders, the schools were to be open to tuition-paying students of whatever denomination, and instruction, while strongly religious, was to be non-sectarian. In these respects Article One was unambiguous:

> Since the originators and contributors to the said fund are of the people called Schwenkfelders, they regard the undertaking as theirs and desire that the trustees elected for control of the fund and supervision of the schools may at all times be prudent and reputable men of the said community. But the idea and intention is that the said school system shall be open to the children of the parents of any denomination, whoever they may be, under this condition that they pay for the instruction of their children, and that they and their children shall regulate and conduct themselves according to the necessary regulations hereby presented, as well as those that may be made hereafter by the trustees hereinafter mentioned. Whereby, however, the impartial instruction according to the religion of each as much as relates to the schools shall not be hindered.

That fall teacher John Davis, for a salary of 20 pounds and board, conducted a school in the Upper District for six months in the home of Christopher Schultz, and in the Lower District John Doerbaum, for a salary of 10 pounds and board, light, and fuel, conducted a six-month term in the home of George Anders. The next year the first school house was erected near the site of the later Towamencin Meeting House. School sessions in the Upper District continued to be held in private homes until erection of the combined school and meeting house at Hosensack in 1790. Combined school and church buildings then followed in Washington Township, near Clayton, in 1791, and at Kraussdale in 1813. A school house at Salford, built in 1828, preceded the later meeting house.

The school system reached perhaps its highest efficiency and influence when the school at Hosensack opened in 1790 with George Carl Stocks as teacher. A native of Halle an der Salle, Germany, he was competent to conduct the study of higher mathematics along with the usual German, English, Latin, and Greek. He was a man of high moral principles and a strict disciplinarian. Financial stringency forced his departure after two years, but he had charted the course the school would follow until it gave way to the public school system around 1840. Hosensack Academy alumni were prominent in Schwenkfelder and community leadership positions for the next fifty years, at which time new needs and new stirrings among the Schwenkfelder community brought into being the present Perkiomen School. As financial pressures increased, and after several teachers in the lower grades introduced reading passages of an objectional nature, teachers began more often to be chosen from the Schwenkfelder ranks, particularly from those serving as ministers.

Financial pressures developed during the revolution when loan interest and repayments were made to the school fund in depreciated continental currency which, however, was legal tender. In 1780, upon the expiration of the original sixteen years, the house-fathers voted to continue the schools on a voluntary contribution basis, with contributions graduated according to capacity to pay. This arrangement continued until 1823 when a distinctly Schwenkfelder system, after fifty-eight productive years, gave way to subscription schools formed by community residents who banded together to hire a teacher and provide for a local school. Subscription schools, in their turn, were discontinued when tax-supported free public elementary schools, legislated in Pennsylvania in 1834, became operative in the area soon after 1840. For some years the income of about $85 from the remains of the school fund was used to pay for supplies and repairs of local schools, but after 1854 it was devoted principally to publication of books and tracts. The trustees finally decided to distribute the remaining amount to the contributors or their heirs, but little of this was accepted. The remainder became the nucleus of the Literary Fund of the Schwenkfelder Church, and was eventually absorbed as part of the Schwenkfelder Library endowment.

The eight-grade curriculum of the tax-supported free public elementary schools, principally of the one-room variety, seemed for a time to satisfy the educational requirements of the area. It was, of course, a rural area with farming by far the predominant source of livelihood. Farm sons could be spared for school for only a limited amount of time. The completed course seems to have served many people quite well and, relative to the times, may have provided as good a preparation for life as the twelve year public school education of later years. The public school, the church and Sunday school, and the popular Hereford and Kraussdale Literary Societies produced in the Schwenkfelder community a surprising number of enlightened and successful individuals.

Toward the end of the century, however, with increasing numbers of young people desiring to pursue college studies, the eight-grade public school preparation became clearly inadequate. Agitation for a secondary school to serve the upper Perkiomen Valley aroused widespread support. At the same time, by the late 1880s the minister of the Upper District churches, Rev. Joshua Schultz, was becoming increasingly handicapped by the infirmities of age. The church leaders desired a seminary-trained minister but felt the congregation too small to support a paid minister without help. When a church committee visited Oberlin College to encourage Oscar Kriebel to undertake seminary training, he at first demurred. He had had several years of experience and felt confident of his ability to teach but was uncertain of his inclination or talent for the ministry. Legend attributes the obvious compromise to the vision of Oscar Kriebel's older cousin, Howard Kriebel, who proposed Oscar undertake a dual career. You want to teach and the community needs a school. The church needs a pastor. Serve both needs. Gradually the idea took hold.

Oscar Kriebel went on to Oberlin Seminary, and after completing two years there arranged to complete his seminary training abroad. He first surprised his friends by marrying Corinne Miller, of Castalia, Ohio, the wedding announcement concluding: At home "The University of Leipsic, Germany, after October 15, 1891" (in actuality the University of Berlin). Meanwhile Howard Kriebel journeyed to Worcester on October 17 to present the school proposal to the Schwenkfelder fall General Conference. The proposal was fortuitously timed, striking the Conference during the same period of creative energy that gave birth to the *Corpus Schwenckfeldianorum* publication project and the establishment of the Conference Mission

Board. Howard W. Kriebel, Edwin K. Schultz, Frank K. Schultz, Daniel Y. Meschter, Charles S. Anders, William H. Anders, and Aaron Snyder were appointed a committee to look into the matter of establishing a private secondary school under the jurisdiction of the Schwenkfelder Church. So strong was the sentiment favoring a school that by the following spring Conference the committee reported subscriptions amounting to $9,317.50. They further reported that a suitable facility in which to conduct the school could be purchased for $3,500 and recommended Rev. O. S. Kriebel to serve as headmaster as well as pastor of the Upper District congregations.

Dr. Clement Weiser, minister of the New Goshenhoppen Reformed Church, had earlier sensed the need and dreamed the vision of a secondary school to serve the area. He inspired his East Greenville neighbor, Charles Wieand, who graduated from Franklin and Marshall College in 1874 intending to prepare for the ministry, to undertake the establishment of such a school and continue his studies under Dr. Weiser's direction. Charles Wieand courted a talented lady from Allentown who came to share the vision of the two men, and who furthermore possessed the means to bring it to realization. They married, purchased a tract of land along the railroad on the outskirts of Pennsburg, and built a stately Victorian structure approached from the railroad along a tree-lined lane. They moved into living quarters and used the remaining rooms for class space, library, chapel, dining room, and kitchens. There in 1875 they opened the first school bearing the name Perkiomen Seminary, from which event Perkiomen sometimes traces its origins. Rev. Wieand taught most of the courses, while his wife, in what seems to have been the custom of the day for ladies, taught foreign languages and music. Dr. Weiser helped out where possible.

Whether this school was ahead of its time, or for whatever reason, it failed to attract students in sufficient numbers to defray expenses and seems to have led a precarious existence from the beginning. While Rev. Wieand on his mother's side was descended from Schwenkfelder immigrant Anna Krauss, the school was more oriented to the Reformed Church, and does not seem to have elicited significant support or patronage from the Schwenkfelder community. During a single week of the Christmas recess of 1883 the Wieands lost three of their five children to diptheria. This blow on top of the long financial strain prompted the Wieands to close the struggling school. Rev. Wieand went on to a successful career as minister of a parish in Pottstown. The school property passed through a number of owners and school sessions were twice reopened for short periods. By 1888, however, further efforts were given up and the stately building, unoccupied except by occasional transients or tramps, rapidly deteriorated, becoming an eyesore in the community by day and a terror to the local populace by night. It was this property that the Schwenkfelder committee proposed to purchase.

Perkiomen Seminary

The 1892 spring General Conference adopted the recommendations of the committee in their entirety and the committee was discharged. To administer the new school Conference elected eight trustees and provided that these eight should elect four additional trustees from outside the Schwenkfelder congregations. Drawing heavily on the preamble and fundamental articles of the earlier Schwenkfelder School System, Conference by resolution provided inter alia: The School shall be conducted on evangelical Christian principles. Every class is to devote an hour's recitation to the Bible. All sectarianism is to be avoided. . . . It is the object of well-established Christian schools to instruct the young while still in their teens in godliness, in learning, and in honorableness so that they may become more devout, learned, and reserved.

The property was purchased and that summer the people of the Upper District went to work with vigor to fix up and paint the dilapidated building, cleaning it from basement to attic. All labor was volunteered; no hired maintenance man or crew was to lay hand on the school until 1903, when a single janitor was hired. Oscar Kriebel and his wife returned from Europe and moved into the living quarters of the building. Just under a year from Howard Kriebel's initial proposal to Conference, the school opened on October 3, 1892 with nineteen students on the roll and a faculty of four. Oscar Kriebel taught languages and rhetoric, Howard Kriebel mathematics, Rev. Ephraim B. Clemmer history and natural sciences, and Mrs. Kriebel music. Tuition, kept low as a matter of principle, was $1.00 per week and a day student could receive thirty-nine weeks of schooling for no more than $45 per year. By Christmastime there were twenty-nine students, by commencement time, ninety-six. One student graduated.

With enrolment passing 100 just two years later, on commencement day of 1895 Dr. Kriebel made an impassioned appeal for new and larger quarters. A building committee studied the matter during the summer and determined a satisfactory building could be erected for $30,000—a sum which challenged the school's supporters and flabbergasted the skeptics. But Perkiomen Seminary was an idea whose time had now come and the skeptics failed to reckon with the creative energy of the Schwenkfelders or the resolute determination of the remarkable Schultz family.

Three young Schultz brothers came to Pennsylvania with the 1734 migration. Melchior died without issue. Christopher (Rev. Christopher Schultz) had four children and twenty-nine grandchildren. George had two sons and fifteen grandchildren. They generally married within the Schwenkfelder Vereinschaft and raised large families. The immigrant brothers acquired substantial holdings of land—the capital of a farming economy, and succeeding generations expanded these holdings. In one of his meadows George's great-grandson, Amos S. Schultz (1809-1895) discovered a deposit of clay suitable for the manufacture of bricks. He embarked upon building operations, including construction of the County Line Flour and Grist Mill near Niantic, in Washington Township, a family landmark down to the middle of the twentieth century.

Amos Schultz's son, Edwin K. Schultz, was born in 1848. He attended the local public schools of his time, worked for ten years in his father's grist mill, and then for thirty years successfully farmed one of the family farms and served as president and manager of the Niantic Dairymen's Association. He was a member of the original investigating committee and an original trustee of Perkiomen School. He was elected the school's first treasurer, a position he would hold for the next forty years.

Old Amos Schultz, a product of the early Schwenkfelder school system, had spent some time attending a private academy in Chestnut Hill. He acquired a lifelong habit of reading worthwhile literature and an ardent determination to see that his children enjoyed the benefits of higher education. He was one of the first to offer a contribution toward the new building. Seven members of the Schultz families started off the building fund campaign by pledging $1,000 each. When it was found that only another $3,000 could be obtained, Edwin Schultz, in what he later often referred to as, in human terms, the most profitable investment he ever made, offered to mortgage much of his property to raise the remaining $20,000 needed. In early August ground was broken and by September men were working to connect the new and old buildings. By Christmastime students were occupying "A" floor and by spring all but "C" floor. The entire building was completed during the summer of 1896, confounding the skeptics, who now wondered loudly what the school was going to do with all that unoccupied space. The new building faced Seminary

Ave., which by this time had been cut through the open fields originally adjoining the school property. It wrapped around the original building, which then became the annex, still clearly discernible at the rear of Kriebel Hall, facing the railroad.

By the early years of the twentieth century enrolment was running around 300, with boarding students lodged with neighboring families in the community and day students riding the Perkiomen Branch passenger trains to and from the school. In his 1903 commencement address Dr. Kriebel waxed his most enthusiastic, drawing a picture of a Greater Perkiomen, with a new wing on the boys' dormitory, a new chapel, a new dining room, and a new gym. The gymnasium, urgently needed to permit a real athletic and physical education program, drew first priority. A careful husbanding of school resources and a new solicitation for funds brought the gym into the realm of the possible. Later named for Professor Irwin Kehs, the gym was completed in 1905, providing a two-story gymnasium section, a third floor dormitory section to house fifteen or twenty boys, and recitation rooms and science laboratories in the basement. Duyckinck Hall, a large duplex house adjoining the campus on Seminary Ave., was rented for additional dormitory space. By 1908 the campus included an athletic field with a cinder track and three tennis courts.

Perkiomen historian William Baker, in his 1974 centennial history, *Perkiomen: Here's To You,* aptly characterizes the period from the founding of the school down to the First World War as the "Golden Days" of Perkiomen, and goes on in considerable detail to paint a most appealing picture of the atmosphere and campus life of those days.

The three-year curriculum—Preparatory, Junior, and Senior—offered the student three options: a general course for those anticipating no further study, a teacher training curriculum for those planning to go directly into teaching, and a classical course, heavy in Greek and Latin, with mathematics and a year of German, for those going on to college. The student body included a large segment of serious-minded students for whom attendance at Perkiomen represented a valued opportunity and a special privilege. Many worked their way through by waiting on tables and doing a variety of jobs to pay their way.

The classical course, attracting sixty to seventy students each year, soon gained wide recognition for the school. Led by Elmer Johnson and Maxwell Kratz of the class of 1895, both of whom earned high scholastic honors at Princeton, Perkiomen graduates generally achieved creditable records at the leading colleges of the day. A Philadelphia Public Ledger reporter wrote in 1912:

> Perkiomen has sent more honor men to Princeton in the last twelve years than any other school. Nearly three quarters of these honor students were entirely self supporting . . . and such excellent students they proved they soon attracted the attention of the Princeton authorities. . . . Professor George McClean Harper wrote to say that Perkiomen was the best preparatory school in the United States.

The faculty included such memorable members as Prof. Elmer Jacoby, teacher of mathematics from 1900 to 1909 and vice-principal before moving on to Central High School in Philadelphia; Prof. D. Montfort Melchior, teacher of history from 1903 to 1912 and vice-principal after 1909, trustee from 1937 to 1951, frequent speaker on special occasions and a distinguished teacher for many years at Girard College, Philadelphia; and Charles K. Meschter, teacher of mathematics from 1896 to 1912.

The school also served to infuse the leaven of culture into the entire Upper Perkiomen Valley. An early rhetoric class soon developed into the Adelphian and Philomathean Societies, which not only conducted debates on timely topics but attracted distinguished speakers to the campus. During the first two decades of the twentieth century Charles and Eleanor Weirich headed Perkiomen's excellent music department, which attracted many musically-gifted students to the school. In addition they molded singers from within and outside the school into an Oratorio Society, which introduced to the community an oratorio repertory, particularly Handel's Messiah. Then in 1908 violinist David Croll joined the faculty and within a year had formed the Perkiomen Symphony Orchestra, which performed three or four times each year, frequently with guest soloists. The orchestra's first program, presented in the gymnasium on May 23, 1909, included Haydn's sixth symphony, Mendelsohn's Wedding March, and Mozart's overture to The Abduction From The Seraglio. The visiting Ben Greet Players attracted large audiences as they presented Shakespeare plays on a stage specially set up on the back campus.

The moving force in Perkiomen's explosive development was, of course, the personality and dedication of its principal, Dr. O. S. Kriebel. As he traveled the dusty country roads in his horse and buggy on pastoral visits he never missed an opportunity to encourage the young people to extend their education by enrolling in Perkiomen. As a member of the Schwenkfelder Mission Board, he actively promoted the Philadelphia and Norristown missions as well as Schwenkfelder interest in foreign missions. As a member of the Publishing Committee and secretary of the Board of Publication he labored diligently on behalf of the *Corpus* publication effort, the *Schwenkfeldian*, and later the *Genealogical Record*. He was the author of several theological texts, a loyal alumnus of Oberlin College, and a frequent visitor to other school and college campuses. In all these activities he built up a wide circle of influential personal friends, many of whom lent their prestige by their commencement addresses, and inextricably bound together the interests of school, church, and community.

Dr. Kriebel had a strong sense of mission. He simply could not deny a deserving candidate admission to Perkiomen for lack of ability to pay. He was quick, some trustees thought too quick, to grant scholarship aid or working grants. At the same time he strove mightily to maintain high academic standards and was loath to hold down instruction expenses. As a result, even in good years the school generally operated at a small deficit. When enrolment fell off for any reason, substantial deficits had to be funded. Here the school came to rely heavily upon the support of its alumni. There were repeated drives to build up an endowment fund, income from which would have eased budgetary pressures, but all too often immediate financial needs took precedence and time and again endowment goals had to be pushed into the future.

Edwin K. Schultz and his wife Amanda Schultz, a descendant of immigrant Rev. Christopher Schultz, had six children who lived into their teens, and every one graduated from Perkiomen Seminary. Amos Schultz's nephew, Levi G. Schultz (1851-1916) had eight children, all of whom graduated from Perkiomen. George Schultz's descendants included Dr. Elmer Ellsworth Schultz Johnson, Eugene Schultz, husband of Dr. Selina Schultz, and Perkiomen trustee and benefactor, Elmer K. Schultz, engaged in the insurance business in Philadelphia, all of whom graduated from Perkiomen, and Andrew Schultz Berky, trustee and headmaster of the school during the 1960s. Alumni records for the period before World War I list 57 Schultzes, 26 Kriebels, 19 Meschters, 14 Anders, 13 Bechtels, 10 Hoffmans, 9 Berkys and 9 Bielers, to say nothing of graduates with less common Schwenkfelder names. All of the Schwenkfelder ministers of the first quarter of the twentieth century and a great many of the denomination's lay leaders attended Perkiomen and came under the spell of its headmaster. The debt of twentieth-century Schwenkfelders, and of the Schwenkfelder denomination, to Perkiomen School and Dr. Kriebel is beyond calculation. While the school served a broader community as well, early Schwenkfelder graduates formed a solid core of grateful and loyal alumni, who came repeatedly to the aid of the school.

In 1898 Edwin K. Schultz was elected a director of the National Bank of Boyertown and from 1905 to 1922 served as its president. So cautious was he in investing money that it is said he never lost a penny through investment in fraudulent or "get-rich-quick" schemes. He served as the first moderator of the consolidated Schwenkfelder church at Palm. As president of the Schwenkfelder Board of Publication he drew his family into a leadership role in financing the publication of the *Corpus Schwenckfeldianorum*. On two later occasions his personal credit was pledged to secure bank loans to permit the school to continue operating. Likewise, the Levi Schultz family repeatedly came to the aid of the school. During the 1960s this family was responsible for the erection of Schultz Dormitory.

By the 1880s the wooden boxes put together by undertakers began to give way to more substantial factory-made caskets. On May 8, 1893 the Boyertown Burial Casket Co. was inaugurated and members of the Schultz, Gerhard, and other Upper District Schwenkfelder families became early shareholders. As this company expanded and enjoyed considerable success during the early twentieth century, these shares attained very substantial value. Inherited land, holdings of Casket Co. shares, and shares of the National Bank of Boyertown, made up substantial family fortunes, lending substance to the dedication of school alumni.

The "Golden Days" peaked just before World War I with the celebration of Perkiomen's twentieth anniversary in 1912 and the dedication of the new Carnegie Library in the fall of 1913.

Although libraries for secondary schools were not included in Andrew Carnegie's philanthropic guidelines, persistent appeals from Dr. Kriebel finally achieved an exceptional gift. In 1906, perhaps feeling the conditions would prove prohibitive, Mr. Carnegie relented and pledged a grant of $20,000 to Perkiomen for construction of a library building on campus on the condition, first of all, that the school raise an equal sum as an endowment and secondly, that the school be free of debt. The next six years required all of Dr. Kriebel's powers of persuasion to meet these conditions, requiring the raising of a combined total of just under $60,000. A final desperate plea to the community featured in Town and Country brought the goal within sight.

The prospect of realizing this long sought goal dominated the twentieth anniversary celebration ceremonies during commencement week of June 23, 1912. On Tuesday afternoon class reunions attracted a large turnout of alumni, who celebrated that evening at a banquet in the gymnasium, which ran into the early hours of Wednesday. On Wednesday morning Ex-Governor Edwin Stuart delivered the commencement address. A special train from Philadelphia swelled the crowd for the anniversary exercises in the afternoon. During the afternoon exercises Mr. Frederick Heydrick, son of Judge Christopher Heydrick, was recognized, as the Judge had made a $9,000 contribution to the Library Fund, the largest such gift. Then it was announced that Dr. E. C. Jacobs of Norristown had pledged the $300 necessary to complete the fund and the assembled multitudes enthusiastically joined in signing an "Anniversary Song," written by Dr. Kriebel.

By fall of the next year the library building had been completed and on Thursday, November 20, 1913 one of the largest and most distinguished assemblages in the history of the school—some 400 strong—gathered in the main auditorium of the new building for dedication ceremonies. With Dr. Kriebel presiding, Rev. Heebner offered the invocation and Mr. Edwin K. Schultz, chairman of the Building Committee, accepted the keys to the building from the contractor and turned them over to Dr. Kriebel. Dr. Kriebel then introduced Dr. John Grier Hibben, president of Princeton University, who warmed the hearts of those attending by saying:

> There is nothing that can affect the welfare of Perkiomen Seminary in any way that is not of interest to Princeton University. . . . The young men who have come to us from Perkiomen Seminary have always brought a peculiar strength and spirit into our midst, so we feel that we are really indebted to you for the increased power of young manhood that has come to us; and when we hear that you are to have this additional scholarly and intellectual equipment for your school, we all rejoice with you.

Ex-Governor Samuel W. Pennypacker spoke, presenting Dr. Kriebel with two rare Schwenckfeld volumes to be added to the historical collections to be housed on the second floor of the building. A number of other speakers brought greetings. The ceremonies continued in the evening with community representatives participating and Prof. Croll's school orchestra furnishing the music.

The "Old Guard" had one more fling during the twenty-fifth anniversary commencement week festivities in June of 1917. Fifty-four seniors appeared at the Sunday evening Baccalaureate services, for the first time wearing caps and gowns. The alumni gathered in force for their traditional class reunions and alumni banquet. Commencement exercises and celebration of the anniversary were combined on Saturday morning with Dr. Russell H. Conwell, founder of Temple University and author of the famous lecture, "Acres of Diamonds," speaking on the need for moral preparedness in the current war. Dr. J. M. Anders gave the anniversary address, followed by greetings from a long list of distinguished visitors and past members of the school faculty and administration. The exercises extended for over four hours.

Perkiomen School

The people of the Upper Perkiomen Valley came largely from Germanic backgrounds and the dawning prospect of war with their old fatherland stirred deep emotions. Lingering strains of pacifism and isolation from world affairs only added to their discomfort. The emotional conflict, however, posed no problem for Dr. Kriebel, who had lived in Germany and perhaps acquired a clearer perception of Germany's militant nationalism. He was a vocal and energetic supporter of the war effort. He preached and lectured on patriotic themes, promoted Liberty Bond drives, and served as a local district Food Administrator and member of the Montgomery County Advisory Committee to the War Council of Philadelphia. At the request of the student body military drill was instituted at the school. The signing of the armistice precipitated a spontaneous, flag-waving parade into town and a Friday holiday to allow students to join in celebrations with their families. During commencement exercises in 1919 a Memorial Tablet in front of Kriebel Hall was unveiled by Dr. Kriebel with appropriate ceremonies. It listed nine Perkiomen men who had given up their lives for their country during the war.

With enrolment declining, especially among female boarders, the trustees in the spring of 1916 voted three changes to bring the school program more into tune with the times. First, the name "Perkiomen Seminary," with its theological connotations, was changed to the more general "Perkiomen School." A separate program was inaugurated for boy boarders, who now took over all of Kriebel Hall, preparing the way in a few years for "Perkiomen School for Boys." And finally, a separate Junior School for boys in grades three to eight, housed in Kehs Hall, was organized with its own director. Under Mr. Kehl Markley, who became director in 1919, this school provided critical enrolment support, attracting an increasing number of boys, many from single-parent homes, who went on to complete eight or nine years at Perkiomen.

Enrolment for the fall term of 1917 was off about 25 percent and in 1918 plummeted to 102. Operation of the school involved fixed costs which could not readily be adjusted to fluctuating enrolment. The resulting declines in tuition income quickly produced staggering operating deficits. Had it not been for the Junior School, the school might then and there have been forced to close its doors. As it was, school debt exceeded $50,000 by 1919, and only the personal endorsement of treasurer Edwin K. Schultz convinced the banks to continue extension of credit for operating funds.

With the opening of the fall term in 1919 the clouds of the war years began to disperse, and spirits to revive. One hundred ninety-seven boarders, including a full complement of Junior School boys, taxed the dormitory capacity of both Kriebel Hall and Kehs Hall, with some boys squeezed three to a room. Missing, however, were the 100-plus day students of pre-war years, many of them presumably drawn to the free public high schools. Tuition rates were raised from a range of $450 to $550 for boarders, depending upon the floor level, to $600 to $750. Day school rates continued at $100.

Not the least daunted, Dr. Kriebel at once launched a Memorial Endowment Fund Campaign, seeking $50,000 to discharge the school debt and $100,000 to augment the school's minuscule endowment fund. The alumni, under the energetic leadership of Rev. Gottschall, still teaching history at the school, for the first time formed regional alumni clubs and pledged to raise $30,000 toward the goal. The trustees undertook to raise another $30,000 and Dr. Kriebel sought the balance from individual Schwenkfelders and other contacts. At the commencement exercises in June 1922 Dr. Kriebel announced that $104,000 had been pledged toward the Memorial Campaign and expressed his hope that the sum of $150,000 would be realized. His prophecy received immediate encouragement. Mrs. John Meigs from the Hill School, who had generously praised the school in her address, stepped forward and handed Dr. Kriebel a check for $5,000 from Philadelphia philanthropist Mrs. Edward Bok. Subsequent reports suggest, however, that securing pledges sometimes proved easier than collecting the amount pledged.

The 1922 Commencement marked the thirtieth anniversary of the school. Forty-four seniors graduated. Rev. Gottschall did some research and reported that over the thirty years 1,240 had graduated from Perkiomen, of whom 800 had gone on to 142 different schools and colleges, 166 into business, 168 into teaching, 44 into medicine, 44 into the ministry, 29 into law, and 27 into engineering; 19 had become principals of schools and 11 farmers; altogether 52 trades and professions had been entered.

As the years passed the school extended its reach for students farther beyond the local area. The 1927 enrolment included students from nine states besides Pennsylvania, and students from Persia, Dominican Republic, Guatemala, Venezuela, Denmark, and Cuba. At the 1928 Commencement the Valedictory speech was given by Louis Midence of Guatemala and the Salutatory by Mr. A. M. Abrahamian of Teheran, Persia. An increasing contingent of boys from the coal regions around Wilkes Barre raised the standing of Perkiomen football teams; basketball, soccer, and tennis also prospered during the decade. Total enrolment fluctuated between 175 and 200, this being the practical capacity of the dormitories.

Daily chapel and Sunday evening worship services were traditional elements of the school week. With the development of a more heterogeneous student body, arrangements had to be made for students of Catholic and Jewish faiths to attend worship services of their own persuasion in the town. Within the student body the YMCA played a predominant role, organizing receptions for new students, conducting regular midweek evening services, and assisting in the Sunday evening services. Rev. Gottschall, Rev. Heebner, and after 1926 Rev. Lester Kriebel regularly assisted in these endeavors. While never absent in spirit, Dr. Kriebel's increasing preoccupation with fund raising left the day to day running of the school to vice principals.

The decade of the twenties witnessed a continuing struggle, only marginally successful, to place the school on a firm financial foundation. By this time the school was predominantly a college preparatory school, competing with numerous similar schools, many of which had superior physical facilities and enjoyed the benefit of significant endowment income. At Perkiomen a vicious cycle developed. Tuition generally could not be expected to cover costs and, in the absence of endowment income, operating deficits recurred, absorbing the proceeds of fund-raising contributions and frustrating efforts to increase endowment. A larger student body would have spread overhead charges and eased budget pressures, but with reduced day-school enrolment dormitory capacity effectively limited the student body. Dr. Kriebel viewed the school in terms of the worthy students who were given a chance to rise above their sometimes limited family circumstances and persisted in granting financial aid wherever a good student could not otherwise attend. The trustees had perforce to keep a watchful eye on the financial condition of the school. As the decade unfolded tensions between headmaster and trustees developed, sometimes bringing relations close to the acrimonious stage. By 1922 Dr. Kriebel had served for thirty years as headmaster and pastor and was approaching 60 years of age. At no time during those years had the school been operated free of financial pressures and the persistent necessity to plead for funds had sapped his energy and taken its toll on his health. During the commencement exercises in June 1921 he showed visible signs of exhaustion and on doctor's orders he and Mrs. Kriebel spent the summer in Europe. By fall he returned refreshed. Both he and Perkiomen now seemed to take a new lease on life.

In 1922 Junior School director, Prof. Markley, as he was universally known, organized Camp Minnehaha as an independent venture. Forty to fifty boys, Prof. Markley, and three or four Perkiomen seniors or faculty members, serving as counselors, spent eight summer weeks in large army tents with wooden floors, camped along the Perkiomen in a meadow below the covered bridge at Markley's mill. The old mill dam across the Perkiomen provided a delightful, rustic setting for a swimming hole, and for boating and canoeing. Along with nature study and fishing, a baseball diamond, two tennis courts, a basketball court, and a volleyball court provided for actively competitive sports. A nearby house on a hill beyond the meadow served as kitchen and dining room. The present writer spent eight healthful and beneficial summers in this delightful setting, including the summer of 1925 when, after days of heavy rain, the Palm dam burst and sent a wall of water rushing down the creek, inundating the tents to a depth of some four feet. Lamentably, the bucolic setting is now obliterated under many more feet of water backed up from the Green Lane Dam of the Philadelphia Suburban Water Company and the covered bridge has been demolished. The camp served some Perkiomen students for whom a return home was for some reason impractical. It also served to draw campers into the school body. The camp was discontinued early in the depression when Mr. Markley left the Perkiomen faculty.

By 1925 the school debt had been significantly reduced and some $44,000 added to the endowment fund. At the December meeting of the trustees the indefatigable Dr. Kriebel unveiled elaborate plans for a "Greater Perkiomen" of the future, requiring a $450,000 building fund and a $500,000 endowment fund drive.

Kriebel Hall was now more than thirty years old and simple maintenance required continual attention. The basement dining hall, with its antiquated kitchen facilities, was inadequate, approaching the point of presenting a health hazard. Dr. Kriebel envisioned facilities along the following lines: a wing on the south side of Kriebel Hall to house a new 300-seat dining hall with kitchen facilities on the ground floor and dormitory accommodations on the second and third floors for fifty-four boys and two instructors; a north wing to house laboratory facilities and recitation rooms; a tower on the main building—always existing on paper but now required to balance the two new wings; a Junior School building; an infirmary; a swimming pool; and a central heating plant. Increased dormitory capacity would spread overhead over a larger number of students and provide more leeway in the operating budget. In the light of Perkiomen's needs Dr. Kriebel's proposals were not unreasonable.

During January of 1927, to restore his increasingly fragile health, Dr. Kriebel vacationed in Florida. By commencement time he was back in force, enlarging on the Greater Perkiomen theme. Architects had determined there was not sufficient space between Kriebel Hall and the railroad to accommodate the new wings originally contemplated and the focus of Dr. Kriebel's plans had changed. As reported by the *Schwenkfeldian*, "In the afternoon Dr. Kriebel led a 'Pilgrimage' to the proposed new site for the Greater Perkiomen School on his farm, one half mile west of the present campus, on a rise of land that was 'providentially made' for the School of the future, commanding a sweep of view scarcely equaled anywhere. It is proposed to maintain the present building equipment for a Junior School, to devote the new plant to the Preparatory Department. Within five years we may expect to see our vision realized."

By the spring trustees' meeting in 1928 several contributions had been announced, including one from the Levi G. and Elizabeth S. Schultz Estate. The endowment fund balance was reported as $80,000. A committee raising funds to eliminate current school bank borrowing reported some progress. The nation was prosperous, the school full and solvent. At the close of the meeting the ever-optimistic Dr. Kriebel remarked, "Tonight I have more hope in the stability and future of Perkiomen School than I ever had."

All this, of course, began to change the next year as the nation began its descent into the Great Depression. Professor Baker has characterized the first half of the decade of the 1930s as "Survival Years," and comments that "The greatest tribute that may be rendered the school is the fact that Perkiomen did survive, and this at a time when a multitude of similar institutions did not." Applications dropped as families could not see their way clear to raise private school tuition funds, although enrolment was for a time propped up by expanded grants and scholarships, on the theory that a part paying student was better than an empty bed. In 1932, however, enrolment dropped by some 25 percent, bank debt edged up to $54,000, and once again only the personal intervention of treasurer Edwin K. Schultz kept the school in operating funds.

At the fall General Conference in 1931 Dr. Kriebel noted that 1932 would mark the fortieth anniversary of the school. He proposed raising a "Contribution" of $40,000 to aid the school in its depression-intensified financial squeeze. Dr. Kriebel, however, was to be spared both the Anniversary Celebration and the severe financial crisis of the next several years. On Friday, February 12, 1932 he planned a business trip to Philadelphia. Not feeling well, he consulted the school physician Dr. Derr and took to his bed, suffering from a serious intestinal obstruction. On Monday, accompanied by Dr. Derr, Kehl Markley drove him to Graduate Hospital at the University of Pennsylvania in Philadelphia, where his lifelong friend and Perkiomen trustee president, Dr. James M. Anders was still the respected professor emeritus of medicine. That evening an operation was performed. The following afternoon Dr. Kriebel passed away. Mrs. Kriebel and Dr. Anders were present to comfort his final hours. On Friday afternoon Rev. Lester Kriebel led the Perkiomen community in funeral services in the school chapel and the student body paid their last respects. On Saturday afternoon, before an audience that overflowed both church and Sunday school facilities, Rev. Harvey Heebner preached the funeral sermon in the Palm Schwenkfelder Church, following which Dr. Kriebel's body was laid to rest in the adjoining cemetery. Dr. Samuel K. Brecht, knowledgeable on the subject, concluded his *Schwenkfeldian* obituary with the statement, "In the death of Dr. Kriebel the Schwenkfelder Church has lost the greatest leader it has had since the arrival of the Schwenkfeldian exiles in 1734."

On August 1, 1932 Mr. Edwin K. Schultz, having completed forty years in the position, resigned as treasurer and, as if to emphasize the passing of an era at Perkiomen, he died on January 4, 1933.

Following Dr. Kriebel's death the trustees rallied and at a special meeting held in Norristown on February 23, 1932 unanimously affirmed their intention to carry on. At a second meeting held in Philadelphia, thirty-year-old Rev. Webster Schultz Stover was elected headmaster, to assume his new duties as of June 1, 1932. His task was formidable on two counts. To step into the shoes of Dr. Kriebel was challenge enough. To maintain school operations in the economic circumstances of the time might well have overwhelmed a less venturesome soul. His credentials were impressive. The Schultz in his name confirmed a degree of Schwenkfelder lineage. He was a graduate of Ursinus and of Union Theological Seminary and had earned a Ph.D. from Columbia in the field of educational administration. He was a practising ordained minister, a college teacher, and the author of several books in the field of education. At the fall Conference in 1932 he reported an enrolment of 140 students and asked that a $40,000 Fortieth Anniversary Contribution to the school in honor of Dr. Kriebel's administration for this period of years, be raised as an urgent necessity. He energetically sought out new students and cut expenses by some 25 percent. There were payless paydays, but most faculty and staff were happy to have board and a roof over their head at a time when alternate jobs were all but nonexistent. Rev. Stover's term was held to three years out of a disagreement with the trustees, but it served a productive transition period. The school survived the depth of the depression. Upon Rev. Stover's somewhat abrupt departure in October of 1934, Mr. Irwin Kehs, Perkiomen's distinguished mathematics teacher, was designated acting headmaster.

By the fall of 1934 it seemed as though the long downward slide may have touched bottom, providing opportunity for an effort at reconstruction. Tuition was increased modestly and there was a small rise in enrolment, the first upward movement since the onset of the depression. In April of 1935 the trustees elected Clarence Tobias as Perkiomen's third headmaster. Officially installed at the June Commencement, he was a graduate of the University of Pennsylvania and had earned a Master's degree in philosophy from Haverford College. For eight years he had served as head of the department of science and religion at Friends Central School. At the time he was serving as secretary of Guildford College, a Quaker college near Greensboro, N.C. His religious roots were Quaker and it was the Quaker, Dr. Rufus Jones, himself a student of Schwenckfeld, who supported the new headmaster and encouraged him to accept what could have been a most difficult assignment in a most difficult time. He had also studied at the Episcopal Divinity School in Philadelphia and his theology tended toward this branch of the Christian faith. In 1939 he would, in fact, be ordained as a priest in the Protestant Episcopal Church. Dr. Tobias seemed particularly qualified in scholarship, administrative ability, and qualities of mind and heart, to carry on the administration of the school in the Christian tradition of Dr. Kriebel.

The school plant had badly deteriorated. In 1931 trustee Wayne

Meschter paid an industrial painting contractor, desperate for work for himself and his men, to paint the entire outside of the school buildings. Funds for maintenance were limited and for improvements virtually nonexistent. Mr. Tobias and Financial Secretary Wayne H. Rothenberger attacked this problem with vigor. Interior walls in Kriebel Hall were replastered and repainted. Twenty-five-watt electric bulbs, installed to save electricity, were replaced with brighter bulbs, dispensing some of the interior gloom. The old coal ranges in the kitchen were removed, the floor and walls tiled, and new kitchen equipment installed. Through the generosity of Mr. Elmer K. Schultz of Philadelphia the chapel was completely remodeled, refinished, and endowed. A new organ, new seats, floor covering, and venetian blinds were installed. On October 10, 1936 the chapel was rededicated as the Lloyd H. Schultz Memorial Chapel, in memory of Mr. Schultz's son, Lloyd, Perkiomen 1911, who passed away in December of 1935. A club room was furnished. In 1940 Elmer Schultz donated some 3,000 hardy flowering plants, shrubs, and trees for an arboretum south of the headmaster's house. Once again through the generosity of a trustee the exteriors of the school buildings were painted. Gradually the atmosphere of neglect was dispelled. By the fall term of 1939 the school, with an enrolment of 143, was again operating more normally.

Dr. Tobias was a thoughtful, intellectual, and educated man. He was interested in pedagogy and had a keen perception of the process of education. He paid particular attention to the faculty and through his wide connections recruited qualified replacements as necessary. He strove to accommodate the school curriculum more towards the needs of the students of his time. The old role of the school as a center of culture in the Upper Perkiomen Valley had been neglected, and Dr. Tobias once again drew into the community interesting and inspiring lecturers, art exhibits, and forums on international topics of interest. During his term of office the physical plant was rehabilitated; more importantly, the spirit and morale of the school was restored after the trauma of Dr. Kriebel's departure and the ravages of the depression. The period of reconstruction under Dr. Tobias's vigorous and competent leadership was interrupted by American entrance into World War II, when students were drawn away by family necessities or directly into the armed forces, and the remaining 100 students consisted disproportionately of Junior School boys. In January of 1944 Dr. Tobias surprised and disappointed the trustees by announcing his resignation to pursue his career in the Protestant Episcopal Church. He left the school notably stronger than when he arrived, but post-war administration would be left to others.

The trustees once again turned to a man of Quaker background, electing as the school's fourth headmaster Mr. Albert E. Rogers, a graduate of George School and Haverford College, with a Master's degree from the University of Pennsylvania. His seven-year term once again marked a period of transition. By the end of war the old faculty had been largely dispersed and new faculty lacked the old traditions. Student morale was low although the school was full, largely as a result of an influx of G.I. veterans seeking to brush up their neglected academic skills before going on to college. Of 110 members of the 1947 graduating class, seventy-three were former members of the armed forces. The school's seventy-fifth anniversary in 1950 passed with only the most modest celebration. There were plans for the future but they remained more wish than reality. In fact there was great concern over the future of the school once the wave of veterans subsided. A long range planning committee, however, focused on demographic trends and projected better days ahead. In January of 1951 Mr. Rogers resigned to accept a proffered position elsewhere.

There were indeed to be better days ahead. At a special meeting held on April 3, 1951 the trustees appointed Mr. Stephen W. Roberts Perkiomen's fifth headmaster. A varsity athlete and co-captain of his college football team, Mr. Roberts had a background of twenty years in teaching, coaching, and administrative work, principally during an eight-year stint at Wayland Academy and Junior College, Beaver Dam, Wisconsin, where he was particularly successful in the area of development. Steve and his wife Eleanore were outgoing, energetic, and gregarious individuals, who infused new vitality into all areas of the school community. The sixteen years of the Roberts era witnessed the rise of a new and greater Perkiomen far beyond even the dreams of Dr. Kriebel.

As if to try the mettle of the new headmaster, almost immediately upon his arrival the twenty-six-year-old heater in Kriebel Hall expired. A two-year fund-raising campaign was required to pay off the $31,000 cost of the new heater. Under Mr. Roberts' tutelage, however, this crisis served as something of a rallying point, drawing forth trustee, alumni, and parent support for the school. Mr. Gunard O. Carlson, president of the G. O. Carlson Co., a stainless steel distributor in Coatsville, Pa., was elected president of the Board of Trustees. The Carlsons had lost their only son early in his life and compensated for their grief by sending boys to Perkiomen, initiating scholarship funds, and generally assuming a leadership role among the trustees. Mr. William Eshelman, a soon to be retired textile executive from Mohnton, Pa., was elected president of the Alumni Association and, with Mrs. Roberts as an indefatigable corresponding secretary, soon organized long-neglected regional alumni meetings, started a tradition of annual Homecoming Days for alumni, and initiated an Annual Gift Fund drive which, in its first year, 1954, raised $30,000. In 1953 Mr. Martin Dellinger was elected president of a newly-formed Parents' Association.

In the fall of 1951 only 121 students were enrolled, but the next year enrolment began a steady climb, until by the 1955 term 197 students were enrolled and some 150 applicants were turned away. Rehabilitation of the physical plant became an urgent priority. Beginnings were small but a steady momentum developed. First the parents campaigned for $60 contributions to purchase new mattresses for the beds. Then new beds were purchased, and early in 1954 the Alumni Association sponsored a three-year program to redecorate and refurnish dormitory rooms. South Cottage was completely renovated, the chapel was redecorated, and a new athletic field on recently-acquired land was graded. In the fall of 1955 a planning committee consisting of five board members and five alumni was appointed to make a complete study of the future needs of the school, with special reference to the physical plant. The Parents' Association started raising funds for a much-needed social and recreation center, dedicated in 1957 as Roberts Hall, and for a $113,000 addition to the rear of Kehs Hall—the first new building on the Perkiomen campus in forty-four years since the dedication of the Carnegie Library in 1913.

In 1952 Mr. Irwin Kehs, professor of mathematics since 1909 and more recently director of studies, resigned and Mr. Ralph Hossman began his thirty-odd-year service in the latter capacity. A six-day school week was instituted with Saturday morning classes, and Wednesday and Saturday afternoons freed for athletics and other special events. The extracurricular program worked well during the spring and fall terms, but was severely handicapped during the winter when students had to travel to a public school gymnasium in town for athletic activities. A course in the Bible was introduced and, as enrolment increased, the social science department was expanded from six sections to nine and a course in Problems of Democracy added. A student government was organized and special speech classes provided. Mrs. Roberts and Gordon Edy, Glee Club director, revived the musical traditions of Perkiomen. A Dramatic Club, a Bridge Club, a Science Club, a Spirit Club, and a Varsity Club were organized, the latter sponsoring an annual Perkiomen Blue and Gold dinner to raise money for athletic equipment. By 1957 the three main student publications—the *Perkiomenite,* the *Griffin* and the *Profile*—were once again appearing regularly.

The 1955 graduation exercises attracted a particularly large and spirited crowd of alumni, including the Fiftieth Anniversary class of 1905 and their distinguished classmate, Dr. Frank Laubach, who gave the commencement address, challenging the graduates to a life of service. At the 1958 Commencement General Carl A. Spaatz, USAF retired, formerly chief of staff for the Allied Air Forces during World War II and a graduate of Perkiomen class of 1908, was awarded the Perkiomen Key. The patient efforts of Steve and Eleanore Roberts were beginning to bear fruit in a new spirit of pride in the institution and concern for its development. Steve Roberts delivered detailed reports at each Schwenkfelder Conference, urging support for "Your School," and in 1955 the school played host to the spring Conference. He also served as a Sunday school teacher at the Palm church, always seeking to keep the needs of the school before the Schwenkfelder congregations.

The launching by Russia of the Sputnik satellite in 1957 redirected the attention of the nation to the quality of education. Preparatory schools such as Perkiomen seemed especially situated to serve the need for better prepared college applicants. The 1958 summer school enrolled 102 students for eight weeks of intensive study, including a special "Reading-Thinking-Writing" program to develop study skills. With the existing facilities largely rehabilitated, by the end of the decade attention turned to three pressing needs—an adequate dining hall, science laboratories attuned to the new emphasis on science education, and a field house with swimming pool to facilitate a year-round physical education program. In the fall of 1959, with 200 boarders and sixteen day students enrolled, the Parents' Association took the lead with a campaign to raise $150,000 to $200,000 for a new Dining Hall. By spring ground had been broken. In 1961 the annual fee was increased from $2,050 to $2,250 and school operations appeared solidly in the black.

The January 26, 1962 trustees' meeting was preceded by dinner in the new Dining Hall, built at a final cost of $340,000, toward which the Parents' Association had raised around one half. In the discussion that evening the remaining debt was all but forgotten when it was announced that Mr. and Mrs. Walter Hollenbach of Jersey City, N.J. had made a gift to Perkiomen of $300,000 for a new science classroom and laboratory building, to be known as "Hollenbach Science Hall." The excitement was contagious and the trustees

undertook to raise funds for a new dormitory building to house about
forty-five students and a single and a married faculty member, thus
completing the first phase of plant development—a dining facility, a
new dormitory, and a science and classroom building, with a total
estimated cost of approximately $1,000,000. With the looming
increase in administrative tasks, in 1960 trustee Andrew Berky was
named chairman of the Development Committee and in 1962 as
assistant headmaster to assist Mr. Roberts. The library and the school
initially shared Andy's time and salary.

"Mr. Perkiomen," Walter Hollenbach entered Perkiomen as a
student teacher in 1898 and was graduated the following year. He
then went on to Princeton and prepared for the teaching profession.
He followed this for forty-four years, first in Trenton and then in
Jersey City where, in 1929, he was elected principal of two elementary schools, a position which he held until his retirement in 1947.
Living simply, he early began accumulating, a few shares at a time, a
portfolio of common stocks, which in the post-war era rose in value to
constitute a seven-figure estate. A loyal alumnus of Princeton, it is
said he never missed a Princeton home football game. With no
children and his interest in Perkiomen renewed, he first promised to
include Perkiomen in his will on an equal basis with Princeton, and
was then persuaded to make lifetime contributions.

On November 9, 1963 some 600 visitors attended two significant events. In the morning assistant headmaster Berky presided over
the cornerstone laying for Schultz Dormitory, a $175,000 unit to
house thirty-eight students and two masters, built with funds contributed by the family of Levi G. and Elizabeth S. Schultz, and by
Webster Schultz of Plainfield, N.J. In the afternoon the Hollenbach
Science Hall was dedicated, with Walter and Kathryn Hollenbach
making the presentation, accepted by Dr. Gunard O. Carlson, president of the trustees. Two life-sized oil paintings of the donors were
unveiled in the foyer of the new building by Mr. William Eshelman,
now director of development.

Mr. Hollenbach became more and more involved in the life of
the school and at a special meeting of trustees held February 7, 1964 it
was announced that he had offered a challenge gift of $225,000 to
launch a campaign for the erection of a gymnasium and field house on
the campus within two years. In April of 1965 the Hollenbachs added
another $225,000 to the field house fund. There were, it is true,
voices of caution. After all, the war baby boom would pass, tuition
was escalating, and who could say what the future held. The expanded campus would have to be staffed, heated, and maintained. On

the other hand, there seemed no doubt that suitable athletic facilities would stand Perkiomen in good stead, might even be crucial, in competition for students once the baby boom passed. Construction proceeded on the field house as well as on the long delayed trustees' dormitory, the two buildings adding another million dollars to the development program.

The trustees' dormitory went up quickly, and was ready for occupancy for the fall term of 1967. Originally dedicated as Trustees Hall, it was later rededicated Ruhl Hall, when a bequest from the estate of Penrose Ruhl of Lancaster, Pa. offered some timely relief from Perkiomen's debt burden.

The Hollenbach Field House, a splendid facility and the crowning glory of the Perkiomen campus, was ready for dedication on Alumni Day, May 27, 1967, bringing to a close the explosion of brick and mortar development. Sadly, the headmaster whose dreams and efforts had sparked this decade of Perkiomen development did not remain on campus to see the Field House completed or Greater Perkiomen fulfilled. Stephen Roberts had been suffering from a cardiac condition as early as 1955, and the doctors had advised him to slow down! In March of 1966, while returning with Mrs. Roberts from a school convention in Atlantic City, he became seriously ill and was compelled to retire for several months' convalescence. Later, after doctors' reports advised a long convalescence, he resigned. During his tenure school enrolment had risen from 121 to 290 and six new buildings had been constructed. He had brought to splendid realization Dr. Kriebel's dream of a Greater Perkiomen.

As if to emphasize the passing of an era, President Gunard Carlson resigned. In July of 1966 Lloyd Schultz was elected president of the trustees. In April of 1966 Andy Berky was elected treasurer, in July acting headmaster, and in January of 1967, headmaster. Andy's report as headmaster to the fall General Conference perhaps best sums up the situation of the school at this time, as the young people of the nation were swept along by radical winds of change:

This year we established a new all-time high of 293 students and 31 faculty members. . . . Ninety-six seniors graduated in June and each and every one of them received acceptance in colleges and universities across the country. Our summer school under the direction of Assistant Headmaster Jack Rothenberger followed the successful pattern of recent years. . . . Our brand new athletic center is completely operative and Perkiomen is now in a splendid position to offer facilities comparable to most boarding schools in the East. You will probably be relieved to know that we do not have any current plans for the physical expansion of the

School. Indeed, this last go round has been quite vigorous and as I indicated last year, we are still several hundreds of thousand dollars short of being out of debt. Over the past five years, more than two million dollars has been expended on physical plant development and we must pause to catch our breath before we can take a further look ahead. As all of you know, the cost of living continues to creep upward and this gives us our own special brand of difficulty.

This is not the easiest of all possible times to be working with young men. There are many strange winds blowing through the fabric of our society these days. How do you come to grips with Vietnam, city riots, teacher strikes, hippies, the explosion of knowledge and the deterioration of family structures? This is not an easy life and there are no easy answers, but I feel that Perkiomen is making a sustained, conscientious effort to be an island of stability and purpose and dedication through all of these wayward currents.

We try to be worthy of your continued interest and support—and without it, we would surely perish. Come visit the School when you can. I have a hunch you will be glad you did.

By the next year the general revulsion among young people against the necessary discipline and regimentation inherent in boarding school life produced an alarming drop in applications, and for the next two years, in enrolment. Lowered admission standards were reflected in a more militant student body, challenging the very standards upon which Perkiomen was founded. With general inflation, the costs of maintaining and operating the expanded campus, and the interest on lingering construction debt, the financial situation of the school once again hit a downward cycle.

Sensing the trend, Andy Berky in 1968 assumed a new position as president of the school, to devote his entire energies to matters of finance, alumni affairs, and development. Rev. Jack R. Rothenberger, chaplain and assistant headmaster, was elected headmaster. A year later Jack accepted a call from the Central Schwenkfelder Church and James Orville Brown, an experienced private school administrator, succeeded him. Jack Rothenberger and James Brown wrestled mightily with problems of the new student attitudes and, while forced repeatedly to beat strategic retreats especially challenging for Schwenkfelder pastor Rothenberger, they managed to spare Perkiomen the open confrontations between students and administration which occurred on many campuses, while still preserving the fundamental moral and spiritual values to which the school was dedicated. In 1969, to support lagging enrolment, coeducation returned to Perkiomen with the admission of five venturesome girls. Somewhat to the surprise of traditionalists, increasing female enrolments of succeeding years generally raised the social tone of the student body and presented no significant special problems. In 1971 Mr. Brown introduced the "February Experiment," under which classes were suspended for a trimester and all students engaged in supervised independent study. Interestingly, while the experiment was generally credited as a success, the following year the student body willingly acquiesced in a return to a more structured curriculum.

Meanwhile, financial pressures forced the school to resort to radical surgery. In the spring of 1970 one third of the faculty was dropped, with those remaining selected not so much for seniority as for their capacity to live on campus and handle extra activities. Once again the loyalty of alumni came to the rescue of the school, this time in a dramatic series of bequests, first of some $50,000 from the estate of Seth Arden Bardwell of the class of 1901, then from the estate of Penrose H. Ruhl of the class of 1903, and finally from the estate of Amy Kline Huttel of the class of 1905. In settlement of the latter bequest a large block of Halliburton common stock was transferred to the school just about the time the shares began a dramatic rise in value, increasing six-fold between their low of 1970 and their high at the end of 1973. Over one million dollars was provided the school from these bequests. They could not have arrived at a more opportune time, for the energy squeeze of 1973 was about to take its special toll in the operation of the school.

In 1971 Andy Berky initiated a Centennial Fund Program, designed to raise much-needed annual giving funds as well as additions to the endowment. This drive ran into the 1973-1974 economic downturn and produced only modest results. During the school year ending June 30, 1977 the school engaged a professional fund-raising organization and embarked upon a Second Century Fund drive. As if to demonstrate the axiom that people will contribute toward a prospective project but lack enthusiasm to contribute toward debt reduction or even endowment, this undertaking proved something less than successful as fees to the professional fund-raising organization exceeded proceeds of the solicitation, thereby further adding to the burden of school debt.

In 1972 Mr. James Brown resigned to accept a proffered position at St. Andrew's School in Delaware. The trustees elected Mr. Howard Deischer as interim headmaster. Mr. Deischer, a resident of Emmaus and a retired Emmaus High School principal, was well acquainted with the Schwenkfelders, as his sister Mae had married Dr. Claude A. Schultz, Jr. and joined the Palm Schwenkfelder

Church. A mature and experienced administrator, he had served on the faculty of Emmaus High School from 1929 to 1963 and as principal for his last ten years there. He had then served as mathematics teacher on the Perkiomen faculty and was intimately conversant with the problems of the school. Under his administration a calm, experienced, and efficient expertise was applied, which consolidated and made workable the innovations of the previous years. By 1973 things were definitely looking up and in the spring Andy Berky, having supplied courageous leadership through some of the most tumultuous years in the history of the school, resigned to pursue other activities. The fall term of 1974 opened with 111 male and 38 female boarding students, and 49 male and 19 female day students, for a total enrolment of 217 students, and a faculty of 14 male and 7 female full-time teachers.

Mr. Deischer served for three years, well beyond the initial call to duty. During his final year a search committee conducted a careful canvas for a new headmaster. As of July 1, 1974, Mr. John Hewett became Perkiomen's tenth headmaster, beginning what might be called the present era. Mr. Hewett, 43-year-old son of a lifelong private school teacher and administrator, had earned a bachelor's degree in American history and literature from Williams College and an M.A.L.S. in literature from Wesleyan College in 1963. After a four-year term of active duty as an officer in the U.S. Navy, he had served on the staff of the Gilman School in Baltimore, Md., and for seven years as headmaster of the Bordentown Military Academy in Bordentown, N.J., and its successor, Bordentown/Lenox School in Lenox, Mass. It seemed to the committee that his background and experience would particularly qualify him to guide the school in areas of curriculum development, teacher supervision, student affairs, college placement and guidance counseling, and admissions interviewing and testing. Charles Read, Andy Berky's brother-in-law and president of the trustees, welcomed Mr. Hewett and his wife Lisa in Parents' Hall at a reception attended by members of the faculty and trustees, their wives, and other guests on May 24, 1974.

Mr. Hewett's ten-year term as headmaster, continuing as of this writing, has been a welcome relief from the turnover of the previous decade. As if to fulfill the perceptions of the search committee, internal school administration, while certainly not without its problems, has generally proceeded on a steady course. Somewhat reminiscent of Dr. Kriebel, Mr. Hewett appeared to place first priority on faculty quality and compensation incentives and on scholarship assistance for worthy students. The result was an uninterrupted string of operating deficits during his first eight years in office, bringing the school by the early 1980s once again to the limits of borrowing available from the banks, although careful segregation of endowment funds and market appreciation of investments raised endowment funds to over $600,000. Under severe pressure from the trustees and from an education committee of the Schwenkfelder Conference, operating costs were brought under a measure of control and the year ending June 30, 1982 closed with a small new addition to surplus.

In the fall of 1982 the school year opened with an enrolment of only 190 students and another large deficit appeared in prospect. Once again drastic measures were undertaken. Faculty and staff salary cuts were accepted with surprisingly good grace, some additional students were enrolled during the year, and a strict austerity program squeezed out an encouraging surplus at year end. When school opened in the fall of 1983 national agitation over the quality of education helped support enrolment of 228 students and Perkiomen's prospects noticeably brightened. A large prospective budget surplus permitted not only restoration of salary cuts, but reimbursement for salaries not received during the previous year as well as an expanded program to make up for maintenance deferred during the years of financial stringency. A kind Providence does indeed seem to keep watch over Perkiomen's finances.

The most eloquent testimony to the service rendered by Perkiomen School over the years has been the support of dedicated alumni, largely Schwenkfelder during the early years of the century, embracing a broader spectrum of alumni during more recent decades. Besides the capital gifts and bequests herein noted as well as many others, during the last ten years annual giving to the school has increased each and every year, rising from around $60,000 during the early 1970s to a record $145,000 in the year ending June 30, 1983. The strong annual giving support reflects in some measure momentum carrying over from the development work of the Roberts era, the persistent cultivation of potential donors by Bill Eshelman and Samuel Roeder, and the organizing efforts of Andy Berky. However, recent totals also reflect credit upon the present administration, the activity of the current director of development, Mr. Brian Thomas, and the sensitive admissions promotion of his wife Sue.

While tuition of $7,800 seems high, it is not that much out of line with current college tuition, and may well represent, in today's economy, no greater family sacrifice than the $500 tuition of the early 1900s. National concern over the quality of education suggests that another cycle of revival of Perkiomen's fortunes may well be under way, this time unburdened by the necessity for brick and mortar expansion, although a self-standing school chapel, keystone of a truly Schwenkfelder preparatory school and cherished dream particularly of Rev. Rothenberger, remains unrealized.

Perkiomen stands today as a monument to the determination, dedication, and sacrifice of a host of twentieth-century men and women of vision and courage, Schwenkfelders and non-Schwenkfelders alike. It is indeed a hardy institution, seemingly with an inherent instinct for survival whatever the storms of change. In the future as in the past the Schwenkfelders and loyal friends of Perkiomen will surely secure the perpetuation of this worthy institution.

Chapter Eleven

Schwenckfeld Manor

In the Schwenkfelder homelands of southeastern Pennsylvania, time-honored tradition bound together three family generations, "tilling the soil" on family farmsteads. By mid-twentieth century, however, the family unit was evolving into a two wage-earner suburban family, providing neither opportunity for useful activity nor personal security for elderly family members. At the same time people were living longer and "Senior Citizens" were making up an expanding segment of the population. Led by the Quakers and Mennonites, church denominations began to sponsor retirement communities and lifetime health care facilities. Schwenkfelder humanitarian traditions beckoned their participation. Dr. Paul T. Bergey, a practicing chiropractor and member of the Lansdale congregation, took the lead in informal discussions urging a "Schwenkfelder Home."

During the 1950s General Conference Moderator Wayne C. Meschter, with aging Schwenkfelder ministers particularly in mind, made a $5,000 personal contribution to the Mennonite Home at Frederick with the understanding that this would assure a place and defray the entrance fee for at least a few Schwenkfelders seeking admittance. At the General Conference held in Lansdale on October 18, 1958 Andrew S. Berky reported for a special committee appointed to consider a Schwenkfelder home for the aged. The committee estimated that a building to accommodate twenty-five to thirty people would cost between $100,000 and $150,000. The committee noted that less than 50 percent of the residents in the Mennonite Home were Mennonites and suggested that their facility might serve the immediate needs of the Schwenkfelder community. Here the matter seemed to rest for the moment.

The subject was again considered at the General Conference held at Palm on May 21, 1960. To study the matter further Moderator J. Herbert Weber appointed a committee made up of Dr. Paul T. Bergey and Paul S. Bieler, co-chairmen, and John K. Snyder, John S. Clemens, J. Herbert Weber, Vincent W. Nyce, Wayne C. Meschter, Rev. Jack R. Rothenberger, and Rev. Martha B. Kriebel. This committee held preliminary conversations with an architect and with legal counsel and made inquiries as to possible sources of financing, including the Federal Housing and Home Finance Agency in the Department of Housing and Urban Development (H.U.D.). It appeared funds could possibly be available for a properly constituted project. Co-chairman Bergey attended the annual congregational meeting of each of the several churches to outline possible options and to urge attendance at the 1961 spring General Conference, when a formal proposal would be considered. That conference voted $400 to permit the committee to continue its study.

A questionnaire was mailed to all church members. At the fall Conference on October 21, 1961 Dr. Bergey reported the results of the survey, which were generally favorable to the concept. After discussion, this conference took the first concrete step to further the project by authorizing the committee to set up a non-profit corporation to receive money and hold real estate for the purposes outlined. It also appropriated funds to cover immediate expenses.

Thus encouraged, the committee promptly moved ahead. On petition to the Court of Common Pleas of Montgomery County, Advanced Living, Inc. was incorporated without assets on May 10, 1962 under the Nonprofit Corporation Law of the Commonwealth of Pennsylvania. The initial incorporators—who also were to serve as directors until their successors were elected—and charter member officers were as follows: Paul T. Bergey, President; Harold G. Kerper, First Vice-president; Dr. John B. Jacobs, Second Vice-president; J. Herbert Weber, Secretary; Warren S. Kriebel, Treasurer; John S. Clemens, Neil L. Conver, Esq., Vincent W. Nyce, John K. Snyder, Paul S. Bieler, Wilbur C. Kriebel, Rev. Jack R. Rothenberger. All of the incorporators were members of the Schwenkfelder churches except for Dr. John B. Jacobs, local physician, and Neil L. Conver, the Lansdale attorney who had been assisting the committee.

After careful consideration, a committee of Harold Kerper, Vincent Nyce, and John Snyder drew up a set of bylaws. Following the precedent of Perkiomen School, the bylaws provided for a Board of fifteen directors, each serving a term of three years, nine to be appointed by the General Conference of the Schwenkfelder Church—the project sponsor, and the remaining six to be elected at the discretion of the nine so appointed. Article IV clearly stated the corporate purpose "shall be to provide housing and/or convalescent care for senior citizens on a non-profit and non-sectarian basis." It was the original intent of the directors to pursue housing and convalescent care simultaneously, but time, experience, and unforeseen circumstances forced modification of this ambitious undertaking.

A drive for funds within the membership of the Schwenkfelder congregations was inaugurated in June of 1962 and by October of 1963 contributions of approximately $35,000 had been received. This fund was augmented by a gift of $10,000 from the Charity Fund as approved by General Conference on October 19, 1963. A search for a suitable tract of land identified 21.42 acres of level land located at the corner of Weikel Road and Allentown Road in Towamencin Township, which was purchased for $45,000, paid in full at settlement on April 11, 1964. Interestingly, this tract is believed at one time to have been part of the land holdings of early Schwenkfelder horse breeder and land speculator, Hans Heinrich Yeakel, whose holdings also included the site of the Hosensack Schwenkfelder Meeting House.

Following the purchase of the land, Advanced Living, Inc. found itself badly in need of funds. Five acres of land deemed excess were sold for $15,000 to provide the board with working capital.

At this point the directors were faced with a crucial decision. They would clearly have preferred private financing. This would have avoided bureaucratic regulation which initially proved burdensome indeed. It would also have permitted more flexible operation of the facility, particularly as to entrance qualifications and priority of admittance. Experience during the 1962-1963 fund drive, however, simply did not suggest that the necessary equity base could be raised within the Schwenkfelder community. Somewhat reluctantly, therefore, in 1964 an application was filed for Federal Government aid under the Housing and Urban Development program for senior citizens.

While the completed project eventually proved quite acceptable, the heavy hand of bureaucracy during the development of the project almost exhausted the patience of its most enthusiastic supporters. Three years would elapse before site approval was received, nine years before a loan agreement was actually executed, and ten years before the first resident could be moved in. The present model facility stands as a monument almost as much to the persistence as to the initial vision of its promoters.

Immediately the directors were informed that while the financing applied for was available for low- and medium-income housing, there would be no funds for convalescent care. This goal had to be abandoned. Then the H.U.D. agency found the site "not urban" and site approval was witheld "because of the relative isolation of the location." It soon became apparent that the directors required the assistance of a financial consultant versed in the intricacies of government procedures for project and loan approval. The firm of Mullen and Lonegan Associates, Inc. of Philadelphia, with extensive experience in urban renewal, community planning, and development programming, was engaged. Mr. John A. Smyth, an employee of this firm, later carried on in his individual capacity. The firm of Howell Lewis Shay and Associates, also of Philadelphia, which had designed the North Penn High School, was engaged as architect. The offices of U.S. Representative Richard S. Schweiker rendered valuable assistance during the long and sometimes frustrating negotiations with the government agency. It was pointed out that the rural location held down the initial property investment and Advanced Living, Inc. covenanted to provide residents with regular bus service to churches, shopping centers, and other facilities nearby. In April of 1967 the site was approved for fifty dwelling units to serve low-middle-income elderly persons.

There followed six years of seemingly endless negotiations with H.U.D. and the Federal Housing Administration. The agency questioned the initial feasibility letter and then lost the revised letter. When approval seemed imminent, no funds were available. When funds became available, the proposed specifications were found to require revision. Cost estimates were questioned and the Washington cost estimator failed to appear as scheduled. In the meantime, however, an application was filed with the newly created Pennsylvania State Department of Community Affairs for a planning loan and on September 15, 1970 the spirits of the directors were considerably quickened when a check in the amount of $45,943 was received, making funds available for continuing architectural fees and other incidental expenses.

At long last, on March 8, 1973 Advanced Living, Inc. entered into a formal agreement under which the government participated in a 100 percent mortgage loan for $892,000 under the section 236 housing program for senior citizens.

Construction bids were received and a contract awarded to Altemose Construction Co. of Center Square, Pa., at a low bid of

$692,700. Not included were $15,000 for an elevator and the costs of improvements providing utility services for water, sewer, and electricity. Impressive ground-breaking ceremonies were held on Sunday, April 1, 1973. Mr. Harold Kerper, who had succeeded Dr. Bergey as president of Advanced Living, Inc., extended an opening welcome, followed by responses from Mr. Vincent Nyce, moderator of the Schwenkfelder General Conference, Dr. John B. Jacobs, supervisor, Towamencin Township, Father Thomas A. Murray, president of the North Penn Ministerium, Mr. Warren Kriebel, representing Schwenkfelder descendants, and Mr. James R. Whiteman of the Altemose Construction Company. Rev. Rothenberger offered a prayer of consecration as the first shovels of earth were turned and Helen Kriebel led those assembled in singing "Now Thank We All Our God."

With construction underway, a special committee of non-board members, appointed to recommend a suitable name for the facility, selected "Schwenckfeld Manor." The name honored the devout and scholarly Caspar Schwenckfeld von Ossig, whose ministry of concern for others is embodied in its purpose. Emphasizing the historical relationship, the name was spelled with the second "c" included, as in his name and in *Corpus Schwenckfeldianorum,* rather than dropped as in Schwenkfelder Library, the individual church names, and the *Schwenkfeldian.*

But the trials and tribulations of the directors had not yet run their course. With construction proceeding ahead of schedule, the building under roof, and interior drywall installation under way, on the night of November 5, 1973 an explosion of unknown origin demolished much of the interior of the building, causing damage estimated at $100,000. The non-union general contractor had experienced difficulties with union organizations on other projects and it was believed some such connection may have been involved. While the cost of repairing the damage was covered by insurance, the incident delayed the completion of the project by more than two months.

The building, providing forty-eight efficiency apartments, sixteen one-bedroom apartments, social room, lobby, arts and crafts room, and office was finally completed. The first resident, Mrs. Fyetta Fields, moved in on May 15, 1974, ten years and five days from the incorporation of Advanced Living. Vincent W. Nyce, chairman of the Building Committee, a member of the Norristown Schwenkfelder Church, and at the time recently retired as business manager at the Norristown State Hospital, was appointed the first administrator. For several months he was assisted by volunteer workers from the several churches. Miss Mary Jane Bosler, a recent honor graduate of Penn State University and a member of Wentz U.C.C. Church of Worcester, Pa., was employed as secretary. She was later designated assistant administrator.

By mid-October all sixty-four apartment units were occupied. Dedication exercises were set for October 19, 1974. Harold Kerper presided, Rev. Krick offered the invocation, and Robert S. Ballentyne, a resident, Vincent Nyce, administrator, and a Towamencin Township official made remarks. The address of the afternoon was delivered by The Honorable Edwin G. Holl, Pennsylvania State Senator. Robert M. Krauss rendered a moving solo, "Bless this House," and Rev. Jack Rothenberger, associate pastor of the Central church and member of the board, led in a prayer of dedication and offered the benediction.

The initial project had not been in operation very long before the board realized that it was too small for efficient operation. Gratified by the enthusiastic acceptance of the project and undaunted by their early difficulties, the board in December of 1975 filed an application with H.U.D. for a reservation of $3,000,000 to construct a second unit providing an additional 150 apartments. Profiting from experience and backed by their favorable track record, this project moved forward more expeditiously. On September 3, 1976 the board was notified that Schwenckfeld Manor had been selected from a long list of applicants for an additional 100 apartments. The architectural firm of Vaughn Associates of Yardley, Pa., was selected to design the proposed facility. The plans were submitted to several union and non-union contractors. On the basis of a low bid of $2,783,980 a contract was awarded to the Frank H. Wilson Co., a union shop contractor of Ardmore, Pa. A formal letter of approval for the project was received on December 6, 1977.

Appropriate ground-breaking ceremonies were held in a snowstorm on January 9, 1978 and, after a short delay occasioned by severe winter weather, construction got under way on March 20. Despite some shortages of building and electrical supplies, construction generally proceeded without undue difficulties. New residents started to occupy portions of the building in May of 1979, only a year after construction began and just five years after the first Schwenckfeld Manor unit opened.

Services of dedication of the new facility, Schwenckfeld Manor East, were held Sunday afternoon, May 20, 1979. President Harold Kerper presided over the outdoor service held under threatening skies with several hundred people in attendance. Rev. Krick gave the invocation, Gerald Kriebel played a trumpet solo, Vincent Nyce and Herbert Weber performed the cornerstone-laying ceremony, Rev. Martha Kriebel, by this time minister of the U.C.C. congregation in Collegeville, delivered the dedicatory sermon, Rev. Jack Rothenberger offered the prayer of dedication, Kenneth Kratz, Jr. introduced key individuals, Joel Bieler sang "Bless This House," and Rev. Arlan Bond gave the benediction. The assembly was particularly privileged to hear the address of the afternoon delivered by Schwenkfelder, The Hon. Richard S. Schweiker, at this time serving his second term as U.S. Senator from Pennsylvania and an interested patron from the inception of the Schwenckfeld Manor project.

Schwenckfeld Manor East consists of 107 one-bedroom rental apartments, one two-bedroom apartment for the building superintendent, community room and kitchen, nurse's office, hobby shop, recreation room, arts and crafts room, laundry, self-improvement room, two elevators, lobby, and offices. The total amount of the direct government loan was $3,271,100.

Schwenckfeld Manor and Schwenckfeld Manor East are linked together by an attractive solarium and operated as a single facility. They were financed, however, under different government housing programs and the rent structures and loan payments are quite different. The initial Schwenckfeld Manor unit was financed under the so-called section 236 program for senior citizens. The 7 percent mortgage is held by the First Family Federal Savings and Loan of Lansdale, Pa. It is amortized over forty years during which time Advanced Living, Inc. makes the principal payments plus 1 percent interest, while H.U.D. subsidizes the remaining 6 percent interest. The rentals are computed by the H.U.D. agency and are determined by the cost of operation, excluding the 6 percent interest subsidy. When the facility opened in 1974, residents paid $111.27 monthly for an efficiency apartment and $128.44 for a one-bedroom apartment. In 1983 these rates were $175 and $195 respectively.

The section 236 program was discontinued before application was made for the second project. Schwenckfeld Manor East was financed under the Section 202 Section 8 program for housing for senior citizens, under which the government subsidizes the renter. The rent for each tenant is fixed at 30 percent of income. The government pays the balance to make up the market rental of the apartment, which in 1983 was $407 per month per apartment. The total subsidy in this program amounts to approximately $25,000 per month, or $300,000 per year. Both mortgages will be paid off in forty years, at which time Advanced Living, Inc. will hold the properties free and clear.

Advanced Living, Inc. initially made annual contributions totaling $12,600 to Towamencin Township, Towamencin Volunteer Fire Department, Volunteer Service Medical Corps, and the North Penn Visiting Nurse Association, these amounts appropriated in lieu of real estate taxes. The real estate tax exemption was challenged by the Board of Assessment Appeals of Montgomery County and in the courts. The exemption for the first unit was confirmed but effective July 1, 1982 Advanced Living, Inc. began paying real estate taxes on the Schwenckfeld Manor East property, where the renter rather than Advanced Living, Inc. is subsidized.

Shortly after the second unit was completed Vincent W. Nyce, who had served both as administrator and chairman of the Building Committee, asked to be relieved of some of his demanding responsibilities. The Board of Directors then appointed as administrator William Swartzendruber, a graduate of Goshen College and an active layman in the Blooming Glen Mennonite Church. Mr. Nyce continued to render valuable service as administrative consultant. As a tribute to his untiring efforts on behalf of Schwenckfeld Manor, the Board of Directors purchased an oil portrait permanently hung in his honor in the lobby of the East Building.

As of 1983 Mrs. Evelyn Moyer served as secretary-bookkeeper and Shirley Wilson as office clerk. Mary Bosler MacDonald continued serving as part-time assistant administrator and Vincent Nyce as part-time administrative consultant. The reception desk and hobby shop were staffed by volunteer residents. Pat and Diane Mayers, members of the Lansdale church, served as building superintendents in the East building, and Norman Cressman, a member of the Towamencin Mennonite Church, served in the West Building.

While the residential buildings proved attractive and quite adequate, the Board soon realized that a garage or utility building was necessary to complete the complex. In harmony with the existing architecture, a three-bay masonry garage was designed by Vaughn Associates of Yardley, Pa. A firm construction estimate of $52,000 was received from Frank H. Wilson, Inc., the general contractor for Schwenckfeld Manor East. Not satisfied with this proposal, the board contacted the officials of the nearby North Montco Vocational Technical School. They immediately recognized this as a learning project for their pupils in the building trades. Advanced Living, Inc. paid for the materials and incidentals, the school provided the supervision and labor, and an admirably satisfactory unit was completed in 1981 at a cost of slightly over $20,000. It now houses all the outdoor equipment and the vans used to provide transportation for the residents.

More than 200 deserving senior citizens reside at Schwenckfeld Manor, where they can live with dignity and self-respect among folk having common interests. They are relieved of anxiety over personal care in the event of sickness or simply the infirmity of old age. At the same time an active residents' organization, which meets regularly and functions through resident officers and committees, takes care to see to their social well-being by providing a program of interesting and stimulating activities. The oft-expressed grateful appreciation of residents amply rewards the initiators and present managers of this exemplary venture in Christian stewardship.

In 1981 several members of the Board of Directors of Advanced Living, Inc. were approached by members of the Board of Directors of Wyncote Home of Jenkintown, Pa., to consider the possibility of a joint low-income housing effort. The Wyncote Home, an entity of the United Church of Christ, owned seventy acres of land adjacent to the New Goshenhoppen U.C.C. Church in East Greenville, Pa. Such a project seemed needed in the area and the site would be convenient for Schwenkfelders residing in the Upper District. Board members Bieler, Kurtz, Rothenberger, and Kerper were appointed to meet with four members of the Wyncote board to investigate the matter further.

The Board of Advanced Living, Inc. felt that the idea had considerable merit. The fall General Conference at Palm on October 18, 1981 authorized Advanced Living, Inc. to pursue with Wyncote Homes, Inc. the possibility of a jointly sponsored, government-subsidized housing project to serve senior citizens in the Upper Perkiomen Valley. The original site proved impractical but an alternative site in Red Hill was acquired and project development was undertaken.

On June 23, 1983 Upper Perkiomen Manor, Inc. made application to H.U.D. for funding and in September the project was approved under the Section 202 Section 8 subsidy program for senior citizen housing. The facility will include twenty-five efficiency apartments, seventy-five one-bedroom units, and other amenities generally following the pattern of Schwenckfeld Manor. Loan authority in the amount of $4,250,000 has been reserved for the project, especially noteworthy since only 330 units were awarded in all of eastern Pennsylvania and the State of Delaware combined. Plans call for construction to begin in the summer of 1984 with completion and initial occupancy in mid-1985.

The Schwenckfeld Manor project, with all its initial difficulties and frustrations, has provided valuable experience and guidance in the development of both Upper Perkiomen Manor and Meadowood, the total-life-care facility under development on the Schweiker homestead property close by the Central Schwenkfelder Church. Schwenckfeld Manor board members Paul S. Bieler, Harold G. Kerper, Stanley M. Kurtz, and Rev. Jack R. Rothenberger serve as directors, and Stanley M. Kurtz of the Palm Schwenkfelder Church serves as president of Upper Perkiomen Manor. Schwenckfeld Manor board members Rev. Jack R. Rothenberger serves as vice-chairman, Harold G. Kerper as secretary, Vincent W. Nyce as treasurer, and Ellis D. Anders as a director, of Meadowood.

The need for caring communities in which senior adults can live in dignity and security and where the pressures of aging and health care are eased seems ever more pressing amid the volatile social change of the later years of the twentieth century. In Schwenckfeld Manor, Upper Perkiomen Manor, and Meadowood the Schwenkfelders have made an exemplary commitment to serving this need. The Schwenkfelder Church faces at once an opportunity and a challenge—to extend its Christian ministry in meaningful ways to this more specialized segment of the church membership and of the community.

Chapter Twelve

The United Schwenkfelder Choir

Just over fifty years ago a group of choir members from each of the Schwenkfelder churches gathered together and, under the direction of Mr. Raymond Seeberger, chorister of the Philadelphia church, prepared the cantata, "Prayer and Praise" by L. W. Ballard, which they presented at the Palm church on October 29, 1927. Formal organization followed in 1928. Since that time, besides presenting annual concerts, the United Choir has been featured on the program of many Schwenkfelder special events.

During 1928 the United Choir sang on May 6 at the special service marking the tenth anniversary of the Lansdale church and in December at a concert during the celebration of the thirtieth anniversary of the Philadelphia church. During the 1934 Bicentennial Celebration the afternoon program at the Palm church on Saturday, September 23, was devoted to the choir's presentation of Handel's "Messiah," with an introductory commentary on Handel's life and work by choir participant Rev. Robert J. Gottschall. As a part of the young people's program in the evening of the same day the choir rendered the stirring anthem "Festival Te Deum," by Dudley Buck. In August of 1934 and again in August of 1976 the choir furnished the accompanying music for the drama, "Faith of Our Fathers." On November 22, 1936 the choir sang at the homecoming celebration for Miss Flora Heebner upon her return from China on furlough. When "This is Your Life, Rev. Robert J. Gottschall" was presented at Stewart Junior High School, Norristown, Pa., in 1955, honoring him for his forty years as pastor of the Norristown church, the choir sang several of his favorite anthems. They also honored him for his many years of service to the choir.

The United Choir has presented concerts each year except for the years of World War II, 1942-1945. Until 1956 programs were comprised of sacred music encompassing the entire church year and titled the "Four Seasons." Since 1956 annual programs have been presented on the first Sunday in December, featuring anthems of the Advent and Christmas seasons.

Raymond C. Seeberger of the Philadelphia church directed the choir from 1927 to 1950 and through his imagination, encouragement, and inspiration the choir grew in numbers and musical ability. From 1950 to 1973 there followed three other Schwenkfelder musicians who directed the choir: Helen Ruth Kriebel of the Lansdale church, and Margaret Rothenberger Scheid and Robert M. Krauss of the Central church. Other directors have included Joel Anderson (1971), Leonard Murphy (1972-1973), Lee de Mets (1974), Stanley Clattenberg (1975-1976), Donald C. Eby (1977-1980), Roger A. Dean (1981), and Edward Bieler of the Palm church (1982 to the present).

Many fine accompanists have served the choir faithfully and well, notable among them being Mae Bieler Schultz who provided piano accompaniments for choir concerts for thirty-seven years, from 1935 to 1972. Memorable also were the bass solos of Raymond Stong, who saw service as an accompanist as well. For nineteen years the organist for the concerts was Dorothy Hungate, the choir director of the Lansdale Schwenkfelder Church.

Vocal soloists for the concerts have frequently been drawn from members of the choir, although noted singers of the area have served as guest soloists. Robert M. Krauss distinguished himself as tenor soloist on numerous occasions. Many programs have included special music by instrumentalists in solo or groups. The choir joined the Roxborough Symphony Orchestra in 1934 to present a spring concert at the Roxborough High School and in 1972 and 1973 combined with the members of the North Penn Symphony Orchestra, who were directed by Leonard Murphy, to present their annual Christmas program. Setting the mood for other Christmas concerts were bell choirs from St. James Methodist Church of Olney (1961—1962—1963), St John's United Church of Christ, Nazareth (1968), Jerusalem Lutheran Church of Schwenksville (1968), the Nativity Lutheran Church of Reading (1970), and the bell choir of the St. John's Lutheran Church of Boyertown (1982).

The choir has been well served by many capable officers. Outstanding in years of service was Paul R. Snyder, who was president for eighteen years and held other offices for several additional years. As publicity chairman for almost twenty years, Miss Irma A. Schultz made the choir and concerts well known to the people of the surrounding area, swelling attendance at the concerts. The choir initially was made up of choir members from the Schwenkfelder churches. More recently the membership, which at times has exceeded 100 voices, has embraced members from neighboring churches, in 1976 including singers from nine denominations and sixteen individual churches.

Rehearsals are held at the Central Schwenkfelder Church each Monday evening during the months of September, October, and November to prepare for the annual December concert. Participants have greatly enjoyed the broader fellowship with choir members from other churches and particularly the stimulation of raising their voices in selections more effectively presented by the larger chorus.

In retrospect, perhaps the concert most vividly remembered by early participants was that reported in the *Schwenkfeldian* of June 1932:

> The Combined Choirs of the denomination sang in concert on Conference evening, June 1, under the leadership of Mr. Raymond Seeberger. Seventy-five voices were in this chorus. The rendition of "The Heavens Are Telling" was accompanied by thunder and lightning, thus adding to its impressiveness.

Chapter Thirteen

The Society of the Descendants of the Schwenkfeldian Exiles

During the years following World War I, as Dr. Brecht and his staff collected information preparatory to publication of the 1923 edition of the *Genealogical Record,* questionnaires and requests for family information were mailed to many hundreds of family representatives. These requests piqued the interest of immigrant descendants not only in genealogy but in the history and activities of the Schwenkfelders. Dr. Brecht received a great many inquiries seeking both specific and general information, many from individuals residing at a distance and not directly involved in the Schwenkfelder church or Schwenkfelder activities.

In search of family details, Dr. Brecht called upon Judge William Wagener Porter, a prominent Philadelphia attorney and briefly a judge in the Montgomery County courts. Judge Porter was the son of an equally prominent Philadelphia lawyer and Justice of the Supreme Court of Pennsylvania; both were descendants of Schwenkfelder immigrant Anna Wagener (Wagner). Dr. Brecht mentioned the number of inquiries he was receiving, prompting Judge Porter to recall that Judge Christopher Heydrick, who had sparked his own interest in his Schwenkfelder antecedents, had advocated the forming of an organization similar to the "Mayflower Society" of the descendants of those Schwenkfelders who arrived on the St. Andrew. Judge Porter offered to participate if a sufficient number of descendants would prove interested in the project. Dr.

Brecht passed the proposal along to Dr. James M. Anders, who responded enthusiastically.

At the call of Dr. Anders, a meeting of a few interested persons was held December 15, 1920 at the City Club to consider formation of such a society. Those present were Dr. Anders, Dr. Brecht, Judge Porter, J. E. Burnett Buckenham, M.D., Ralph Getelman, M.D., Mr. Wayne Meschter, Mrs. Linwood L. Righter, and Mr. Elmer K. Schultz. After discussion, on motion of Judge Porter the meeting was organized for business; Judge Porter was called upon to preside and Dr. Buckenham to act as secretary pro tem. A committee was appointed to draw up a constitution and another to prepare a slate of officers. Dr. Anders is credited with proposing the name, "The Society of the Descendants of the Schwenkfeldian Exiles." Despite four formal attempts over the years to change or shorten it, the name has proven so accurately descriptive of the society that no satisfactory substitute has been devised. The society retains its original name to this day, although it is commonly shortened simply to "The Exile Society."

Slightly larger groups met at the office of Judge Porter on December 28, 1920 and again on February 8, 1921. They adopted a constitution and elected Dr. Anders president, Judge Porter first vice-president, Owen J. Roberts, Esq. second vice-president, Dr. Buckenham secretary, and Dr. Getelman treasurer. Dr. Brecht was appointed chairman of a membership committee, Mr. Elmer Schultz of a finance committee, Dr. Buckenham of a history committee, and Dr. Getelman of an entertainment committee, the latter being responsible for arranging the public meetings—a spring meeting at a country location of historical interest and a fall meeting at a central Philadelphia location. The business of the society was handled by a Board of Governors of nine members, serving rotating three-year terms. The constitution provided, inter alia:

> Section II. The objects of this Society are the preservation of the history of the Schwenkfelder religious exiles, and of their descendants in America, and the promotion of social intercourse among its members now and hereafter. Section III. Any loyal American citizen of good character, a descendant through one or both parents of the Schwenkfelder immigrants who came to Pennsylvania between 1731 and 1737, shall be eligible for membership.

A list of 125 charter members presented by the secretary was approved and one name added, to bring the total to 126. Thereafter membership was to be by application to a membership committee, whose certification as to eligibility was required before election to membership. Membership increased slowly but steadily, reaching 218 at the end of the society's first decade.

The first formal meeting of the society was held in the assembly hall of The Historical Society of Pennsylvania, 1300 Locust St., Philadelphia, Friday evening, April 29, 1921, with 180 persons present. The meeting was called to order by the president, Dr. James M. Anders, who, after extending a cordial welcome stated, "Without doubt, this organization will prove to be a means of disseminating valuable and welcome information among the present and future generations of Schwenkfeldian offspring; it will also increase sympathy and friendliness between persons who are connected by ties of blood and humanity." He then introduced the nation-famed orator, the Hon. Hampton L. Carson, who discussed in a broad way the position and influence of Schwenckfeld and the Schwenkfelders in the early life of Pennsylvania, pointing out that "Schwenckfeld and his doctrines were of a mild, humane sort, much like those instilled by William Penn, the founder of this commonwealth."

Dr. Anders, Judge Porter, Dr. Getelman, Dr. Buckenham, and Dr. Brecht, who served as genealogist and scrutinized qualifications for membership, provided energetic leadership during the first decade of the society's existence. Individually they were interested in and informed about their heritage. They seemed to derive genuine pleasure from their association with like-minded colleagues in the activities of the society. While busy men, they all seem to have found time to attend regular meetings of the Board of Governors, usually held in Judge Porter's central city office. They were prominent and respected in their professions, enjoyed wide circles of acquaintances, and were able to attract equally prominent and learned speakers. The scholarly papers presented were regularly printed in the *Exile Herald*, the society's news bulletin. The Philadelphia meetings were quite formal, black tie affairs, over which Dr. Anders presided, contributing gracious and felicitous remarks. Judge Porter was famous for his extemporaneous remarks, always appropriate and frequently memorable for their wit. Dr. Brecht was the most prolific contributor, reporting on his historical and genealogical researches into the history of the Schwenkfelder immigrants and their early descendants in Pennsylvania.

The fall meeting held November 13, 1931 in the Bellevue-Stratford Hotel marked the society's tenth anniversary. Dr. Anders prepared and delivered a lengthy review of the activities of the society during the ten-year period. Obvious notes of satisfaction, pride, and pleasure, which even the following necessarily sketchy review may suggest, permeated his address.

The second meeting was held at the Norristown home of Judge John Faber Miller on October 8, 1921, at which time Judge Porter presented an interesting dissertation on the early history of Silesia. Dr. Brecht read extracts from correspondence between the Schwenkfelders and the Mennonites in Holland during the years 1722 to 1726.

The next year Dr. Thomas L. Montgomery, librarian of the Historical Library of Pennsylvania, spoke on the topic "The Beginnings of Pennsylvania," relating a fascinating account of the adventures of the first white man, a Frenchman, to come into the State from the north and the story of two daughters who were captured by the Indians and taken far west but later returned to their homes. Dr. Johnson described valuable manuscripts, artifacts, and heirlooms from the Schwenkfelder Library collection. In November Dr. O. S. Kriebel spoke on "Hosensack Academy" and the early Pennsylvania school system. The Hon. John Weaver, ex-mayor of Philadelphia, spoke on "Reformers by Force—and by Practice."

The spring meeting of 1923 was held at the home of Henry S. Kriebel in North Wales, with Judge J. Ambler Williams discussing historical events in Montgomery County. Mr. Herbert Heebner Smith spoke on "The Exiles Still Instruct Us," appealing to the various family groups to organize into clans and found scholarships for worthy students at Perkiomen School. Dr. Brecht spoke on "The Migrations of the Schwenkfelders," giving an account of the first migration from the Harpersdorf area to Berthelsdorf in Saxony. That fall Rev. Harvey K. Heebner presented a highly interesting and successful sketch of "Balzer Hoffman." Mrs. James Starr gave an address on the "Immigration of Religious Sects" to America and the founding of early churches in Philadelphia.

The spring meeting of 1924 was held at Perkiomen School. Dr. Brecht presented a paper on "The Heritage of the Schwenkfeldian Exiles," and Dr. Cheesman A. Herrick, president of Girard College, gave an interesting and illuminating address on "The German Redemptioners," citing their heartrending hardships, from which the Schwenkfelder immigrants mercifully were spared. At the fall meeting Judge Porter gave a lively description of the proclamation issued by Frederick II of Prussia petitioning the Schwenkfelders to return to Silesia, continuing "I have a feeling of pride and warmth in my heart when I say that not one went back, and you will look in vain for any other society, or any other group of religious exiles in this country, to which such a thing happened." Dr. George P. Donehoo, former State Librarian, addressed the society on the subject, "Pennsylvania as a Mecca for the Exiles of European Oppression in the Eighteenth Century."

The annual meeting held in the Schwenkfelder Historical Library on May 23, 1925 was addressed by Rev. Dr. William J. Hinke of the Auburn Theological Seminary. Dr. Hinke, an authority on the history of the Goshenhoppen Charge, "delivered a masterly and scholarly address" on "The Schwenkfelders in Pennsylvania." The fall meeting was addressed by Judge John Faber Miller and by Franklin Spencer Edmunds, Esq., well known Philadelphia attorney, who spoke on "Penn's First Charter."

On June 5, 1926 the society celebrated the 200th anniversary of the Schwenkfelder flight from the Harpersdorf area by presenting in the gymnasium of Perkiomen School a pageant depicting in ten scenes events from the migration of the Schwenkfelders and the early years in Pennsylvania. The descriptive narrative was prepared by Dr. Samuel K. Brecht and read by Miss Frances Maxwell. Mrs. Carlotta Hoffman served as director, assisted by Mr. Wayne Rothenberger as stage manager and committees from each of the churches. One-hundred-fifty persons participated. The pageant committee was headed by Mr. Herbert Heebner Smith, who then had prepared an illustrated booklet showing pictures of each scene, listing the cast and including generous notes. It was the recollection of this event that prompted Rev. Hoffman's suggestion leading to the pageant "Faith of Our Fathers" presented in Salford grove during the 1934 Schwenkfelder Bicentennial Celebration and again in the auditorium of the North Penn High School during the nation's bicentennial celebration in 1976.

The fall meeting in 1926 was addressed by Charles Beaty Alexander, president of the State Society of the Cincinnati, on the subject "Kaspar von Schwenckfeld, His Life, Christology and Theology" and by Judge Joseph Buffington, President Judge of the U.S. Circuit Court of Philadelphia, on the topic "The Strife for Individuality."

On June 4, 1927 the society met in the Memorial Chapel at Valley Forge to hear addresses by the Rev. Dr. W. Herbert Burk, host for the occasion, and by William H. Kirkpatrick, Judge of the U.S. Federal Court for the Eastern District of Pennsylvania. Dr. Brecht contributed a paper on "The Part Played by the Exile Descendants in the History of Valley Forge." The fall meeting heard Chester N. Farr, Jr. Esq., again addressing the topic of "The Schwenkfelders and

Frederick the Great." Mr. Edward W. Hocker, associate editor of the *Germantown Independent-Gazette* spoke on "Revolutionary Landmarks in the Schwenkfelder Territory." He showed pictures of the Christopher Yeakle log cabin formerly at Mermaid Lane and Germantown Ave., the Washington headquarters at the Joseph Schultz home in Worcester, and other sites of historic importance during the revolutionary period in Schwenkfelder territory.

The spring meeting of 1928 was held at the Salford Meeting House and addressed by Prof. Charles K. Meschter of Moravian College, Bethlehem, on the subject "Pioneers in American Ideals." Mrs. John L. Farrell, society governor, spoke on her investigations which identified the south side of Walnut Street, then Pier No. 10, as the spot where Captain John Steadman landed the band of Schwenkfeldian exiles off the "St. Andrew" in 1734. Mrs. Farrell's continuing research into this subject suggested the Bicentennial ceremonies held at this location in 1934. Once again Dr. Brecht participated with a paper on "Salford, an Historical Center of the Exiles." The fall meeting, again held in the assembly hall of the Historical Society of Pennsylvania, heard the Hon. Frederic A. Godcharles, formerly state librarian, on "Exiles in Pennsylvania History," dealing particularly with the Scotch-Irish as pioneers and their conflicts with the Indians. Rev. Lester Kriebel spoke on "Glimpses of Silesia," illustrating his talk with pictures of Schwenkfelder homes in Silesia and in Saxony taken during his visits there.

In the spring of 1929 the society met at Ursinus College to hear a "highly intellectual presentation" by its president, Dr. George L. Omwake on the subject, "Ancestry and Civilization." Mr. Herman L. Collins (The *Inquirer*'s "Girard") spoke on "Early German Newspapers in Pennsylvania." "His address bristled with points of interest. He pointed out that the Pennsylvania German, as a distinct racial group, has almost reached the point of extinction.... Where once Pennsylvania had scores of German newspapers, it today has a scant eight in this entire commonwealth of more than 9,000,000 inhabitants. . . . In Berks, with its fine metropolis of Reading of 125,000 population, you find two Polish and one Italian newspaper, but miracle of miracles, not a German."

The 1929 fall meeting heard Herman V. Ames, professor of history, University of Pennsylvania, discuss "Some Characteristics of the Immigration to the Colonies in the Eighteenth Century" and Rev. Charles W. Carroll, D.D. on "The Pilgrim Spirit."

In May of 1930 the society met on the John K. Heebner farm to hear Rev. Heebner on "Traditions, Genealogical and Historical, of the John K. Heebner Homestead, in Worcester, Montgomery County, Pennsylvania." Prof. Brecht spoke on "Abraham Wagner, the Pioneer Physician and Philanthropist," presenting Dr. Wagner's "Practice Book" containing medical formulas which he employed in the ministrations to his patients. In the fall Dr. Josiah H. Penniman, provost of the University of Pennsylvania, spoke on "The Importance of Preserving Traditions." Rolland Johnson addressed the subject of "Memorial Markers in the Homeland," laying the groundwork for the markers erected there during the Bicentennial Celebration.

In the spring of 1931 Dr. Brecht presented a paper on "John Krauss and the Hosensack Academy," describing John Krauss, a prominent surveyor, organ builder, inventor, and astronomer, as the most distinguished graduate of the school. Rev. Elmer F. Krauss spoke on "Descendants, Yes: Ascendants," asking the question, "Have we descended or ascended from the ideals set by our ancestors?" Dr. Johnson led a pilgrimage to the Schwenkfelder cemeteries at Kraussdale, Hosensack, and Washington.

Having reviewed the activities of the society during its first ten years of existence, during which he was a principal moving spirit, Dr. Anders concluded his 1931 talk with the following remarks:

> Finally, it will have been observed that this Society has kept in mind two major objectives: One, to procure and preserve an account of the lives and activities, public and private, of the Schwenkfeldian Exiles before, during and after migrating to America, as well as of their earlier descendants, and, Two,
>
> To preserve a record of contemporaneous happenings which form a clear background or setting that will enable succeeding generations to better appreciate the historical significance of the part played by our ancestors near and remote, in the development of our national life.

Dr. Anders begged to resign as president in 1931 and was immediately elected president emeritus for life. He was succeeded by second vice-president, Mr. Herbert Heebner Smith. As the bicentennial year approached, however, Mr. Smith asked to be relieved as president to devote his time to publicity for the 1934 events. Dr. Anders was unanimously drafted to serve as president during the year 1934, so that he could lend his prestige and gracious presiding manner to the Philadelphia events of the Bicentennial Celebration. He also delivered a paper on the life of Schwenkfelder John Frederick Hartranft, at one time Governor of Pennsylvania, at the fall meeting in 1933. His interest in the activities of the society was ended only with his death in 1936.

In Chapter 1 we have already reviewed at length the society's enthusiastic participation in the 1934 Bicentennial Celebration.

After 1934 Mr. Smith resumed the office of president. In his place as second vice-president the Board of Governors elected Mrs. Caroline Roberts Huber, daughter of Judge and Mrs. John Faber Miller and wife of John Y. Huber, Jr., president of the Keebler Baking Co. of Philadelphia. In 1937 Mrs. Huber succeeded Mr. Smith as president, in which office she served until 1944. Dr. Buckenham continued as secretary until his death in 1937; Dr. Getelman as treasurer until 1954. Mrs. Alice Meschter Hostetter was elected secretary in 1938 and served as president from 1945 to 1953.

Until the disruptions arising from World War II, the activities of the society generally followed the pattern established under Dr. Anders' leadership. Fall meetings were held on Friday evenings in Philadelphia at the Bellevue-Stratford or Ritz-Carlton hotels. Spring meetings were held at the Palm church, Ursinus College, the Historical Library at Pennsburg, and at the Salford Meeting House. From 1942 to 1946 the fall meetings were held at the Old Customs House, 420 Chestnut St., then being restored under the guidance of the Carl Schurz Foundation, for which it served as headquarters. At the 1942 meeting Dr. Wilbur I. Thomas of the foundation welcomed the group to the house and gave an interesting résumé of the history of the building and the work to restore it and open it to the public.

At the fall meeting in 1934 Mr. Meschter showed moving pictures of the Bicentennial Pilgrimage to Silesia; at the following spring meeting Mr. Oscar Schultz showed his movies of the cemetery monument unveilings and of the pageant.

In the fall of 1935 Henry S. Borneman, Esq. presented a paper on "Pennsylvania Illuminated Manuscripts." Mr. Borneman began collecting Fraktur with a specimen given to him by his grandmother and for sixty-three years exercised careful discrimination in steadily expanding his collection. In 1943 he was president of the Pennsylvania German Society and an exhibit drawn from his collection was displayed in the rooms of the Carl Schurz Memorial Foundation in the Old Customs House. The fall meeting of the exile society was held there and Mr. Borneman gave a most enlightening discussion of his collection and the specimens exhibited.

On May 26, 1934 the society welcomed to the Salford Meeting House Dr. Rufus Jones, professor of philosophy at Haverford College and well-known Quaker scholar and author, who spoke on "The Eternal Gospel—A Religion of the Spirit." He returned in 1940 to speak on "The Central Idea of the Spiritual Reformers." In closing he remarked that he was sorry he could not claim immigrant descent and qualify for membership in the society, whereupon Mr. Wayne Meschter moved that Dr. Jones be made an honorary member of the society and the motion was unanimously adopted.

Because of war-time gas rationing, spring meetings usually held in the country were eliminated from 1942 to 1945. Spring meetings were resumed with the 1946 meeting held at Salford Meeting House and addressed by noted architect G. Edwin Brumbaugh speaking on "The Ephrata Cloister Restoration." For the fall meeting Mrs. Huber suggested a renewed emphasis on spiritual concerns and Rev. Andrew Mutch, minister emeritus of the Bryn Mawr Presbyterian Church spoke on "The Religious Challenge in American Citizenship Today."

With the distractions of the war and the interruption in meetings, interest in the activities of the society waned and attendance at the meetings declined. In March of 1947 the Board of Governors held a lengthy discussion on the future of the society. At this time the Harpersdorf refugee relief project held the attention of the Schwenkfelder community and the governors decided to dispense with meetings and turn the money so saved over to the relief fund. In December of 1947 the president, Mrs. Hostetter, sent out a letter appealing for relief contributions, enclosing with it lengthy extracts from the many letters received from the refugees describing their condition and expressing their heartfelt thanks for the aid received. On Saturday evening, November 13, 1948 at the Old Customs House Mr. Meschter showed color movies of the refugees and their circumstances taken during his and Spencer's inspection trip to Germany, from which he had just returned.

At the February board meeting there was further consideration of disbandment, but William and Wilbur Kriebel moved to carry on and a spring meeting in 1949 at Salford was arranged with Millard E. Gladfelter, provost of Temple University, speaking on "A Goodly Heritage." No meetings were arranged during the following two years.

By 1952 the Schwenkfelder Historical Library collections had been moved into the new Schwenkfelder Library building and Mr. Andrew S. Berky had been installed as director. The Exile Society adopted the library as its headquarters and elected Mr. Berky its secretary-treasurer. The interests and objectives of the two organizations closely paralleled each other. The society, with its broader list of members, complements the library organization. The new library facility generated increased interest in Schwenkfelder heritage and history, reflected also within the Exile Society. The new secretary-treasurer inaugurated a series of meetings which continued without interruption until 1967. A single meeting was arranged each year, in the spring at the library until 1961; thereafter in the fall at various appropriate locations. A meeting sponsored jointly by the society and the Palm Schwenkfelder Church at the Kraussdale Meeting House in the fall of 1967 brought this era to a close. No further meetings were held until 1975, although at no time was the society disbanded.

At the spring meeting of 1952 Andy exhibited some interesting items from the library collection. The next year the society heard from Cornelius Weygandt, "dean of all authorities on the Pennsylvania Dutch," whose books "began the movement which projected our Dutch background into national prominence," speaking on "The Place in America of Things Pennsylvania Dutch." Immediately prior to this public meeting, the Board of Governors was reorganized. Wilbur C. Kriebel was elected president, Owen J. Roberts first vice-president, William F. Kriebel second vice-president, and Andrew S. Berky secretary-treasurer. A membership drive in the fall of 1953 more than doubled the membership. Initially there had been a single class of membership with annual dues of $3.00. In 1929 Life Memberships were made available for a single fee of $50 (now $75). During the depression an inactive membership with annual dues reduced to $1.00 had been set up to accommodate members residing at a distance and unable to attend meetings regularly. This membership class was now eliminated. The costs of printing and postage had increased and in addition appropriate items published or reproduced by Schwenkfelder Library were being regularly mailed to society members. The eligibility requirement of descent from an immigrant of 1731-1737 remains in effect, but in September of 1975 the governors established a class of associate membership to accommodate nondescendants interested in the society and the somewhat broader activities of the library.

Programs for the annual spring meetings included a talk by Henry S. Borneman, Esq. titled "Some Reflections on Pennsylvania House Blessings"; by Mr. Guy Reinert, former secretary of the Pennsylvania German Folklore Society, on "Pennsylvania Dutch Decorated Barns"; by Rev. William J. Rupp on "Bird Lore among the Pennsylvania Dutch"; by Olive Zehner, curator of the Ephrata Cloisters and folk art editor of *The Pennsylvania Dutchman,* on "The Pennsylvania Way of Life"; an illustrated talk by Andrew Berky on his trip to Germany in the interests of the *Corpus* publication; by Samuel Edgerton, Perkiomen School art instructor and former Fullbright Fellow to Lingen Gymnasium, Germany, on "The Resto-

ration of Famous Philadelphia Landmarks (The Philadelphia Mall)";
and an illustrated talk by W. Kyrel Meschter reporting on a goodwill
tour of the Holy Land.

The meeting to be held in 1961 was delayed until October 14 to
permit presentation by Andrew Berky of a report on his visit to the
old Schwenkfelder homelands in Silesia, at this time a part of Poland,
behind the iron curtain. About eighty members heard Andy's report
of his sometimes tense experiences. The cycle of meetings then
continued with fall meetings in 1962 at the Salford Meeting House,
with Dr. Don Yoder, professor of religious thought, the University of
Pennsylvania, speaking on "The Meeting House Tradition in
Pennsylvania"; in 1963 at the Kraussdale Schwenkfelder Meeting
House, with Fritz Eberhard addressing the fine art of bookbinding,
on which he is a nationally recognized authority; in 1965 at the
Hosensack Meeting House to celebrate the 200th anniversary of the
location of a Schwenkfelder school at the site and the 175th anniver-
sary of the construction of the first place for public worship built by
the Schwenkfelders in America; in 1966 at the library, with Marcus
Aurelius Mensch, son of the late Irwin P. Mensch, lecturing on the
Schwenkfelder Treasure Book illuminated by his father; and in 1967
at the Kraussdale Meeting House, with a historical sketch of the
Krauss family organ builders by Ella Krauss Althouse and a historical
sketch of the Kraussdale Meeting House by society vice-president,
Eugene Arlen Schultz, son of Dr. Selina Schultz.

During the 1934 Bicentennial Celebration the society had
installed a plaque commemorating the site of the landing of the 1734
immigrants. During the early 1960s the society was made aware that
the building on which this plaque had been mounted was scheduled
for demolition in 1965 to make way for the new Interstate 95 highway
and the Penn's Landing promenade. Vice-president Eugene Schultz
was appointed to negotiate its recovery and it was duly returned to the
Schwenkfelder Library and refurbished to await remounting following completion of the Penn's Landing development. The plaque was
mounted on a column of the Penn's Landing development and dedicated September 19, 1976 with the Hon. Richard S. Schweiker
giving the dedicatory address. Three years later it was pried loose
from its mounting and stolen, presumably to be melted down for
recovery of the heavy brass from which it was made. Fortunately, an
aluminum copy was held in the library, from which a new plaque was
cast and reset upon the same column along the river's edge, this time
firmly embedded in the concrete pillar with epoxy cement. It is still
prominently visible at the historical site.

By the late 1960s, with Andy's attention deeply absorbed in the affairs of Perkiomen School, interest in the society waned. From 1967 to 1975 no public meetings were held, although no move was made to disband the society and annual dues were regularly billed and paid by many members. Dr. Claude A. Schultz, Jr., library president, became impatient with this situation, feeling strongly that the society could serve a most useful purpose in a "Friends of the Library" capacity. He recruited Dr. Sherman L. Gerhard as secretary-treasurer, who was charged with updating the membership list and generally breathing new life into the society. Dr. Gerhard is a son of Prof. Elmer Gerhard, translator of the *Erläuterung* and an editor of *Schwenckfeldiana*. Upon his retirement as a physicist at the Picatinny Arsenal in Dover, N.J., Dr. Gerhard returned to Hellertown, Pa., near the place of his birth, joined the Palm Schwenkfelder Church, and renewed his interest in the history of his family and of the Schwenkfelders.

At a September 20, 1975 meeting of the Board of Governors Dr. Gerhard reported 60 dues-paying members, 27 life members and a mailing list of 165 names. Officers were elected as follows: Waldo Johnson, grandson of Dr. Elmer Johnson, president, Sara Bieler vice-president, and Sherman Gerhard secretary-treasurer. Board members elected for a one-year term were Irma Schultz, Waldo Johnson, and Wilbur Kriebel; for a two-year term J. Herbert Weber, Ruth Harris, and Dr. Claude Schultz, Jr.; and for a three-year term, Kyrel Meschter, Sara Bieler, and Helen Gerhard. At the public meeting held that afternoon in the meeting room of the library, Rev. Jack Rothenberger spoke on "Silesia after 250 years," illustrating his talk with slides taken during the 1972 pilgrimage group's visit there.

The society made regular contributions toward the operating expenses of the library and in addition cooperated in the printing and distribution of a number of books. In 1978 the society published Dr. Peter Erb's translation of *The Spiritual Diary of Christopher Wiegner*. In 1979 it printed Sherman Gerhard's translation of Siegfried Knörrlich's 1963 memorial booklet under the title *The Refuge Church in Harpersdorf, Silesia*. Library publications were generally distributed to society members.

With the 1923 edition of the *Genealogical Record* outdated, there were repeated requests for a new edition. Since the number of family members increases in geometrical progression and since not less than three generations had intervened since 1923, such a publication was hardly a feasible undertaking. However, a committee of the society under Mrs. Ralph Bieler undertook to record recent family genealogical information where available. A family record form was prepared on which current information could be entered. The forms were then numbered to permit reference to the 1923 record and systematically filed at the library. A sizeable collection of more recent genealogical data has been accumulated.

Society governors worked closely with General Conference in the effort to reestablish with the current Polish authorities Schwenkfelder title to the Viehweg plot in Harpersdorf. While title could not be secured, the Schwenkfelders were successful in having the plot designated as a historical site and placed under the protection of the state, with the Schwenkfelders making annual payments for maintenance from a fund already deposited with a Polish government agency. Efforts are under way to have an aluminum plaque attached to the rear of the monument with identification in the Polish language.

During the first week of October 1982 Dr. Sherman Gerhard and Dr. Fritz Richter traveled to Vienna to search the state archives for the seventeen petitions presented to the court of Emperor Charles VI by the 1721 Schwenkfelder mission seeking relief from the Jesuit persecutions of the Schwenkfelders in the Harpersdorf area. Since Dr. Richter's visit there with the 1977 pilgrimage group he had sought to trace the state archives in which they would probably have been included and was determined to track them down. Unfortunately it was demonstrated to the satisfaction of the two travelers that the records in question had been stored in the Palace of Justice which was destroyed by fire around 1927.

In September of 1983 Mr. Gerald Kriebel was elected president, Dr. Ruth Harris vice-president, and Martin L. Kriebel secretary-treasurer. A show-and-tell program at the fall meeting presided over by Gerald and Helen Kriebel attracted a capacity audience. Members exhibited artifacts passed down through their families and related fascinating stories relating to them. The spontaneous enthusiasm generated at the meeting was reminiscent of Dr. Anders' remarks at the society's first meeting. The organization did indeed "prove to be a means of disseminating valuable and welcome information among the present and future generations of Schwenkfeldian offspring" and increase "sympathy and friendliness between persons who are connected by ties of blood and humanity."

The fall meeting of the society during the 250th anniversary year of 1984 is being planned in conjunction with a Colloquium on Schwenckfeld and the Schwenkfelders to be sponsored by Schwenkfelder Library. The meeting is scheduled for Saturday afternoon, September 22. Rev. Frederick Weiser will present a slide-illustrated lecture on Fraktur from the library's extensive and unique collection. With a popular subject and a uniquely qualified speaker, the society looks forward to an outstanding meeting at which the traditional objectives of the society will be well served.

Chapter Fourteen

Schwenkfelder Theology: A Twentieth Century Perspective

Theological traditions are not immutable bodies of belief and practice; they evolve over time, shaped by forces from within and from without. All Christian traditions are rooted in the words of Scripture and influenced to a greater or lesser degree by the commentaries of the Church Fathers and the creeds of the early church councils. Protestant traditions are differentiated by the thought and writings of the reformers from whom they trace their origins. As Protestant theological traditions have been passed on through history they have been further influenced by other factors: religious, intellectual, social and political forces outside themselves with which they have had to come to grips; the quality of pastoral and theological leadership and the means by which pastors are chosen and trained; the educational methods chosen to pass on the tradition; and the commitment of members to understanding and maintaining their tradition.

Schwenkfelder theology is not greatly different from other theologies in any of these matters. It has consistently turned to the Scriptures (both the Old and the New Testaments) as its authority, yet it has not neglected the common Christian tradition of the early church. It has maintained the use of the Apostles' Creed in its worship and holds with other Christians to the central teachings of the first four church councils. Its particular form has been shaped by the thought and life of Schwenckfeld and his associates. Even Schwenckfeld's thought passed through stages of development, and it has not been passed on since his time without further change. By the early seventeenth century Schwenkfelder theology had shifted its primary concern from discussions over the person and work of Christ and the sacraments to commentary on the effects of redemption in the individual believer's life; by the beginning of the eighteenth century the impact of Pietism can be seen.

After the migration entirely new influences had their effect in shaping Schwenkfelder thought and worship. Their early school and meeting houses reflected the influence of Mennonite and Brethren designs. In 1782 they organized themselves into a "society," thereby making the first move toward institutionalizing their religious position. Almost from their first arrival in America they were deeply concerned about the training of their youth and the quality of their leadership, and as a result initiated a school system, wrote catechisms and theological compendia, and reprinted the works of their founder. In the next century, as they began to lose the German language, they supported translations of the major books of their tradition. By the twentieth century (against the earlier express will of Schwenckfeld himself) they had formed a "church" and were practicing the sacraments.

In the earlier chapters we have outlined the framework within which twentieth century Schwenkfelder theology developed. It remains to review more closely the specific content of that theology and to reflect on the forces which have shaped it. To do so, however, it will be useful to consider some of the major theological developments during the first 150 years of the Schwenkfelders in America so as better to understand the structure of Schwenkfelder theology in this century.

Schwenkfelder Theology to the End of the Nineteenth Century

It is now a commonplace to speak of the radical change which has affected every aspect of twentieth century life, including the religious aspect, but it is important to remember that that change was already well underway in the century preceding this one. For Schwenkfelder theology change was occurring dramatically by the 1884 celebrations and had in fact been initiated by those men and women who reflected on their responsibilities much earlier, in the 1780s, some few fifty years after their first arrival in America. The formal treaty of peace between Great Britain and the American Colonies had not yet been signed when in 1782 the Schwenkfelders made what was for them a monumental decision. On August 17, 1782 a "statement of principles " of the Schwenkfelder Society, which earlier had been worked out in detail by Christopher Schultz, was accepted and subscribed to by all members. This statement came to be known as the constitution of the Schwenkfelder Society.

Twentieth century readers will approach this document to sift from it an understanding of the political and social structure of the organization for which it was written, but in this they will be disappointed. What faces the reader of the Schwenkfelder constitution is not a chart of administrative responsibilities, but a theological treatise. It opens with a definition of a society member: "Every person who wishes to be a member of this society is to be deeply concerned to have a proper foundation and an approved model [ideal]." The foundation is that out of which members are to act and the model is that toward which they are to aspire. Both, we are told, are the same: the love of God. The foundation is the nature of God in which "one beholds first of all love, as that excellent outflowing virtue which binds God and man together." If members concern themselves with remaining on this foundation they will necessarily "unite themselves and maintain their unity in the bond of perfection" and their "one, single immovable chief design will be and remain: (a) the glory of God and (b) the advancement of the general good of each fellow member." This "chief design" will be the ideal toward which they will move.

The framework in which societal membership is to be carried out is "public worship." In such worship the word of God is fostered and doctrine is expounded. If this is to be properly done there must be persons among the members "who can understand, practice, and expound the doctrine; otherwise it would lie dead." What is of particular interest in this statement is the understanding of "worship" on the part of the Schwenkfelder Society. For the Schwenkfelders of this early period worship does not consist alone in the activities carried on within a worship setting as constituted by a Sunday morning meeting in a meeting house, home or church, but includes all the actions of the members throughout the week.

Particularly to be emphasized is the "instruction of youth." Those persons who are to carry the primary responsibility of leadership are to understand their task as the "exercising of commendable discipline," but it must always be remembered that this task of leadership cannot be upheld by a few individuals; "each and every member must through good regulations take part in the said exercise and supervision," and conferences must be appointed "according to the convenience of the time, and the demands of the circumstances of the general good."

In 1850 it was agreed that "the circumstances of the general good" called for such a conference and for a rethinking of the religious structures within which Schwenkfelders were living. As a result, on October 19 of that year a number of bylaws to the original constitution were passed which were intended to further the work of the Society and to deal with changed circumstances. The Revolutionary War was now long past, the era of Jacksonian enthusiasm was at an end, and it must have been clear to even the least perceptive members of the group that struggles over the slavery issue and the problem of states' rights were reaching a crisis.

A number of attempts were made to reacquaint Schwenkfelder members with the writings of Schwenckfeld. In 1806, 1819, 1820, 1830, 1858 and 1859 editions of works by the Silesian nobleman were published in Allentown, each edition comprising a large print run. But it was clear that these were not meeting the need because of the increasing loss of the German language among the Schwenkfelders. It must therefore have been with joy that the Schwenkfelder leadership received the translation of *Schwenckfeld's Heavenly Balm and the Divine Physician,* including his treatise on *The Threefold Life,* done by R. F. Anspach in 1858.

Even more significant than the loss of the German language was the impact of American revivalism. The revivalistic movement had begun early in the century and under the leadership of such dynamic men as Charles Finney it was already beginning to reshape popular American religious thought. It had not yet reached the extremes of the later nineteenth century when it would attract whole families away from the Schwenkfelder community, but revivalism's emphasis on dynamic preaching must have called some members of the Society to question their own practice of reading set sermons from the sixteenth-century works of Erasmus Weichenhan. The revival movement then sweeping through the United States, with its obvious anti-Catholic, anti-ritual bias, must have caused other members to feel embarrassed with the practice of genuflection and standing for the Gospel then observed at worship services.

The 1850 bylaws looked first to the role of teachers within the society. It was essential, they pointed out, that persons be elected to the ministry (paralleled with teachers interestingly enough) "who were able to understand, exemplify [the traditional Schwenkfelder interest in the "effect" of a life of faith is here again pressed], and expound doctrine." Likewise great attention was given to the need for education in the community, with a section on the manner of selection and the responsibilities of school trustees, and on the support of the poor, with a discussion on the role of the deacons and the director of the poor fund. The emphasis on education indicates the felt need on the part of Schwenkfelders of the time that their members be well trained to think through the implications of the new world they faced; the concern with deacons and the poor fund reflects their continued concern with mutual aid and the Gospel admonition to care for the needy.

The 1850 bylaws also indicate that the community had already begun to question the traditional Schwenkfelder teaching on the Stillstand, the cessation of the Lord's Supper as initiated by Schwenckfeld in the 1520s. Schwenckfeld's doctrine of the Supper as a spiritual eating is maintained but no mention is made of not participating; there is a section in the treatment of the theme which may have been placed in the text to allow persons in the community who still held firmly to the Stillstand to uphold it: what is suggested is that the practice of the Supper is correct if and only if it is practiced with exactitude according to the doctrine of scripture as outlined earlier in the article. Christian love must be manifested in its practice "as the infallible evidence of the right use. . . . Without this it is pure delusion and coarse idolatry with which no true believer can stain himself."

When the bylaws of 1850 were accepted, the dynamism of Joshua Schultz, perhaps the most important Schwenkfelder leader of the nineteenth century, was already being felt. Schultz continually pressed for the implementation of the bylaws and in 1882, just two years before the celebrations of the 150th anniversary which were to have so significant an effect on the community, he published them along with the original constitution in German and English. Schultz was a highly learned man. In spite of the opposition of his father he had become a minister in the Schwenkfelder Society on December 26, 1842. He continued in the role for fifty years until his death in 1892, stricken during a funeral service in the Kraussdale Meeting House in the same pulpit in which he had preached his initial sermon.

Throughout his life Joshua Schultz was deeply concerned with maintaining central Schwenkfelder doctrines, particularly the traditional position of the community with regard to the glorification of Christ, the reading of the Scriptures according to their spiritual sense, and the spiritual interpretation of the Supper. It was in support of such principles that he carried out a lengthy epistolary debate in the pages of the *Neutralist* in 1858 with the Upper Hanover Reformed Church pastor, Daniel Weiser. The debate was reprinted in

Lansdale in 1861 under the title *Open Correspondence* and along with Schultz's later 1875 publication of tracts on the Sacraments by the first two Schwenkfelder pastors in America, George Weiss and Balzar Hoffmann, it offered Schwenkfelders additional information about their religious position and a respect for it. His work demonstrated to Schwenkfelders that their theology could after all be defended with clarity and grace. Joshua Schultz appears as well to have played an important role in the various publications of Schwenkfelders—during the years he was in office the editions of Schwenckfeld's works already noted and new printings of Christopher Schultz's *Catechism* and of the *Constitution and Bylaws* of 1850 appeared. It might well have been under Schultz's prodding as well that the Rupp translation of Christopher Schultz's *Catechism* was published in 1862. In a very significant way Joshua Schultz established the ideal of leadership which was to follow the Schwenkfelders into the twentieth century—the ideal of a learned scholarly pastor concerned with the maintenance of the tradition of which he was a part and the application of the deepest insights of that tradition to the practical matters facing the parishioners he was called to serve.

Schwenkfelder Theology at the Turn of the Twentieth Century

There can be little doubt that the most important single element shaping the development of Schwenkfelder theology in the twentieth century was the decision in 1884 to proceed with publication of a critical edition of Schwenckfeld's works. That project would be with the Schwenkfelders until its completion in 1961 and would force every Schwenkfelder pastor and parishioner to be mindful of the thought and life of the founder. The theology of Schwenckfeld always played a role in Schwenkfelders' theological reflection, but that reflection was seldom the result of mere historical interest—almost always it was directed to particular practical, contemporary problems. In the late nineteenth and early twentieth centuries the problem which was most present to Schwenkfelders was the growing impact of the evangelical movement.

This concern looms large in two works by Dr. O.S. Kriebel, the leader who was to shape the form of the Schwenkfelder church and its theology in the early twentieth century. On Sunday, March 12, 1905 Dr. Kriebel preached a sermon which lasted an hour and twenty minutes on the theme "Christian Perfection." In spite of its length he tells us that the audience was "large and appreciative." Within a very short time he had expanded the sermon and published it under the title *A Discourse on Sanctification versus Christian Perfection.*

By the time this book was published a good number of Schwenkfelders had already been attracted away by the Evangelical church and other similar groups, who among other things were emphasizing the need for Christian perfection on the part of all believers. The Schwenkfelders had been concerned with Christian behavior from the earliest time. Schwenckfeld had himself refused to follow Luther in the beginnings of the Reformation because he did not see any improvement in the lives of the persons turning to Protestantism and away from Catholicism. He therefore insisted that the new life of faith must of necessity be followed by good works of love for God and neighbor if it was to be true faith. It is accordingly not surprising that 200 years later, when Lutheran Pietism was enunciating similar doctrines, the Schwenkfelders underwent a renewal within the context of that Pietist awakening. The Schwenkfelders did have serious differences with the Pietists as can be seen in the battles between themselves and the Moravians on the estates of the Lutheran Pietist Count von Zinzendorf in the 1730s, but the fact remains that it was to Zinzendorf's estates that they were attracted and that those who fled to the nearby town of Görlitz soon attended the services of the Lutheran Pietist Melchior Schaeffer who was preaching there.

There was, however, a major difference between the Schwenkfelder insistence on growing daily more in the image of the glorified Christ and the perfectionism being preached vociferously by some evangelicals at the turn of the twentieth century. As Oscar Kriebel put it: "I believe the doctrine of Christian perfection to be misleading in its meaning, unscriptural in its scope, unattainable in actual experience, and pernicious in its practical results." Against this perfectionism he upheld a doctrine of Christian sanctification, of "Christian growth and development." Such growth, "which is the normal process of every earnest believer's life, presupposes a state of mind and heart which is not perfect, which is capable of improvement, and which is continually approximating perfection but will never realize it in this life."

Before developing his argument, Kriebel noted that in 1845 Joshua Schultz before him had opposed the perfectionism of the Evangelical church. Quoting Wesley, Kriebel pointed out that perfectionism supposed that of "grown Christians it can be affirmed that they are perfect as to be freed from evil thoughts and evil tempers." This doctrine, he went on to insist, has no scriptural basis whatever and brings about numerous practical difficulties, chief among them being the spiritual arrogance it begets in those who believe they are perfect and the despair it forces upon those who know they are not. It leads to spiritual pride and self-satisfaction, it makes light of sin and easily excuses transgression, it engenders the contempt and distrust of others, and it is subversive of the highest stimulus of Christian growth and development. Perfectionism should not be confused with sanctification as upheld in the Schwenkfelder tradition. Sanctification presupposes a lack of perfection, an openness to growth, and a deep sense of humility. It is open to divine aid, to following after Christ, the model or ideal spoken of in the 1782 constitution, and to pressing toward the mark.

How seriously Dr. Kriebel perceived the threat of the Evangelical movement can be seen in his work *Conversion and Religious Experience* written just two years later and once again arising out of a series of sermons he had preached. In this work he took up the question of conversion and the repeated evangelical claim that any true conversion must be instantaneous and deeply felt. Once again he endeavored to avoid any doctrine which disparaged growth and which suggested that one could reach a point beyond which there was no need to continue. Such teachings, he felt, disparaged the promise of God's grace and discouraged Christian love, upholding an idea that the Christian could reach a plateau on which, having arrived, he or she could rest. In 170 pages he went on to treat the subject in depth.

In his opening paragraph he sums up his argument. "There is a natural life and a spiritual life" and conversion is "a necessary and essential experience for the enjoyment of a true spiritual life.... Conversion marks the point of transition from the natural to the spiritual life." In his work he considers it as a "radical change of heart and life for those who have lived in conscious sin and disobedience." There are many, however, who do not live a conscious life of sin. "For the child of Christian parents and Christian training" conversion is a "gradual unfolding and development of the religious nature." "For the confirmed sinner a radical change of heart and life in conversion is an absolute necessity. For the growing child of Christian parents and training a more quiet and gradual but no less marked change of spiritual life may be, and under normal conditions ought to be, experienced through proper Christian culture and education."

Dr. Kriebel then goes on to discuss the need for conversion in the one who has led a life of conscious sinfulness. It is evident that this is not his main concern, since he devotes only 20 pages to the topic and then moves on to treat the issue which is of greater interest to him and the Schwenkfelders of his day, the conversion "process" in relation to Christian nurture within the church. He regularly speaks of conversion in this case arising out of proper Christian "culture and education." Later readers may be confused regarding his meaning of the word culture, which for him is used in its original sense of cultivation, as in "the cultivation or nurture of plants," and with his word "education" which he uses in a sense enunciating both the academic and practical aspects of education.

Typically Schwenkfeldian is his summation of the argument: "The child is to be regarded as belonging to God's spiritual household." The term conversion is used for both the conversion of the sinner and that of the child within the church, because in the conversion of the child "the same results are achieved and the same ends are reached and consequently the same spiritual activities must be assumed as being at work as in the more radical and striking kind of conversion. The end is the same—the genuine spiritual life—the Kingdom of God on earth.... The all important thing is that the human soul should lead the life of the spirit and should show forth the fruits of the spirit in a life of unselfishness and true Christian holiness."

At the time Dr. Kriebel was writing these books the tracts known as *The Fundamentals* from which the Fundamentalist movement would later take its name were circulating. The debate between the Fundamentalists and the Social Gospel group had begun but the battle of the Fundamentalists and the Modernists was not yet underway; that was to have its greatest impact twenty years later. Although it is a temptation to do so, Dr. Kriebel's books are not to be interpreted in the context of these controversies. What concerned him most was not the defeat of other religious positions as much as the nurture of the Schwenkfelder tradition. Although he seldom mentions Schwenkfelders explicitly, it is clear to any student of his writing that they are always present in his thought.

His central concern with the Schwenkfelder tradition was shared by his colleague Howard W. Kriebel, although the two differed greatly in their form of expression. H.W. was not primarily interested in theology and education as was O.S.; his interest was history. If we read O. S. we seldom hear the name of Schwenckfeld, and yet everything that he wrote was imbued with the thought of the Silesian nobleman. When we read H.W., in particular his *The Schwenkfelders in Pennsylvania,* we hear only the name of Schwenckfeld and of the Schwenkfelders. We suppose too quickly that he was solely interested in history and cared little for the present. Nothing could be further from the truth. At the conclusion of his study of the Schwenkfelders in Pennsylvania we come upon a chapter which is far more than history. It is in fact a call for the Schwenkfelders to return to the basis of the theology which has shaped their thought and his throughout the years he is describing.

But one can hardly read Howard Kriebel's book, and the last chapter in particular, without reflecting on the change which occurred within the Schwenkfelder tradition in the years of which he wrote. What is the common tradition to which he is calling his fellow believers back? That tradition was an amalgam of many traditions. The theology of Christopher Schultz was shaped by Reformed Pietism, the principle of non-bearing of arms was not Schwenckfeld's, and the notion of a society seems to have been greatly shaped by Quaker concepts. In Howard Kriebel's day Schwenkfelders had returned to the practice of the Supper (fiercely opposed by earlier members of the group), and had given up the principle of the non-bearing of arms (as is clear in a comparison of the 1850 constitution and the 1898, 1902, and 1912 *Formula for the Government and Discipline of the Schwenkfelder Church*). Yet Howard Kriebel clearly felt that there was a common theme running through all of the Schwenkfelder tradition to which the community was being called to return. At times one has the sense that neither he nor Oscar Kriebel was willing to accept the fact that the tradition had changed.

The notion of a common Schwenkfelder tradition is strong among all those persons who worked on the *Corpus Schwenckfeldianorum.* In the introduction to the first volume there is an insistence that Schwenckfeld's position remained ever the same. The theme is taken up again and again in the numerous writings of Selina Schultz. Yet better than anyone these scholars must have known the changes through which Schwenckfeld's thought developed. The sacramental discussions of the 1520s had moved to the christological speculations of the 1530s and to numerous other problems treated in later years. The Schwenckfeld who insisted that his followers should found no church was still angered late in his life when one of his "followers" refused to admit that he was a Schwenkfelder. What the editors were insisting on was that there was a spirit in Schwenckfeld's theology which, in spite of the surface changes, remained ever the same, and that that spirit could be called upon in a most practical way to face the questions facing the church in the contemporary period.

It is difficult for us to imagine the effect of the arrival of Vol. I of the *Corpus* in 1907. The Schwenkfelders had been waiting for it for twenty-three years and had wrenched it from the hands of Hartranft only after commissioning Elmer Johnson to Germany to speed up the editorial process. It contained only five documents and was 661 pages long. How many Schwenkfelders read the volume through is difficult to say, but they did read the additional fifty pages of the introduction to the work, an introduction which, like H.W. Kriebel's book, appears to be primarily concerned with describing history, but which is in fact theological. The introduction to the *Corpus* is not so much a description of Schwenckfeld's theology as an interpretation of it. That interpretation lies at the roots of the works of almost every later Schwenkfelder writer.

Which one of the editors was primarily responsible for the introduction is difficult to say; they signed it as a group. It is likely that Hartranft played a central role in composing the piece, but the later work of the associate editor Elmer Johnson demonstrates that he was fully in agreement with the orientation of the introduction and the later writings of Selina Gerhard Schultz demonstrate her adherence to the principles of the introduction as well.

What contemporary students of the Radical Reformation consider to be the central issues in Schwenckfeld's thought, the editors of the *Corpus* pass over in one line: "We shall not begin with any particular point of christology nor with the sacraments nor yet with the inner Word in conflict with the outer word." Rather, they begin with a detailed discussion of Schwenckfeld's individualism, an individualism which perhaps owes as much to the ideals of America in the early twentieth century as to the Schwenckfeld of the sixteenth. Nor do the editors fear to preach:

> Schwenckfeld said, I must think for myself and so must every man; I must act for myself, another cannot act for me if my deeds are to have any weight, or if I am to meet the moral ends of my being. How else can I give an account for myself or of myself to God, or how can I treat my neighbor properly, unless I reform myself, consider my duty to both? ... Each individual must be trained to be clear in his mental and moral judgments; his education should not stultify and devitalize his consciousness of self but increase its intelligence and self-control, otherwise none is capable of meeting the sacrifices and rendering the services which society requires.

In passages such as these the careful reader of the introduction sometimes hears the tones of Horatio Alger speaking more clearly than those of the Silesian nobleman, even though the sentiments are those of the sixteenth century Reformer.

Next to individualism the *Corpus* editors declared that Schwenckfeld was primarily concerned with the fundamental rights

of the laity, then the principle of individual freedom, the brotherhood of all men, and the right of religious assembly, all of which
topics held particular interest for citizens of a democratic republic.
(Interestingly enough, they close their introduction with a nationalistic reference to the two nations of the eagle, "imperial"
Germany and republican America, indicating their specific "political" intention.)

The more explicitly theological tenets which are ascribed to
Schwenckfeld also appear to be chosen more because of their applica-
bility to the times than for their primary importance in understanding the life and times of Schwenckfeld. It is difficult to read the
section on Schwenckfeld's distinction between the spirit and the
letter without being immediately aware of the struggle over that
topic which was then being initiated between Fundamentalists in
America and their liberal opponents; the points raised regarding
Schwenckfeld's opposition to speculation in theology and his demand
for ethical and social betterment seem to fit the same mode. It is only
after this discussion, more directly applicable to the America of the
early nineteen-hundreds, that the editors finally take up the central
Schwenckfeld teaching on the person and work of Christ but when
they do so they avoid reference to the controversial topic of the
celestial flesh and they discuss the matter in less than one-tenth the
space that they have devoted to any one of the the topics earlier
mentioned.

After the publication of the first volume of the *Corpus,* however,
that edition had its impact on Schwenkfelder theology more as
representing an ideal than as offering further practical interpretations
of the work of the founder for the Schwenkfelder community. Fewer
and fewer Schwenkfelders, and more significantly, following the
second World War fewer and fewer Schwenkfelder pastors could read
German, particularly the German of the early sixteenth century. In a
practical sense it was not until the 1970s that the most important
Schwenckfeld treatises began to be published in fine English translations by Fred A. Grater, and by that time theology itself and popular
American religion was no longer directing attention to historical
sources as a primary wellspring for new life.

It was as if that problem had already been foreseen by a
Schwenkfelder pastor in the 1930s, however. In 1931 Rev. Levi S.
Hoffman published his delightful volume, *The Christ We Love.*
Hoffman is a particularly fascinating writer, with a rhetorical skill
which had a deep impact on the members of the church of his day (in
spite of their sometime dismay with the length of time he was

accustomed to display it!). In a very real way his work sums up the Schwenkfelder ideal, albeit without continual explicit reference to the founder. Although it does not appear so on the surface, *The Christ We Love* is an "historical work" in the spirit of H.W. Kriebel. Its words, according to its subtitle are "An Unknown Voice From the Echoes of the Pilgrim Exiles of the St. Andrew of 1734." Its central concern is with the practical Christ and with practical Christianity, and in this it reflects the concern of Schwenkfelders from the time of Schwenckfeld himself through Daniel Suderman in the seventeenth century, Martin John, Jr. at the end of the seventeenth century, George Weiss, Balthasar Hoffmann and Christopher Schultz in the eighteenth century, Joshua Schultz in the nineteenth century and O. S. Kriebel and the scholarly editors of the *Corpus* in the twentieth century.

In his opening lines Hoffman deliberately moves away from a speculative theology to what is better referred to as affective theology. "The Christ who loves us," he writes, "is always the same; but the Christ we love is constantly changing. He is as different as the individuals who observe, esteem and worship Him. His attributes are as manifold as our human powers of conception." "Books are constantly being written," he goes on to say, "to portray the theological, the historical, the orthodox, the radical and the biblical status of Christ." These works are the works of academics, writes Hoffman who, true to his Schwenkfelder heritage, turns to write on the "practical Christ whom the common people love."

But if Hoffman is anti-theoretical he is not anti-theological. What he believes he is doing is writing theology, albeit not speculative theology: "In so far as theology tends to stereotype thought and action; in just so far it falls short of its design. For theology aims to clarify the noblest truths, not to retard progress." *The Christ We Love* is written to spur on progress, individual and social, and it does so in twelve chapters, poetic inspirational essays intended to help the laity deal with the confusions facing them in a newly developing scientific, rational and secular world.

The central issue which Hoffman takes up in the volume is to demonstrate how spiritual reality shines through all the normal aspects of life. "We have never heard the angels sing but for many years we have listened to His messengers...singing anthems about the Christ child." The singers on Christmas eve are as significant to Hoffman as the angels themselves. All about us are gleams of heavenly glory. To this glory the astronomers and all the natural scientists testify. It is "difficult to impart clear conceptions of deep mysteries" in the physical universe, but the marvel of Christianity becomes "more astounding and more fascinating" as we "stop long enough to view and to grasp the whole situation." The telescope does not make God more distant; it testifies to his proximity. We must come to see nature "through Christ's eye" and then its newness and its glory will become clear and radiant. In Christ divinity was "personalized in humanity." Those who participate in his redemption must participate in it in action, not in theory alone; "Christ did not live like a recluse as did John the Baptist—he associated with people." Even though he is no longer physically present among men, one can hear his whispers from eternity—"Whispers from eternity or where the beyond breaks through" portray "how Christ in a spiritual way is keeping in touch with his own today." Christ "affiliates individually," and in good Schwenkfeldian style, Hoffman goes on to point out, "Christ is ever present and ever coming," not lost in the history of ancient texts or put off into the far distant and unreachable future. He is present, inspiring the dynamic actions of men and women and inspiring the perpetual emotion of the soul.

Schwenckfeld and his early associates in Silesia were among the first reformers to develop the catechetical method and well in keeping with his Schwenkfelder heritage Hoffman wrote a catechism to better explain to the youth of his day the central issues of the Christian faith as he saw them. His catechism is dedicated to O.S. Kriebel and the mark of that earlier writer is clear in it. His method, he points out, is the Socratic one; his catechism is not a simplistic list of questions which expect an immediate and correct answer from the student. Rather, following Socrates, Hoffman wishes through repeated questions to lead his pupils "to grasp the nature of the subject... he desire[s] to teach." His catechism is not a legalistic treatise telling young people what they ought to or what they ought not believe. The questions contain "endless possibilities" and are intended to draw the students out into the practical application of the truths of the Christian faith. Thus he writes:

> You may study religions and know their contents, you may peruse books and acquire facts, you may attend lectures and ascertain knowledge; but you are never educated and cultured unless that knowledge has become a part of you and you are capable of using and imparting it effectually. Now religion may be a belief or a system of faith and worship; but Christianity is a life.

Hoffman then goes on to follow through his principles, outlining the beginning of the faith (Entering the Gates), and discussing the nature of God (his abode, his character, his attributes, his personality, his fatherhood). In his section on the nature of man we see the influence of O.S. Kriebel most clearly. Both Kriebel and Hoffman use the word "culture" to describe the formation of the Christian from a child to an adult, and both, in good Schwenkfeldian fashion, expect that there will be a difference between those nurtured or cultured in the church and those who are converted to Christianity from outside the church. Fully Schwenkfeldian too is Hoffman's treatment of the idea of spiritual growth. Created in the image of God all individuals possess spiritual powers at birth, powers which must be developed in the home and in the church so that there may result a spiritual unfolding and a divine fruition. Central to this fruition is the person and work of Christ and the outpouring of the Holy Spirit. The Church, scriptures and sacraments are all aids in this "ascent" which begins with a spiritual awakening, and continues under the guidance of Christ in true discipleship and growth. The final section in the catechism outlines the end of such life in the world in which all believers find themselves.

Schwenkfelder Theology at Mid-century

With the work of Levi Hoffman, the pastoral and theological tradition begun by Joshua Schultz and O.S. Kriebel comes to an end. No better can this finality and new beginning be seen than in the *Handbook for Instruction of Catechumens in the Schwenkfelder Church* written in 1954 by Robert J. Gottschall, pastor of the Norristown church. Hoffman had made very few comments regarding Schwenckfeld in his catechism, understanding the tradition of which he was a part to have a directive not a prescriptive function. Thus he did mention Schwenckfeld briefly in his introduction but not again until the close of the work where he outlined the main tenets of Schwenckfeld's teaching as earlier listed in Vol. I of the *Corpus.* With Gottschall and the end of the second World War this pattern changes.

Gottschall's work begins with two lengthy chapters on the Schwenkfelder church and on the founder, including in appendices the distinctive beliefs of Schwenckfeld and a brief history of the Schwenkfelder church. Each chapter opens with a prayer chosen from the work of Schwenckfeld. This move toward the catechism as an educational tool in teaching children the facts of the theology and the church is also evident in the central portion of the catechism proper, which devotes lengthy sections to a historical survey of the Bible and various translations and to the history and present form of the

Christian church and Christian worship. Special attention is devoted to the unity of the church, a theme which Hoffman and Kriebel, in a more traditional Schwenkfeldian form, took for granted. The introduction of Gottschall's catechism proper still deals with the topic "Becoming a Christian" and attends to the child who has grown up in the church, but the idea of Christian "culture" in the Kriebel sense is lacking and much greater emphasis is placed on conversion. The doctrinal aspect of the work is emphasized by the early discussion of the Apostles' Creed in the fourth chapter and the designation of specific points to be believed in the discussion of the Trinity.

Only ten years after Gottschall published his catechism, Selina Schultz had her volume *Caspar Schwenckfeld von Ossig: A Course of Study* printed. The piece had been released earlier in mimeographed form and proved a useful tool for catechetical work. It is still regularly used for catechetical instruction and its use marks the furtherance of the model of instruction initiated with the Gottschall *Handbook*. In the Schultz piece the historical aspect is even further emphasized and the concern is primarily in educating members in understanding the distinctive marks of their tradition. One must be careful not to ascribe a false intent to either Gottschall or Schultz. Neither was attempting to destroy the earlier tradition, nor was either opposed to the stance taken by Hoffman which emphasized the practical Christ against the theoretical Christ as known in the theologies of history. Both Gottschall and Schultz realized, however, that the traditional base of the church was changing. Persons from other than Schwenkfelder backgrounds were joining the church and as the base was changing, historical knowledge which Kriebel and Hoffman could take for granted as passed on through the family could no longer be postulated. They thus felt the great need to emphasize it. The problem was, however, that since their volumes were the only ones at hand, they came to be used as the only approach and, tragically, no writers came to the fore to write volumes which spoke to the times in the way Joshua Schultz, O.S. Kriebel and Levi Hoffman had done.

Ironically, this insistence on designating specifically the Schwenkfelder content of belief in the catechism of the church came just a few years before the Schwenkfelder pastorate at large would be chosen less and less from Schwenkfelder families and have less and less training in Schwenkfelder theology. The Palm Church pastoral committee in 1959 noted the difficulties of attracting a new pastor who would have to leave the denomination in which he was trained and to reorient his thinking to the beliefs and traditions of his new charge. Dual ordination by the Schwenkfelder General Conference and the United Church of Christ resulted as a practical compromise, though hardly an attractive solution.

During the first half of the twentieth century all Schwenkfelder pastors, with the minor exception of Rev. Gottschall, came from Schwenkfelder families. They were drawn together by their common backgrounds and home training. All came under the spell of Dr. O.S. Kriebel at Perkiomen and the influence of this common experience can hardly be overemphasized, especially since there existed no specifically Schwenkfelder theological seminary in which they could pursue their studies. Hartford Theological Seminary, with the *Corpus* connection and with Dr. Elmer Johnson active on the faculty for many years, perhaps came closest to offering training oriented toward Schwenkfelder theology and history. Rev. Hoffman, Rev. Lester Kriebel and (later) Rev. Rothenberger were strongly influenced by their studies there. Rev. Heebner shared with Dr. O.S. Kriebel the undergraduate study experience at strongly religious Oberlin College. Rev. Heebner and Rev. Gottschall shared seminary training at Union Theological Seminary in New York City. They matured as pastors sharing congenial theological beliefs and a common respect for their Schwenkfelder heritage.

Following the second World War this pattern changed radically as pastors were drawn from more widely disparate backgrounds. Reverends Jacksteit, Byron, Sharp, Wagner and Luz were trained in the Baptist tradition; Martha Kriebel and Ronald Krick at Lancaster Theological Seminary; Pastors Bradshaw, Braund and Wagner at the Yale School of Divinity; Lockhart, Chandler and Johanson at Crozer Theological Seminary; and Rev. Bond at Evangelical Congregational School of Theology at Myerstown, Pa. Only Rev. Hohlfeld benefited from the broadening experience of study abroad.

The two pastors after the time of Gottschall and Schultz who did take special interest in writing tended to follow their historical interests, in all likelihood influenced as well by the "rebirth" of the Schwenkfelder Library, with its new building and director, in the early 1950s. But these writers were not locked into history. They did endeavor to make the historical works which they were writing relevant to their day. Nevertheless, it must be emphasized that they began with history and suggested the practicalities. They did not, as did men like O.S. Kriebel and Levi Hoffman, begin with the practicalities of theology and suggest (or take for granted) the historical tradition within which they were writing. Rather the later writers returned explicitly to the tradition of H. W. Kriebel. Thus

Rev. Martha Kriebel's *Schwenkfelders and the Sacraments* is explicitly concerned with the "perpetuation of [the Schwenkfelder Church's] unique contribution to Christian thought." She is writing history, but is doing it in the same manner as H. W. Kriebel—as an explicit "sermon" to her contemporaries. She is aware of the crisis facing the church with the calling of non-Schwenkfelders to the pastorate and the discussions underway to affiliate with the United Church of Christ. Her explicit purpose in writing the book is "to present a historical survey of the sacraments," but she wishes to do so in a way "that will enable members of the Schwenkfelder Church to appreciate their heritage, and then to relate it to their church life today and to their ecumenical conversations."

Less explicitly "historical" than Martha Kriebel's work, but nonetheless within the same framework, are the writings of Rev. Jack R. Rothenberger: his Master's thesis, published by the Board of Publication in 1967 as *Caspar Schwenckfeld von Ossig and the Ecumenical Ideal,* and his Doctor of Ministry study on the Schwenkfeldian theory of "Erkenntnis Christi." In the earlier work he is concerned with what he considers the basic task of the Schwenkfelder Church, namely, "to seek for an experiential-spiritual religion which will enable its members to translate the Christian faith from the first century through the mill of history by way of the sixteenth century to the present ecumenical movement in order to inspire the world to become the Household of God." "What matters most," Rothenberger concludes, returning to a central Schwenkfeldian theme, "is that the individual seeker of truth should seek honestly for life's meaning and life's sources in Christ."

His conclusion is addressed not so much to the general reader as to the Schwenkfelder reader. "What responsibility rests upon the 2,500 Schwenkfelders who comprise the five congregations of Schwenkfelder descendants today?" he asks. His answer deserves to be quoted in full:

First—They must recognize that the Church of Jesus Christ cannot be known or seen from the outside. One has to get inside to really be creatively alive. One has to become involved. He has to have a direct, personal encounter with God here and now. It is not enough simply to stand in the reflected light of a great heritage. One must seriously ask: Is this heritage ending or is it being continued through me? Am I helping to reflect the Light of the World who illuminated Caspar Schwenckfeld?

Second—As Schwenckfeld attempted to be the physician of a dissected church in his day, so his followers need to become a healing force in the divided church of today wherever they may live. They must be engaged in all ecumenical concerns, recognizing that mere outward unity is not enough.

Third—As Schwenckfeld remained a layman and spoke with prophetic voice to the clergy of his day, so all his followers today must re-examine the meaning of the "priesthood of all believers" and become intelligently concerned about the unity of Christ's Church by witnessing to it and working for it no matter what they do to "earn their living."

Fourth—As Schwenckfeld saw that the need of his day was to rededicate the outward church to the depth of spiritual reality and thus became a great leader in showing the way to unity in Christ by helping to educate and raise up valiant leaders, so the Schwenkfelder Church of today must raise up leaders from within its own ranks and must make its people aware of its profound spiritual heritage so that the cause of Christ may continue in unbroken line.

Fifth—As Schwenckfeld would not compromise spiritual truth for the sake of mere outward peace and concord, so the Schwenkfelder church of today must guard against a too easy compromise of its tradition for mere convenience. Church merger may well be the next step for the Schwenkfelder church, but this must be carefully studied and prayerfully derived.

Sixth—As Schwenckfeld allowed the Holy Spirit to guide him through the Scriptures to the living Word of God, Jesus Christ, so the Schwenkfelder Church must direct its people to the same Word who alone can give life meaning and purpose. The Schwenkfelder Church must reemphasize the "conventicle" method of serious Bible study, discussion and prayer.

Seventh—As Schwenckfeld sought to avoid coercion, so the Schwenkfelder people must avoid being imprisoned by their traditions and must sincerely and honestly seek to learn from their tradition how to make new application of spiritual truths to the conditions of today.

The basic task of The Schwenkfelder Church, as of all churches, is to seek for an experiential-spiritual religion which will enable its members to translate the Christian Faith from the first century through the mill of history, by way of the sixteenth century, to the present ecumenical movement in order to inspire the world to become the Household of God. Schwenckfeld gave no blueprint for the ecumenical church, but he did direct us to the only source of Christian unity—Jesus Christ.

Caspar Schwenckfeld von Ossig, 1489-1561, was a Christian nobleman and truly a "Confessor of the Glory of Christ" seeking the unity of his Church. He was "superbly out of date." We must not forget, however, that no one man or institution possesses the whole truth. Man's hope today is, as was affirmed by the early Christians as well as by Schwenckfeld, in simply belonging to the way Christ gave us. What matters most is that the individual seeker of truth should seek honestly for life's meaning and life's source in Christ.

Dr. Rothenberger's "answer" is consistent with the answer that would have been offered by his forefathers in the tradition. It is also a contemporary theological statement which may appropriately bring to a close this chapter and this narrative history of Twentieth Century Schwenkfelders.

APPENDIXES

A   Officers of General Conference

B   Schwenkfelder Ministers

C   Moderators of the Schwenkfelder Churches

D   Church Membership

E   Sunday School Enrollment

F   Sunday School Average Attendance

Statistics for the earlier years are as reported to the General Conference and printed in the *Schwenkfeldian*. Records are subject to some inconsistencies.

Statistics for later years are as furnished by church representatives. Figures marked with an asterisk (*) are estimates, as no reported figures were available.

Appendix A

Officers of General Conference

The Schwenkfelder Church

YEAR	MODERATOR	VICE-MODERATOR	SECRETARY	TREASURER
1900	Edwin H. Schultz		H. W. Kriebel	n.a.
1901	William A. Schultz		Jesse S. Kriebel	
1902	Edwin H. Schultz		H. W. Kriebel	
1903	William A. Schultz		Jesse S. Kriebel	
1904	Edwin H. Schultz		H. W. Kriebel	
1905	William A. Schultz		Jesse S. Kriebel	
1906	Edwin K. Schultz		H. W. Kriebel	
1907	n.a.		Jesse S. Kriebel	
1908	Edwin K. Schultz		Eugene Schultz	
1909	Daniel M. Anders		Jesse S. Kriebel	
1910			Amos H. Schultz	
1911	Edwin K. Schultz		Samuel K. Brecht	Amos S. Anders
1915			Jesse H. Snyder, Jr.	
1918	John H. Schultz			
1919			Samuel K. Brecht	
1926				George K. Brecht
1927	Dr. James M. Anders	Wayne C. Meschter		
1932	Wayne C. Meschter	Oscar S. Schultz		
1937		Ernest A. Heebner		
1938			Wilbur C. Kriebel	
1942				J. Herbert Weber
1953		J. Herbert Weber		Lester S. Heebner
1958	J. Herbert Weber	John K. Snyder		
1961		Dr. Paul T. Bergey		
1965		Vincent W. Nyce	Mrs. Nevin Kelly, Jr.	
1971	Vincent W. Nyce	Gerald H. Kriebel	Florence C. Schultz	
1977		Andrew C. Anders		
1978	Andrew C. Anders	Paul L. Bergey		Ellis W. Kriebel
1981		Paul S. Bieler		
1983	Paul S. Bieler	Andrew C. Anders		

Appendix B

Schwenkfelder Ministers

YEAR	UPPER DISTRICT	MIDDLE DISTRICT	PHILADELPHIA	NORRISTOWN	LANSDALE
1900	O. S. Kriebel	William S. Anders			
		George K. Meschter			
		Edwin S. Anders			
1902			H. A. Bomberger		
1903			E. E. S. Johnson		
1904				George K. Meschter	
1905			Supply		
1906			Harvey K. Heebner		
1907		George K. Meschter			
		Edwin S. Anders			
1908		Edwin S. Anders			
1909				Robert J. Gottschall	
1910		Edwin S. Anders			
		Levi S. Hoffman			
1912				Jerry A. Swingle	
1914				Supply	
1915				Robert J. Gottschall	
1916					Levi S. Hoffman

Year					
1932	O. S. Kriebel Lester K. Kriebel				
1933	Lester K. Kriebel				
1937		Levi S. Hoffman			
1938					Levi S. Hoffman J. Maurice Hohlfeld
1939					J. Maurice Hohlfeld
1947					Lester Kister
1949					Edgar T. Chandler
1954					Jack R. Rothenberger (Int) Arthur F. Wagner (Int)
1956					Jack R. Rothenberger
1958	Supply	Levi S. Hoffman William B. Bradshaw			
1959	Martha B. Kriebel Howard Kriebel	William B. Bradshaw Levi S. Hoffman			
1960	Martha B. Kriebel	Arthur F. Wagner (Int) Levi S. Hoffman			
1961		Eric T. Braund Levi S. Hoffman			
1963		Eric T. Braund Levi S. Hoffman Berthold Jacksteit (Y)	Ernest Moritz		William E. Cameron, Jr.
1964				Ronald Lockhart Robert Gottschall (E)	
1965			James G. Serdy	David R. Crowle Robert Gottschall (E)	Jack R. Rothenberger

1966		Berthold Jacksteit			
		Levi S. Hoffman			
1967		Berthold Jacksteit			Larry O. Bechtol
		Arthur F. Wagner			
		Levi S. Hoffman			
1968				David R. Crowle	
1969			F. Havis Davis (Int)		Andrew Johanson
			William E. Maddox		
1970		Berthold Jacksteit	F. Havis Davis (Int)		
		Jack R. Rothenberger			
		Arthur F. Wagner			
1971		Berthold Jacksteit			Arlan Bond
		Jack R. Rothenberger			
1972	Ronald Krick		T. Arnold Brooker		
1974				Frank Sharp (Int)	
1975		Berthold Jacksteit		Herbert Dewees	
		Jack R. Rothenberger			
		Thomas E. Byron			
1976		Jack R. Rothenberger			
		Thomas E. Byron			
		Berthold Jacksteit (E)			
1980		Jack R. Rothenberger			
		Thomas E. Byron			
		Linda M. Vanderhoof			
		Berthold Jacksteit (E)			
1982	Ronald Krick				
	David Luz				
1983		Jack R. Rothenberger			
		Thomas E. Byron			
		Berthold Jacksteit (E)			

Appendix C

Moderators of the Schwenkfelder Churches

YEAR	UPPER DISTRICT	MIDDLE DISTRICT	PHILADLEPHIA	NORRISTOWN	LANSDALE
1900	Edwin H. Schultz	William A. Schultz			
1902			Dr. James M. Anders		
1904				George K. Brecht	
1909		Daniel M. Anders			
1913		Charles S. Anders			
1918	Amos K. Schultz				Homer Kriebel
1919		n.a.			Homer Kriebel
					William Cassel
1920					Raymond Dresher
1921		George K. Kriebel, Jr.			
1922		n.a.			
1927					Charles K. Rittenhouse
1937		Ernest A. Heebner	Wayne C. Meschter		J. Roscoe Anders
1948	Claude A. Schultz, Sr.				
1949					Ernest Hunsberger
1950					J. Roscoe Anders
1953		Warren S. Kriebel			Paul T. Bergey

Year					
1955					Samuel Freed, Jr.
1960	William N. Schultz				Willard Bergey
1962		Lester S. Heebner			
1963			William Ayre	C. Harold Beideman	
1965				Harry Felton	
1966		Harold G. Kerper			
1968			Michael Beauford		
1969	Stanley Kurtz		Edward Simpson	Vincent W. Nyce	
1970		Andrew C. Anders	Donald Chestnut		Gladstone Smith
1971				Harold Beideman	
1972					Paul L. Bergey
1973				Raymond M. Nyce	
1974			Clifton Brooker		
1975	Foster Schultz	John H. Graham			
1977	Ray Rothenberger				Waldo Johnson
1978				Kenneth Slough, Jr.	
1982	Ralph M. Bieler			P. Frank Anders	
1983		Fred Seipt			

Appendix D

Church Membership

YEAR	PALM	CENTRAL	PHILADELPHIA	NORRISTOWN	LANSDALE	TOTAL
1905	217	403	68			688
1910	211	449	181	54		895
1915	250*	481*	242	75		1,048
1920	262	483	373	137	81	1,336
1925	295	482	437	205	143	1,562
1930	299	506	447	309	172	1,733
1935	351	509	457	386	181	1,884
1940	387	535	460	483	232	2,097
1945	417	563	460	552	256	2,248
1950	466	602	460	611	298	2,437
1955	542	689	300*	656	337*	2,524
1960	538	860	200*	600*	340*	2,538
1965	585	1,034	50*	527	362	2,558
1970	620	1,128	75*	427	281	2,531
1975	637	1,226	125*	374	313	2,675
1980	638	1,372	125*	300	300	2,735
1982	624	1,405	125*	294	314	2,762

Appendix E

Sunday School Enrollment

YEAR	PALM	WORCESTER	TOWAMENCIN	CENTRAL	PHILADELPHIA	NORRISTOWN	LANSDALE	TOTAL
1905	241	201	328		225			995
1910	194	221	317		357	115		1,204
1915	373*	230*	400*		450*	151		1,604
1920	364	234	308		502	247	205	1,860
1925	421	217	392		628	429	425	2,512
1930	408	190	314		560	519	217	2,208
1935	383	193	361		521	611	212	2,281
1940	380	198	378		466	760	259	2,441
1945	371	231	389		311	680	198	2,180
1950	416	233	367		325	601	200	2,142
1955	380*			745	250*	310	200*	1,885
1960	391			818	200*	340	175*	1,924
1965	425			782	150*	301	150*	1,808
1970	354			691	100*	183	150	1,478
1975	264			646	100*	109	124	1,243
1980	219			538	100*	75	135	1,067
1982	212			537	100*	84	161	1,094

Appendix F

Sunday School Average Attendance

YEAR	PALM	WORCESTER	TOWAMENCIN	CENTRAL	PHILADELPHIA	NORRISTOWN	LANSDALE	TOTAL
1905	92	n.a.	n.a.		140			
1910	80*				150	51		
1915	160*				175*	78		
1920	160*				180*	97*		
1925	215	125	202		188	155	145*	1,030
1930	244	130	200		180	215	143	1,112
1935	246	147	209		163	229	145	1,139
1940	230	125	227		152	275	165	1,174
1945	217	107*	200*		79	182	117	902
1950	248	131	215		75*	177	128	974
1955	248*			402	70*	177	123	1,020
1960	246			478	65*	199	135*	1,123
1965	244			426	50*	155	124	999
1970	175*			378	50*	81	60	744
1975	127			360	50*	53	84	674
1980	108			336	50*	57	90	641
1982	105			339	50*	46	106	646